Watch *How to Study the Bible's Use of the Bible Video Lectures* on your favorite devices

To access a free first session of this video study, scan the QR code or go to **ZondervanAcademic.com/Seven-Choices**

Full access to the complete video study is available through a MasterLectures subscription. For a free 7-day trial or to register for a monthly subscription simply go to MasterLectures.com.

MASTERLECTURES

How to Study the Bible's Use of the Bible offers readers a front row seat to key developments in the study of Scripture's engagement with Scripture. Schnittjer and Harmon help readers navigate choices that that confront readers of the Bible's interconnections. Jam-packed chapters trace the implications of a guiding claim that the New Testament's use of the Old follows interpretive practices that already matured within the Old Testament.

MATTHEW LYNCH, associate professor of Old Testament, Regent College

"Scripture interprets Scripture" is an age-old Protestant hermeneutical rule of thumb; the NT use of the OT is a newer, and burgeoning, academic field. Schnittjer and Harmon argue compellingly that undergirding both notions is inner-biblical exegesis, specifically, the OT use of the OT, a relatively neglected topic. They also present a strong case for viewing the OT use of earlier Scripture as a primary resource for the NT use of the OT—and for Jesus's own biblical interpretation. This was, for me, an eye-opening examination of the hermeneutical choices every student must make to understand the Bible's use of the Bible, a matter of no little theological import for all who profess biblical authority.

KEVIN J. VANHOOZER, research professor of systematic theology, Trinity Evangelical Divinity School

This incisive study directs any student of the Bible to hone and fine-tune their methodology when considering the relationship between the Old and New Testaments. Schnittjer and Harmon call for a connected approach that pays as much attention to the Old Testament's use of itself as it does to the New Testament's use of its existing scripture. They weave their way through a myriad of scholarly suggestions to present a strong toolbox of seven hermeneutical choices that the careful student can select and apply to biblical texts, many of which form case studies in this book. Frequently asked questions and study questions accompany this invaluable guide to a Christian appreciation of the subtleties of the progressive revelation of scripture in its plain sense, a scripture that is God-given and God-inspired, that is thoroughly biblical in its exegetical tendencies, and that is ultimately fulfilled in the New Testament's messianic exegesis.

PROFESSOR KATHARINE DELL, professor of Old Testament literature and theology, University of Cambridge

Schnittjer and Harmon have provided a valuable resource on the Bible's use of the Bible. They expand the discussion past the New Testament's use of the Old to include the use of the Old in the Old. They don't try to force one system but allow the text to drive their conclusions. This allows for a nuanced and non-reactive survey of current debates that will be a help to pastors, students, and scholars for many years to come.

PATRICK SCHREINER, associate professor of New Testament and biblical theology, Midwestern Baptist Theological Seminary

Those who have appreciated Gary Schnittjer's ground-breaking *Old Testament Use of Old Testament* will welcome this study. Gary has teamed up with New Testament scholar Matthew Harmon to produce a "how to" book outlining a carefully designed method for understanding how the Bible uses the Bible. Right up front the authors state a foundational principle that drives their approach, namely, that the Old Testament's use of the Old Testament "provides a model and a guide for the use of scripture in the New Testament." I am impressed with the breadth of their research and the precision of their analyses. Readers will appreciate user-friendly features like case studies and a glossary of definitions for key terms. The book is well-designed for use as a course text, with study questions and a Zondervan link to a variety of pedagogical aids. I heartily recommend it as a text for hermeneutics courses and as an invaluable guide for those trying to navigate this sometimes-bewildering field of study.

ROBERT B. CHISHOLM, JR., chair and senior professor,
Old Testament studies, Dallas Theological Seminary

They have done it again—*How to Study the Bible's Use of the Bible* by Gary Schnittjer and Matthew Harmon is a fountain of wisdom for biblical interpretation! Modeled on the exegesis employed within Israel's own scriptures, this book ably offers an eminently useful workshop for understanding how the Bible's revelation unfolds organically. *How to Study the Bible's Use of the Bible* forms a needed corrective to a variety of hermeneutical errors even while deftly guiding readers into the deep riches and beautiful layers of the biblical canon. This book is a must-have for pastors and Bible students.

L. MICHAEL MORALES, professor of biblical studies,
Greenville Presbyterian Theological Seminary

In the crowded field of books on the NT use of the OT, this volume by Matt Harmon and Gary Schnittjer stands out by extending the issue to include the OT use of the OT. This added dimension enhances our appreciation of the unity of biblical revelation. Harmon and Schnittjer are especially focused on providing students of the Bible a method to apply to the issue. Many "case studies" flesh out this approach to methodology.

DOUGLAS MOO, professor of biblical studies, emeritus, Wheaton College

In this exciting new book by two of the great masters of biblical intertextuality studies, Gary Edward Schnittjer and Matthew S. Harmon set out for students and scholars alike both the *why* and the *how* of the discipline. The rigor and clarity of this book is the sort that only emerges after years of meticulous, detailed study. In a field where intertextuality is often located in the eye of the beholder, the authors are to be thanked for opening up the technicalities of the discipline in such an accessible way. Through methodological discussion and worked examples, they have, in effect, provided a roadmap for the next generation of biblical scholars. This is a book I will return to again and again.

HELEN PAYNTER, executive director, Centre for the Study of Bible and Violence

This book addresses an important and neglected area of intertextual studies. Providing a clear introduction to and explanation of key hermeneutical choices that need to be considered by readers of the Bible as a unified text with progressive revelation, Schnittjer and Harmon show how interpretive decisions directly impact exegetical findings. Readers will be challenged to think critically about issues, reflect on their implicit assumptions, and recognise the deep complexity of this task. Filled with model examples, study aids, discussion questions, and an expansive glossary, this work is ideal as a course text and for those interested in this subject regardless of their knowledge of ancient languages.

SEAN ADAMS, professor of New Testament and ancient culture, University of Glasgow

Schnittjer and Harmon have done a monumental service to students of Scripture in *How to Study the Bible's Use of the Bible*. Relying on exhaustive research and detailed case studies, the authors walk the reader through the often-imposing process of determining the use of Scripture within Scripture. The result is not just a practical handbook, but a thorough overview of the state of the question and a wealth of exegetical insight on particular texts. For anyone interested in biblical exegesis, this book is essential.

ALAN D. HULTBERG, associate professor of New Testament, Talbot School of Theology

Most Christians know that the OT relates to the NT in some way—but how? Schnittjer and Harmon provide seven interpretive choices that serve as a useful guide for the student of Scripture. Most importantly, they begin with how the OT uses the OT, before looking at how the NT uses the OT. The overall effect is to show the organic progress of revelation. Whether one agrees with everything the authors propose in their hermeneutical approach, reading this book will stimulate further thinking and discussion in the whole area of inner-biblical interpretation.

JONATHAN GIBSON, associate professor of Old Testament,
Westminster Theological Seminary, Philadelphia

This book provides students with an accessible entry point into seven important conversations in how to understand the ways that biblical authors read Scripture. Drawing upon and then distilling key secondary literature, Schnittjer and Harmon offer an indispensable resource for students and pastors interested in the topic.

MADISON N. PIERCE, associate professor of New
Testament, Western Theological Seminary

Gary Edward Schnittjer's and Matthew S. Harmon's project, *How to Study the Bible's Use of the Bible*, is a treat. Rarely does a project glean from the OT's use of the OT and apply those insights into the apostles' use of the OT. They evaluate contemporary approaches, offer a way forward, and wisely articulate seven hermeneutical choices for the reader.

BENJAMIN L. GLADD, executive director of The
Carson Center at the Gospel Coalition

Schnittjer's and Harmon's book contributes to the exciting, complex, and often debated field of hermeneutics. Schnittjer and Harmon write in clear prose, provide straightforward aims, give insightful case studies, offer thought-provoking study questions, communicate with an accessible style, and offer an informative glossary of key terms. Even when readers disagree with their exegesis, examples, arguments, method, analysis, or conclusions, students, scholars, and others interested in hermeneutics will still learn much about how to study the Bible's use of the Bible.

JARVIS J. WILLIAMS, professor of New Testament interpretation, The Southern Baptist Theological Seminary

Can a textbook also advance scholarship? This one does. Schnittjer and Harmon take the exploration of Scripture's use of Scripture to the next level by identifying weak areas and problematic approaches in previous scholarship, especially the widespread neglect of the Old Testament's use of the Old Testament. I expect to return to this volume again and again. It's methodologically rigorous, with clear examples in every chapter. The book will benefit advanced students who are ready to build on the basic foundation of their Hermeneutics 101 as well as career scholars who want to keep growing.

CARMEN JOY IMES, associate professor of Old Testament, Talbot School of Theology

This is an instructional book to teach students how to interpret the use of the OT in the OT and the use of the OT in the NT. This itself is an advantage, since most books on this general subject deal with the NT use of the OT. The two need to be put together, since the NT's use of the OT is based on hermeneutical patterns of the OT's use of the OT. Therefore, the latter enlightens the former. Among helpful chapters are those on presuppositions underlying the NT's use of the OT, how to detect allusions, and on descriptions of the various kinds of OT in the OT uses and NT of the OT uses. The two authors are well-experienced and skilled in this area. This book will especially be useful for upper-level master's seminars, ThM seminars, and doctoral seminars. In this respect, I am happy to recommend this book.

G. K. BEALE, professor of New Testament, Reformed Theological Seminary, Dallas, Texas

HOW TO STUDY THE BIBLE'S USE *of* THE BIBLE

HOW TO STUDY THE BIBLE'S USE *of* THE BIBLE

Seven Hermeneutical Choices for the Old and New Testaments

GARY EDWARD SCHNITTJER

MATTHEW S. HARMON

ZONDERVAN ACADEMIC

How to Study the Bible's Use of the Bible

Published in Grand Rapids, Michigan, by Zondervan. Zondervan is a registered trademark of The Zondervan Corporation, L.L.C., a wholly owned subsidiary of HarperCollins Christian Publishing, Inc.

Requests for information should be addressed to customercare@harpercollins.com.

Zondervan titles may be purchased in bulk for educational, business, fundraising, or sales promotional use. For information, please email SpecialMarkets@Zondervan.com.

Library of Congress Cataloging-in-Publication Data

Names: Schnittjer, Gary Edward, 1965- author. | Harmon, Matthew S., author.
Title: How to Study the Bible's Use of the Bible: Seven Hermeneutical Choices for the Old and New Testaments / Gary Edward Schnittjer, Matthew S. Harmon.
Description: Grand Rapids, Michigan: Zondervan Academic, [2024] | Includes bibliographical references and index.
Identifiers: LCCN 2024009829 (print) | LCCN 2024009830 (ebook) | ISBN 9780310142454 (softcover) | ISBN 9780310142461 (ebook)
Subjects: LCSH: Bible--Hermeneutics.
Classification: LCC BS476 S333 2024 (print) | LCC BS476 (ebook) | DDC 220.601--dc23/eng/20240320
LC record available at https://lccn.loc.gov/2024009829
LC ebook record available at https://lccn.loc.gov/2024009830

Cover design: Tammy Johnson
Interior design: Sara Colley

Printed in the United States of America

24 25 26 27 28 LBC 6 5 4 3 2

CONTENTS

ABBREVIATIONS

AB	Anchor Bible
ABC	*Assyrian and Babylonian Chronicles*. Albert K. Grayson. Texts from Cuneiform Sources 5. Repr., Winona Lake, IN: Eisenbrauns, 2000
ABD	*Anchor Bible Dictionary*. Edited by David Noel Freedman. 6 vols. New York: Doubleday, 1992
ANEP	*The Ancient Near East in Pictures Relating to the Old Testament*. 2nd ed. Edited by James B. Pritchard. Princeton: Princeton University Press, 1969
ANET	*Ancient Near Eastern Texts Relating to the Old Testament*. Edited by James B. Pritchard. 3rd ed. Princeton: Princeton University Press, 1969
ApOTC	Apollos Old Testament Commentary
ARAB	*Ancient Records of Assyria and Babylonia*. Daniel David Luckenbill. 2 vols. Chicago: University of Chicago Press, 1926–1927. Repr., London: Histories & Mysteries of Man, 1989
ArBib	The Aramaic Bible. 19 vols. Collegeville, MN: Liturgical Press, 1987–2004
ARI	*Assyrian Royal Inscriptions*. Albert Kirk Grayson. 2 vols. Weisbaden: Harrassowitz, 1972–1976
AT	Author's translation
ATNTS	*Ancient Texts for New Testament Studies: A Guide to the Background Literature*. Craig A. Evans. Peabody, MA: Hendrickson, 2005
b.	Babylonian Talmud
BBR	*Bulletin for Biblical Research*
BBRSup	Bulletin for Biblical Research Supplements
BDAG	Danker, Frederick W., Walter Bauer, William Arndt, and F. Wilbur Gingrich. *Greek-English Lexicon of the New Testament and Other Early Christian Literature*. 3rd ed. Chicago: University of Chicago Press, 2000
BDB	Brown, Francis S., S. R. Driver, and Charles A. Briggs. *A Hebrew and English Lexicon of the Old Testament*
BECNT	Baker Exegetical Commentary on the New Testament
BFE	*Bound for Exile: Israelites and Judeans Under Imperial Yoke*. Mordechai Cogan. Jerusalem: Carta, 2013

BHK[3]	*Biblia Hebraica*. Edited by R. Kittel. Seventh ed. Stuttgart: Wurttembergische Bibelanstalt, 1951 [*BHK*[3] includes upper apparatus (minor variants) and lower apparatus (proposed alternative readings—preferred readings and/or conjectural emendations)]
BHQ	*Biblia Hebraica Quinta*. Edited by Adrian Schenker et al. Stuttgart: Deutsche Bibelgesellschaft, 2004– [apparatus classifies variants and notes preferred readings but does not offer conjectural emendations (with no witnesses)]
BHS	*Biblia Hebraica Stuttgartensia*. Edited by Karl Elliger, Wilhelm Rudolph, et al. 5th ed. Stuttgart: Deutsche Bibelgesellschaft, 1997 [one combined apparatus with minor variants interspersed with proposed alternative readings—preferred readings and/or conjectural emendations]
BNTC	Black's New Testament Commentaries
BQASTJL	*Biblical Quotations and Allusions in Second Temple Jewish Literature*. Armin Lange and Matthias Weigold. Journal of Ancient Judaism Supplements 5. Göttingen: Vandenhoeck & Ruprecht, 2011
BQS	*The Biblical Qumran Scrolls*. Eugene Ulrich. 3 vols. Leiden: Brill, 2012
BSac	*Bibliotheca Sacra*
BZNW	Beihefte zur Zeitschrift für die neutestamentliche Wissenschaft
CAD	*The Assyrian Dictionary of the Oriental Institute of the University of Chicago*. Chicago: The Oriental Institute of the University of Chicago, 1956–2006
CBPDSS	*A Catalog of Biblical Passages in the Dead Sea Scrolls*. David L. Washburn. Text-Critical Studies 2. Atlanta: Society of Biblical Literature, 2002
CBQ	*Catholic Biblical Quarterly*
CNTTS	Center for New Testament Textual Studies
CNTUOT	*Commentary of the New Testament Use of the Old Testament*. Edited by G. K. Beale and D. A. Carson. Grand Rapids: Baker Academic, 2007
ConBNT	Coniectanea biblica: New Testament Series
COS	*The Context of Scripture*. Edited by William W. Hallo and K. Lawson Younger, Jr. 4 vols. Leiden: Brill, 2003, 2017. Vol. 1, *Canonical Compositions from the Biblical World*; Vol. 2, *Monumental Inscriptions form the Biblical World*; Vol. 3, *Archival Documents from the Biblical World*; Vol. 4, *Supplements*
CšD	Songs of David in *OTPMNS*
CTR	*Criswell Theological Review*
CTU	*The Cuneiform Alphabetic Texts from Ugarit, Ras Ibn Hani, and Other Places*. Edited by Manfried Dietrich, Oswald Loretz, and Joaquin Sanmartín. Münster: Ugarit-Verlag, 1995
DCHR	*Dictionary of Classical Hebrew Revised*. Edited by David J. A. Clines. Sheffield: Sheffield Phoenix Press, 2018–

DNTUOT	*Dictionary of the New Testament Use of the Old Testament*. Edited by G. K. Beale, D. A. Carson, Benjamin D. Gladd, and Andrew D. Naselli. Grand Rapids: Baker Academic, 2023
DSSB	*The Dead Sea Scrolls Bible*. Martin Abegg, Jr., Peter Flint, and Eugene Ulrich. San Francisco: HarperSanFrancisco, 1999
DSSSE	*The Dead Sea Scrolls Study Edition*. Edited by Florentino García Martínez and Eibert J. C. Tigchelaar. 2 vols. Leiden: Brill, 1997, 1998
DTTBYML	*A Dictionary of the Targumim, the Talmud Babli and Yerushalmi, and the Midrashic Literature and II*. Edited by Marcus Jastrow. London; Luzac, 1903
E	English Bible verse numbers
EBC	Expositor's Bible Commentary
ESV	English Standard Version
ETL	*Ephemerides Theologicae Lovanienses*
Even-Shoshan	*A New Concordance of the Bible*. Edited by Abraham Even-Shoshan. Jerusalem: Kiryath Sepher, 1990 [Hebrew]
FAT	Forschungen zum Alten Testament
FDSS	*The Dead Sea Scrolls: Major Publications and Tools for Study*. Edited by Joseph A. Fitzmyer. Rev. ed. Resources for Biblical Study 20. Atlanta: Scholars Press, 1990.
Frg. Tg.-P	Fragmentary Targum-Paris. Pages 3–89 in *Translation*. Vol. 2 of *The Fragment Targums of the Pentateuch According to their Extant Sources*. Edited and translated by Michael L. Klein. Analecta Biblica Investigationes Scientificae in res Biblicas 77. Rome: Biblical Institute Press, 1980
Frg. Tg.-V	Fragmentary Targum-Vaticanus. Pages 90–199 in *Translation*. Vol. 2 of *The Fragment Targums of the Pentateuch According to their Extant Sources*. Edited and translated by Michael L. Klein. Analecta Biblica Investigationes Scientificae in res Biblicas 77. Rome: Biblical Institute Press, 1980
G	LXX verse numbers
GKC	*Gesenius' Hebrew Grammar*. Edited by Emil Kautzsch. Translated by Arthur E. Cowley. 2nd ed. Oxford: Clarendon, 1910
H	Hebrew Bible verse numbers
HALOT	*The Hebrew and Aramaic Lexicon of the Old Testament*. Ludwig Koehler, Walter Baumgartner, and Johann J. Stamm. 2 vols. Leiden: Brill, 2001
HNTUOT	*Handbook on the New Testament Use of the Old Testament*. G. K. Beale. Grand Rapids: Baker Academic, 2012
HUB	*Hebrew University Bible*
IBHS	*An Introduction to Biblical Hebrew Syntax*. Bruce K. Waltke and Michael O'Connor. Winona Lake, IN: Eisenbrauns, 1990
IBUB	*Index of the Bible's Use of the Bible*. Gary Edward Schnittjer. Grand Rapids: Zondervan Academic, forthcoming

ICC	International Critical Commentary
ISBE	*International Standard Bible Encyclopedia*. Edited by Geoffrey W. Bromiley. 4 vols. Grand Rapids: Eerdmans, 1979–1988
JAOS	*Journal of the American Oriental Society*
JBL	*Journal of Biblical Literature*
JBTS	*Journal of Biblical and Theological Studies*
JETS	*Journal of the Evangelical Theological Society*
Joüon	Joüon, Paul. *A Grammar of Biblical Hebrew*. Translated and revised by T. Muraoka. 2nd ed. with corrections. Rome: Pontifical Biblical Institute, 2011
JPSC	Jewish Publication Society Bible Commentary
JPSTC	Jewish Publication Society Torah Commentary
JSNT	*Journal for the Study of the New Testament*
JSNTSup	Journal for the Study of the New Testament Supplement Series
JSOT	*Journal for the Study of the Old Testament*
JSOTSup	Journal for the Study of the Old Testament Supplement Series
JTI	*Journal of Theological Interpretation*
K&D	Keil, Carl Friedrich, and Franz Delitzsch. *Biblical Commentary on the Old Testament*. Translated by James Martin et al. 25 vols. Edinburgh, 1857–1878. Repr., 10 vols. Peabody, MA: Hendrickson, 1996
KC	Kerux Commentaries
LCL	Loeb Classical Library
LEH	Lust, Johan, Erik Eynikel, and Katrin Hauspie, eds. *Greek-English Lexicon of the Septuagint*. 3rd ed. Stuttgart: Deutsche Bibelgesellschaft, 2015
LHBOTS	Library of Hebrew Bible/Old Testament Studies
LNTS	Library of New Testament Studies
LXX Cambridge	*The Old Testament in Greek*. Edited by Alan England Brooke, et al. 8 vols. Cambridge: Cambridge University Press, 1906–1935
LXX Göttingen	*Septuaginta, Vetus Testamentum Graecum*. Göttingen: Vandenhoeck & Ruprecht, 1931–
LXX HPTAT	Septuagint Hebrew parent text (*Vorlage*) alignment by Emanuel Tov in *CATSS Hebrew/Greek Parallel Text*. Emanuel Tov. Philadelphia: University of Pennsylvania, 2005 (*CATSS* = *Computer Assisted Tools for Septuagint Studies*)
LXX Rahlfs	*Septuaginta*. Edited by Alfred Rahlfs. Rev. ed. Robert Hanhart. Stuttgart: Bibelgesellschaft, 1935, 2006
m.	*The Oxford Annotated Mishnah*. Edited by Shaye J. D. Cohen, Robert Goldberg, and Hayim Lapin. 3 vols. New York: Oxford University Press, 2022
MFM	*Myths from Mesopotamia*. Rev. ed. Stephanie Dalley. New York: Oxford University Press, 2000
Midr.	Midrash (+ biblical book)
MT	Masoretic Text

NA[28]	*Nestle-Aland Novum Testamentum Graece*. 28th ed. Edited by Holger Strutwolf et al. Stuttgart: Deutsche Bibelgesellschaft, 2012
NAC	New American Commentary
NASB	New American Standard Bible
NET	New English Translation
NETS	*A New English Translation of the Septuagint, and Other Greek Translations Traditionally Included under that Title*. Edited by Albert Pitersma and Benjamin G. Wright. New York: Oxford University Press, 2007
NGTD	*Notes on the Greek Text of Deuteronomy*. John William Wevers. Atlanta: Scholars Press, 1995
NGTE	*Notes on the Greek Text of Exodus*. John William Wevers. Atlanta: Scholars Press, 1990
NGTG	*Notes on the Greek Text of Genesis*. John William Wevers. Atlanta: Scholars Press, 1993
NGTL	*Notes on the Greek Text of Leviticus*. John William Wevers. Atlanta: Scholars Press, 1997
NGTN	*Notes on the Greek Text of Numbers*. John William Wevers. Atlanta: Scholars Press, 1998
NICNT	New International Commentary on the New Testament
NICOT	New International Commentary on the Old Testament
NIDNTT	*New International Dictionary of New Testament Theology*. Edited by Colin Brown. 4 vols. Grand Rapids: Zondervan, 1975–1978
NIV	New International Version
NIVAC	New International Version Application Commentary
NJPS	New Jewish Publication Society Bible
NovT	*Novum Testamentum*
NovTSup	Supplements to Novum Testamentum
NRSVue	New Revised Standard Version Updated Edition
NSBT	New Studies in Biblical Theology
NTGECM	*Novum Testamentum Graecum Editio Critica Maior*
NTS	*New Testament Studies*
NTUOT	*New Testament Use of Old Testament*. Edited by Gary Edward Schnittjer. Grand Rapids: Zondervan Academic, forthcoming
NTUOTPL	*New Testament Use of Old Testament in Parallel Layout*. Edited by Gary Edward Schnittjer. Grand Rapids: Zondervan Academic, forthcoming
OTP	*Old Testament Pseudepigrapha*. Edited by James H. Charlesworth. 2 vols. New York: Doubleday, 1983, 1985
OTPMNS	*Old Testament Pseudepigrapha: More Noncanonical Scriptures*. Edited by Richard Bauckham, James R. Davila, and Alexander Panayotov. Grand Rapids: Eerdmans, 2013
OTPSI	*A Scripture Index to Charlesworth's The Old Testament Pseudepigrapha*. Steve Delamarter. Sheffield: Sheffield Academic, 2002

OTUOT	*Old Testament Use of Old Testament.* Gary Edward Schnittjer. Grand Rapids: Zondervan Academic, 2021
OTUOTPL	*Old Testament Use of Old Testament in Parallel Layout.* Gary Edward Schnittjer. Grand Rapids: Zondervan Academic, forthcoming
PE	*The Persian Empire: A Corpus of Sources from the Achaemenid Period.* Amélie Kuhrt. New York: Routledge, 2007
POT	*The Apocrypha and Pseudepigrapha of the Old Testament.* Vol. 2 *The Pseudepigrapha.* Edited by R. H. Charles. Oxford: Clarendon Press, 1913
PTR	*Princeton Theological Review*
R&H	*A Concordance to the Septuagint.* Henry A. Redpath and Edwin Hatch. Oxford: Clarendon, 1892
RINAP	Royal Inscriptions of the Neo-Assyrian Period. Vol. 3.1, *The Royal Inscriptions of Sennacherib, King of Assyria (704–681 BC), Part 1.* A. Kirk Grayson and Jamie Novotny. Winona Lake, IN: Eisenbrauns, 2012
Roth	Roth, Martha T. *Law Collections from Mesopotamia and Asia Minor.* 2nd ed. Atlanta: Society of Biblical Literature, 1997
RT	*The Raging Torrent: Historical Inscriptions from Assyria and Babylonia relating to Ancient Israel.* Mordechai Cogan. Jerusalem: Carta, 2008
SBJT	*Southern Baptist Journal of Theology*
sec.	section
SFAC	*Stories from Ancient Canaan.* 2nd ed. Edited and translated by Michael D. Coogan and Mark S. Smith. Louisville: Westminster John Knox, 2012
SIRL	*A Scripture Index to Rabbinic Literature.* Edited by Caleb T. Friedeman. Peabody, MA: Hendrickson Academic, 2021
SP	(Samaritan Pentateuch) *Der hebräische Pentateuch der Samaritaner.* Edited by August Freiherrn von Gall. 5 vols. Giessen: Töpelmann, 1914–1918
SP-Eng	*The Israelite Samaritan Version of the Torah: First English Translation Compared with the Masoretic Version.* Edited by Benyamim Tsedaka. Grand Rapids: Eerdmans, 2013
SP-G	*The Samaritan Pentateuch: Genesis.* Edited by Stefan Schorch. Berlin: de Gruyter, 2021
SP-L	*The Samaritan Pentateuch: Leviticus.* Edited by Stefan Schorch. Berlin: de Gruyter, 2018
Str-B	Strack, Hermann Leberecht, and Paul Billerbeck. *Kommentar zum Neuen Testament aus Talmud und Midrasch.* 6 vols. Munich: Beck, 1922–1961
Str-BEng	Strack, Hermann Leberecht, and Paul Billerbeck. *A Commentary on the New Testament from the Talmud and Midrash.* Edited by Jacob N. Cerone. Translated by Andrew Bowden and Joseph Longarino. 3 vols. Bellingham, WA: Lexham, 2021–22

SwJT	*Southwestern Journal of Theology*
TAD	*Textbook of Aramaic Documents from Ancient Egypt.* 4 vols. Edited and translated by Bezalal Porten and Ada Yardeni. Winona Lake, IN: Eisenbrauns, 1986–1999
TBA	*The Bible in Aramaic Based on Old Manuscripts and Printed Texts.* Edited by Alexander Sperber. 4 vols. Leiden: Brill, 1959
tc	textual criticism
TCGNT	*A Textual Commentary on the Greek New Testament.* 2nd ed. Bruce M. Metzger. New York: United Bible Societies, 1998
TCHB[4]	*Textual Criticism of the Hebrew Bible.* 4th ed. Emanuel Tov. Minneapolis: Fortress, 2022
Tg. Neof.	Targum Neofiti in ArBib, vols. 1–5
Tg. Ps.-J.	Targum Pseudo-Jonathan in ArBib, vols. 1–5
THGNT	*Tyndale House Greek New Testament.* Edited by Dirk Jongkind. Wheaton, IL: Crossway, 2017
TJ	*Trinity Journal*
TJSVC	*The Torah: Jewish and Samaritan Versions Compared: A Side-By-Side Comparison of the Two Versions with the Differences Highlighted.* 2nd ed. Edited by Mark Shoulson. Leac an Anfa, Co. Mhaigh Eo, Éire: Evertype, 2008
TLC	*Treaty, Law, and Covenant in the Ancient Near East.* Kenneth A. Kitchen and Paul N. J. Lawrence. 3 vols. Wiesbaden: Harrassowitz Verlag, 2012
TOTC	Tyndale Old Testament Commentaries
TRENT1	Instone-Brewer, David. *Traditions of the Rabbis from the Era of the New Testament. Volume 1, Prayer and Agriculture.* Grand Rapids: Eerdmans, 2004
TRENT2a	Instone-Brewer, David. *Traditions of the Rabbis from the Era of the New Testament. Volume 2a, Feasts and Sabbaths: Passover and Atonement.* Grand Rapids: Eerdmans, 2011
UBS[5]	*The Greek New Testament.* United Bible Societies. 5th ed. corrected. Edited by Barbara Aland et al. Stuttgart: Deutsche Bibelgesellschaft, 2019
WTJ	*Westminster Theological Journal*
ZECNT	Zondervan Exegetical Commentary on the New Testament
ZECOT	Zondervan Exegetical Commentary on the Old Testament

INTRODUCTION

The Bible's use of the Bible is a foundational part of both the unity and diversity of God's revelation. It appears in central biblical passages and, thus, intersects with exegesis, biblical theology, and systematic theology, which each provide avenues for applying the biblical teachings to the Christian life.

Yet studying how biblical authors use earlier scriptures can be challenging. It requires hermeneutics, Old and New Testament introduction, and background studies. English Bible readers as well as those who have the advantages that come from studying the biblical languages need to apply themselves to a wide range of difficult interpretive issues.

This book presents seven hermeneutical choices to study the Bible's use of the Bible in both testaments. This book is a hands-on, "how to" guide to this area of study.

Here is a preview of this introduction:

What's at Stake?
Getting Started
Seven Hermeneutical Choices
How to Use This Book
A Note to Students
A Note to Professors

WHAT'S AT STAKE?

Failure to adequately understand scripture's use of scripture undermines responsible exegesis and distorts the progressive revelation of redemption.

Biblical authors frequently use earlier scriptures to present new teachings. In this sense, the Bible's use of the Bible is a vital organ of progressive revelation. Advancement of revelation does not start with the New Testament. Rather, the authors of the New Testament who exegete scripture work along an already ancient and well-worn path, namely, the exegesis of scripture within the Old Testament. This exegesis—the Old Testament's use of the Old Testament—provides a model and a guide for the use of scripture in the New Testament.

Though the study of scripture's use of scripture makes up an important part of responsible interpretation, many people have a fuzzy or incomplete understanding of what this entails. One scholar says the ideal for interpreting scripture by scripture is reading scripture the way Jesus and the New Testament use the Old Testament.[1] This is fine as far as it goes, but, ironically, neither Jesus nor the authors of the New Testament start there. Rather, they interpret the Old Testament the way the Old Testament interprets itself—as it had been for more than a thousand years before the days of Jesus. Understanding how the Old Testament interprets itself and how, in turn, Jesus and the New Testament continue this interpretive tradition is part of responsible exegesis.

GETTING STARTED

So where does one begin? This section provides definitions and basic elements that need to be carefully considered before moving into the following chapters. Readers may wish to mark elements in this introduction and refer back as needed as well as note the Glossary near the end of this book.

Advancement of revelation refers to the progressive revelation of God's redemptive will that culminates in the teaching, death, and resurrection of the Messiah. Beginning in the Torah Yahweh adds "supplementary" teachings and "modifications" that "advance" divinely given authoritative instructions.[2] God's prophets advance Torah's revelation by "explaining, exhorting, enforcing, above all things *evolving* the spiritual kernel from the objective external form."[3] Geerhardus Vos says: "The Bible contains besides the simple record of direct revelations, *the further interpretation* of these immediate disclosures of God by inspired prophets and apostles."[4]

An **organic view of revelation** opposes a mechanical view wherein biblical authors are detached from their personalities and their historical contexts. Biblical authors are not mindless stenographers.[5] Vos emphasizes that Jesus

1. See Vanhoozer, *Biblical Authority*, 127.

2. Vos, *Mosaic Origin*, 89, 131, 140. Vos makes these points even as he argues against the kind of developmentalism celebrated by source-critical studies of the Pentateuch.

3. Ibid., 168, emphasis added.

4. Vos, "Inaugural Address," 33, emphasis added.

5. A point made by Bavinck, *Reformed Dogmatics*, 1:431. Also see Vos, *Biblical Theology*, 188; Barrett, *Canon, Covenant and Christology*, 18–20.

approached the Old Testament as "an organic expression" of God's will, being sensitive to "the progressive development of revelation."[6]

Scriptural exegesis of scripture requires three things: identifiable donor text(s), identifiable receptor text(s), and identifiable exegetical outcome(s). **Donor texts** refer to cited scriptural contexts and **receptor texts** refer to citing scriptural contexts. **Exegesis** can be defined narrowly as explaining or more broadly as explaining, expanding, enhancing, connecting, extrapolating, and the like. This study uses exegesis in its broader sense. The terms exegesis and interpretation are interchangeable.

The present study's focus on **the Bible's use of the Bible** is limited to Old Testament use of Old Testament and New Testament use of Old Testament. The study of the New Testament use of earlier New Testament contexts can be profitable. Yet we have limited this book to how authors of both testaments use the Old Testament. This can provide a basis to consider the New Testament's use of itself.[7] In recent decades much attention has been dedicated to New Testament use of the Old. Study of the Old Testament use of scripture has been widely ignored by scholarship of the New Testament use of scripture.[8] This neglect contributes to the confusion that plagues this area of study. The evidence shows that authors of the New Testament closely studied Israel's scriptures. It should surprise no one that they modeled their own use of scripture on scriptural exegesis within Israel's scriptures. In every chapter the present study emphasizes the use of scripture within Israel's scripture as a resource for making sense of the New Testament's use of scripture.

There are a couple of concepts that play a larger role in the use of scripture within Israel's scriptures because they were composed over a period of a thousand years. **Canonical consciousness** refers to the emerging awareness of the authority of earlier scriptural traditions by later scriptural authors. Biblical authors make explicit the authority of earlier scriptural traditions by citation formulas such as "as it is written." Caution is required because of authorized updating, such as Genesis looking back to the establishment of Israel's kingdom and Deuteronomy referring back to the conquest of the land of promise (Gen 36:31; Deut 2:12). Authorized updating includes the headings on the prophets and psalms, as well as the proverbs of Solomon edited by Hezekiah's scribes (Prov 25:1). Determining which text used the other in the Old Testament can be very challenging.

---

6. Vos, *Biblical Theology*, 359.

7. For examples of NT use of NT, see, e.g., Blomberg, "Quotations, Allusions, and Echoes," 129–43; Miller and Murawski, *1 Peter*, 42–44; *NTUOT*, each ch. ad loc.

8. See *OTUOT*, 849–56; Schnittjer, "Long-Lost Grandparent Texts," 27–31.

When studying Old Testament use of Old Testament, the single criterion for determining **direction of dependence** is an interpretive allusion with the right kind of evidence. The evidence may be verbal, syntactical, and/or contextual. Every case needs to be evaluated individually and carefully. But something more than simply a parallel is required to determine direction of dependence within Israel's scriptures. The necessary evidence may include an interpretive blend, splitting and developing, or any element that identifies the donor and/or the receptor text.[9]

Biblical parallels run on a sliding scale from quotation/citation to paraphrase to allusion to echo to thematic similarity. **Allusion**, **paraphrase**, and **quotation** are author-intended. It is not necessary to say author-intended allusion because there is no other kind. Echoes are too subtle to determine if the parallel is purposeful or coincidental, like figures of speech, stock phrases, and refrains. In this study, allusion—with the sense of "purposeful reuse"—is also inclusive of paraphrase and quotation.[10] The issue of detecting allusions will be taken up in detail in Chapter 3.

Whenever this book refers to **verbal parallels** it indicates the same roots or words in the Hebrew, Aramaic, or Greek scriptures. Though this book is accessible to English Bible readers, it is everywhere based on the scriptures in their original languages.

Biblical allusions may be unmarked or marked. **Marked** refers to explicit acknowledgment of dependence of any sort, including the commonplace "as it is written." Though marked and unmarked allusions themselves tend to function identically, marking allusions makes the authority of the donor text overt for author and readers.[11]

This book affirms a **plain sense** reading of the redemptive revelation of scripture.[12] Plain sense reading accepts that authors mean what they say and

9. See extended explanation with examples in Schnittjer, "Going Vertical," 121–22 and *OTUOT*, xxviii–xxxiv.

10. For "purposeful reuse," see Schultz, *Search for Quotation*, 222; cf. 222–24.

11. *IBUB* indicates all cases of marking by citation formulas in both testaments—the specific wording in the original and in translation are indicated in *OTUOTPL* and *NTUOTPL*. For evaluation of the function of citation marking, see *OTUOT*, 633–37.

12. So also Beale, "Apostolic Hermeneutics: Description and Presuppositions," *DNTUOT*, 64. Vanhoozer refers to this as "grammatical-eschatological" interpretation (*Mere Christian Hermeneutics*, 24, 176–80, 182, et passim). Plain sense and redemptive-historical interpretation should not be set against each other. In a Five Views book on hermeneutics, the advocates for the historical-grammatical (Blomberg) and redemptive-historical (Gaffin) views rightly affirm each other's approaches. See Blomberg, "Historical-Critical/Grammatical," 140, and Gaffin, "Redemptive-Historical," 176. Gaffin admits that "grammatical-historical" interpretation is a prerequisite of a redemptive-historical approach to revelation. The differences between Blomberg and Gaffin in the Five Views book seem to come down to disagreements over this or that passage within a basically shared framework.

that their writings can be understood by ordinary conventions of interpretation. This applies to what should characterize modern interpretation as well as the exegesis by biblical authors within the scriptures. Plain sense hermeneutics is often referred to by modernists as grammatical-historical interpretation. We have no problem with this modernist language or this view, though we prefer the expression plain sense. This means biblical writings and passages are taken on their own terms: narrative as narrative, legal standards as legal standards, prophetic discourse as prophetic discourse, poetic expression as poetic expression, letters to collectives as letters to collectives, irony as irony, figurative language as figurative language, and so forth, including the ways the scriptures use earlier scriptures in all their genres and rhetorical strategies.

Plain sense redemptive reading accents two sides of the work of the Spirit—revelation and interpretation. Revelation of scripture is God-given, as is its interpretation that appears within both testaments. Consider what the narrator says about Ezra:

> He [Ezra] was a scribe who was an expert in *the Torah of Moses* that **Yahweh the God of Israel had given**. . . . Ezra had inclined his heart to study *the Torah of Yahweh*. (Ezra 7:6b, 10a AT)

The expressions "Torah of Moses" and "Torah of Yahweh" are interchangeable (see italics above) because revelation mediated by ordained delegates is given by Yahweh (see bold).[13]

Peter likewise emphasizes both sides of the work of the Spirit. The Spirit's revelation by the prophets and his illumination to the preachers are redemptively shaped—note the apostle's twofold emphasis on the Spirit signified by broken underlining.[14]

> Concerning this salvation, the prophets, who spoke of the grace that was to come to you, searched intently and with the greatest care, trying to find out the time and circumstances to which the Spirit of Christ in them was pointing when he predicted the sufferings of the Messiah and the glories that would follow. It was revealed to them that they were not serving themselves but you, when they spoke of the things that have now been told you by those

13. For a similar point, see 2 Kgs 18:12—"**The voice of Yahweh** their God . . . *all which Moses* the servant of Yahweh *had commanded*" (AT, emphasis added). And see discussion on the "instrumentality" of Moses in Morales, *Numbers 1–19*, latter portion of sec. on "Who composed the book of Numbers?" in "Introduction" (forthcoming).

14. See Miller and Murawski, *1 Peter*, 75.

> who have preached the gospel to you by the Holy Spirit sent from heaven. (1 Pet 1:10–12a, emphases added)

Yet the God-givenness of scriptural revelation and its redemptive interpretation do not contradict the realities of strenuous study of the scriptures by Ezra and by the prophets (see underlining in both passages above).[15]

A plain sense approach does not set aside interpretive complications and complexities. Just the opposite. The manifold difficulties attached to the Bible's use of the Bible all need to be taken seriously on their own terms, without some other hermeneutical filter to deflect and/or compartmentalize the difficulties. A plain sense approach does not seek out a clever hermeneutical device to "solve" all of the difficulties. A plain sense reading is not a method or technique. Accepting a plain sense reading is not an attempt to solve all of the difficulties of the Bible's use of the Bible. Doug Moo is correct when he says that interpreting difficult cases of the scriptural use of scripture "cannot be reduced to a single formula."[16]

To say that the biblical authors used plain sense exegesis will likely raise the eyebrows of anyone who has wrestled with challenging cases of the Bible's use of the Bible. The way biblical authors interpret earlier scripture will be demonstrated in detail in Chapters 1–7. For now, it is enough to say that when later biblical authors—of either testament—interpret earlier scriptures according to the very ways these earlier scriptures interpret themselves, this is nothing other than plain sense exegesis. The authors of the New Testament did not invent a new hermeneutic. They followed the well-worn interpretive path used by prophets, psalmists, narrators, visionaries, and sages of Israel's scriptures. These Old Testament authors did not invent this way of interpretation either. They interpret Torah in the same ways Torah interprets Torah.

The broad generalizations in the previous paragraph are not important of themselves. They merely offer an invitation to wrestle through the seven choices in the next seven chapters. Then it would help to work through difficult cases of the Bible's use of the Bible for oneself to see how the choices work. Students in our courses on Old Testament use of Old Testament and New Testament use of Old Testament routinely adjust their thoughts after they actually get their hands dirty with the Bible for themselves. Working with the biblical evidence will provide a good basis to disagree or agree or modify the generalizations of the previous paragraph.

---

15. On the need for the Holy Spirit and study for Christian interpretation, see Harmon, *Asking the Right Questions*, 50, 102.

16. Moo, "Problem of *Sensus Plenior*," 209.

As noted above, plain sense exegesis does not remove interpretive difficulties. There are a few cases in scripture that are difficult for any and every approach, including a plain sense reading. The small minority of potentially noncontextual cases of the Bible's use of the Bible may be considered exceptions to the norm of many hundreds of contextual uses of scripture.[17] But even in the cases listed in the first footnote of this paragraph, the exegesis of the receptor text is compatible with the meaning of the donor text in some sense.[18]

Studies of the Bible's use of the Bible typically frame themselves as **author-oriented/diachronic** or **reader-oriented/synchronic** approaches. Diachronic (through time) studies focus on the text-author dialectic and synchronic (at one time) studies focus on the text-reader dialectic. Unfortunately, most studies have failed to attach their approaches to aims, thus eliminating any meaningful generalization by labels like diachronic and synchronic. In broad terms, diachronic approaches may serve textual or excavative aims.[19] Diachronic studies with excavative aims move away from the biblical text seeking something else, like theoretical authorial elements such as theoretical editorial layers, theoretical sources, theoretical scribal culture, and theoretical life settings, and to establish dates of all of these. Diachronic studies with textual goals work with the same evidence to evaluate what the author has put together.[20] Synchronic approaches may serve readerly or textual aims. Synchronic studies with readerly aims vary widely. They may put texts into conversation with unrelated ancient or modern texts or films or seek to produce a history of reception. Synchronic studies with textual aims focus on the final form of the text, like how a New Testament author read a scroll of Israel's scripture in its received form.[21]

To a greater extent, the present study employs a diachronic approach restricted to textual aims to evaluate scriptural interpretation of scripture. Evaluating biblical evidence this way means thinking with the author based on available evidence. To a lesser extent, the present study uses a synchronic approach restricted to textual aims. This means focusing on biblical authors

17. Here is a combined list of possible noncontextual interpretation uses of scripture: Ezek 16:53–57//Deut 29:23[22 H]; Matt 2:15//Hos 11:1; Matt 2:17–18//Jer 31:15; Matt 27:9–10//Zech 11:12–13; Acts 2:16–21//Joel 2:28–32[3:1–5 H]; Acts 2:25–32//Ps 16:8–11; Acts 2:30//Ps 132:11; Acts 15:16–17//Amos 9:11–12; Rom 10:5//Lev 18:5; Rom 10:6–8//Deut 30:11–14; 1 Cor 9:9–10//Deut 25:4; 1 Cor 10:1–4//Exod and Num passim; 2 Cor 3:13–18//Exod passim; Gal 3:12//Lev 18:5; Gal 3:16//Gen 12:7; Gal 4:21–31//Gen passim; Eph 4:8//Ps 68:18; Eph 5:31–32//Gen 2:24; Heb 7//Gen 14; 1 Pet 1:24–25//Isa 40:6–8. See *OTUOT*, 323; Beale, *Right Doctrine*, 389; Vlach, *Old*, 73.

18. See Moo, "Problem of *Sensus Plenior*," 209–10; Beale, *Right Doctrine*, 389.

19. The term "excavative" comes from Alter, *Art of Biblical Narrative*, 14.

20. See "authorship" in Glossary, and for more detail, see *OTUOT*, 890.

21. For detailed explanation of diachronic and synchronic approaches to the Bible's use of the Bible with illustrations and references, see Schnittjer, "Going Vertical," 124–26. Also see *OTUOT*, xxxiv–xxxvi.

as readers of earlier scripture based on the evidence in the received form of the scriptures.

Figural or **typological patterns** refer to intentional scriptural shaping to draw selective expectational analogies between persons, events, institutions, procedures, oracles, or a combination of these, within the historical framework of progressive revelation. Unlike allegory, only *selective* analogous elements get reused in typological patterns in scripture.[22] Some typological patterns are forward-looking and expectational, and other donor texts are non-expectational in themselves, with the backward-looking pattern recognized by the receptor text in light of its fulfillment. Both forward-looking and backward-looking typological patterns are fulfilled by the events presented in the receptor texts.

Many scholars ask (and answer in different ways): **Can we as moderns interpret scripture the way the biblical authors did?** No and yes. No, only divinely appointed authors can advance biblical revelation by exegesis. Yes, insofar as biblical authors use plain sense exegesis, so too can modern interpreters.[23]

SEVEN HERMENEUTICAL CHOICES

The next seven chapters work through hermeneutical choices necessary for responsible interpretation of the Bible's use of the Bible. These chapters are followed by detailed Case Studies that put all of it together step by step.

Working through seven choices to study the scriptural use of scripture is different than either "methods" or "views." For starters, the seven choices build on the basics. This book does not review what we all learned as students in an introductory course on hermeneutics (here referred to as "Hermeneutics 101"). Instead, the present study takes the next step and narrowly focuses on the special issues of interpreting the Bible's use of the Bible. Students are encouraged to review the textbook from their introductory hermeneutics course or any other such textbooks like *Asking the Right Questions* (Harmon), *Studying Scripture by Its Connections* (Schnittjer), *Scripture as Communication* (Brown), *Grasping God's Word* (Duvall and Hays), and *How to Read the Bible for All Its Worth* (Fee and Stuart).

Many **methods** to study the New Testament use of scripture tend to focus on interpretive activities that are presented in Hermeneutics 101. The core of three leading methods (by Greg Beale, by Craig Evans, and by Klyne Snodgrass, respectively) is to study the donor text in its context and the receptor text in

22. See Moo, *Old*, 380; *OTUOT*, 862.

23. Similarly, Moo, "Problem of *Sensus Plenior*," 206; Carson, "Apostolic Hermeneutics: Present-Day Imitation," *DNTUOT*, 64. Contra Longenecker, *Biblical Exegesis*, xxxv.

its context—just like Hermeneutics 101 (these three methods are analyzed in detail in the Case Studies of the Bible's Use of the Bible near the end of this book). The present study affirms these hermeneutical basics as an excellent starting place. Yet, the methods do not touch on many of the hermeneutical choices presented in the next chapters.[24] For example, the three methods do not give dedicated attention to how Old Testament use of Old Testament provides a resource for New Testament use of Old Testament.[25] Yet, this is a critical consideration since scriptural interpretation within Israel's scriptures provided models and guidance for the authors of the New Testament.

How can modern interpreters understand the New Testament's use of scripture without studying the scriptural exegesis within the Bible of Jesus and the apostles? The present study emphasizes the Old Testament's interpretation of itself as a resource to study New Testament use of scripture.

Choices are also different than **views**. Sometimes books and articles have presented competing hermeneutical views of the New Testament use of scripture.[26] Unfortunately, all of the views in the footnote fail to account sufficiently for the foundational role of the Old Testament use of scripture that sets the course for New Testament authors. But if that deficiency is set aside for a moment, the views often overlap and talk past each other. Contrasting this view and that view implies that each view has a one-size-fits-all approach. But that is not how the scriptures work.

Each interpreter's view is made up of many choices. At the end of one book of three views on interpreting the New Testament use of scripture, the editor provides a chart of choices showing where all three views agree and where only two of the three agree.[27] The views, therefore, are not mutually exclusive but are made up of many choices—frequently agreeing with the opposing views. And trying to wield a one-size-fits-all view against the wide variety of scriptural situations naturally explains why one view works well for some scriptures and another view works better for other scriptures.

---

24. These approaches give attention to some of the issues of the seven choices of the present work, namely, interpretive presuppositions (Beale, Snodgrass); detecting allusion (Beale, Evans); extrabiblical texts (Beale, Evans, Snodgrass); and typological patterns (Beale). Yet even these issues are mostly approached in terms of the basics of introductory hermeneutics courses. None of the three methods gives dedicated attention to the other choices presented herein (connected approach; advancement of revelation; vertical context; and prosopological exegesis). See Table 8-A in the Case Studies of the Bible's Use of the Bible near the end of this book; and see Evans, "Function of the Old Testament," 170–71; Snodgrass, "Use of the Old Testament," 222–23; and *HNTUOT*, 42–43; Beale, "Method," *DNTUOT*, 520–26.

25. Beale mentions the importance of Old Testament interpretation of scripture three times (*HNTUOT*, 47, 97, 98).

26. See Bock, "Evangelicals: Part 1," 209–23; idem, "Evangelicals: Part 2," 306–19; Lunde and Berding, *Three Views*; Vlach, *Old in the New*; Tabb and King, *Five Views*.

27. See Berding, "Conclusion," 240. Also see Vlach, *Old in the New*, 24, 25, 39, 40, et passim.

There is no need to get stuck with a view that has preselected all the choices.

Responsible interpretation needs to get more granular and make interpretive choices one at a time. There is no domino effect with the choices in this book. Each hermeneutical choice needs to be made no matter what a person decides for the other six choices and irrespective of a person's view, approach, or method of study. While this book advocates for specific choices in each chapter, the reader who disagrees with one, some, or all the preferences of this book will still benefit by consciously making the decisions needed for responsible interpretation.

The next seven chapters work through **seven hermeneutical choices** narrowly targeting the special interpretive challenges of studying the Bible's use of the Bible.

Not all the choices are of the same sort. Choices 1 and 2 are global choices that consider approaches to the use of scripture in the two testaments and how to handle meaning and context. The choice in Chapter 1 focuses on hermeneutical presuppositions (why), while the choice in Chapter 2 targets hermeneutical mechanics (how). **Chapter 1** presents a choice between approaches that sequester the use of scripture within Israel's scriptures and the New Testament as things unto themselves versus a connected approach. The present work advocates for a connected approach. The choice in **Chapter 2** is between those approaches that adjust meaning and/or adjust context in the case of the Bible's use of the Bible versus advancement of revelation. The present study rejects adjusting meaning and/or adjusting context and emphasizes advancement of revelation. These first two choices are highly contested, with careful scholars taking a range of opposing positions.

Chapters 3 through 7 target a series of choices on particular aspects of studying the Bible's use of the Bible. **Chapter 3** tackles the choice between detecting allusion as an art versus as a science. The chapter takes a both/and approach. While detecting allusions is more an art than a science, empirical standards provide guardrails to avoid errors. In the case of New Testament allusions, the textual basis of the donor text must be determined, especially between the Hebrew and Greek scriptures. As elsewhere, this chapter will suggest a path for English Bible readers to make use of English translations of Hebrew, Aramaic, and Greek texts. **Chapter 4** considers the choice between horizontal context (verses surrounding the text) and vertical context (allusions to earlier scriptures). Though the vast majority of studies of the Bible's use of the Bible limit their attention to horizontal context, the present study promotes a both/and approach, explaining what is lost by ignoring vertical context. The choice of **Chapter 5** is a matter of emphasis between biblical and extrabiblical parallels. Much is at stake in getting the emphasis correct.

Chapters 6 and 7 work through sharply contested areas of scriptural use of analogical patterns in earlier scriptures. **Chapter 6** takes a both/and approach over and against those who claim that typological patterns are always forward-looking and those who say they are always backward-looking. But it is not as simple as combining approaches. There are many moving parts that require great care to avoid gross misunderstandings. The choice in **Chapter 7** builds on Chapter 6 by targeting a particularly challenging area of typological interpretation in scripture, namely, a choice between exegesis confined to the historical context of donor texts versus historical and prosopological exegesis. Prosopological exegesis refers to analogical speech (inclusive of typological speech), that is, a biblical author reading an earlier biblical speech in the light of a new character—whom the speech is by, about, or to. This contested, and frequently misunderstood, biblical phenomenon needs to be approached with patience.

The interrelated nature of progressive revelation in the scriptures means that there is significant overlap between the seven choices. They have been sorted out here for the sake of working out these challenging issues. For example, typological patterns are very common in scripture and will come up briefly in many chapters, by necessity. But dedicated attention to the hermeneutical challenges of interpreting typological patterns in scripture appears in Chapter 6.

All of the next seven chapters attend to, in different degrees, use of scripture in both testaments. All seven chapters end with one or more brief case studies. This book tilts toward hands-on study rather than interpretive theories. There are many places where this study wades into hermeneutical debates. But this book is committed to hermeneutics serving scriptural studies, not the other way around. This means readers will find plenty of concrete examples from the scriptures along the way, as well as more detailed cases at the end of each chapter.

After the seven choices, the **Case Studies of the Bible's Use of the Bible** bring together the entire process of studying the Bible's use of the Bible. These case studies take a "how to" approach, step by step.

HOW TO USE THIS BOOK

The main text of this book is accessible to students and ministers of the word of God. This book only uses biblical languages (**Hebrew**, **Aramaic**, and **Greek**) when necessary for students who study these. Everything in the main text is translated so that **English Bible** readers can easily follow the discussion. In addition, the Case Studies of the Bible's Use of the Bible near the end of this book include guidance for English Bible readers alongside guidance for those who study the biblical languages.

This book uses **default translations** of scripture and other ancient literature. Unless stated otherwise, scripture is presented in the NIV. Other defaults include: Hebrew Bible from *Biblia Hebraica*; LXX from Göttingen in most cases (Pentateuch, Prophets, Psalms), otherwise from Rahlfs; translation of LXX from NETS; Greek New Testament from NA[28]; Qumran biblical texts from *BQS*; Qumran sectarian texts from *DSSSE*; Apocrypha from NRSVue; and pseudepigrapha from *OTP*. This book puts Hebrew Bible verse references, when different from English versions, in square brackets []—except Exod 20 and Deut 5, for which only English Bible references are cited.[28]

Specialized terminology is legion in studies of the Bible's use of the Bible. Students new to this area of study should be aware that many scholars define terms in their own ways. This book includes a **Glossary** for quick reference. The **Bibliography** offers full details to locate resources cited in brief in the footnotes. Page numbers are used for print resources, and for e-resources chapter numbers and/or section headings are used when possible. Use of resources is limited to English whenever possible. Items appearing in the **Abbreviations** are not included in the bibliography.

Study questions appear at the end of the seven chapters of this book, as well as this Introduction and the Cases Studies of the Bible's Use of the Bible.

A NOTE TO STUDENTS

The Bible's use of the Bible can be subtle, complicated, and complex. Virtually every issue is sharply contested. You will do well to take your time.

If you are new to the study of the Bible's use of the Bible, please exercise caution. Initial provisional decisions made with humility and with a willingness to reevaluate after working through difficult scriptures can help. For views that do not seem correct, please take the time to consider them from the point of view of those who espouse these views. This can go a long way to clearing up confusion. Discussing the challenges with other students and your professor can be helpful.

28. See *OTUOT*, xlv, n. 61.

Please look up scripture references and study the larger contexts of the passages cited in this book. Hermeneutical decisions always need to be tested against the scriptures.

Students of Old Testament or New Testament should devote equal time to the examples of both testaments in this book. Ignoring earlier or later stages in progressive revelation almost always leads to interpretive deficiencies.

The Case Studies of the Bible's Use of the Bible near the end of this book provide step-by-step explanatory models that illustrate how to do the research needed to interpret the Bible's use of the Bible. After reading the case studies, it is recommended that you go to the library and look through the reference tools mentioned in the cases.

A NOTE TO PROFESSORS

The Case Studies of the Bible's Use of the Bible (immediately after Chapter 7) offer step-by-step examples that students can use to do the research needed to produce a paper.

We advocate for specific choices in each chapter rather than straddling fences. Informed disagreement is welcome. This book is designed around learning outcomes by helping students make the choices necessary for responsible interpretation—whether they agree with none, one, some, or all of the choices for which this book advocates.

Resources are available at no cost to professors who use this book as a required text. See TextbookPlus at ZondervanAcademic.com for the following aids:

- Visuals Aids
- Quizzes and exams
- Questions suitable for student assignments or class discussions
- Suggested syllabi for courses on Old Testament use of Old Testament, New Testament use of Old Testament, and the Bible's use of the Bible
- Suggested unit on the Bible's use of the Bible for syllabi of courses on hermeneutics, Old Testament studies, or New Testament studies
- Instructions for research papers on Old Testament use of Old Testament and New Testament use of Old Testament
- Quiz and discussion questions for the videos that go with this book sold separately

Study Questions

1. In what sense is the Bible's use of the Bible a vital part of progressive revelation?
2. What is the shortcoming with the ideal of interpreting scripture the way Jesus and the apostles interpret it?
3. Define the following: advancement of revelation; organic view of revelation; donor text; receptor text; exegesis; marked; plain sense reading.
4. What is the difference between allusion and echo?
5. What does it mean to say scriptural use of scripture is characterized by plain sense exegesis?
6. Where does the Bible's use of the Bible begin, and why is this important?
7. What are typological patterns within scripture?
8. What are the problems with the hermeneutical elements emphasized by the leading methods of studying the New Testament use of scripture?
9. What is the problem with one-size-fits-all hermeneutical views of the scripture's use of scripture?
10. How do hermeneutical choices relate to and differ from hermeneutical views?

CHAPTER 1

SEQUESTERED VERSUS CONNECTED

This chapter presents a choice between sequestered and connected approaches to scriptural exegesis within scripture.

Scholars sequester scriptural exegesis in each testament by treating it unto itself and without regard to the use of scripture in the other testament. Because scholars sequester the use of scripture in the Hebrew Bible and the New Testament for different reasons, they will be treated separately in the next two sections. This will be followed by this chapter's preferred choice for a connected approach to the Bible's use of the Bible and a brief case study.

This chapter argues that the shared presuppositions of the exegesis of scripture across the two testaments of the Christian Bible are connected by Jesus's exegesis of scripture. Students should exercise caution. The choice to sequester each testament dominates scholarship.

CHOICE—SEQUESTERING SCRIPTURAL INTERPRETATION WITHIN ISRAEL'S SCRIPTURES

Prominent scholarship focuses on select cases of scriptural interpretation within Israel's scriptures that anticipate Second Temple sectarian and/or late rabbinic exegesis. There is nothing wrong with this narrow agenda except when it eliminates attention to the rest of exegesis within Israel's scriptures. The tendency to sequester interpretation within Israel's scriptures needs to be evaluated.

No treatment of exegesis within Israel's scriptures has been more influential than that of Michael Fishbane. His *Biblical Interpretation in Ancient Israel* presents scriptural interpretation within Israel's scriptures as anticipating postbiblical rabbinic exegesis. The book's opening and closing sections on biblical interpretation by scribal interventions and in visionary contexts frame its important middle sections. The two middle sections focus on legal exegesis (halakic) and narrative exegesis (haggadic) within Israel's scriptures. The middle sections collate cases of scriptural interpretation to show their affinity with the two great streams of halakic and haggadic exegesis preserved in classic rabbinic literature—Mishnah, Talmud, Midrashim, and much more. Fishbane closes the Introduction to the book with a leading question:

> Is it possible that the origins of the Jewish exegetical tradition are native and ancient, that they developed diversely in ancient Israel, in many centres and at many times, and that these many tributaries met in the exile and its aftermath to set a new stage for biblical culture which was redirected, rationalized, and systematized in the lively environment of the Graeco-Roman world?[1]

Fishbane frames the exegesis of Israel's scriptures in the Gospels and letters of the New Testament as "something new, something not 'biblical'" in contrast to the exegesis of scripture within Israel's scriptures.[2] In the same context he acknowledges that rabbinic Judaism with its Talmud, Christianity with its New Testament, and Islam with its Quran represent three streams of postbiblical exegesis of Israel's scriptures. This sleight of hand does not make explicit that the controlling framework for rabbinic Judaism is Torah—written Torah and oral Torah (see Glossary)—emphasizing the legal and narrative categories of exegesis Fishbane investigates. By contrast, scripture constitutes the authoritative framework for Christian doctrine. These factors help strengthen the continuity Fishbane sees between exegesis within scripture and rabbinic exegesis, as well as isolate these from the early Christian exegesis within the New Testament.

The thematic organization of examples of exegesis in Israel's scriptures into the two central sections of Fishbane's *Biblical Interpretation* aptly demonstrates the kinds of exegesis that appear in legal and narrative interpretive traditions of rabbinic Judaism. The book seems to confirm the continuity suggested in the question Fishbane posed at the end of his Introduction (see above). But the organization of the book makes it vulnerable to criticisms.

An early reviewer perceptively criticized the diversity of Fishbane's haggadic section because it is too wide. He deduced that the haggadic section "is not the sort of category one would come up with *unless* one were working backwards

1. Fishbane, *Biblical Interpretation*, 19.
2. See ibid., 10.

from the rabbinic ones."[3] The reviewer went on to make a more damaging criticism that amounts to accusing Fishbane of rigging the apparent continuity between biblical and rabbinic writings. The reviewer suggested that the purpose of the opening section on scribal exegesis is to collate cases of biblical exegesis that do not fit neatly in the two middle sections. He says Fishbane uses the opening section "as a separate category" in order to "enable 'aggadic exegesis' to maintain its basically rabbinic dimensions."[4]

Observing the similarities between late rabbinic exegesis and interpretation within Israel's scriptures is not a problem of itself. But the selection and organization of exegesis within Israel's scriptures that resembles Second Temple sectarian and late rabbinic interpretive traditions skew the evidence. More than thirty-five years later, Christian scholars use Fishbane's study to sequester exegesis within Israel's scriptures.

Fishbane's *Biblical Interpretation* provides the basic resource for guiding Christian students in *How Scripture Interprets Scripture* by Michael Graves. The five case studies Graves offers do not satisfy the expectation generated by the book's subtitle: *What Biblical Writers Can Teach Us about Reading the Bible*. For example, Graves approaches Ezra 9–10 and Neh 13 by an uncritical adoption of Fishbane's racial/ethnic interpretation of the intermarriages, ignoring the biblical evidence of apostasy marriages. Graves helpfully alerts readers to the donor texts pointed out by Fishbane (Deut 7; 23; Lev 18). But instead of engaging the details, Graves's six-page discussion offers a summary of Ezra-Nehemiah.[5] Graves, like Fishbane, only attends to one side of Ezra-Nehemiah's handling of others. In spite of the Bible's consistent use of two kinds of others—excluded others and included others—many scholars wrongly collapse these into one category. Graves investigates passages concerning excluded others and ignores passages concerning included others.[6] In short, Graves limits "what biblical writers can teach us" to the selective rabbinic-oriented guidance of Fishbane's *Biblical Interpretation*. Graves does not show his readers that Isaiah, Ezekiel, and Ezra-Nehemiah each promote two kinds of others—excluded others and included others—in continuity with the same twofold teaching in Torah.[7] Graves does not mention that the restoration assembly of Ezra-Nehemiah

3. Kugel, review, 275, emphasis original.

4. Ibid., 276.

5. See Graves, *Scripture*, 57–63.

6. See ibid., 61, n. 38; cf. Fishbane, *Biblical Interpretation*, 142–43, n. 98; *OTUOT*, 249, n. 74.

7. See *OTUOT*, 238–41, 247–50, 339–46, 655–64, 677–79 esp. the tables on 240 and 341. Also see scriptural texts from the same biblical books—Torah, prophets, postexilic narratives—on excluded others (Exod 12:45; Deut 23:3–6[4–7 H]; Isa 52:1; Ezek 44:9; Ezra 4:1, 4; Neh 10:30[31 H]) and included others (Exod 12:48–49; Deut 23:7–8[8–9 H]; Isa 56:3–7; Ezek 14:7; 47:22–23; Ezra 6:21; Neh 10:28[29 H]); cf. entries on these texts in *OTUOTPL*.

welcomed outsiders who turned to the covenant of Yahweh (Ezra 6:21; Neh 10:28[29 H]), including them within the "seed of Israel" (Neh 9:2 AT).[8] In sum, it is easy to agree with Graves's plan to let the scriptural use of scripture guide thematic theological interpretation of scripture. But filtering out all of the Bible's use of the Bible that does not fit the profile of rabbinic-like exegesis sequesters these contexts of Israel's scriptures away from the New Testament, or at least makes them seem like strange misfits.

Though the scholarship of the New Testament use of scripture has primarily been content to ignore exegesis within Israel's scriptures, in rare publications this scholarship turns to it. A collection of essays on *Methodology in the Use of the Old Testament in the New*[9] opens with an essay by Susan Docherty seeking to provide insight from interpretation in the Hebrew Bible. Docherty approaches exegesis in the Hebrew Bible according to the rabbinic categories established by Fishbane.[10] This follows a similar pattern in previous studies, such as Hubbard's and Longenecker's, that use Fishbane's approach to exegesis as a resource for New Testament studies.[11] Likewise, Vermes's study surveys "midrash" in the Hebrew Bible as precursor to the midrash of Second Temple sectarians—the lone representative of exegesis within Israel's scriptures to appear in *The Cambridge History of the Bible*.[12]

The underlying reasons why scholarship on the New Testament use of scripture prefers focusing exclusively on examples of exegesis within Israel's scriptures akin to Second Temple sectarian and rabbinic interpretation are not hard to detect. Anyone can page through an assortment of overviews of the New Testament use of scripture in the present and past couple of generations and see what they include and what they exclude. They exclude comparisons to exegesis within Israel's scriptures. They almost invariably include a discussion of how the New Testament authors depend on Second Temple sectarian and rabbinic exegetical tendencies (see next section and Chapter 2).[13]

The studies by Docherty (2020) and Graves (2021) mentioned in the preceding paragraphs appeared thirty-five and thirty-six years after Fishbane's *Biblical Interpretation* (1985). This signals the complicity from many quarters

8. See Schnittjer, *Old Testament Narrative*, 203–4.

9. Allen and Smith, eds. *Methodology in the Use of the Old Testament in the New*.

10. See Docherty, "Crossing Testamentary Borders," 12–15.

11. See Hubbard, "Inner-Biblical Exegesis," 125–39; Longenecker, *Biblical Exegesis*, xxvii–xxviii.

12. See Vermes, "Bible and Midrash," 199–231.

13. See, e.g., Lindars, "Place of the Old Testament," 62; Ellis, *Paul's Use of the Old Testament*, 139–47; Longenecker, *Biblical Exegesis*, xxii–xxvi; Barrett, "Interpretation of the Old Testament," 383–89; Motyer, "Old Testament," 582; Evans, "Function of the Old Testament," 165–69; Snodgrass, "Use of the Old Testament," 214–20; Bock, "Scripture Citing Scripture," 259–63; Allen, "Introduction," 9; Moyise, *Old*, 11–25. An exception is *HNTUOT*, 47, 97, 98.

of scholarship to sequester the study of interpretation within Israel's scriptures. There has been a long commitment to narrowly focus on a small sampling of cases that reinforce the interpretive biases of scholarship.

A study of cases of exegesis within Israel's scriptures that resemble late rabbinic interpretation is not at issue. Rabbinic exegesis does depend on exegesis within Israel's scriptures. The problem derives from exclusively targeting and organizing interpretive elements that resemble rabbinic interpretation. Something more is needed.

The continuities Fishbane detects between exegesis in the Hebrew Bible and in rabbinic writings may be exaggerated. Stemberger argues that the kind of atomistic exegesis practiced within classic rabbinic interpretation requires both a "closed canon" and "an absolutely fixed text."[14] This stands at some distance from the emerging canonical consciousness evident in the exegesis within Israel's scriptures.

The alternative choice offered in this chapter (below) approaches exegesis within both testaments of the Christian Bible in a connected manner. The point has nothing to do with reading New Testament exegesis of Israel's scriptures back onto the donor texts. The donor texts need to retain their historical integrity alongside their later interpretations within both testaments. Israel's scriptures should be approached on their own terms rather than overlaying them with categories of Second Temple sectarian and rabbinic exegesis.

One path forward is an inductive study of exegesis within Israel's scriptures.[15] This can proceed section by section, book by book, one passage at a time.[16] The study of the Bible's use of the Bible envisioned here is inclusive of the entire Christian Bible. The advantages of a book-by-book, case-by-case approach include investigating the various tendencies of exegesis within Israel's scriptures according to a scroll-by-scroll framework that approximates the way in which they were contextualized for the authors of the New Testament.

In sum, the majority choice is to approach select cases of interpretation within Israel's scriptures organized by Second Temple sectarian and/or late rabbinic exegesis. This narrow agenda has effectively sequestered scriptural exegesis within Israel's scriptures. An alternate choice promoted in this chapter is approaching the use of the Bible in the Bible book by book through the entire Christian Bible.

---

14. See Stemberger, "From Inner-biblical Interpretation," 194, 195.

15. An inductive approach is suggested by Johnson, *Old Testament in the New*, 26.

16. See Vos, "Inaugural Address," 21–24; and see *OTUOT*, xlii.

CHOICE—SEQUESTERING SCRIPTURAL INTERPRETATION WITHIN THE NEW TESTAMENT

Overview. Dominant scholarship of the New Testament use of scripture has sequestered this field of study as a thing unto itself. This section will summarize the situation and provide evidence to illustrate the problem.

Studies of the New Testament's use of scripture have, with rare exceptions, ignored the resources of scriptural interpretation within Israel's scriptures.[17] In recent days, a few studies have begun to notice the lack of attention to scriptural interpretation within Israel's scriptures.[18] These glimmers of awareness that something is missing provide hope for the option proposed in this chapter (next section below).

Arthur Keefer evaluates what counts as "Old Testament context" in three approaches to the New Testament use of scripture by Craig Evans, by Klyne Snodgrass, and by Greg Beale.[19] The importance of the list of eight aspects of Old Testament context cannot be pursued here.[20] The present concern is the glaring absence of discussion regarding scriptural exegesis within the Old Testament. In spite of hundreds of cases of exegesis within Israel's scriptures, many of which serve as donor texts for the New Testament use of scripture, New Testament studies has all but ignored this natural resource.[21]

In an extremely rare exception, a book on the Bible's use of the Bible entitled *It Is Written: Scripture Citing Scripture* is coedited by an Old Testament scholar and a New Testament scholar.[22] The book features four chapters on the Old Testament in the Old Testament, five chapters on between the testaments, and nine chapters on the Old Testament in the New Testament. I. Howard Marshall's twenty-one-page introduction to the book focuses almost entirely on

17. On the lack of attention to scriptural exegesis within Israel's scriptures, see *OTUOT*, 848–56; Schnittjer, "Long-Lost Grandparent Texts," 27–31; idem, "What's Old?" 62, 79. For exceptions that include attention to exegesis within Israel's scriptures as a resource for study of the New Testament use of scripture, see, e.g., Bruce, *This Is That*, 11–22, et passim; Shepherd, *Text in the Middle*, 7–166; Beale, "Colossians," in *CNTUOT*, 844, 853, 855; Shively, "Israel's Scriptures," 238–39, 245–46, et passim.

18. See Allen and Smith, "Introduction," 1; Docherty, "Crossing Testamentary Borders," 11–12; *HNTUOT*, 47, 97, 98. And see the series of entries on OT books in *DNTUOT* ad loc.

19. See Keefer, "Meaning and Place," 73–85, esp. 75; Evans, "Function of the Old Testament," 170–71; Snodgrass, "Use of the Old Testament," 222–23; *HNTUOT*, 41–54. Beale mentions the importance of OT use of the OT in three places (*HNTUOT*, 47, 97, 98).

20. Keefer summarizes what OT contexts scholars of the NT use of scripture focus on: (1) grammatical/linguistic; (2) surrounding verses; (3) similar texts elsewhere; (4) major sections of the OT, esp. a single book; (5) OT themes; (6) divine redemptive-historical actions; (7) historical context of the OT authors; and (8) mental intentions of the original author ("Meaning," 84).

21. See *OTUOT*, 849–56; Schnittjer, "Long-Lost Grandparent Texts," 27–31; idem, "What's Old?" 62, 79.

22. See Carson and Williamson, eds., *It Is Written*.

the New Testament use of scripture except for a single sentence. The sentence epitomizes the disconnect of the entire field of study: "We shall, however, steer clear of one problem which is the subject of the first major section of the book, namely the use of the OT in the OT."[23] No statement more clearly explains the problem that lies under and prevails over the scholarship of the New Testament use of the scriptures.

Marshall begins his introduction by evaluating Dodd's proposal for the New Testament's contextual use of the Old Testament.[24] Marshall does well to revisit Dodd's important proposal as a way to frame the larger subdiscipline of the New Testament use of scripture. Conversely, in a different introductory study, F. F. Bruce decided not to reevaluate Dodd's thesis, with which he concurs, but to go in a different direction that more closely aligns with the approach taken up below.[25]

Bruce rejects the claim that Old Testament scholarship needs to confine itself to the original meaning of the Old Testament without consideration of how the New Testament makes use of it. Though Bruce agrees with the importance of attending to the original context of the Old Testament, he warns against the tendency to "atomize the Christian scriptures." He contends that the New Testament use of the Old is not a correct starting point because "the Old Testament is also interpreted in the Old."[26] Bruce presents a series of case studies of the Old Testament use of the Old Testament unfolding into the New Testament use of the Old Testament.[27] In spite of Bruce's effort, this kind of approach remains widely neglected.

A student new to the study of the scriptural use of scripture may find it strange that the scholarship of the New Testament use of scripture ignores the use of scripture within the apostles's Bible. It raises a question. Why?

Long ago laity, students, and scholars became aware that the New Testament authors use scripture in unusual ways. Less investment in the Old Testament by students and laity naturally increases the seeming strangeness of interpretation of scripture in the New Testament, which was modeled after interpretation within Israel's scriptures. Professors began teaching one thing in introductory courses on biblical hermeneutics and something else in courses on the New Testament's use of scripture.[28] Studying two approaches to proper

23. Marshall, "An Assessment," 2.

24. See ibid., 2–8; cf. Dodd, *According to the Scriptures*.

25. See Bruce, *This Is That*, 11.

26. Ibid. for both quotations in this paragraph.

27. See ibid., 22–114.

28. For an example of two approaches to hermeneutics—ours and theirs—by the same scholar in the same book of essays, see Bock, "Opening Questions," 23–32 and idem, "Scripture Citing Scripture," 255–76.

hermeneutics—ours and theirs—undergirds an attitude of tolerance for the increasingly idiosyncratic ways of explaining New Testament interpretation of scripture within the discipline. The discovery of sectarian Second Temple Jewish interpretations of the Hebrew scriptures commonly known as the Dead Sea Scrolls as well as the rise of new literary approaches, both in the mid-twentieth century, increased the isolation of the study of the New Testament use of scripture with its own hermeneutics.

One scholar claims that New Testament authors show "no sign of a direct interest in the Old Testament for its own sake." In this view the Old Testament is never "leading the way, nor even guiding the process" because it is the "servant" of the New Testament.[29] This view asserts a complete break between interpretation in the two testaments of the Christian Bible.

The scholarship of the New Testament use of scripture possesses a self-awareness that the interpretive tendencies of the authors of the New Testament together make up a hermeneutic that is something unto itself. A dictionary entry on "Old Testament in the New Testament" articulates the self-sequestering of the dominant scholarly outlook (a view that the entry strives against):

> Many New Testament scholars maintain that the New Testament use of the Old Testament *works within a closed logical circle*: it depends on Christian presuppositions and reads the Old Testament in a distinctly Christian way (even if employing Jewish methods of exegesis), often doing violence to the true meaning of the Old Testament texts employed.[30]

The reason for characterizing the New Testament hermeneutic as a closed system unto itself is its dependence on "Christian presuppositions" and "Jewish methods of exegesis." Explaining the presuppositions that sequester the hermeneutics of the New Testament use of scripture dominates many overview essays and introductory books from the past few generations up to the present.

Presuppositions. The present discussion will limit its focus to so-called Jewish *presuppositions* that scholars have detected to try to explain *why* the New Testament interprets scripture as it does. Part of the next chapter will unpack so-called Jewish *interpretive strategies* that scholars use to understand *how* the New Testament uses scripture.

Scholarship often claims that the unusual hermeneutical tendencies appearing in the New Testament use of scripture stem from borrowing contemporary

29. Lindars, "Place of the Old Testament," 64, 66.
30. Motyer, "Old Testament," 582, emphasis added.

Jewish sectarian and rabbinic presuppositions. Here are three of the presuppositions most frequently identified as "Jewish" (or rabbinic, or the like):[31]

- Interrelationship of the individual and the collective (corporate solidarity)
- Now and not yet fulfillment
- Correspondence in history (typological patterns)

It is easy to agree that the earliest Christians are influenced by Jewish perspectives. They are Jews. But the argument that the theological presuppositions of the apostles as temple-going Jews caused them to approach Israel's scriptures in a stilted way misses the actual source of the presuppositions. Each of the three so-called Jewish sectarian and/or rabbinic presuppositions in the previous paragraph calls for pushback because Second Temple Jews and New Testament authors inherited these presuppositions from the same place—Israel's scriptures. In other words, they are not "Jewish" or "rabbinic" but biblical presuppositions. The next section begins by providing evidence of the source of these exegetical presuppositions in the Old Testament.

CHOICE—CONNECTING THE BIBLE'S USE OF THE BIBLE

The present study advocates study of the Bible's use of the Bible in a connected way. This view opposes the majority choices: to sequester scriptural exegesis within Israel's scriptures as exclusively setting the stage for biblical interpretation of the rabbis, as well as sequestering the New Testament's use of scripture as something unto itself with its own hermeneutic. As noted above, there are numerous hermeneutical mechanics interrelated to both of the sequestering choices that will be unpacked in the next chapter (how). The present purpose is to explain the presuppositions that support a connected approach to the Bible's use of the Bible as well as to identify that the Messiah's teaching connects these exegetical presuppositions in the two testaments (why). Please notice the commonplace biblical presuppositions—those used by New Testament authors mentioned above—that function within Israel's scriptures themselves.

31. See, e.g., Ellis, "How the New Testament Uses the Old," 209–14; idem, *Old Testament in Early Christianity*, 101–21; Snodgrass, "Use of the Old Testament," 214–18; Bock, "Evangelicals: Part 2," 312–13; idem, "Scripture Citing Scripture," 261–63. For an approach to these presuppositions closer to the one offered here, see *HNTUOT*, 53, 96–97; Beale, "Did Jesus and His Followers Preach Right Doctrine," 392; idem, "Apostolic Hermeneutics: Descriptions and Presuppositions" *DNTUOT*, 51–57; idem, "Method," *DNTUOT*, 525.

Interrelationship of the individual and the collective in Israel's scriptures. The interrelationship between individual identity and responsibility and collective identity and responsibility runs through Israel's scriptures. That is, it is not an invention of Second Temple sectarian or late rabbinic exegesis, though they also use it.

The constant interchange between "you" singular and "you" plural is integral to the Torah's presentation of legal responsibility for the individual and the collective alike—as one, so the whole and vice versa. The commonplace intermixture of singular and plural appears in every legal collection of Torah.[32] In many cases, the shift between plural and singular occurs within the same verse. Consider the following typical example, including an overly wooden translation to bring out the intermixture:

> **You personally** shall not mistreat or oppress a residing foreigner, because **you collectively** were residing foreigners in the land of Egypt. **You collectively** shall not abuse any widow or orphan. If **you personally** abuse them at all when they cry out to me I will certainly listen. My anger shall blaze and I will kill **you collectively** with the sword, and **your collective** wives will become widows and **your collective** children orphans. (Exod 22:21–24[20–23 H] AT)

The same kind of interplay between individual/collective identity and responsibility, commonplace in Torah, continues throughout exilic and postexilic scriptural contexts.[33]

The individual and collective interplay appearing in the New Testament's use of scripture should not be surprising. The evidence overwhelmingly suggests that the authors of the New Testament carefully and constantly studied Israel's scriptures. The fact that ancient Jews of all sorts interchanged individual and collective senses when interpreting Israel's scriptures should be expected since ancient Jews of all stripes read and studied Torah. And that is what Torah does. The shared outlook concerning the individual and collective can be explained without any direct dependence of the New Testament authors upon Jewish sectarian or rabbinic ideology. The individual and collective interchange would be a natural view of any ancient person who studied Israel's scriptures—it is how Israel's scriptures operate.

Now and not yet fulfillment in Israel's scriptures. There is confusion about fulfillment as now and not yet by some scholars of the New Testament

32. See Schnittjer, "Say You, Say Ye."

33. See Schnittjer, "Individual versus Collective," 113–32. This phenomenon is not unique to Israel's scriptures but appears in other ancient Near Eastern writings. See idem, "Say You, Say Ye," n. 5.

use of scripture. One scholar claims now and not yet fulfillment is an exegetical innovation, unique to New Testament exegesis of scripture with no parallel in Second Temple Jewish literature.[34] Another scholar says the New Testament authors shared their now and not yet view of eschatological fulfillment with the sectarians of the Judean desert.[35] Both of these proposals distort the evidence. Scriptural exegesis within Israel's scriptures features now and not yet fulfillment.

Zechariah uses a now and not yet perspective regarding the fulfillment of earlier prophecy concerning Jerusalem. Yahweh declares that he has returned to Jerusalem after the prophesied seventy years (Zech 1:12–16).[36] At the same time, Zechariah can look to a day when Yahweh will return to dwell in Jerusalem (8:3). Ezra-Nehemiah opens with the edict of Cyrus as the fulfillment of Yahweh's word through Jeremiah (Ezra 1:1). Yet the Levitical intercessors still define the returned exiles as "slaves" in need of a new work of God (Neh 9:36). The now and not yet outlook of the returned remnant is part of their struggle with their identity and their placement within God's prophetic will.[37]

The authors of the New Testament and the Judaisms of their day should be expected to share commonplace outlooks of Israel's scriptures. The use of now and not yet eschatological perspective does not require New Testament authors to approach Israel's scriptures with a foreign set of presuppositions that they borrowed from Second Temple sectarians. This kind of explanation seems to have things turned around. It seems more likely that late Second Temple Jewish interpretations of Israel's scriptures, including those of the authors of the New Testament, share a now and not yet eschatological perspective with the early Second Temple scriptural interpretations appearing within Israel's scriptures themselves.

Typological patterns in Israel's scriptures. Some scholars consider typological patterns in the New Testament use of scripture as part of the mindset shared with or borrowed from the sectarians of the Judean desert.[38] It seems more likely, based on their great differences, that Second Temple sectarians and New Testament authors independently adopted the use of typological patterns from Israel's scriptures. Whereas sectarian commentaries

34. See Bock, "Scripture Citing Scripture," 263; idem, "Single Meaning, Multiple Contexts," 111.

35. See Snodgrass, "Use of the Old Testament," 216.

36. See *OTUOT*, 446–47.

37. See Schnittjer, *Ezra-Nehemiah*, ad loc. (forthcoming). Also see Ulrich, *Now and Not Yet*, 6–7, 25. For additional examples of now and not yet in Israel's scriptures, see Beale, *John's Use of the Old Testament*, 130–31; Gladd, "Mystery" *DNTUOT*, 555.

38. See Ellis, "How the New Testament Uses the Old," 201–12; Bock, "Scripture Citing Scripture," 262; Snodgrass, "Use of the Old Testament," 215.

imposed allegorical analogies verse by verse, biblical typological patterns are highly selective.[39]

Isaiah's expectation for a return from Mesopotamian captivity resembled Israel's wilderness trek in Torah (Isa 11:15–16; 40:3–4; cf. Exod 23:20–21). Solomon's temple does not resemble the tabernacle in every point. In Kings the glory coming into the temple at its dedication retroactively caused the tabernacle to be a pattern of the temple (1 Kgs 8:10–11; cf. Exod 40:34–35; 2 Chr 5:11–14).[40] The cases of typological patterns in scripture require careful attention and will be taken up in Chapter 6.

The point at hand is that the strong family resemblance between the use of *selective* typological patterns in the Old and New Testaments undercuts claims that New Testament authors borrow a nonselective Jewish sectarian mindset to allegorically superimpose these patterns onto Israel's scriptures. The strong evidence of the New Testament authors closely studying Israel's scriptures corroborates this conclusion.

In sum, the evidence suggests that both Second Temple Jewish writers and New Testament authors employ commonplace exegetical presuppositions of Israel's scriptures. This evidence affirms the need to rigorously compare the overlap between the use of scripture by the authors of the New Testament and their contemporaries, *but not in isolation.*

Shifts. Important shifts in New Testament scholarship have begun to realign study of the New Testament use of scripture with Israel's scriptures. Pausing to take note of selected proposals confirms the problem of sequestering the New Testament's use of scripture observed above.

N. T. Wright devotes numerous books to the ways different Second Temple Jewish groups appropriated Israel's scriptures toward themselves. Wright's model suggests different frameworks within which competing Jewish factions (Pharisees, separatist sectarians, Sadducees, priests, aristocrats, ordinary Jews, early Christians) reprioritized the place of Israel's scriptures within their respective identities.[41] One of Wright's more contested claims for all ancient Jews is enduring exile.[42] For Wright, Paul reads Israel's

39. The running "commentaries" of the sectarians of the Judean desert (e.g., Pesher Habakkuk/1QpHab) are known as pesharim. For a list, see Wold, "Old Testament Context," 117. Pesher exegesis is discussed in Chapter 2 below. On the "strict selectivity" of typological patterns in the New Testament, see Moo, *Old Testament in the Gospel*, 380; *OTUOT*, 861–63.

40. On the exegetical use of typological patterns in Israel's scriptures, see *OTUOT*, 715–16; Brettler, "Israel's Scriptures," 69–74; Fishbane, *Biblical Interpretation*, 350–79. And see Boda's discussion of "recapitulative historiography" ("Legitimizing the Temple," 316–17), a term he borrows from Dillard and Longman, *Introduction to the Old Testament*, 174.

41. See Wright, *New Testament and the People of God*, 181–214, 371–417.

42. See ibid., 268–71. See interaction in White, "N. T. Wright's Narrative Approach," 191–95.

scriptures as a framework of the covenant narrative of Israel that comes to its climax in Jesus.[43]

Richard Hays makes the case that all four evangelists present their narrative interpretations of Christ "within the matrix of Israel's scriptures." The Gospel writers, each in different ways, narrate "the story of Jesus as the continuation and fulfillment of Israel's story."[44] Yet, for Hays, the evangelists do not read Israel's scriptures forward toward the Messiah. The Gospel writers read backwards, connecting the Christ to Israel's scriptures in figural ways.[45] Hays also sees Paul as interpreting Israel's scriptures by an "ecclesiotelic" (church-as-goal) reading.[46] Paul does not apply Israel's scriptures directly. They are "refracted through the hermeneutical lens provided by God's action in the crucified Messiah and in forming his eschatological community."[47]

Francis Watson argues that the function of Israel's scriptures for Paul comes from his approach to the Pentateuch as a whole. Galatians 3 draws on the unconditional, universal promise of salvation in Genesis (Gal 3:8; cf. Gen 12:3), the coming of the law in Exodus (Gal 3:17; cf. Exod 20), the conditional promise of life for observing the commandments in Leviticus (Gal 3:12; cf. Lev 8:5), and the curse of the law upon the disobedient in Deuteronomy (Gal 3:10; cf. Deut 27:26).[48] Watson suggests that Paul sees the conditional law as contradicting the promise of salvation. "For Paul . . . the unconditional promise to Abraham is at odds with the law's conditional promise, which is itself at odds with the later declaration that this conditional promise can never be realized."[49] Watson rejects Wright's and Hays's views that Paul uses the Torah as the first part of a storyline that culminates in the gospel of Messiah. Instead, for Watson, Paul interprets the Pentateuch as creating a contradiction that is only resolved by the gospel of Christ.

The views of Wright, Hays, and Watson are representative of a renewed sensitivity toward the role of Israel's scriptures as it pertains to their use in the New Testament. The present point does not require pushing back against or making adjustments to the problems of these diverse proposals. It is enough to observe that the choice promoted in this chapter is not alone in rejecting the long tendency to sequester the New Testament's use of scripture. Unlike the

43. See Wright, *Paul*, 1453; also see Macaskill, "Israel's Scriptures," 124.

44. Hays, "Canonical Matrix," 53.

45. See Hays, *Reading with the Grain of Scripture*, 78–81; cf. his full-length works: idem, *Reading Backwards*; idem, *Echoes of Scripture in the Gospels*.

46. See Hays, "On the Rebound," 94.

47. Hays, *Echoes of Scripture in the Letters of Paul*, 169. Also see Macaskill, "Israel's Scriptures," 125.

48. See Watson, "Scripture," 191–92; idem, *Paul*, 473–78.

49. Watson, "Scripture," 192; cf. idem, *Paul*, 22.

views of Wright, Hays, and Watson, however, the present choice is not restricted to the New Testament. It seeks to connect the study of scriptural exegesis in the entire Bible. All of this raises a question.

What triggered the New Testament's adoption of the exegetical presuppositions it borrowed from exegesis within Israel's scriptures? The teaching attributed to the Messiah in the New Testament adopts exegetical presuppositions from Israel's scriptures in distinctive ways that appear across the New Testament. That is, interpretation of scripture by the Messiah connects exegesis within the two testaments of the Christian Bible. The same three presuppositions of scriptural interpretation within Israel's scriptures summarized above can show how these are mediated to the New Testament in the teachings of Jesus.

Interrelationship of the individual and the collective in the Messiah's exegesis of scriptures. The Messiah's exegesis of scripture uses a commonplace presupposition in Israel's scriptures of the interrelationship of the individual and the collective (corporate solidarity or representation).

The Messiah based his extended interpretation of the figure like a son of a human being on the collective interpretation within Dan 7 itself. The celestial attendant explains that the figure of one like a human being symbolized the holy people of the Most High. Compare the vision and its interpretation by the celestial attendant.[50]

> [The vision:] I saw one like a human being coming with the clouds of heaven. . . . **He was given dominion,** glory and **a kingdom**; all nations and peoples of every language worshiped him. *His dominion is an everlasting dominion* that will not pass away, and his kingdom is one that will never be destroyed. (Dan 7:13b, 14 AT)

> [The explanation:] Then **the kingdom, dominion** and greatness of all the kingdoms under heaven **will be given to** the holy people of the Most High. *His kingdom will be an everlasting kingdom*, and all rulers will worship and obey him. (7:27 AT; cf. v. 18)

Bold signifies the dominion and the kingdom that is given to the one like a human being in v. 14 whom the celestial attendant identifies as the people of the Most High in vv. 18 and 27. The Messiah's exegetical intervention in Mark 13 does not violate the presuppositions of the vision. The wild animals of the

50. See Schnittjer, *Old Testament Narrative*, 175–76.

vision symbolize both kings (individuals) and kingdoms (collectives) (Dan 7:17, 23).[51] The Messiah advances revelation by identifying the one like a human being not as a collective but as an individual who gathers the collective people of God by his celestial delegates:

> [Jesus to his followers:] At that time people will see *the son of a human being coming in clouds* with great *power* and *glory.* And he will send his celestial agents and gather his elect from the four winds, from the ends of the earth to the ends of the heavens. (Mark 13:26–27 AT; cf. Matt 24:30–31; Luke 21:27)

The Messiah's interpretation of the individual and collective sense of the figure like a human being in Dan 7 includes a further collective application. He extends the rule of the son of a human being upon his throne to twelve thrones for his followers to sit upon and judge the tribes of Israel (Matt 19:28).[52]

The Messiah's interpretive allusions to the servant in the context of Isaiah's new exodus likewise presuppose the interchange between the individual and the collective (Mark 10:45; cf. Isa 41:8–9; 44:1, 21 [collective]; 53:10–12 [individual]; 57:14–21 [collective]).[53] The New Testament letters latched onto the individual servant's humiliation as an example for the collective to follow (e.g., Phil 2:5, 7; 1 Pet 2:21–25). The Messiah's identification of himself with the servant figure of Israel stands in contrast to the interpretation in Psalms of Solomon (first century BCE). Notice the collective identity of the servant who needs to be delivered by a royal figure: "See Lord, and raise up for them their king, the son of David, to rule over *your servant Israel*" (Pss. Sol. 17:21, emphasis added). The issue is not the individual versus collective identity of the servant but that the royal figure and the servant figure refer to one and the same Messiah in the New Testament, as opposed to their differentiation in Pss. Sol. 17.

In sum, the Messiah's exegesis of scripture advances revelation based on the interrelationship of the individual and the collective already present within Israel's scriptures. In this way the Messiah's exegesis of scripture connects scriptural exegesis within Israel's scriptures and the New Testament.

Now and not yet fulfillment in the Messiah's exegesis of scriptures. The exegetical allusions to Deut 30:4 and especially Zech 2:6[10 H] in Mark 13:27 build on the presupposition of now and not yet fulfillment in Israel's scriptures. Notice that the catchword "heavens" in Deut 30:4 and Zech 2:6[10 H]

51. See France, *Jesus and the Old Testament*, 170.

52. See ibid., 66.

53. On the individual and the collective in Isa 53:10 and 57:14–21, see *OTUOT*, 244–46.

provides a mechanism for the Messiah to bring together this interpretive blend (emphases signify allusion).

> Even if you have been banished to the end of the heavens, from there Yahweh your God will gather you and bring you back. (Deut 30:4 AT)
>
> "Come! Come! Flee from the land of the north," declares Yahweh, "for I have scattered you to **the four winds of heaven**," declares Yahweh. (Zech 2:6[10H])
>
> And he will send his celestial agents and gather his elect **from the four winds**, from the ends of the earth to the ends **of the heavens**. (Mark 13:27 AT)

The issue at hand is the shared now and not yet perspective of initial fulfillment in the early Second Temple days of Zechariah and the late Second Temple days of the Messiah. Zechariah and Messiah both proclaimed a message in the land to the remnant who had returned concerning the scattered remnant that will be regathered.[54] The Messiah's advancement of revelation includes the larger expectational scheme in which he places the regathering with the coming of the son a human being (see above).

The series of exegetical uses of Zechariah and Malachi (both from a time earlier in the Second Temple) in the Messiah's teaching suggests similar kinds of now and not yet fulfillment as when the prophecies were first uttered.[55] Following the exegesis of Jesus and scriptural exegesis within Israel's scriptures, New Testament authors went on to apply now and not yet fulfillment to many other uses of scripture.

Typological patterns in the Messiah's exegesis of scriptures. The mechanics of typological patterns in scriptural exegesis will be the focus of a later choice (see Chapter 6). The present concern is typological patterns in the Messiah's scriptural exegesis to connect the use of typological patterns in exegesis within Israel's scriptures and within the New Testament.

The Messiah's use of Isa 6:9–10 to explain the function of his narrative riddles as obstructing the acceptance of his message (Matt 13:14; Mark 4:12) builds on the pattern of Isaiah's own obstructing ministry. The function of Isaiah's ministry of obstruction as a pattern is affirmed when Messiah says of the auditors of his parables: "In them is fulfilled the prophecy of Isaiah"

54. See France, *Jesus and the Old Testament*, 64.

55. See Zech 13:7 in Mark 14:27 (cf. Matt 26:31); Mal 3:1 in Matt 11:10 (cf. Luke 7:27); Mal 4:5[3:23 H] in Matt 17:10–11.

(Matt 13:14a).[56] But use of this pattern does not start with the Messiah's riddles.

Yahweh's commission of Isaiah's ministry of obstruction in Isa 6:9–10 exegetically advances Moses's interpretation of the obstruction of Israel (bold signifies verbal parallels with the receptor text Isa 6:9–10 not quoted here).[57]

> Moses summoned all the Israelites and said to them: **Your eyes have seen** all that Yahweh did in Egypt to pharaoh, to all his officials and to all his land. With **your own eyes you saw** those great trials, those signs and great wonders. But to this day Yahweh has not given you a **heart** that understands or **eyes that see** or **ears that hear**. (Deut 29:2–4[1–3 H] AT)

In this way the commission of Isaiah functions as a self-conscious, heightened reenactment of the pattern of obstruction of Israel in Moses's generation. Likewise, the riddles of the Messiah function as heightened reenactment of the pattern of obstruction of Isaiah's ministry. These recurring typological patterns interconnect the advancement of revelation in the Bible's use of the Bible.

Though the New Testament sometimes reworks typological patterns already used as such in Israel's scriptures, other cases initiate new typological allusions based on the same presupposition of recurring redemptive patterns—new creation, new exodus, new Moses, new David, new covenant, new Jerusalem, and so on.[58] These New Testament authors follow the Messiah's interpretations of scripture that activate typological patterns.

In sum, the Messiah extends typological exegesis within Israel's scriptures, as well as identifying other typological patterns, in his exegesis of scripture. The moderate use of typological patterns within Israel's scriptures and the Messiah's teachings sets the precedent for widespread exegesis of typological patterns in scripture by the authors of the New Testament.

Earlier studies, following Dodd, looked to the teaching of Jesus as citing single verses as pointers to large segments of the Hebrew scriptures of which they are a part.[59] Dodd said, "These sections were understood as *wholes*, and particular verses or sentences were quoted from them rather as pointers to the whole context than as pointers constituting testimonies in and for themselves."[60]

---

56. See France, *Jesus and the Old Testament*, 68; Powery, *Jesus Reads Scripture*, 142, n. 252; cf. 144–45.

57. See *OTUOT*, 224, 878 (concealing revelation network).

58. See *HNTUOT*, 20–22; von Rad, *OT Theology*, 2:372–74, 382–84.

59. See Dodd, *According to the Scriptures*, 110; Ellis, *Paul's Use of the Old Testament*, 113; France, *Jesus and the Old Testament*, 226; Beale, "Did Jesus and His Followers Preach Right Doctrine," 390–91. Allison criticizes Dodd's list of OT texts favored by the NT ("Old Testament in the New," 480–84).

60. Dodd, *According to the Scriptures*, 126, emphasis original.

The choice favored by the present chapter agrees with Dodd's proposal and also its premise, namely, that the teachings of the Messiah connect the exegetical advancements of revelation in Israel's scriptures and the New Testament.

The exegetical presuppositions surveyed above show that the authors of the New Testament follow the lead of the interpretations of scripture attributed to the Messiah. Both Jesus and the authors of the New Testament adopt the exegetical presuppositions running through Israel's scriptures. Consider a tiny fraction of cases of Old Testament exegesis of Old Testament by receptor texts that are further reinterpreted in the New Testament:[61]

- Blessing of Judah (Gen 49:8–12; cf. Rev 5:5)
- Ten Commandments (Exod 20//Deut 5; cf. Rom 13:9)
- Love thy neighbor (Lev 19:18b; cf. Mark 12:31)
- Prophet like Moses (Deut 18:15; cf. Acts 3:22–23)
- Song of Moses (Deut 32; cf. Rom 12:19)
- Davidic promise (2 Sam 7; cf. Heb 1:5)
- New exodus (Isa 40:3–5; cf. Luke 3:4–6)
- Last servant song in Isaiah's new exodus (Isa 53; cf. Acts 8:32–33)
- Temple as house of prayer for all peoples (Isa 56:1–7; cf. Mark 11:17)
- New covenant (Jer 31:31–37; cf. Heb 8:8–12)
- Psalms of the Davidic covenant (Pss 2; 110; 132; cf. Mark 12:36; Acts 2:34–35; 4:25–26)
- Resurrection (Dan 12:2–3; cf. Acts 24:15)

These are not peripheral cases. Even this partial list points to the dependence of the New Testament upon exegesis within Israel's scriptures. In at least eighty cases, the New Testament interpretively alludes to Old Testament contexts that are themselves receptor texts alluding to still earlier Old Testament scriptures.[62] These cases are dwarfed by a large number of Old Testament passages that serve as donor texts to both Old and New Testament receptor texts.[63] This evidence demonstrates extensive study of exegesis within Israel's scriptures by Jesus and the authors of the New Testament. All of this explains why shared presuppositions connect exegesis across both testaments of the Christian Bible.

Suggestions for study of connected scriptural exegesis of scripture. The point at hand is not about discovering biblical allusions to the Bible. That

61. This list is adapted from Schnittjer, "Long-Lost Grandparent Texts," 28. For a longer list see *OTUOT*, 866–67.

62. See Schnittjer, "Long-Lost Grandparent Texts," 31, n. 6.

63. For hundreds of cases, see *IBUB*.

will be taken up in Chapter 3, along with many suggestions regarding how to do so. The issue here concerns approaching the use of scripture within the two testaments of the Bible in a connected way. What are starting places for the student new to scriptural interpretation of scripture?

First, the beginning student can get a sense of the use of scripture in a biblical book like Deuteronomy by surveying the book-by-book hermeneutical profiles of the use of scripture in Torah in *OTUOT*.[64] This can highlight the distinctions and importance of Deuteronomy's contribution to exegesis within Torah. This background is useful to study the exegesis in Deuteronomy or to study the exegesis of Deuteronomy by later Old and New Testament receptor texts. One can get a sense of Matthew's use of scripture by comparing the hermeneutical profiles of the Gospels in *NTUOT*. The same kind of comparison can help with the use of scripture by the prophets, postexilic narratives, and New Testament letters. This often-overlooked but easy-to-do comparison can quickly set an investigation in a more fruitful direction.

It may help to consider the earlier scriptural contexts to which a biblical author typically turns—the lists in *IBUB*, *OTUOT*, and *NTUOT* are arranged for this kind of comparative overview. Are there clusters? Recurring genres? Similarities or differences in the kinds of contexts from which donor texts are drawn?

Second, it can be worthwhile to consider exegesis within the entire biblical book when studying a particular case within it, like Kings or Ephesians. This may include reading a broad overview,[65] an introductory case-by-case evaluation of interpretive allusions of the entire book,[66] and an introductory overview of the use of scripture in the book in a detailed commentary.[67]

Third, it is worth checking if the donor or receptor texts are interpreted by other biblical texts or are part of an interpretive network (networks are explained in Chapter 4).[68] Networks can alert interpreters to broader interpretive momentum and other potential influences or dependence.

Fourth, at some point investment should be made in less studied contexts. Studies of New Testament use of scripture do not tend to focus on Ezra-Nehemiah or Chronicles because of the lack of direct citation of these texts in the New Testament. This is unfortunate. Ezra-Nehemiah and Chronicles

64. See *OTUOT*, 3 (Gen), 17–20 (Exod), 39–40 (Lev), 57–59 (Num), 78–88 (Deut).

65. See respective entries in *DNTUOT*.

66. See respective chapters in *OTUOT*, *NTUOT*, and *CNTUOT*.

67. See, e.g., Wray Beal, *1 & 2 Kings*, 32–33; Cohick, *Ephesians*, 55–57.

68. See *IBUB* or the lists in the opening of the chapters of *OTUOT* and *NTUOT*. On networks, see *OTUOT*, 873–84, and see index, 885–87; *NTUOT*, ad loc. For a similar suggestion, see Imes, "Scripture Interprets Scripture."

include large storehouses of exegesis of scripture from an earlier part of the Second Temple period. Many of the exegetical tendencies that appear during a later part of the Second Temple period in the New Testament follow after those in Ezra-Nehemiah and Chronicles.[69] The underlying point of this suggestion is to avoid being too nearsighted in study agendas. In many cases, what students consistently ignore explains the deficiencies in their exegesis, theology, and ministries.

CASE STUDY

Using the same hermeneutical presuppositions, Israel's scriptures and the New Testament frequently interpret and advance the revelation of the very same donor texts. The importance of the case of the new exodus stems from the explicit forward-looking expectation in Isaiah of Israel's return from Mesopotamian captivity (Isa 11:15–16). The series of exegetical advances—Isaiah's use of Exodus, Malachi's use of Exodus and Isaiah, and Mark's use of Exodus, Malachi, and Isaiah—have been explained in detail elsewhere, so only a summary will be included here.[70]

In the background of Exod 23:20 and its several receptor texts, in Israel's scriptures and the Gospel of Mark, stands Moses's pleading with Yahweh not to send his messenger but for Yahweh's own glory to go with Israel (Exod 33:3, 12–20).[71] The threat of judgment against Israel's rebellion in Exod 23:21 overlaps Isa 40:10 and, even more strongly and somewhat ironically, Mal 3:1b–2. The call to repentance by John the baptizer and the Messiah in Mark 1:4 and v. 15 demonstrates continuity with the series of exegetical interventions in the receptor texts of Exod 23:20 in Israel's scriptures. All of these factors need to be considered. Notice the series of verbal allusions signified by emphases, as well as alternate references to God signified by broken underlining:

> See, I am sending a messenger ahead of you to guard you along the way and to bring you to the place I have prepared. (Exod 23:20 AT)

> *A voice of one calling: "In the wilderness prepare the way for Yahweh; make straight in the wilderness a highway for our God."* (Isa 40:3 AT)

69. See, e.g., *OTUOT*, 871.

70. See ibid., 234–36, 468–69; *NTUOT*, ad loc.

71. On the exchange between Yahweh and Moses in Exod 33, see Schnittjer, *Torah Story*, 237–38.

> "**I will send** my **messenger**, who **will prepare** ***the way*** **ahead of** me. Then suddenly the Lord you are seeking will come to his temple; the messenger of the covenant, whom you desire, will come," says Yahweh Almighty. But who can endure the day of his coming? Who can stand when he appears? For he will be like a refiner's fire or a launderer's soap. (Mal 3:1–2, v. 1 AT)

> . . . as it is written in Isaiah the prophet: "**I will send my messenger ahead of you**, who **will prepare** your **way**—*a voice of one calling in the wilderness, 'Prepare the way for* the Lord, *make straight paths for* him.'" (Mark 1:2–3)

Isaiah's exegetical intervention in Isa 40:3 plays off the conventional interchange between the individual and the collective. Since Yahweh had agreed to go with his people and not merely send a messenger (Exod 33:14; cf. vv. 2–3; 23:20), Isaiah focuses on preparation of the way in the desert for Yahweh (Isa 40:3).

The exegetical advances of Mal 3:1 and Mark 1:2–3 pertaining to the identity of the messenger and the one whom he goes before need attention. By reading Isa 40:3 against Exod 23:20—two texts already connected by interpretive allusion—Mal 3:1 extends the expectation by identifying the function of the messenger who goes before "me," referring to Yahweh (Mal 3:1). The messenger that goes before needs to prepare a people already back in the land whose rebellion has incited God's judgment (Mal 3:2). This helps explain using judgment language—fishers of people (Jer 16:16)—to characterize the role of Messiah's followers (Mark 1:17).[72]

Mark extends the expectation further still by identifying the messenger who goes before as John the baptizer and identifying the Messiah with the God of Israel.[73] Malachi and Mark both advance revelation based on preexisting interpretive connections within earlier scriptures. The categorical and definitive advancement of revelation in this series of exegetical allusions comes by Mark interpreting Israel's scriptures in the light of the revelation of God in the Messiah and by interpreting the Messiah according to Israel's scriptures.

The series of exegetical interventions with Exod 23:20–21 illustrates all three of the hermeneutical presuppositions surveyed above. Israel as "you" in Exod 23:20 is eventually assigned to "Yahweh" in Isa 40:3, to "me" in Mal

72. Also see Ezek 29:4; Amos 4:2; Hab 1:14–15; cf. Isa 37:29. So also Tucker, *Malachi*, 116.

73. See Hays, *Reading Backwards*, 19–21; idem, *Echoes of Scripture in the Gospels*, 23, 62–63; Bauckham, *Jesus and the God of Israel*, 219, and see also pp. 32–51 on Isa 40–55 in the NT, though Bauckham does not treat Mark 1:3 there.

3:1, and to "you" the Messiah in Mark 1:2.[74] This relies at minimum on the interrelationship of the individual and the collective since Yahweh agreed to go with the people. The expectation for the messenger to prepare the way in Mal 3:1 rests on now and not yet fulfillment. Malachi and his rebellious constituents had already returned to Jerusalem, which sets up the ironic allusion to Yahweh coming in judgment on them there. The exegetical allusions in Isa 40:3, Mal 3:1, and Mark 1:23 each work by typological patterns in their respective donor texts. The trek through the wilderness (Exod 23:20–21) serves as a pattern of the return from exile (Isa 40:3; cf. 11:15–16), both of which serve as ironic patterns for the return of Yahweh in judgment on his people already returned to the land (Mal 3:1), all of which serve as translucent overlaid patterns for the gospel mission of the Messiah (Mark 1:2–3).

In sum, the series of exegetical interventions with Exod 23:20–21 shows how interpreters can study earlier scriptures with later biblical authors. This allows students to study exegesis connected across the entire Christian Bible.

Study Questions

1. In your own words, what is the choice at issue in this chapter?
2. Why do most scholars sequester scriptural interpretation within Israel's scriptures?
3. What is Michael Fishbane's goal in studying interpretation within Israel's scriptures? How did he organize his research to accomplish this goal?
4. Why do most scholars sequester scriptural interpretation within the New Testament?
5. Why does the dominant scholarship of the New Testament use of scripture neglect the study of the interpretation of scripture within Israel's scriptures?
6. Why is it incorrect to refer to the hermeneutical presuppositions of the New Testament as Jewish or rabbinic or the like?
7. What is the relationship between individual and collective identity and responsibility in Israel's scriptures?
8. Why did now and not yet prophetic fulfillment appear within the later parts of Israel's scriptures?

74. For explanation of this kind of typological maneuver (prosopological exegesis), see Chapter 7.

9. How does the New Testament use of scriptural typological patterns line up with or against the use of the same within Second Temple sectarian writings and within Israel's scriptures?
10. How does the Messiah advance revelation based on the interpretive presuppositions evident within Israel's scriptures?
11. What hermeneutical presuppositions are at work in the series of exegetical interventions in Exod 3:20; Isa 40:3; Mal 3:1; and Mark 1:2–3? How so?

CHAPTER 2

ADJUSTING MEANING AND/OR ADJUSTING CONTEXT VERSUS ADVANCEMENT OF REVELATION

The choice in this chapter overlaps with the choice in the previous chapter. Chapter 1 emphasizes hermeneutical presuppositions (why), and Chapter 2 focuses on hermeneutical mechanics (how). Both of these choices undergird responsible exegesis.

Most scholars adjust meaning and/or adjust context to try to fix the problem they sense with the way the biblical authors interpret earlier scriptures. This chapter presents scriptural exegesis of scripture as a subset of the progressive revelation of God's redemptive will. This makes the long line of adjustments to meaning and/or adjustments to context by modern interpreters unnecessary and unhelpful. Responsible interpretation of the Bible's use of the Bible is not dependent upon clever and ever-more-nuanced hermeneutical theories. This chapter will work through many of the prominent adjustments to meaning and/or context that have been proposed to "solve the problem" of the Bible's use of the Bible.

CHOICE

The choice between, on the one side, adjusting meaning and/or adjusting context, and, on the other side, advancing revelation may not seem to go together at first. They do. The situation of this complicated issue calls for an apples and oranges choice.

In one of my (Schnittjer's) doctoral seminars, Darrell Bock said that all questions have the answers built into them. The idea that even the questions that drive our research affect the outcomes should be taken seriously by all students. Bock suggests that viable research starts by learning to ask the right questions.[1]

The present chapter contends that one of the questions many scholars of exegesis within scripture have been arguing about is the wrong question. This has been especially true of scholarship of the New Testament's use of scripture. The confusion rests in part on ignoring the thousand years of scriptural exegesis within Israel's scriptures that lead up to the use of scripture in the New Testament.[2] Instead scholars ask, in essence, how meaning and/or context need(s) to be adjusted to fit what New Testament authors are doing when they interpret scripture. Proposals about the meaning of meaning and/or how to adjust context are legion. Many proposals are too clever.

The problem is not about finding a sophisticated adjustment to meaning and/or context. Exegesis of scripture within scripture advances revelation. This opens the way to evaluate plain sense interpretation used by biblical authors.

The critiques in this section get to the point. The manifold complications and posturing by which the proponents set up their views can only be mentioned here if and when it bears on key issues of adjusted meaning and/or adjusted context as it applies to the Bible's use of the Bible. All of the proponents of these views of adjusted meaning and/or context have much to offer on interpreting scripture. Most of these views work better on certain cases but not so well on others. The point here has nothing to do with disagreements over the interpretation of this or that verse. The present criticism is of hermeneutical theories that redefine meaning and/or context in order to explain how the biblical authors interpret earlier scriptures. An attempt is being made to take each view in its best sense. Readers are invited to look up the resources mentioned in the footnotes for further details about the approaches.

The first couple of views come from or concern Jewish interpretation. These are followed by several approaches that come from trying to resolve difficulties in the New Testament's use of earlier scripture. The small sampling of views here is representative of many others.

Michael Fishbane **opposes** the right of prophets to mediate **progressive revelation**, especially in the case of the instructions of Torah. Fishbane posits that to count as exegesis a biblical allusion needs to include some kind of innovation. But he denies the right of the biblical authors to use their interpretations to develop Torah. Thus, Fishbane privileges legal revelation in Torah

1. Bock makes a similar point in "Opening Questions," 26. Also see Harmon, *Asking the Right Questions*, 63.

2. See Schnittjer, "Long-Lost Grandparent Texts," 27–31; idem, "What's Old?" 62, 79; *OTUOT*, 849–56.

as invulnerable to the kinds of adaptations allowable in lesser varieties of revelation. This suggests a different, higher kind of meaning in Sinai revelation than other scriptural revelation.

Fishbane claims the marking in 1 Kgs 11:2—"about which Yahweh had told the Israelites" (AT)—is a false citation of the law of devoting and of the law of the assembly in the beginnings of Deut 7 and 23. He says that the author wrongly expands the list of the nations of Canaan to include the Ammonites, Moabites, Egyptians, and Edomites "in terms of intermarriage!"[3] Notice the interpretive blend (bold signifies allusion to Deut 23, underlining signifies allusion to Deut 7, broken underlining signifies an addition, and italics signify marking):

> King Solomon loved many foreign women along with **pharaoh's daughter, Moabites, Ammonites, Edomites**, Sidonians, and Hittites, [2]from the nations *of which Yahweh had said to the Israelites*, "You **shall not come into them**, and they **shall not come into you**, otherwise they will turn your heart after their gods." Solomon clung to them in love. (1 Kgs 11:1–2 AT)

One problem with Fishbane's view is the inclusion of the Sidonians (see broken underlining above), who do not appear in the lists of forbidden peoples in Deut 7 or 23. The narrator's interpretive paraphrase in v. 2 does not get at the ethnicity of the wives but that they have rejected the covenant by clinging to the gods of their homelands (see vv. 5–8). The narrator of Kings interprets the sense of the Torah prohibitions not in ethnic but covenantal terms. This includes treaty wives from any people, such as the Sidonians, if they worship other gods. The authority of the narrator of Kings to advance revelation by exegetical intervention is affirmed by Nehemiah when he cites this precedent in condemning the apostasy marriages that are a sign of the failure of the restoration (Neh 13:26–27).[4]

Fishbane's denial of a place for authorized exegesis extends to prophets like Jeremiah. He claims that Jeremiah acts "presumptively" when he adds a false citation formula to his own innovation to the Sabbath commandment in Jer 17. The presumption, says Fishbane, is claiming a revelatory status to his own innovation by marking it with "thus says Yahweh." He concludes that ancient Israel's prophets need "to camouflage and legitimate" their exegetical innovations.[5]

---

3. Fishbane, *Biblical Interpretation*, 125–26.

4. See Schnittjer, *Old Testament Narrative*, 137–38; idem, "Overview of Composite Citations," forthcoming; idem, "Bad," 43–44; *OTUOTPL*, ad loc.

5. See Fishbane, *Biblical Interpretation*, 134. Fishbane acknowledges that these so-called presumptuous interpretations of laws later become scripture themselves.

It is easy to appreciate the rightful extolling of the place of Torah revelation at the headwaters of Israel's scriptures. Yet prophets who interpret Torah revelation are not presumptive but necessary according to Moses himself (Deut 18:18–22; see case study below). More importantly, Fishbane does not observe that the alleged presumptive citation formula is not only inserted by Jeremiah, but this twofold marking is carried over from Deuteronomy. The evidence that Jer 17 cites Deut 5 versus Exod 20 also includes the use of "be careful" (שׁמר) in Deut 5:12 and Jer 17:21 but "remember" (זכר) in Exod 20:8. Notice the double marking in both the Mosaic and prophetic interpretations of the Sinai revelation (bold signifies marking and broken underlining signifies interpretive expansions):[6]

> Be careful of the Sabbath day by keeping it holy, **as Yahweh your God has commanded you**. Six days you shall labor and do all your work, but the seventh day is a sabbath to Yahweh your God. On it you shall not do any work, neither you, nor your son or daughter, nor your male or female servant, nor your ox, your donkey or any of your animals, nor any foreigner residing in your towns, so that your male and female servants may rest, as you do. Remember that you were slaves in Egypt and that Yahweh your God brought you out of there with a mighty hand and an outstretched arm. Therefore **Yahweh your God has commanded you** to observe the Sabbath day. (Deut 5:12–15, vv. 12, 14–15 AT)

> **Thus says Yahweh**: You need to be careful not to carry a load on the Sabbath day or bring it through the gates of Jerusalem. Do not bring a load out of your houses or do any work on the Sabbath, but keep the Sabbath day holy, **as I commanded your ancestors**. Yet they did not listen or pay attention; they were stiff-necked and would not listen or respond to discipline. (Jer 17:21–23, v. 21 AT)

Both Moses and Jeremiah advance revelation by interpretive expansions of their donor texts as signified by broken underling. And both use citation formulas signified by bold to frame their expanded and enhanced exegetical applications of the Sabbath command. The authority of Yahweh granted to Moses and to Jeremiah undercuts accusations of presumption on their parts.

The view that the revelation of the law to Moses at Mount Sinai cannot be advanced by divine revelation stands at odds with biblical revelation even in

6. See *OTUOT*, 275.

Torah, and even at Sinai itself. Deuteronomy self-identifies as "Torah explained" (Deut 1:5; cf. 6:1).[7] And Yahweh reinterprets a series of instructions from the Ten Commandments (Exod 20:1–17) and the covenant legal collection (Exod 21–23) in the covenant renewal legal collection (34:11–26)—all at Sinai and all within the same book that first presents the Sinai revelation. Moses goes on to present interpretive advancements to three of the Ten Commandments in Deut 5.[8] There is no book of Torah that lacks interpretive interventions with divinely proclaimed commands. The exegesis of Torah in Torah sets the precedent for exegesis by prophets and other divinely authorized delegates (see case study below).

Scholars often claim that authors of both testaments use **atomistic exegesis**. This refers to receptor texts that lift verses, phrases, or even words out of their biblical contexts and interpret them without regard to their context of origin.[9] These proposals are sharply contested. The following several adjustments to context and/or meaning offer mechanisms that utilize atomistic exegesis.

Scholarship of the New Testament use of scripture often contends that New Testament authors use **"Jewish," "rabbinic," or "midrashic" exegesis**. Prevailing perspectives regard the New Testament authors as mimicking sectarian Jewish genres, embracing Second Temple Jewish interpretive traditions, and employing rabbinic, midrashic, and sectarian exegetical techniques.[10] One scholar claims that radical sectarian exegesis is "the dominant manner" of the New Testament's use of Israel's scriptures.[11] These trends in scholarship suggest the dependence of the New Testament authors upon Jewish, rabbinic, and sectarian exegesis (Figure 2-A). Some go further, insinuating that New Testament authors accessed Israel's scriptures as mediated by Second Temple interpretive traditions.[12]

These prevailing views in the scholarship of the New Testament use of scripture fail to take into account the most important evidence, namely, scriptural exegesis within Israel's scriptures.

The evidence of scriptural exegesis within Israel's scriptures provides the underlying reason for most similarities between Second Temple interpretive

---

7. See ibid., 78–86.

8. See Schnittjer, *Torah Story*, 406–7.

9. See Stemberger, "From Inner-biblical Interpretation," 197.

10. See Docherty, "New Testament Scriptural Interpretation," 7–18; Henze and Lincicum, "Introduction," 9. Also see Wilcox, "On Investigating," 233–43.

11. Longenecker, "Can We Reproduce the Exegesis of the New Testament?" 17.

12. One linear model proposes: OT revelation → nonrevelatory Second Temple literature → NT revelation (Bateman, *Hebrews*, 59, by permission). Also see Longenecker, *Biblical Exegesis*, xxiii–xxvi.

Figure 2-A: Prevailing View of New Testament Dependence on Jewish Exegesis

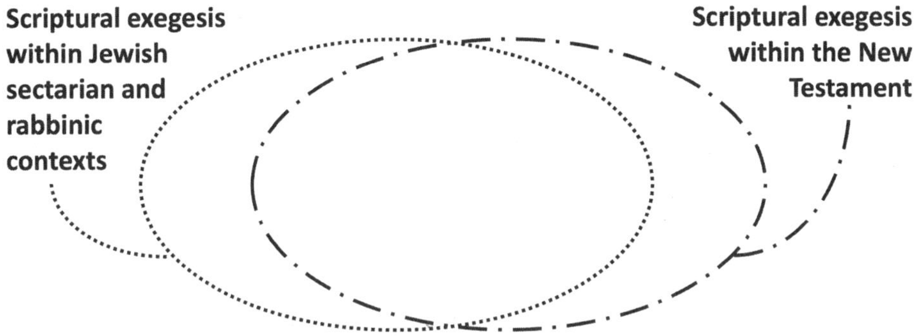

traditions and the New Testament use of scripture. The agreement between New Testament and Second Temple Jewish scriptural exegesis should be expected because they are both following exegetical models they found within the scriptures that they studied.[13] Figure 2-B inserts scriptural exegesis within Israel's scriptures as what should be the primary starting point for evaluating ancient exegesis in Second Temple interpretive traditions and

Figure 2-B: New Testament and Ancient Jewish Dependence on Exegesis within Israel's Scriptures

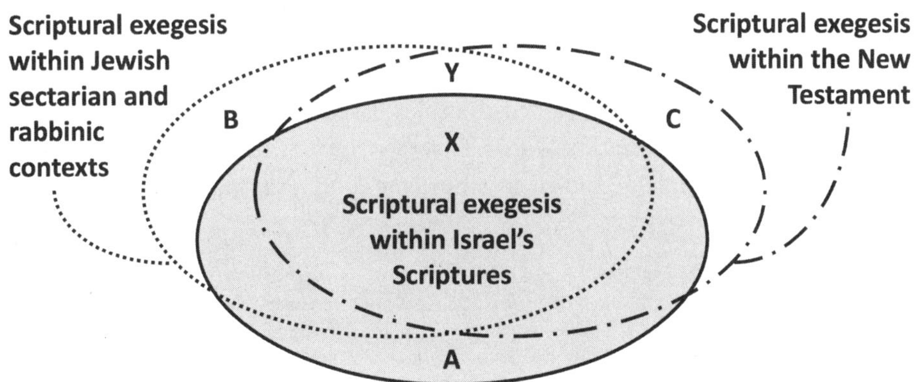

the New Testament. While this figure makes a broad point and is not to scale, it does try to show that most (X) of the exegetical tendencies shared between various Second Temple traditions and the New Testament are not

13. Zakovitch demonstrates that ancient extrabiblical interpretation mimicked scriptural exegesis within Israel's scriptures ("Inner-biblical Interpretation," 61).

sectarian or rabbinic—they are biblical. The exegetical similarities not shared with the interpretive traditions within Israel's scriptures (Y) are a much rarer commodity.[14]

Scholarship should continue the important work of comparing the exegetical traditions of the New Testament and other Second Temple Jewish streams of interpretation (see Chapter 5). Yet, a major adjustment is needed. The starting place needs to be scriptural exegesis within Israel's scriptures upon which all brands of ancient Jewish and early Christian interpretation depend. A few scholars have begun to notice this void.[15] These hopeful glimmers stand out against the prevailing adjustments of context.

In sum, distorted conclusions arise from adjusting context by excluding the evidence of exegesis within Israel's scriptures (Figure 2-A).

Many scholars claim that New Testament authors use rabbinic exegesis—adjusting context atomistically—by adopting the seven so-called **rules of interpretation of Hillel** (active ca. 30 BCE–10 CE).[16] Use of Hillel's rules in New Testament interpretation of scripture is often referred to as "Jewish" or "rabbinic" or "midrash."[17] These widespread claims distort the evidence.

They are not really rules, and Hillel did not invent them from scratch. Richard Hays says they are not "rules for interpretation" but that they describe "imaginative operations" the rabbis could perform in the act of interpretation of scripture.[18] While this may be correct about how the rules are used in late rabbinic literature, it does not explain their origin. David Daube claims that Hillel's rules are not Jewish but Hellenistic, since they exhibit tendencies similar to Hellenistic rhetoric.[19] The parallels Daube surveys illustrate common operations of logic, but they do not reveal the source of the rules.

Hillel apparently developed the rules based on observations of varieties of scriptural interpretation within Israel's scriptures, especially Torah. Since this has been explained in detail elsewhere, only examples of the two most

---

14. See *OTUOT*, 858–65.

15. See Docherty, "Crossing Testamentary Borders," 11–22; Tooman, "Scriptural Reuse," 39; Shively, "Israel's Scriptures," 238–39, 245–46, et passim; Harmon, "OT Use of the OT: Comparison with the NT Use of the OT," *DNTUOT*, 586–93; Beale, "Method," *DNTUOT*, 522; and the entries on each Old Testament book in *DNTUOT*.

16. See, e.g., Docherty, "Israel's Scriptures," 149–50; Ellis, *Paul's Use of the Old Testament*, 41; Barrett, "Interpretation of the Old Testament," 383–84; Longenecker, *Biblical Exegesis*, 20–21; Bock, "Scripture Citing Scripture," 259–60; Bateman, *Early Jewish Hermeneutics*, 9–21, 119, 245.

17. The term "midrash" means interpretation. The genre of ancient Judaic writings known as midrash commonly includes imaginative backstory and clever gap-filling to biblical traditions. See a list in Kugel, *Traditions of the Bible*, 926–28.

18. See Hays, *Echoes of Scripture in the Letters of Paul*, 12.

19. Daube, "Rabbinic Methods," 240.

important rules can be offered here.[20] Lesser to greater (*qal vahomer*) refers to exegetical expansions with the logic of "how much more." If you shall love the residing foreigner, how much more your neighbor (Lev 19:33–34, 18)? If tending to the animal of one's enemy is required, how much more the animal of one's fellow citizen (Exod 23:4–5; Deut 22:1–4)? Argument deduced by analogy (*gezerah shevah*) refers to exegetical extrapolations by deductive logic. If Yahweh protected Israel when they were residing foreigners and slaves in Egypt crying out to Yahweh, then he mandates protection of residing foreigners, widows, and orphans who may cry out to him (Exod 3:7; 22:21–23[20–22 H]; Deut 24:17–19). If landless widows, orphans, and residing foreigners need help, then Levites also need help since they do not inherit land (Deut 14:29; 26:13). These examples show that these commonplace interpretive tendencies within Israel's scriptures observed by Hillel can be based on contextual exegesis.

Like Hillel, authors of the New Testament naturally leaned toward exegetical tendencies they learned from Israel's scriptures, which they studied carefully and persistently. Second Temple and later rabbinic interpretation should also be expected to mimic the sorts of interpretive tendencies that appear frequently in the Bible.

In sum, the Bible's uses of the Bible that serve as the bases of the rules observed by Hillel are not imaginative midrash, Jewish, or rabbinic. They are biblical. New Testament authors and later rabbis applied these interpretive tendencies in distinct ways.

Much confusion stems from claims that New Testament exegesis relies on **pesher.**[21] The Aramaic term comes from the root *p-sh-r* (פשר, similar to the biblical Hebrew term פתר), which has the basic sense of "interpret." The genre of pesher writings from sectarians of the Judean desert offers eschatological interpretation line by line through select biblical texts.[22] Because they treat every verse, the interpretations become very allegorical. Like the sectarian pesharim, New Testament authors sometimes apply Israel's scriptures to themselves

20. All seven hermeneutical tendencies observed by Hillel appear commonly within Israel's scriptures. See *OTUOT,* 860, n. 69.

21. See, e.g., Ellis, *Paul's Use of the Old Testament*, 139–47; Lindars, "Place of the Old Testament," 62; Barrett, "Interpretation of the Old Testament," 387–89; Longenecker, *Biblical Exegesis*, 54–58, 113–16, 180–84, cf. 24–30; Bock, "Scripture Citing Scripture," 260–61; Bateman, *Hebrews*, 55–60; idem, *Early Jewish Hermeneutics*, 115–16. Though Bock sees pesher in the New Testament, he complains about Longenecker's ill-defined and excessive labeling of passages as "pesher exegesis" ("Evangelicals: Part 2," 313). Moo accuses Longenecker of calling "any 'direct' application" of scripture in the NT "pesher" ("Problem of *Sensus Plenior*," 193). This corresponds to Longenecker speaking of "a pesher type of interpretation" and a "pesher attitude" among New Testament authors (*Biblical Exegesis*, 54, 113, 181).

22. See, e.g., the Habakkuk Commentary/1QpHab and 4QpNah/4Q169. On continuous versus thematic pesharim, see Devorah Dimant, "Pesharim, Qumran," *ABD* 5:245–48. For a list of Qumran pesharim, see Wold, "Old Testament Context," 117.

within the latter days of scriptural fulfillment. But the New Testament use of typological patterns exhibits a "strict selectivity," only adapting the applicable parts of the donor context to the receptor text.[23] Selectivity characterizes Old and New Testament use of typological patterns versus nonselective sectarian allegorical interpretation. This sharp contrast of interpretive tendency has often been ignored in eager attempts to detect Jewish influences in the New Testament.[24]

New Testament scholars frequently claim that the introductory formulas "this is what was spoken" of Joel 2:28–32[3:1–5 H] in Acts 2:16 and "this is the stone" (AT) of Ps 118:22 in Acts 4:11 depend on sectarian pesher exegesis.[25] The tendency to gloss elements with kindred formulae appears frequently in Israel's scriptures (emphases added to the following examples).

> Then Melchizedek king of Salem brought out bread and wine. *He was* [הוּא] priest of God Most High. (Gen 14:18)

> David and all the Israelites marched to Jerusalem (*that is, Jebus* [הִיא יְבוּס]). The Jebusites who lived there. . . . (1 Chr 11:4, underlining signifies verbal parallel with donor text in 2 Sam 5:6)

> "*This is its interpretation* [זֶה פִּתְרֹנוֹ]," Joseph said to him. "The three branches are three days." (Gen 40:12 AT)

> "*This is its interpretation* [זֶה פִּתְרֹנוֹ]," Joseph said. "The three baskets are three days." (40:18 AT)

> [Daniel:] "*This* [דְּנָה] was the dream, and now we will tell *the interpretation* [*pshr*; פִּשְׁרֵהּ] to the king." (Dan 2:36 AT)

The first example, from Gen 14:18, is an interpretive gloss by the narrator to explain the king's other role. The second example, from Chronicles, glosses the identity of Jerusalem in David's day as he interpretively paraphrases the conquest of the city from 2 Sam 5. The last three examples come from the interpretation of dreams by Joseph and Daniel that, along with interpretations

---

23. See Moo, *Old Testament in the Gospel*, 380.

24. For a detailed comparison of sectarian pesharim and New Testament exegesis, see *OTUOT*, 861–63.

25. See Ellis, "How the New Testament Uses the Old," 707–8; Longenecker, *Biblical Exegesis*, 181; Bock, *Acts*, 211–12.

in Ezekiel, Zechariah, and elsewhere in scripture, likely serve as precursors for the pesharim of the Second Temple sectarians.[26] The New Testament's use of Daniel, Ezekiel, and Zechariah as tributaries of eschatological interpretation may be more important to explaining its interpretive tendencies than the less aligned exegetical techniques of the sectarians of the Judean desert.

Evaluating exegesis within the Second Temple Jewish setting is essential to responsible interpretation of the Bible's use of scripture (see Chapter 5). The problems described above stem from taking sectarian and late rabbinic interpretive tendencies and inserting these into the New Testament while simultaneously ignoring the Old Testament use of scripture that sets the precedents for most of the cases involved (see Figures 2-A and 2-B above). This twofold problem is epitomized by one scholar who claims both that contemporary Jewish exegesis is the "proper background" of New Testament interpretation of scripture and that New Testament authors never ask, "What does this mean?" of scripture when they take it out of context for their own ends.[27]

In sum, the comparisons between New Testament and other ancient Jewish interpretive trends offer little or no insight when the interpretive traditions of Israel's scriptures are ignored. Many of the similar interpretive tendencies in the New Testament and their sectarian contemporaries can be traced back to analogous exegesis within Israel's scriptures. The adjustment of context to exclude the use of scripture within Israel's scripture in favor of exclusively Jewish sectarian and rabbinic interpretive tendencies confuses the situation.

Before moving on, the great variation of what some scholars mean by **noncontextual exegesis** needs to be noted. Ben Witherington III views New Testament authors as sometimes using Israel's scriptures in contextual ways and sometimes in noncontextual ways.[28] But his explanation of noncontextual use can be a problem. In the case of Ps 41:9 in John 13:18, Witherington says it is noncontextual, even though the language of the verse fits both contexts. "In the psalm the person in question was ill and his 'friends' stopped eating with him; not so at the Last Supper in the case of Jesus and Judas."[29] Witherington complains that the psalmist has sinned against Yahweh, among other differences between the psalmist and the Christ, which excludes a contextual use

26. Most of these examples and the connection between biblical dream interpretations and pesharim are from Fishbane, *Biblical Interpretation*, 44–46; idem, *Biblical Text*, 223–24; cf. 216, and a series of ancient Near Eastern parallels at 218–22.

27. Lindars, "Place of the Old Testament," 61, 64.

28. See Witherington, *Torah*, 358; idem, *Isaiah*, 353; idem, *Psalms*, 327, 330.

29. Witherington, *Psalms*, 328.

of the psalm in John 13.[30] Witherington's expectation for multiple alignments would be appropriate for pesher or an allegorical use of Ps 41. But his complaint against partial alignment between the donor and receptor context fails to take into account the decided selectivity of typological patterns throughout the Christian Bible (see Chapter 6).

Atomistic or noncontextual exegesis includes vast numbers of **"exegetical motifs"** functioning outside their contexts of origin within ancient Jewish literature. James Kugel suggests that ancient exegetical motifs travel far and wide by word of mouth, often becoming connected together.[31] Kugel thinks the reasons for these exegetical interventions primarily come from within the biblical text rather than from the historical context of ancient interpreters.[32] For example, ancient interpreters sought to solve the apparent problem of killing all creatures in Noah's flood, not just sinful humans, by detecting clues within scripture. The relations between the sons of God and daughters of humans in Gen 6:2, 4 provided an analogy suggesting to these ancient interpreters that the animals must have transgressed by mating outside their own species.

> Even animals were so corrupted with those not of their species, horse with donkey and donkey with horse and snake with bird, as it says, "For all flesh had gone astray. . ." [Gen. 6:12]. It does not say "all humans" but "all flesh," therefore, "And he destroyed all of creation which was on the face of the earth, from man to beast. . . ." [Gen. 7:23] (*Midrash Tanḥuma, Noaḥ* 12; cf. Jubilees 5:2; 7:24; 1 Enoch 7:5; 4Q201, 3.20 in *DSSSE* 1:402–3)[33]

Although these interpreters begin by reading scripture with scripture, this turns out to be a point of departure for filling in imaginative backstory. This is very different than the imagery of sweeping away all creatures akin to the flood in Zeph 1:2–3 or all creation groaning as though in labor in Rom 8:22. These biblical authors limit their exegetical interventions to what has been revealed in Genesis.

It is easy to express gratitude for the achievements of scholars like Walter Kaiser, Craig Blomberg, and many others, who seek to make sense of the New Testament use of scripture. They remind us to do close readings of the details

30. See ibid., 101–2. Witherington makes the same kind of complaint about many psalms used in the New Testament (see 152–53, 156, 164, et passim). Yet, the sin of the psalmist is acknowledged within Kaiser's decidedly contextual interpretation of Ps 41:9 in John 13:18 (see "Single Meaning," 63).

31. See Kugel, *Traditions of the Bible*, 24–29; idem, "Beginnings of Biblical Interpretation," 21–22.

32. See Kugel, *Traditions of the Bible*, 20–21.

33. As quoted in ibid., 188.

in ways that honor the scriptures in a day of unrestrained criticism.[34] The following paragraphs do not offer a general critique but narrowly focus on the problem of adjusting meaning and/or context in the case of explaining the Bible's use of the Bible.

A couple of elements of **E. D. Hirsch's** views of interpretation need to be explained because many scholars, including Kaiser, make use of these views. Hirsch separates meaning and significance. Hirsch defines meaning as "that which is represented by a text" and significance as "a relationship between that meaning" and any contextual elements.[35] Hirsch later moved meaning outside of texts toward reception ("meaning-for-an-interpreter"), but he retained significance as "meaning-as-related-to-something-else."[36] However, it is the earlier version of Hirsch's distinction between meaning and significance that scholarship of the New Testament use of scripture has in mind.[37] The present study does not take issue with Hirsch's earlier approach itself, only with elements that many scholars add to it.

Kaiser locates the **author's meaning outside of its written context**.[38] This radical move is part of Kaiser's strenuous advocacy for preserving the author's intentions in the reuse of the Old Testament in the New. Kaiser frames his adjustment of meaning within his version of Hirsch's division between meaning and significance. That Kaiser's version of Hirsch's views does not align with the authorial intentions of Hirsch is evident by Kaiser's frequent complaints that Hirsch is not using his own hermeneutic correctly.[39] The ironies of Kaiser's complaints can be set aside here to focus on Kaiser's own adjustment of meaning.

The meaning or author's intentions is not, for Kaiser, to be located in the text the author has written (contra Hirsch's earlier view; see above). Instead, Kaiser insists that meaning is the proposition or principle that needs to be abstracted from what the author has written. This proposition or principle is "timeless" because it exists in the abstract outside of any context. Kaiser says of the New Testament's use of the meaning of the Old: "[T]hose *propositions identified with the text's meaning* as indicated by the author's use of linguistic symbols will need to be the source for making normative decisions."[40] The

34. So too Moo, "Problem of *Sensus Plenior*," 199.

35. Hirsch, *Validity in Interpretation*, 8.

36. See Hirsch, *Aims of Interpretation*, 79–81.

37. See Vanhoozer, *Is There a Meaning in This Text?* 260–62.

38. Walter Kaiser decided not to offer any feedback to the draft version of this chapter he was given.

39. See, e.g., Kaiser, "Single Meaning," 52; idem, *Uses of the Old Testament*, 204; idem, "Current Crisis in Exegesis," 3–4.

40. Kaiser, *Uses of the Old Testament*, 211, emphasis added. Elsewhere Kaiser speaks of "principles" akin to his use of "propositions." See ibid., 226; Kaiser, "Single Meaning," 82. For a generous critique of the problems with Kaiser's approach, see Moo, "Problem of *Sensus Plenior*," 189, 198–201. Vlach adopts

recontextualization of the timeless principle (meaning) in the New Testament, according to Kaiser, is not meaning but significance.

Again and again Kaiser claims that different uses of a biblical teaching mean the same thing as the unexpressed mental intentions of the donor text's human author. He claims later biblical authors mean the same things in their own unexpressed mental intentions even while changing the significances. Kaiser makes this argument about any New Testament use of the Old, for example:

- The law in Deut 25:4 about not muzzling the ox means the same thing as Paul's teaching on support for ministers of the gospel (1 Cor 9:9–12).[41]
- Amos's statement about possessing the remnant of Edom (Amos 9:12) means what James means by "so that all other people may seek the Lord" (Acts 15:17 NRSVue) to refer to uncircumcised Gentiles converting to the Way.[42]
- The psalmist did not speak of himself when he said, "for you will not abandon my soul to Sheol, nor will you let your faithful one see the Pit" (Ps 16:10 AT) but was consciously predicting the resurrection of the Messiah with the same meaning as Peter's and Paul's use of this psalm (Acts 2:27; 13:35).[43]
- Caiaphas's ethnocentric statement about the death of Jesus (John 11:50) means the same thing as John's claim that he died for all people (vv. 51–52).[44]

The present study pushes back in two ways. First, meaning is represented by the text in its context.[45] An author's intended meaning should not be separated from the contextualized expression of it in the written text.[46] The biblical text is authoritative and truthful, not the abstracted propositions deduced by modern

---

and modifies Kaiser's approach by noting that in certain cases the New Testament writers are interpreting the significance and the meaning of the Old Testament context (*Old in the New*, 63). Chou espouses single meaning but says some New Testament uses of scripture are only based on significance, not meaning (*Hermeneutics*, 41; cf. 34). In these ways the views of Vlach and Chou are even more radical than Kaiser's approach, since, for them, "meaning" is doubly severed from the biblical text.

41. See Kaiser, "Single Meaning," 81–87.

42. See ibid., 68–72.

43. See ibid., 75–80.

44. See ibid., 58–59.

45. Though oral speech and written texts share many properties, the present argument narrowly addresses biblical writings.

46. So too Clark, *To Know and to Love God*, 94, 96, and see 91–98. Clark promotes what he calls "soft" principalizing (95).

scholars concerning the unexpressed mental intentions of biblical authors.[47] Second, all scripture advances revelation, including exegetical interventions within scripture. Kaiser affirms progressive revelation. But what Kaiser has in mind is later biblical teachings about something else.[48] Progressive revelation, for Kaiser, does not apply to reuse of scriptural teaching in the scriptures because they mean the same thing outfitted with different significances. Thus, for Kaiser, a later legal collection in Torah, like the torah collection in Deut 12–26, "only enlarges" on the significance of the same teaching in the Ten Commandments but does not include progress of revelation.[49] This contention stands at odds with Moses's claim that he is explaining what Israel needs to do when they get into the land (Deut 6:1; cf. 1:5; 4:44).[50]

In sum, Kaiser affirms that the Old and New Testament authors mean the same thing. The sharp differences that Kaiser senses between them require him to insulate meaning so it is untouched by context. For Kaiser the applications of significance to contexts can differ wildly without having any effect upon the meaning. Meaning, for Kaiser, is the author's unexpressed mental intentions, not textual expression. Meaning, in this view, has no context (it is timeless) because contextualization is the work of significance. Kaiser's adjustment of meaning stands at a distance from the plain sense reading advocated in this study.

Blomberg tentatively uses the term **"double fulfillment"** to refer to a prophecy that is fulfilled both in the day of the Old Testament prophet who uttered it as well as in the New Testament. Blomberg considers Isa 7:14 the clearest example because the foretold birth is fulfilled in Isaiah's own day before the child is grown (Isa 7:1, 15), as well as in the virgin birth of the Messiah (Matt 1:23).[51] Blomberg's view of one thing meaning two things has problems. First, Blomberg identifies Immanuel (Isa 7:14), Mahar-Shalal-Hash-Baz (8:3), and the child born to us (9:6[5 H]) as the same person. But Isaiah's own son, Mahar-Shalal-Hash-Baz cannot be heir to the Davidic throne like Immanuel (7:13) and the child born to us (9:7[6 H]). Second, to say the same utterance means two things in the same context implies a pluralistic view of truth. Elsewhere Blomberg frames the relationship between the two fulfillments more circumspectly, calling the

47. The meaning of the propositions (locutions) of the biblical author in their context (illocutions or illocutionary framework) is authoritative and truthful (inerrant), not abstracted propositions produced by modern interpreters. See "Chicago Statement of Biblical Hermeneutics," 398 (VI). Against approaches that assert philosophical propositions of moderns in place of the verbal expression of scripture, see Vanhoozer, "Semantics of Biblical Literature," 56–67, esp. 63; idem, "Lost in Interpretation?" 96–100, 103.

48. See Kaiser, *Toward Old Testament Ethics*, 60–64.

49. See ibid., 132.

50. See Schnittjer, *Torah Story*, 383–85; *OTUOT*, 78–79, 81.

51. See Blomberg, "Double Fulfillment," 19–21.

fulfillment in Isaiah's day a "partial fulfillment" or a "provisional fulfillment" that foreshadows a greater fulfillment.[52] These are much better ways to explain the meaning of the prophetic utterance. Blomberg freely acknowledges that "double fulfillment" may not be the correct way to frame it.[53]

The context of Isaiah offers help. Isaiah 7–8 includes three sign children: Shear-Jashub (7:3), Immanuel (7:14), and Mahar-Shalal-Hash-Baz (8:3). While Isaiah himself is the father of Shear-Jashub and Mahar-Shalal-Hash-Baz, they cannot be identified with the child born to us (9:6[5 H]) because this figure is a Davidic ruler (9:7[6 H]). The child born to us is part of a deliverance that can be described as a light dawning from Galilee of the nations (9:1–2[8:23–9:1 H]). Matthew may be identifying Immanuel with a child born to us since he cites both Isa 7:14 and 9:1–2[8:23–9:1 H] in relation to the coming of the Messiah (Matt 1:23; 4:15–16).

Detecting a relationship between Isa 7:14 and 9:6[5 H] would naturally be based on catchwords—"Give birth" and "son"—appearing in both contexts. Using catchwords and catchphrases to interpret together two remote donor texts within a receptor text occurs frequently throughout Israel's scriptures. In this case, the expectational framing of "a child is born to us" would naturally cause the sign-child born to the young woman of Isaiah's day (Isa 7:14) to function as a typological pattern for a greater fulfillment of one like a child born to us in Matt 1.[54] The nature of fulfillment (Chapter 3), interpretive blends (Chapter 4), and typological patterns (Chapter 6) will be discussed at length later.

In sum, there is no need to adjust meaning by "double fulfillment." This inherently pluralistic hermeneutic seems to represent a poor choice of wording, since neither Blomberg nor other evangelicals who adopt this approach are pluralists. Instead of finding a label like double fulfillment, these cases of scriptural reuse show a need for greater attention to context.

Sensus plenior is a Latin expression meaning "fuller sense." This view sees the divine author of scripture as having fuller intentions and meaning than the limited intentions and meaning of the human author.[55] In this way the New Testament use of the Old Testament can be said to mean the same thing in both testaments. The human authors of Israel's scriptures were limited by their historical contexts and only meant what they knew from their contextual vantage points. The omniscience of the divine author could simultaneously mean

52. See Blomberg, *Matthew*, 60; idem, "Matthew," *CNTUOT*, 4.

53. Blomberg, "Double Fulfillment," 19.

54. See France, *Matthew*, 57.

55. See Brown, Sensus Plenior *of Sacred Scripture*, 92–93; idem, "Problems of *Sensus Plenior*," 460. Also see idem, "History and Development," 141–62; idem, "*Sensus Plenior* in the Last Ten Years," 262–85.

something much fuller by the very same words. The mysterious extra meaning remained hidden until the teaching, death, and resurrection of the Messiah put the biblical contexts into a new light. The New Testament human authors, then, could use the scriptures according to the divine author's original intentions. In this way the New Testament is saying the same thing as the Old, only more fully.

Sensus plenior is not an exegetical method.[56] It is an explanation of the alleged mechanics of revelation. It adjusts meaning and adjusts context, placing them somewhere external to the context and intentions of biblical authors.

This speculative proposal has garnered many subvarieties. Here are two qualifications by Protestant advocates.[57] First, the Old Testament context should be interpreted in its own right before reading the New Testament use of it back onto the earlier context.[58] That is, the human author's intentions for the earlier scripture need to be respected first. After all, God was pleased to present his word this way within this context. Second, the fuller sense is not different, but extends and develops from the authorial sense of the earlier human author.[59]

S. Lewis Johnson uses sensus plenior to explain Paul and Sosthenes's reuse of a law (bold signifies verbal parallels and italics signify synonyms).[60]

> **Do not** ***muzzle*** **an ox while it is treading out the grain**. (Deut 25:4)

> Who serves as a soldier at his own expense? Who plants a vineyard and does not eat its grapes? Who tends a flock and does not drink the milk? Do I say this merely on human authority? Doesn't the Law say the same thing? For it is written in the Law of Moses: "**Do not** ***muzzle*** **an ox while it is treading out the grain**." Is it about oxen that God is concerned? Surely he says this for us, doesn't he? Yes, this was written for us, because whoever plows and threshes should be able to do so in the hope of sharing in the harvest. (1 Cor 9:7–10; cf. 1 Tim 5:18)

For Johnson, the apostolic interpretation of the law is an *extension* of the Old Testament human author's intention and is an expression of the fuller divine intention inherent in Deut 25:4 all along.[61]

---

56. Contra those who claim sensus plenior is an exegetical method, such as Duane Garrett, "Hosea, Book of," *DNTUOT*, 339.

57. See fuller discussion in Bock, "Evangelicals: Part 2," 306–11.

58. See Johnson, *Old Testament in the New*, 51; LaSor, "*Sensus Plenior* and Biblical Interpretation," 275.

59. See Johnson, *Old Testament in the New*, 50; Moo, *Paul*, 23; Moo and Naselli, "Problem of the New Testament's Use of the Old," 733–34; Packer, "Infallible," 350.

60. See Johnson, *Old Testament in the New*, 47–51.

61. For an interpretation of Deut 25:4 based on an overlooked element of what working cattle eat, see Joel R. White, "Contextual and Noncontextual NT Use of OT," *DNTUOT*, 125. If the observation

It is easy to agree with the premise that God in his omniscience conceives of the later reuse of scripture from the time of the original revelation. However, the fuller meaning apparatus is both unnecessary and unhelpful. The historical unfolding of revelation does not require humans to get inside of God's mind, as if they could. Further, the sensus plenior proposal is not enough in itself but requires secondary hypotheses to repair the problems created by the proposal. For example, some propose that God chose the Old Testament to use the Hebrew language because of its special qualities to carry "hidden meanings."[62] Brown illustrates this point by noting the flexibility of "young woman" (*'almah* עַלְמָה) in Isa 7:14.[63] Brown confuses the issue because Isaiah had a choice in how to express the sign. That Isaiah chose to say "young woman" instead of "virgin" (*betulah* בְּתוּלָה) has nothing to do with an alleged unique capacity of the Hebrew language to carry hidden messages.[64]

Another example of a second speculation to repair the problems of sensus plenior is defining the fuller sense as the canon of scripture.[65] This adjustment of context attempts to accommodate the locus of meaning (the mind of God). This means the teaching gets framed in at least two contexts: the initial revelation of the donor text and the reinterpretation of that revelation within the scripture as a whole that replaces the historical contexts of the donor text and the receptor text. Though this double reading, of sorts, could be helpful by naming concrete contexts, it anachronistically reads back the completed canon into the time of the biblical authors. But there is no author of the Bible who had access to the entire canon of scripture.

Not one.

This means no biblical author of either testament could understand what modern advocates of sensus plenior say the donor text means. Treating the finished canon of scripture as sensus plenior is a severe anachronism that eliminates the historical context and intentions of the authors of scriptural donor and receptor texts.

White highlights is confirmed—that oxen eat forage and cannot digest and so do not eat standing grain—it eliminates the validity of the hermeneutical debate about Paul's use of Deut 25:4.

62. See Brown, Sensus Plenior *of Sacred Scripture*, 125.

63. See ibid., 126.

64. See Barr, *Semantics*, 19; cf. 8–45.

65. See Andrew Naselli, "History of Interpretation: 1800 to Present," *DNTUOT*, 325–26; Moo and Naselli, "Problem of the New Testament's Use of the Old," 736–37; LaSor, "*Sensus Plenior* and Biblical Interpretation," 275. Cf. studies listed in Compton, "Shared Intentions?" 30, n. 42. Also see Vanhoozer, *Is There a Meaning in This Text?* 264–65, where he equates fuller meaning with the whole canon. Though Vanhoozer now rejects sensus plenior as a way to speak of the Bible's use of the Bible (see *Mere Christian Hermeneutics*, 137 discussed below on p. 46), he continues to espouse that the divine meaning is identical to the full canon with reference to the interpretation of the Bible by Christians after the close of the canon (see *Mere Christian Hermeneutics*, 175–77, 194).

An effort to explain how the apostles use a sensus plenior interpretation of scripture versus how modern Christians should interpret scripture sometimes leads to confusion. William Osborne claims that because the story of Israel's scriptures is fulfilled in Christ, because God revealed his redemptive plan in Israel's scriptures, and because of a solidarity between Old Testament Israel and the new covenant people of God, that New Testament authors "freely read" the Old Testament in a figural manner.[66] Osborne tries to walk this back by saying that not "anything goes."[67] Yet, he claims that New Testament authors are essentially saying, "This is actually what Jeremiah meant when he said . . ."[68] Osborne says "a Christian reading . . . must" bring a christological perspective into the Old Testament prophets.[69] By this he means that sensus plenior is not the "*creation* of meaning" but a recognition of "a full canonical meaning of the prophet."[70] It is easy to agree that responsible interpretation by modern Christians requires working out how biblical prophetic teachings fit within the entire Christian canon. But, as noted above, no biblical author of either testament had access to the entire canon. Imposing the full canon into Old or New Testament times as sensus plenior is an adjustment of context and an adjustment of meaning.

Treating sensus plenior as the entire canon can lead to transgressing the fine line between figural and allegorical reading—imposition of later developments. The New Testament authors' interpretation of Israel's scriptures in light of the teaching, death, and resurrection of the Messiah by the Spirit is not the same thing as replacing their incremental advancement of revelation with a postbiblical, full-canon, and developed Christian theology. This reading back into the New Testament context a later context distorts progressive revelation of redemption.

The framing of the issue by Lissa Wray Beal offers some help. She emphasizes that modern Christians should read the Old Testament in its own context before rereading it in "the context of a two-testament canon."[71] Wray Beal distinguishes this whole Bible context from the authors of the New Testament who interpreted Israel's scriptures "guided by Christ's own direction . . . and the Spirit's illumination" as "hermeneutical guides [that] directed them to the Old Testament as revealing Christ, while also anticipating his full revelation

66. See Osborne, "Emulating," 250–51.

67. See ibid., 252.

68. Osborne, "Conclusion," 315.

69. Ibid., 315.

70. Ibid., 317, emphasis original.

71. Wray Beal, "Emulating," 144.

in the New Testament."[72] This helpful distinction removes the anachronism of sensus-plenior-as-canon and acknowledges the advancement of revelation within the scriptures. We will return to this issue after observing one more fuller-meaning approach.

Greg Beale and Ben Gladd take a different approach to fuller meaning. They argue for fuller meaning from the Old Testament itself. They do a contextual study of mystery in Dan 2 and Dan 4 that provides an important part of how mystery functions in the New Testament. The twofold structure of Dan 2 and Dan 4—symbolic vision followed by full interpretation—provides a model for wisdom or revelation that was mostly hidden in the Old Testament but fully revealed in Christ and the New Testament.[73] This model applies not only to the use of "mystery" in the New Testament but also to the revelation of resurrection, christological understanding of the Old Testament, the gospel, and more.[74] Beale and Gladd apply the model of mystery in Dan 2 and Dan 4 to understanding the New Testament use of the Old in general.[75] Though revelation is hidden, it is still "there" in the Old Testament.[76] They say, "Full or complete meaning is indeed actually 'there' in the Old Testament text; it is simply partially 'hidden' or latent, awaiting later revelation, whereby the complete meaning of the text is revealed to the interpreter."[77]

Elsewhere Beale refers to this fuller sense as "cognitive peripheral vision," saying, "Old and NT writers *knew more* than what they explicitly intended to say. . . . If so, there was an explicit intention and implicit wider understanding related to that intention."[78] In pushing back, Moyise repeatedly misstates that in this view biblical authors "say more than they know."[79] But Beale asserts that biblical authors know more than they say.[80]

The major concern is detecting additional meaning unexpressed in the specific text but at the unexpressed edge of the author's mind. Beale does not resort to readerly imagination but seeks the latent intentions in the context of the biblical author's writing. In his words: "In addition to the explicit meaning from the specific text quoted and explicitly attended to by the New Testament author, this contextual meaning may include ideas from the immediate or

72. Ibid. Wray Beal's framing is close to what I have elsewhere called retrospective prospectivity or reading the Hebrew Bible as Christian scripture. See *OTUOT*, xl.

73. See Beale and Gladd, *Hidden but Now Revealed*, 41, 43.

74. See ibid., 289–99.

75. See ibid., 329–34.

76. See ibid., 335.

77. Ibid., 330.

78. Beale, "Cognitive Peripheral Vision," 292, emphasis added.

79. Moyise, "Latency and Respect for Context," 131, 135.

80. See Beale, "Cognitive Peripheral Vision," 271, 292.

nearby OT context that are in mind, as well as ideas from the other OT books that are related to the meaning of the focus text."[81] Looking in the context of the biblical author's writing or in earlier scriptural writings seems more like plain sense exegesis than sensus plenior. Indeed, advocates of sensus plenior reject Beale's approach because he makes the "case from the text itself."[82] We affirm seeking meaning in the text the biblical author has produced.

In sum, scholars adjust meaning and adjust context with sensus plenior to preserve the authorial intention of the donor text by positing that the divine author has more in mind than the human author. This speculation requires additional speculations, such as hidden messages or anachronistic replacement of the historical context and intentions of the human author of the donor and receptor texts with the complete canon. This widely held "solution" does not fix the apparent incongruity. Biblical authors do not know or intend the full extent of what they are saying. Perhaps the attraction of sensus plenior is that its proponents feel like this conjecture-cluster settles everything with the belief that God knows what he is saying even if no biblical author does.

Before moving on, many of the adjustments of meaning and/or context surveyed above focus on the donor text considered individually and the receptor text considered individually. But this only applies to some of the exegetical interventions in the Bible. A very large number of receptor texts are reading one donor text in the light of another, whether in an interpretive blend or based on the vertical context within the donor text or kindred situations.[83] These cases have more going on than interpreting a single earlier scripture in relation to an element in the context of the receptor text. The point being that many of the approaches surveyed above have not explained what is really going on in a large number of receptor texts. These issues are taken up in Chapter 4.

As noted at the opening of this chapter, the choice between many proposals to adjust meaning and/or adjust context and advancement of revelation is a choice between two different kinds of things. An approach that starts with the divine right to **advance revelation by exegetical interventions**, as proposed here, eliminates the need for creative adjustments of meaning and/or adjustments of context.

The approach here agrees with Geerhardus Vos's emphasis on plain sense exegesis employed by Jesus in the context of "progressive development of revelation." He says, "His [Jesus's] hermeneutics were simple and straightforward."[84]

81. Ibid., 273; cf. 275.

82. See Longman, "Christotelic Approach," 81–82. The quotation here is from 81.

83. Similarly, see Macaskill, "Israel's Scriptures," 133.

84. Vos, *Biblical Theology*, 359.

All scripture advances revelation, including its reuse of earlier scriptures. Accepting the scriptural exegesis of scripture as advancement of revelation does not solve all interpretive difficulties. Every case of the use of scripture in the scriptures needs to be approached on its own terms. The problem has never been about finding the proper way to adjust meaning and/or context. Accepting the exegetical advancement of revelation in scripture is both much simpler and much more difficult than any of the "solutions" summarized above.

Yahweh himself sets the precedent for advancing revelation by scriptural exegesis of scripture. Only one of the five divine legal precedent and/or amendment cases can be mentioned here.[85] Yahweh advances revelation by his own authority. At the first Passover celebration in the wilderness, Yahweh responds to the complaints of those excluded from participation because of ritual pollution by an exegetical advancement of revelation (Num 9:6–14). This new circumstance arose based on the glory entering the tabernacle, which necessitated new ritual purity regulations (5:1–4; cf. 19:11, 16; Lev 11–15). These factors were not a concern during the original Passover in Egypt. But a new event in redemptive history triggers the need for additional revelation that is mediated through exegetical advancements.[86] Yahweh goes even further than necessary by also making allowances for persons who are traveling to celebrate Passover in the second month (Num 9:10).

Yahweh's own set of exegetical adjustments to legal standards demonstrates that law serves the covenantal relationship, not the other way around. It also underlines Yahweh's commitment to advancing revelation by means of scriptural exegesis.

An attitude of "Do not question the revealed law of God" stands at odds with Yahweh's precedent-setting exegetical advancements of the law in Torah. Yahweh himself responds to well-founded complaints by advancing revelation.

Yahweh advances revelation in many ways.[87] A small subset of this advancement of revelation comes in the form of exegetical interventions of earlier scriptures by the divinely ordained delegates who authored scripture. Biblical authors who use interpretations of earlier scriptures as part of their

85. The five precedent-setting and legal amendment narratives in which Yahweh himself made advancements of revelation have been known at least since Philo (*Moses 2*, §§192–245; cf. Tg. Neof. and Tg. Ps.-J. at Lev 24:12; Num 9:8; 15:34; 27:5). See Lev 24:10–23 (the blasphemer); Num 9:1–14 (alternate date for Passover); 15:32–36 (the Sabbath breaker); 27:1–11 (inheritance of Zelophehad's daughters); and 36:1–12 (amending inheritance in the case of Zelophehad's daughters). See *OTUOT*, 44–46, 60–61, 66–71.

86. See Morales, *Numbers 1–19*, comment on Num 9:6–7 (forthcoming). Similarly, the new circumstances of inheritance granted to Zelophehad's daughters in Num 27:1–11 created the need for an adjustment of this adjustment in 36:4. See idem, *Numbers 20–36*, comment on Num 36:1–4 (forthcoming).

87. See Athas, *Bridging*, 13.

own scriptural instruction follow the precedent of exegetical advancement of revelation by Yahweh's own scriptural exegesis. The frequency of the Bible's use of the Bible is one index of the deep commitment of biblical authors to reinterpret an earlier scripture rather than exclusively proclaiming new teachings without allusion.

Accepting the advancement of revelation will not produce clean-cut interpretive solutions to all cases of the Bible's use of the Bible. Doug Moo concludes that Peter's interpretation of Ps 16:8–11 in Acts 2 cannot be explained by the psalm according to its plain sense or sensus plenior or severing meaning from significance. Moo says this context, and maybe others, needs to be taken by faith.[88] We agree that knowing when to say I don't know needs to be part of responsible exegesis.

Likewise, it is easy to agree with Moo's criticisms against several varieties of sensus plenior.[89] In pushing back against and seeking to adjust problematic varieties of sensus plenior treated above, Moo points in the direction of the argument made here. He says the "*pregnant sense*" or "'added meaning' that the text takes on is the product of the ultimate canonical shape—though to be sure, *often perceived only on a revelatory basis*."[90] While the affirmation of "ultimate canonical shape" needs to be set aside as anachronistic for every biblical author (see above), Moo's acknowledgment of the need for further revelation—"often perceived only on a revelatory basis"—is a key point. He goes on, "The revelatory stance of the New Testament interpreter of the Old must not be ignored."[91] Though our view is not identical with Moo's, we agree with the revelatory role of receptor texts in both testaments. God advances revelation. He sometimes does so by means of authorized exegetical interventions of the authors of receptor texts. The choice promoted here affirms plain sense interpretation and historical context—with no adjustments—based on organic authorized exegetical advancement of revelation by receptor texts.

The image of a tree gets used by competing viewpoints. One version explains the advancement of revelation in scripture. "The line of revelation is like the stem of those trees that grow in rings. Each successive ring grows out of the preceding one."[92] The figure does well to capture organic continuity of the living and active and not always symmetrical shape of exegetical advances of revelation within scripture. The redemptive relationship with God's people has

88. Moo, "Problem of *Sensus Plenior*," 210–11. For a list of other difficult texts see footnote 17 in the Introduction.

89. Ibid., 201–9. Also see Moo and Naselli, "Problem of the New Testament's Use of the Old," 733.

90. Moo, "Problem of *Sensus Plenior*," 206, emphasis added and Latin expression translated.

91. Ibid.

92. Vos, "Inaugural Address," 39.

many messy details as their identity shifts from slaves to invaders to settlers to subjects of regional kingdoms to homeless exiles to a remnant returned to their ancestors's homeland to a provincial minority in the hinterlands of the empire to marginalized outcasts. The dynamics of progressive revelation, especially through repackaging earlier revelation for a new day of the redemptive relationship, make exegetical allusions to earlier scripture an ideal vehicle for God to speak his will to his wayward people.

Surprising christological fulfillments cast their announcements within Israel's scriptures as unexpected expectations. D. A. Carson notes that while New Testament authors like Paul and his associates insist that plain textual exegesis bears witness to the gospel, they marvel at God's wisdom hidden in plain view. They did so without any apparent awareness of tension.[93] "[T]he Gospel has been announced throughout the Scriptures, yet . . . only fresh revelation, both in the person of Christ and in the illuminating work of the Spirit, unpacks what is there in the text."[94]

In the midst of Kevin Vanhoozer's larger argument for mere Christian hermeneutics—a shared interpretive perspective of all Christians everywhere from the close of the New Testament canon until the second coming of Christ—he introduces two elements that line up with the approach presented here, namely, frame of reference and fuller reference. Vanhoozer defines frame of reference as "the way a reader looks at a text," including presuppositions, values, and questions.[95] He makes the case that the frame of reference controls how interpretive methods function along with their interpretive outcomes. Two persons with different frames of reference can use the same methods on the same texts and come to different interpretive outcomes. Thus, as Vanhoozer says, "Frames matter."[96]

Vanhoozer recognizes that fuller meaning does not get it right. "[W]hat is 'fuller' is not the sense, but the reference, of their [biblical authors'] discourse—not [fuller] meaning but fuller reference."[97] He argues that interpreters need to honor Isaiah's frame of reference because the sense of Isaiah's discourse does not change. "[T]he prophets knew *what they were saying*."[98] Rereading Isaiah within the larger biblical context provides a fuller reference of who and what

93. See Carson, "Mystery and Fulfillment," 426–27.

94. Ibid., 435.

95. Vanhoozer, *Mere Christian Hermeneutics*, 78.

96. Ibid. Vanhoozer here borrows this statement from Scot McKnight, *Five Things*, 149.

97. Vanhoozer, *Mere Christian Hermeneutics*, 137, Latin expressions ("*sensus [plenior]*" and "*referens plenior*") are here presented in English. Vanhoozer acknowledges that he is borrowing the expression "fuller reference" from Elliott Johnson, though Vanhoozer is using it distinctly. See Johnson, "Author's Intention," 428.

98. Vanhoozer, *Mere Christian Hermeneutics*, 137, emphasis original.

he is speaking about. The meaning does not change. The understanding of readers grows within a larger biblical framework.[99]

Vanhoozer's fuller reference closely aligns with the advancement of revelation approach advocated here. It is easy to agree that fuller meaning distorts the situation by adjusting meaning and context to something other than the frames of reference of the authors of the donor and receptor texts. Advancement of redemptive revelation activated by the Bible's use of the Bible overlaps with the idea of a fuller reference identified by the receptor text.

The differences between Vanhoozer's project and the present study need to be registered. Vanhoozer's *Mere Christian Hermeneutics* does not emphasize the Bible's use of the Bible, which is the exclusive focus of the present study. Vanhoozer rightly argues for the closed canon as the proper boundary—a key part of the frame of reference—for mere Christian exegesis. Meanwhile the present study advocates for responsible exegesis of the biblical authors' use of earlier scripture that takes place before there is a closed canon. To use Vanhoozer's language, the complete canon of scripture as the frame of reference applies to zero biblical authors.

The place of emerging canonical consciousness within the biblical authors' frames of reference can help calibrate how advancement of revelation relates to the Bible's use of the Bible across the two testaments. The authors of Israel's scriptures advance revelation by their exegesis of earlier scriptural traditions. That is, earlier scriptural traditions provide an authoritative frame of reference for the advancement of revelation by exegesis in later writings of Israel's scriptures. New Testament authors interpret Israel's scriptures with two authoritative bodies of revelation in their frame of reference: Israel's scriptures inclusive of its exegesis of itself and the teachings of Jesus. Later New Testament authors also make use of earlier New Testament teachings as part of their frame of reference. This evidence points to the way that emerging canonical consciousness contributes to the frame of reference of biblical authors as they interpret earlier scriptures.

Others have observed the way that later biblical authors interpret earlier scripture within the redemptive-historical framework of progressive revelation. The definitive revelation of God in the teaching, death, and resurrection of the Messiah put Israel's scriptures in a whole new light. New Testament authors explain Israel's scriptures in the light of the Messiah whom they interpret according to Israel's scriptures. But the advancement of revelation by scriptural

99. See ibid., 169.

exegesis of scriptures is not new to the New Testament. The interpretation of scripture according to the historical progress of redemption "can be shown to have its antecedents in what the Old Testament itself does with earlier revelation."[100]

In sum, God moves revelation forward by his appointed delegates who author scripture. Scriptural authors frequently present new teachings by exegetical interventions with earlier scriptural teachings. Yahweh himself set the precedent to honor the authority of earlier revelation by interpretive advancements in a new context. This understanding entails no adjustments of meaning and no adjustments of context. Advancement of revelation by scriptural exegesis of scripture makes such adjustments unnecessary. This understanding naturally affirms a plain sense reading of scripture.

CASE—PROPHET LIKE MOSES

This case, and the next, of the Bible's use of the Bible highlights the advancement of revelation.

The expectation for a prophet like Moses stems from the people's own request for Moses to mediate Yahweh's will to the people because they were in fear. In the biblical text, the institution of prophetic mediators in the tradition of Moses began not with a divine decision but with a complaint of the people. The fear-inspiring circumstances of the historic pronouncement of the Ten Commandments from the mountain prompted human petitions that triggered a divine response accepting Moses's mediatorial role—the people had nominated him. Moses's role would be passed down to later prophets (Deut 18:15–18). The series of prophets eventually led to an expectation for a prophet at the level of Moses (34:10–12). Notice on the facing page the series of exegetical expansions within Torah that lead to the expectation for a prophet like Moses (emphases signify verbal parallels).[101]

While both Moses and Yahweh refer to a prophet singular (Deut 18:15), the singular functions in a distributive sense, referring to many prophets or an ongoing prophetic office.[102] Yet the narrator of Deuteronomy draws out an expectation from the subtext of the simile of a prophet *like* Moses. In spite of other prophets like Moses who mediated God's will, there has yet to arise a prophet with the level of revelation or terrifying deeds mediated by Moses

100. Moo, "Problem of *Sensus Plenior*," 205. Also see Schnittjer, "What's Old?" 79–80.

101. These parallels and observations combine elements from Schnittjer, *Torah Story*, 453, with *OTUOT*, 131, 147–48. For a color-coded layout, see *OTUOTPL*, entry on Deut 34:10–12.

102. See Driver, *Deuteronomy*, 227; GKC §126o.

The people . . . said to Moses, "*You tell us* and *we will listen*. But do not have God speak to us or *we will die*." (Exod 20:19 AT)

Yahweh would speak to Moses face to face, as one speaks to a friend. Then Moses would return to the camp, but his young aide Joshua son of Nun did not leave the tent. (33:11 AT)[103]

Has any god ever tried to take for himself one nation out of another nation, by testings, by signs and wonders, by war, by a mighty hand and an outstretched arm, or by awesome deeds, like all the things Yahweh your God did for you in Egypt before your very eyes? (Deut 4:34 AT)

[The people said:] But now, why should we die? This great fire will consume us, and *we will die* if we hear the voice of Yahweh our God any longer. . . . Go near and listen to all that Yahweh our God says. Then *you tell us* whatever Yahweh our God tells you. *We will listen* and obey." Yahweh heard you when you spoke to me, and Yahweh said to me, "I have heard what this people said to you. Everything they said was good. (Deut 5:25, 27–28, v. 27 AT)

[Moses said:] Yahweh your God **will raise up** for you a **prophet like** me from among you, from your fellow Israelites. You must listen to him. 16 For this is what you asked of Yahweh your God at Horeb on the day of the assembly when you said, "Let me not hear the voice of Yahweh my God nor see this great fire anymore, or I will die." 17 Yahweh said to me: "What they say is good. 18 I will raise up for them a prophet like you from among their fellows, and I will put my words in his mouth. He will tell them everything I command him." (Deut 18:15–18, vv. 16, 18 AT)

[Narrator:] Since then, no **prophet has risen** in Israel **like** Moses, whom Yahweh knew face to face, who did all those signs and wonders Yahweh sent him to do in Egypt—to Pharaoh and to all his officials and to his whole land. For no one has ever shown the mighty hand or performed the awesome deeds that Moses did before the eyes of all Israel. (Deut 34:10–12, v. 12 AT)

103. The expression "mouth to mouth" (AT) in Num 12:8 is different than "face to face" in Exod 33:11 and Deut 34:10.

(34:10–12; cf. Exod 33:11; Deut 4:34). The context of the donor text in Deut 4:34 provides a clue to the narrator's interpretation. The line of thought starts with a comparative question: "Has anything so great *as* [כְּ] this ever happened, or has anything *like* [כְּ] it ever been heard of?" (Deut 4:32b, emphasis added) This question points to the catchword "like" in 4:32; 18:15 and suggested to the narrator of Deuteronomy in 34:10 that, to the narrator's day, there has yet to be a prophet like Moses in terms of revelation and terrifying signs.[104]

The narrator of Deuteronomy's exegetical intervention presses the sense of "like" (כְּ). Though the preposition can mean anything from *something like* to *exactly like*, the narrator fills out the sense by expecting the level of revelation and cosmic terrors mediated by Moses.[105] In this way the narrator of Deuteronomy extends revelation by shifting "like" from a prophetic office to the higher ideals of redemption and revelation mediated during Moses's tenure. The narrator does not impose an innovation. Instead, the narrator's exegetical extension stems from interpreting scripture in the light of scripture. Authorized advancements of revelation arise from the authority of prior scriptural revelation.

Notice how this later interpretation in Deut 34:10 retrojects its exegetical outcomes onto 18:15 (see side-by-side comparison above). Peter cites Deut 18:15 but with the sense of the incomparable expected one from 34:10 (Acts 3:22; cf. John 1:21, 45; 6:14; 7:40). Old and New Testament writers often cite a scriptural context that had been interpreted by a later Old Testament receptor text and read the donor text with the later interpretive sense but without citing the receptor text. New Testament scholars say, "Sometimes a NT author may have in mind the earlier OT reference but may be interpreting it through the later OT development of that earlier text."[106] An allusion within the framework of emerging canonical consciousness permanently connects the donor and receptor texts and activates both in relation to their counterparts. That is how scriptural allusions work (see Chapter 4).

In sum, the expectation for a prophet like Moses emerges in a moment of a rightful complaint brought before Yahweh. He responds with grace and institutes a series of prophets like Moses. But the narrator of Deuteronomy reads together multiple donor texts in order to extend revelation on the same fault line, as though asking with the donor texts: Has a prophet like Moses arisen?

---

104. For the problem of the translation of Deut 34:10 as "never since" (NRSVue) and "never again" (NJPS) see *OTUOT*, 148. On the narrator of Deuteronomy, see Schnittjer, *Torah Story*, 389–90.

105. On the function of the preposition of analogy "like" or "as" (כְּ), see GKC §118s; *IBHS* 11.2.9b; Joüon §133g.

106. Beale and Carson, "Introduction," *CNTUOT*, xxiv.

The narrator of Deuteronomy looked backward to establish an expectation that awaited fulfillment by the prophet from Nazareth.

CASE—THE SPIRIT

The Spirit provides enlightenment for exegetical interventions of biblical authors in both testaments. This includes David's exegesis of the promise mediated by Nathan as noted in 2 Sam 23:2 and the interpretation of scripture in relation to the teaching of Jesus by his followers after his resurrection. This latter example will be taken up here.

The Messiah's promise to his followers of enlightenment by the Spirit is broader than but includes exegetical interventions. Jesus said, "But the Advocate, the Holy Spirit, whom the Father will send in my name, *will teach you all things and will remind you of everything I have said to you*" (John 14:26, emphasis added). The Spirit's work of enlightenment helps make sense of the telescoping routinely featured in John (e.g., 2:17, 22; 12:16; 20:9). Notice the exegetical interventions of the postresurrection narration of preresurrection events:

> His disciples *remembered that it is written*: "Zeal for your house will consume me" **[Ps 69:9(10 H)]**. . . . *After he was raised from the dead, his disciples recalled* what he had said. Then they believed the scripture and the words that Jesus had spoken. (2:17, 22, emphasis added)

The narrator of the Fourth Gospel uses telescoping to reinterpret the teaching and events of the Lord's clearing of the temple. In this way Ps 69:9[10 H] provides a typological interpretive foil to reinterpret the events and teachings and advance revelation from an exegetical perspective unavailable to the eyewitnesses of the events. They had the scriptures, but they needed the illuminating work of the Spirit.

The eyewitnesses of the triumphal entry lacked the vantage point to interpret the Messiah's actions in relation to the expectations of the prophets. The narrator explains the retrospective reinterpretation of the events based on scripture:

> Jesus found a young donkey and sat on it, as it is written: "Do not be afraid, Daughter Zion; see, your king is coming, seated on a donkey's colt" **[Zech 9:9]**. At first his disciples did not understand all this. *Only after Jesus was glorified did they realize that these things had been written about him* and that these things had been done to him. (John 12:14–16, emphasis added)

The exegesis of scripture by a biblical author in these cases does not require adjustments of meaning or adjustments of context, even while they are not transparent or straightforward to the eyewitnesses themselves. The events were reinterpreted from a new vantage point. Scriptural exegesis of scripture is a vehicle of progressive revelation. The exegetical advancement of revelation in John is explicitly and self-consciously attributed to the Holy Spirit (cf. 14:26).

The two cases presented here (prophet like Moses and the enlightenment by the Spirit) complement the example offered in the previous section (Yahweh's exegetical legal amendments). All of these point to revelatory advancements activated by scriptural exegesis of scripture.

FAQS

The following questions push back on advancement of revelation as an explanation of meaning and context in the Bible's use of the Bible. These questions are based on those posed by students and scholars as well as hosts of podcast interviews.

If an Old Testament donor text means X in its original context, and a New Testament receptor text says it means Y, do these authors make these claims by their revelatory stance?

There are two problems with the question. First, the question misrepresents biblical realities. If the donor text means X, then the receptor text advances revelation as X or x or X+ or *X* or $\underline{X}$ or X^2 or (X) or ironic-X or X+Y, and so on, but not X means Y. Earlier in this chapter it was noted that Isa 7:14 MT says "the young woman will conceive" (AT) and the LXX which Matt 1:23 quotes says "the virgin will conceive" (AT). These two are in continuity since the LXX, in this case, is based on a Hebrew parent text identical to the MT (see Isa 7:14 LXX HPTAT). Saying one is X and the other is Y implies complete difference. Second, Old Testament receptor texts and New Testament receptor texts operate identically in relation to their donor texts—this is not merely a New Testament issue.

Setting aside these two problems with the question, the answer is no and yes. No, authors of receptor texts use plain sense exegesis. Yes, biblical authors are ordained by God to write his word. Plain sense exegesis by the Spirit's guidance is exactly what an organic view of revelation supposes as opposed to mechanical or dictation theories of revelation.

In the advancement of revelation approach, what is the relationship of the meaning of the donor text and the meaning of the receptor text?

There is a continuity of meaning between the donor text and receptor text. The author of the receptor text interprets the donor text according to its context (including its horizontal and vertical contexts; see Chapter 4) and according to the context of the author of the receptor text. God authorizes every biblical author to advance revelation in all that they write, including their exegesis of earlier scriptures.

The expression "exegetical advancements" seems to indicate that the author of the receptor text is interpreting the donor text. Yet does the author of the receptor text sometimes discover a sense that is not evident from a plain sense reading of the donor text in its original context?

No and yes. No, the reuse of scripture does not change the sense of the donor text in its original context. Yes, the author of the receptor text interprets the donor text by its plain sense as it relates to the historical context of the author of the receptor text, such as Israel's rebellion or the exile or the teaching, death, and resurrection of the Messiah. And in many cases the author of the receptor text interprets the donor text in light of its horizontal and/or vertical context(s) or reads one donor text in the light of another based on a catchword (see Chapter 4). In all of these cases, and more, the advancement of revelation is activated by exegetical interventions with the donor text in the receptor text.

Does the Spirit enable the author of the receptor text to interpret meaning that is legitimately in the donor text but was not evident to the author of the donor text?

Yes and yes. Yes, according to John, Jesus told his followers the Spirit would enhance their interpretive insight after the resurrection (see the discussion of unexpected expectations above, as well as the case studies). And, yes, all scripture, including its exegetical interventions, advances revelation for it is God-breathed. The strong preference of biblical authors for presenting their teaching according to earlier scriptures accounts for the continuity of revelation within the historical advancement of redemption. In all this the Spirit's revelation is mediated organically, not mechanically, by the author.

How does an advancement of revelation approach handle a specific case of the Bible's use of the Bible in relation to how it is handled by dividing meaning and significance or sensus plenior—such as Hos 11:1 in Matt 2:15?

> When Israel was a child, I loved him,
> and **out of Egypt I called my son.**
> [2]But the more they were called,
> the more they went away from me.
> They sacrificed to the Baals
> and they burned incense to images. (Hos 11:1–2, emphasis added)

> So he got up, took the child and his mother during the night and left for Egypt, [15]where he stayed until the death of Herod. And so was fulfilled what the Lord had said through the prophet: **"Out of Egypt I called my son."** (Matt 2:14–15, emphasis added)

Those who divide meaning and significance do so to retain meaning aligned with the author's intentions. As such, this approach asserts that even though Hosea is speaking of a past historical event in Hos 11:1, probably his unexpressed mental intention means it as a prediction. This unexpressed mental intention against the apparent sense of the text builds on the overlap of the individual and the collective with Israel called "son" in Exod 4:22, as well as similar language used of Israel in Balaam's second oracle and of a coming king in his third oracle (Num 23:22; 24:8).[107]

The sensus plenior approach claims Hosea did not intend a prediction and that Matthew assigns an additional meaning that goes beyond its grammatical-historical sense.[108] A proponent of sensus plenior explains that Matthew fits among New Testament authors who "disregarded the main thrust . . . and applied those passages in different ways to suit the different points they were putting across."[109] In this case, Matthew treats Hos 11:1 "as though it predicted a NT occurrence."[110]

The cognitive peripheral vision fuller sense approach emphasizes that in a larger context Hosea affirms a future return from Egypt (Hos 1:10–11; 11:11). "Thus, by extending Hosea's peripheral vision . . . he [Matthew] understood

107. See Vlach, *Old in the New*, 55–56, 140–41; Kaiser, "Response to Enns," 223; idem, *Uses of the Old Testament*, 47–53. Vlach is careful to use hypothetical language (perhaps, if, likely, etc.) in his repeated suggestions that Hosea intended/meant Hos 11:1 as a prediction (56, 141). Kaiser rejects the predictive force of Num 23:22; 24:8 espoused by Vlach and others (*Uses of the Old Testament*, 50–51). In one place Kaiser says Hosea "deliberately chose" the expectational language of 11:1 ("Response to Enns," 223). Elsewhere he says 11:1 is "not a prophecy" and refers to Hosea's intentional presentation of 11:1 as an expectational type (*Uses of the Old Testament*, 52–53).

108. See Thomas, "New Testament Use," 80, 86.

109. Ibid., 83.

110. Ibid., 86.

that the first exodus was a pattern foreshadowing a second, end-time exodus."[111] Matthew, in the periphery of his own mental intentions unexpressed in Matt 2:15 itself, then, reads Hos 11:1 according to Hosea's peripheral mental intentions, not expressed narrowly in Hos 11:1 but expressed elsewhere in his writings, and applies these to Jesus.[112]

A detailed explanation of this case according to an advancement of revelation approach appears in Chapter 6, so only the conclusion can be previewed here. Matthew 2:15 presents a plain sense interpretation of Hos 11:1 in relation to the way Hosea himself uses earlier non-expectational scriptures typologically. Matthew combines this with a fulfillment formula according to their function within Israel's scriptures. In short, Matthew interprets Hosea and Israel's scriptures the same way they interpret earlier scriptures.

If the authors of biblical receptor texts advance revelation by exegesis, is this not the same thing as Richard Longenecker's view that this sort of interpretation is okay for them but not for us?

No. Longenecker is saying that in those cases in which New Testament authors used "Jewish" methods of exegesis, they are operating by a different mindset. The approach of this book is that later biblical authors of both testaments interpret Israel's scriptures in the very ways these earlier scriptures interpret themselves. This book affirms plain sense exegesis by New Testament authors rather than introducing a foreign hermeneutic as Longenecker does.[113]

Isn't exegesis by New Testament authors different than exegesis of earlier scripture by Old Testament authors?

No and yes. They are the same in kind but different in degree.

No, the authors of receptors texts in both testaments use the same kinds of interpretive interventions.

Yes, the degree of revelation in the person and work of the Messiah is on an entirely different scale in the New Testament. This difference in degree is in time—two generations for New Testament versus a thousand years for Old Testament—and the power of revelation in the teaching, death, and resurrection of Jesus. Both factors are crucial.

---

111. Beale, "Cognitive Peripheral Vision," 276; cf. Beale and Gladd, *Hidden but Now Revealed*, 350–51.

112. See Beale, "Cognitive Peripheral Vision," 277; cf. Beale and Gladd, *Hidden but Now Revealed*, 351–52. Thank you to Benjamin Gladd for helpful feedback on this summary.

113. Also see in the Introduction (p. xxvi) the response to: "Can we as moderns interpret scripture the way the biblical authors did?"

Doesn't the distinction between meaning and significance preserve the plain sense of the donor and receptor texts? Doesn't sensus plenior preserve the same meaning and same authorial intention of the donor and receptor texts?

In the case of Hirsch's distinction of meaning and significance, no. If we sever meaning from significance—as it is often practiced by evangelicals who use this approach for the Bible's use of the Bible—then it does not explain the meaning of the donor text in relation to the meaning of the receptor text. This approach only compares the meaning of one to the significance of the other. In one version of this approach, meaning is decontextualized (made "timeless") by being removed from the text, which can only present contextualized significance, with meaning placed unexpressed in the author's mental intentions.

In the case of sensus plenior, no. Sensus plenior is not a method. It is a theoretical framework asserting that the meaning of the donor text is what the divine author intended even though no biblical author understood it as such. One major overlooked issue is that by removing meaning and intention from the author's historical context and putting them somewhere else outside the purview of authors of donor and receptor texts (divine omniscience or a closed canon), it removes exegesis which requires context.

Do all approaches that adjust meaning and/or context by the division of meaning and significance or by sensus plenior cause the same problems in explaining the scriptural interpretation of scripture?

No, not all of these approaches are created equal. These approaches in the hands of interpreters who emphasize responsible plain sense exegesis can be beneficial. But more often these approaches are used to validate reading the receptor text against the sense of the donor text. Reckless uses of these approaches are a problem.

Why would an interpreter make the choice for advancement of revelation if it cannot explain every use of scripture within scripture?

The challenges of the Bible's use of the Bible cannot be removed by clever hermeneutics. Instead, accepting the advancement of revelation in all scripture, including the Bible's exegesis of the Bible, opens the way to think with the authors of donor texts and receptor texts in their historical contexts according to plain sense interpretation.

CONCLUSION

It is understandable that interpreters seek hermeneutical solutions to handle the challenges of the Bible's use of the Bible. But adjustments of meaning and/or adjustments of context seem to undermine the larger reality of the very revelation that the hermeneutical "solutions" were meant to fix. The answer is not to be found in ever-more-clever or sophisticated adjustments to meaning and/or adjustments to context. The path forward is of a different order.

Yahweh advances revelation in many ways according to his own sovereign will. One divinely ordained mechanism for advancing revelation is scriptural exegesis of scripture. The benefits of this variety of progressive revelation include signaling continuity by the revelatory advancements themselves. Again and again the biblical authors look back to look ahead. The biblical authors exegetically advance revelation for a new Moses, new David, new creation, new exodus, new covenant, new heavens and new earth, and more. They interpret the redemptive will of God by means of his former redemptive will.

Here is the point. Yahweh has the right to advance revelation by many means, including scriptural exegesis. This places heavy demands upon interpreters.

Interpreters will do well to think with the authors of biblical receptor texts. In many cases their exegesis of scripture is modeled on earlier cases of scriptural exegesis within scripture. That is, understanding difficult cases of scriptural exegesis of scripture should start by examining kindred cases of exegesis within scripture. This will not solve every difficulty. But it can help to evaluate and explain the reasons for how and why receptors texts handle donor texts as they do.

Study Questions

1. In your own words, what is the choice at issue in this chapter?
2. How does Fishbane adjust meaning and/or adjust context? What are at least two liabilities with Fishbane's adjustment(s)?
3. What does atomistic exegesis refer to?
4. How have Hillel's rules been mischaracterized by scholars seeking a rabbinic basis for New Testament scriptural exegesis?

5. What is sectarian pesher exegesis? In what ways are Acts 2:16 and 4:11 dissimilar from sectarian pesher exegesis but similar to interpretive glosses within Israel's scriptures?
6. How do approaches that separate meaning from significance adjust meaning and/or context? What problem(s) arise from this(these) adjustment(s)?
7. How does double fulfillment adjust meaning? What is the problem with this adjustment?
8. How does sensus plenior adjust meaning and/or context? What is the problem with defining the fuller sense as the canon?
9. How is accepting exegetically activated advancements of revelation different in kind from approaches that adjust meaning and/or context?
10. How does Yahweh himself set the precedent for advancing revelation by scriptural exegesis?
11. How does the expectation for a prophet like Moses illustrate exegetically activated advancement of revelation?
12. According to John's Gospel, what role does the Holy Spirit play in scriptural interpretation by New Testament authors?

CHAPTER 3

DETECTING ALLUSIONS AS ART VERSUS SCIENCE

The actual task of detecting allusions is often approached from two different perspectives. Some interpreters develop extensive lists of strict criteria that must be met for an allusion to be detected. Taken to its extreme, this approach portrays detecting allusions as a strict form of objective scientific study. By contrast, other interpreters approach detecting allusions with an emphasis on the reader's own sensibilities and imagination for making connections between texts. Taken to its extreme, this approach portrays detecting allusions as a largely subjective and artistic act by the reader. In reality, detecting allusions involves both art and science, and understanding this dynamic is a foundational part of studying scripture's use of scripture.

CHOICE

Approaches that emphasize science to the neglect of art when determining allusions often attempt to establish a strict number of overlapping words that must be present. For example, Michael Stead argues that four or more words must be present for a quotation, two or three words for an allusion, and one or two for an echo.[1] Approaching the issue from a different angle, Paul Foster expresses skepticism at the presence of virtually any Old Testament allusions in Colossians because several prominent studies of the topic display what he considers to be significant disagreement over allusions and echoes in that letter, despite using similar methodologies.[2] Such a criticism, however, assumes that detecting allusions and echoes is essentially a scientific process in which using

1. Stead, *Intertextuality*, 22–23.
2. Foster, "Echoes without Resonance," 96–111; idem., *Colossians*, 52–60.

the right method will produce the exact same results. Both of these approaches are too mechanical, albeit in different ways.

By contrast, approaches that emphasize art to the neglect of science when determining allusions often eschew (or at least significantly downplay) criteria for validating potential allusions. For example, Havilah Dharamraj advocates an approach that "intentionally resists speculating about how one text may be dependent on another" in which the reader "is guided by an instinct to create for himself, out of whatever odds and ends he can come by," some kind of connection between two texts.[3] The result is an approach that engages in imaginative free association with little or no constraints.

As Greg Beale helpfully summarizes, "Recognizing allusions is like interpretation: there are degrees of probability and possibility in any attempt at identifying an allusion. Recognition of allusions is not only a science but a literary art (the latter involving an interpreter's intuition), as is the case to some degree in all interpretive decisions."[4]

In the broadest sense, when it comes to studying scripture's use of scripture, the goal is to identify and explain how an earlier text has influenced a later text. But the concept of influence is rather wide ranging, accounting for the entire spectrum of ways that previous scripture affected later biblical authors. As Roy Ciampa rightly notes, it can sometimes be difficult or impossible to distinguish the direct influence of scripture from places where a biblical author has been shaped by the "scriptural background behind words, concepts, idioms, topics, structures, and concerns" found in earlier scripture, "including the many subtle or intuitive ways in which Scripture may be influencing the argument of the text."[5]

Within this broad concept of influence, we can plot out a spectrum that stretches from unambiguous citations (often, though not always, with citation formulas) all the way to thematic similarities, with allusions and echoes somewhere in between.[6] This can be visually represented as in Figure 3-A.

Figure 3-A: Spectrum of Influence

Citation Allusion Echo Thematic Similarities

3. Dharamraj, "Reception-Centered Intertextual Approach," 128–29.
4. Beale, "Old Testament in Colossians," 263.
5. Ciampa, "Scriptural Language," 46.
6. See the Glossary for definitions of each of these terms.

As the figure shows, conceptualizing the different categories as a spectrum means that distinguishing between citation and strong allusions can be difficult (if not impossible). The distinction between weaker allusions and echoes is perhaps even more difficult, though with one key difference. Whereas the amount of evidence present in the receptor text for both citations and allusions indicates intentional dependence on the donor text, with faint allusions and echoes, the intentionality of a reference to the donor text (or texts) is far more difficult to determine.[7] The same is true to an even greater extent when it comes to thematic parallels. With respect to echoes and thematic parallels, then, it is perhaps preferable to speak of previous scripture (whether that be specific texts, common language or idioms, or broader themes) exerting influence over how the later author communicates while allowing that such influence may be working at a subconscious rather than conscious level.

While studying the more subtle ways that earlier scripture has influenced later biblical authors can be very fruitful, our focus is on places where later scripture is dependent on a particular donor text or texts. To be even more specific, our focus is on allusions that have a demonstrable exegetical outcome. Sometimes a biblical author may allude to a previous text in a way that does not produce exegetical outcomes relative to the donor text. Such cases are often examples of literary allusions, which are valuable in their own right. Literary allusions can provide a window into the events, stories, symbols, images, and themes that shape the basic worldview and conceptual framework of the author.[8]

A potential danger with more subtle forms of influence is the possibility of seeing allusions and echoes where they do not exist. Allusions and echoes must be distinguished from a form of free association in which the reader simply connects a donor text and a receptor text without any evidence other than the clever imagination of the reader. At the same time, creating detailed criteria for detecting legitimate allusions and echoes does not guarantee certain results.

Put succinctly, determining the presence of allusions is both an art and a science. It is a science in that establishing clear criteria provides an important consistency of method that looks for evidence of dependence and reduces the likelihood of speculative free association. At the same time, it is an art in that consistent reading and studying of scripture produces a certain kind of sensibility and sensitivity to recognizing connections between texts.

With that conceptual framework in place, we can now explore the specific

---

7. For a helpful discussion of this distinction based on intentionality, see Beetham, *Echoes*, 20–35.

8. These elements are the basic building blocks of biblical theology; see further Hamilton, *Biblical Theology*, 11–91.

kind of evidence one should look for when determining whether a receptor text is in fact dependent upon a donor text.

DETECTING ALLUSIONS

The process for detecting allusions can be divided into three phases.

SEARCHING FOR EVIDENCE

The most important evidence is *shared vocabulary and syntax* between the donor and receptor texts. Bible software can be a significant help in discovering such overlap, but one should not neglect other tools, such as concordances and lexicons. A common benchmark is at least three shared roots or words, with particular emphasis on nouns, verbs, and adjectives, though sometimes the presence of the article, a preposition, or other minor syntactical markers may be significant. But this guideline of at least three words is merely that—a guideline. Some probable allusions can rest on just a single word. For example, the term "flood" (מַבּוּל) appears twelve times in Gen 6–11 and elsewhere only in Ps 29:10a ("Yahweh sits above the flood" AT). The uniqueness of this particular word indicates that an allusion is likely present. When Paul describes his life before encountering Christ on the road to Damascus, he refers to himself as "extremely zealous for the traditions of my fathers" (Gal 1:14, emphasis added). He likely alludes to Phinehas, who killed an Israelite man and Midianite woman engaged in sexual immorality as an act of pagan worship (Num 25:6–9). Because of his actions, "Phinehas . . . turned my anger away from the Israelites. Since he was as zealous for my honor among them as I am, I did not put an end to them in my zeal" (25:11, emphasis added). Even though the two texts share just the one word ("zealous"), the concept of zeal was so uniquely associated with Phinehas in both the Old Testament and Jewish literature that an allusion is probable.[9] Thus, "It seems likely that before his conversion Paul saw himself acting within this tradition of zeal to preserve the purity of God's people in view of dangers from the surrounding gentile culture."[10]

Although often the shared vocabulary will occur as part of the same clause or even phrase, at other times it may occur over a larger span of text. For example, Gen 9 shares a sequence of details that intentionally portray Noah as a new Adam figure (Table 3-B):

9. On this background, see especially Ortlund, *Zeal*, 62–114.

10. Harmon, *Galatians*, 63.

Table 3-B: Selective Parallels between Adam and Noah

Adam (Gen 1–3)	**Noah (Gen 9)**
Be fruitful and multiply and fill the earth (1:28)	Be fruitful and multiply and fill the earth (9:1, 7)
Dominion over all creatures (1:28)	Fear and dread of Noah placed on all creatures (9:2)
Placed in a garden to work and keep it (2:8–15)	Noah is a man of the soil and plants a vineyard (9:20)
Eats from the fruit of the forbidden tree of the knowledge of good and evil (3:6)	Gets drunk from the fruit of his vineyard (9:21)
Covering up nakedness (3:7)	Covering up nakedness (9:23)
Knowledge of shame (3:7)	Knowledge of shame (9:24)
Pronouncement of a curse (3:14–19)	Pronouncement of a curse (9:25)

This extended echo effect over a larger amount of text invites the reader to compare and contrast Noah with Adam. But as a general rule, however, the shorter the span over which the shared vocabulary occurs, the more probable the allusion tends to be.

Unusual or irregular syntax can also indicate the presence of an allusion. That is, sometimes an author retains the syntax of the donor text in the receptor text to alert the reader to the allusion. The irregular syntax in Jer 34:14—using second person singular in a plural context—points to an allusion to the second person singular of Deut 15:12.[11] In this case the receptor text retains the grammar of the donor text, causing the irregularity (underlining signifies verbal parallels to Deut 15:12).

> Every seventh year each of you **[plural]** must free any fellow Hebrews who have sold themselves to you **[singular]**. (Jer 34:14a)

In addition to shared vocabulary and syntax, one should look for *shared structure and sequence.* When a receptor text follows a similar sequence of ideas and/or an (often underlying) narrative structure as that of a donor text, an allusion may in fact be present.[12] As the description suggests, larger amounts

11. See Fishbane, *Haftarot*, 116.

12. For helpful discussion and examples of this kind of dependence, see Beale, *Use of Daniel*, 178–203, 313–20 and idem., *John's Use of the Old Testament*, 75–126.

of text are generally needed to identify this type of influence. It often consists of multiple allusions of varying strength.

In the Old Testament, Numbers uses the pattern of Israel's wilderness wanderings in Exod 15–18 as a template for describing Israel's subsequent wilderness wanderings. Note the following parallels (Table 3-C):[13]

Table 3-C: Recurring Elements in the Wilderness

Journeys	Red Sea to Sinai	Sinai to Kadesh	Kadesh to Moab
Led by cloud	Exod 13:21	Num 10:11	—
Victory over enemies	14	—	Num 21:21–35
Victory song	15:1–18	10:35–36	21:14–15
Miriam	15:20–21	12	20:1
People complain	15:23–24	11:1	21:5
Moses's intercession	15:25	11:2	21:7
Well	15:27	—	21:16
Manna and quail	16	11:4–35	—
Water from a rock	17:1–7	—	20:2–13
Victory over Amalek	17:8–16	—	21:1–3
Moses's father-in-law	18:1–2	10:29–32	—

The similarities between the individual elements and the sequence indicates an intentional effort to draw a parallel between Israel's journey to Sinai and their subsequent wilderness struggles.[14] By repeating similar elements and a similar sequence, Numbers shows that the later generation is just as bad if not worse than their forebears. "In sum, the large-scale repetitions in the major travel and encampment narrative cycles in Numbers connote the tendencies of the two generations toward rebellion in the face of God's ongoing mercies."[15]

---

13. This table is slightly modified from Schnittjer, *Torah Story*, 325, which in turn adapted it from Wenham, *Numbers*, 19.

14. For a detailed presentation of verbal parallels in the texts within Table 3-C, see entry on Numbers "first and second generations in the wilderness" in *OTUOTPL*, ad loc.

15. See further *OTUOT*, 61–63 (quote from 63).

In the New Testament, Greg Beale has argued that the throne room vision of Rev 4–5 has been patterned after Dan 7:9–27. He notes the following parallels (Table 3-D):[16]

Table 3-D: Daniel 7 as a Framework for Revelation 4–5

Parallel	Daniel	Revelation
Introductory vision phraseology	7:9 [cf. 7:2, 6–7]	4:1
The setting of a throne(s) in heaven	7:9a	4:2a [cf. 4:4a]
God is sitting on a throne	7:9b	4:2b
The description of God's appearance on the throne	7:9c	4:3a
Fire before the throne	7:9c–10a	4:5
Heavenly servants surround the throne	7:10b	4:4b, 6b–10; 5:8, 11,14
Book(s) before the throne	7:10c	5:1–10
The "opening" of the book(s)	7:10d	5:2–5, 9
A divine (messianic) figure approaches God's throne in order to receive authority to reign forever over a kingdom	7:13–14a	5:5b–7, 12
The "kingdom" includes "all peoples, nations, and tongues"	7:14a [MT]	5:9b
The seer's emotional distress on account of the vision	7:15	5:4
The seer's reception of heavenly counsel concerning the vision from one among the heavenly throne servants	7:16	5:5a
The saints are also given divine authority to reign over a kingdom	7:18, 22, 27a	5:10
A concluding mention of God's eternal reign	7:27	5:13–14

16. This chart is adapted from *HNTUOT*, 80–81; for detailed discussion, see Beale, *Use of Daniel*, 181–228.

Repeating these elements in the same order (with only a few slight variations) demonstrates that John has used Dan 7 as a blueprint for the throne room vision of Rev 4–5. The slight variations are the result of the "creative expansion of images" that intensify the description of the heavenly servants and make the messianic identity of the Son of Man figure more explicit.[17] "The point of Revelation's use of the Daniel 7 blueprint is to indicate that Daniel's prophecy of the kingdom of the Son of Man and of the saints has been inaugurated in Christ's death and resurrection. In addition to this idea, the judgment mentioned in Dan 7 has also begun fulfillment in Christ, especially in the climactic defeat of the kingdom of evil forces."[18]

A final form of evidence of a possible allusion is *shared thematic or conceptual overlap*. That is, instead of borrowing specific language from a donor text, the receptor text uses a theme/concept expressed in the author's own words. A good example is Gal 4:22, where Paul writes "For it is written that Abraham had two sons, one by the slave woman and the other by the free woman." The citation formula "it is written" signals a clear and unambiguous reference to the Old Testament. But instead of a direct citation or even a verbal allusion, Paul makes a summary statement that is an obvious allusion to Gen 16–21.[19] In the verses that follow, Paul summarizes these chapters, describing both the sons (Ishmael and Isaac) and their respective mothers (Hagar and Sarah) from a theological perspective, and then draws a point of application from those chapters.

Another example of a thematic or conceptual allusion is references to grumbling. In John 6:41 the Jews "grumbled" (ἐγόγγυζον) when Jesus claims to be the bread of life. Combined with the obvious references in the larger context to Israel eating manna in the wilderness (John 6:31–34), the use of this one verb strongly suggests an allusion to Israel's grumbling in the wilderness (cf. Exod 16:2).[20] Indeed, Paul uses this same verb in 1 Cor 10:10 to describe Israel's grumbling in the wilderness. The consistent use of this verb and its cognate noun in reference to Israel's wilderness grumbling make it likely that when Paul exhorts the Philippians to "Do everything without grumbling [γογγυσμῶν]" (Phil 2:14), he is urging them not to be like the Israelites in wilderness.[21]

---

17. *HNTUOT*, 81.

18. Ibid., 82.

19. Another example of an introductory formula that is not followed by a direct citation is Luke 24:46, where Jesus introduces a summary of the OT message with the expression "this is what is written."

20. This allusion is further confirmed by Jesus's reference to himself as the "living bread that came down from heaven" (John 6:51), which likely alludes to Ps 77:24–25 LXX (78:24–25 MT). In retelling the events of Exod 16, the psalmist asserts that Yahweh "gave them the bread of heaven; the bread of angels man ate" (AT). This is a good example of vertical context, which is discussed in Chapter 4.

21. Seven of the eight LXX occurrences of γογγυσμός clearly refer to Israel's grumbling in the wilderness (Exod 16:7, 8 [2x], 9, 12; Num 17:20, 25 [17:5, 10 E]; Isa 58:9 is the exception). The statistics

EVALUATING THE EVIDENCE

Once the evidence is gathered, the interpreter must evaluate it. The starting point is the *volume*;[22] to what extent is there shared vocabulary, syntax, structure, sequence, or themes between the receptor text and the proposed donor text(s)? Both the quantity and the quality of the evidence matters. The greater the amount of shared material between the receptor and proposed donor text(s), the greater likelihood of an allusion. If the shared language occurs multiple places in scripture, the potential allusion may instead be an example of a stock phrase, figure of speech, or a refrain. So how does one tell the difference?

A good example is Jonah 4:2, where the prophet accuses Yahweh of being "a gracious and compassionate God, slow to anger and abounding in love." There is obvious overlap with Exod 34:6, where Yahweh proclaims himself as a "compassionate and gracious God, slow to anger, abounding in love and faithfulness." The similarities could be drawn from nothing more than lyrical diffusion, in which language becomes detached from its original biblical context and becomes a poetic idiom or stock phrase. But a closer look shows otherwise. First, Jonah 4:2 reverses the order of the terms "compassionate" and "gracious" found in Exod 34:6, a technique that invites the reader to pause and consider it for an extra moment.[23] Second, the statement of the king that Yahweh may relent from the threatened destruction (Jonah 3:9–10) alludes to Moses's prayer for Yahweh to relent from the threatened destruction of Israel (Exod 32:12b, 14).[24]

When determining the significance of shared vocabulary, syntax, or themes for a potential allusion, sometimes the rareness of terms can strengthen confidence in the presence of an allusion. The use of "woven together" in only Lev 19:19 and Deut 22:11, combined with contextual parallels, provides strong evidence of an allusion (underlining signifies verbal parallels):[25]

> Keep my decrees. Do not mate different kinds of animals. Do not plant your field with two kinds of seed. Do not wear clothing woven together [שַׁעַטְנֵז] of two kinds of material. (Lev 19:19 AT)

are similar for γογγύζω (eight of thirteen), διαγογγύζω (eight of ten) and γόγγυσις (one of one). The NT usage is far more split: γογγυσμός (three of four: John 7:12; Acts 6:1; Phil 2:14), γογγύζω (five of eight: John 6:41, 43, 61; 1 Cor 10:10 [2x]), διαγογγύζω (zero of two) and γογγυστής (one of one: Jude 16).

22. See Hays, *Echoes of Scripture in the Letters of Paul*, 30–32, for the criteria used in this section.

23. This technique is referred to as Seidel's theory after the scholar who noticed that authors sometimes switch word order in allusions (see Glossary).

24. See *OTUOT*, 404–5. Likewise, the use of "compassionate and gracious is Yahweh" in Ps 103:8 can be seen as an allusion to Exod 34:6 because the revelation to Moses is mentioned in 103:7. But the use of the same phrase in Ps 111:4 may just as likely come from lyrical diffusion as from Exod 34, along with many other uses of this language; for a list of places that use this language, see ibid., 877; cf. 375–76.

25. See "שַׁעַטְנֵז" *HALOT* 2:1610–11; Noonan, "Unraveling," 95–101.

> Do not plant two kinds of seed in your vineyard; otherwise the produce will be holy, both the seed you have sown and the produce of the vineyard. . . . Do not wear clothes of wool and linen woven together [שַׁעַטְנֵז] (Deut 22:9, 11, v. 9 AT)

Another example is Ps 110:4, where Yahweh says to David's Lord, "You are a priest forever, in the order of Melchizedek." This is an obvious allusion to Gen 14:17–24, the only other Old Testament passage to mention Melchizedek (where he is described as both a king and a priest). When Jesus explains why he speaks to the crowds in parables, he responds by explaining that the "knowledge of the secrets of the kingdom of heaven has been given to you, but not to them" (Matt 13:11). The noun "secrets" (μυστήρια) alludes to the use of this term in Daniel, the only Old Testament book in which it occurs. In Daniel this term is consistently associated with God revealing truths about the nature and future of his eternal kingdom (see esp. 2:18–19, 27–30, 47; cf. 4:9).[26]

A second tool for evaluating a potential allusion is *recurrence*. Sometimes an author uses the same donor text elsewhere in the receptor text. Hebrews 1:13 cites Ps 110:1 along with several other Old Testament texts to demonstrate the superiority of Jesus as the Son of God over the angels. This overt citation strongly supports the likelihood of brief allusions to it ("sat down at the right hand") even with no marking in 1:3; 8:1; 10:12, 13; 12:2. The use of the same donor text by the author of the receptor text in a different book can also provide additional support for a potential allusion. During the transfiguration, the voice from heaven identifies Jesus as "my Son, whom I have chosen" and commands Peter, James, and John to "listen to him" (Luke 9:35). This command likely alludes to Deut 18:15, which promises that God will raise up a prophet like Moses and insists "You must listen to him." Confidence in this allusion is strengthened by the clear citation of Deut 18:15 in Acts 3:22–23 and 7:37. Even the use of the same donor text by another biblical author can increase confidence in a potential allusion. The presence of an allusion to Jer 31:31 in both Luke 22:20 ("This cup is the new covenant in my blood") and 2 Cor 3:6 ("He has made us competent as ministers of a new covenant") is further bolstered by the lengthy citation of Jer 31:31–34 in Heb 8:8–12 to introduce a discussion of the new covenant. Citations and allusions by different biblical authors can confirm the significance of the donor text and demonstrate a broader awareness of that text, providing additional support for a potential allusion in the text you are investigating.

---

26. See further the discussion in Beale and Gladd, *Hidden but Now Revealed*, 75.

As a final check, *look to see if others have recognized the potential allusion you have identified* (Resource Guide 3-E). Because scripture has been closely studied for centuries, there is a good chance that the allusion you have detected has been recognized by others. If you do not find your proposed allusion in any of these resources, that does not necessarily mean it is illegitimate. But it should cause you to carefully reevaluate the evidence.

Resource Guide 3-E: Discovering Allusions

- The cross-references in many Bibles provide a good starting point, but particularly NA[28], which also contains an appendix (Loci Citati vel Allegati) listing places where Old Testament texts are cited or alluded to in the New Testament.
- Reference works such as *IBUB*, *OTUOT*, *OTUOTPL*, *CNTUOT*, *NTUOTPL*, and *NTUOT*.
- Many technical commentaries also discuss potential allusions and their significance, though often the depth and detail of such discussions is limited.
- Master index of the NSBT series, available at https://www.thegospelcoalition.org/article/new-studies-in-biblical-theology/. Looking at places where both the donor and receptor texts are discussed can point to helpful insights.

EXPLAINING THE EXEGETICAL OUTCOME

Once the allusion has been confirmed, the interpreter must determine and explain the nature of the exegetical outcome. The goal is to explain how the biblical author uses the donor text. Keep in mind that multiple exegetical outcomes may be present. Biblical authors use scripture in a wide range of ways, making it nearly impossible to create a comprehensive list. But the following are among the most common.[27]

Fulfillment of a direct verbal prophecy. What is directly promised in the donor text is fulfilled in the receptor text, though not always in a straightforward manner (Ezra 1:1//Jer 25:11; 29:10; John 12:15//Zech 9:9).

27. For a similar list with expanded discussion, see *HNTUOT*, 55–93. The discussion that follows has its origins in Beale, "Use of the Old in the Old," 4–10. Beale aligns the exegetical outcomes found in *OTUOT* with his *HNTUOT*, and I have adapted that alignment here as well as used a number of the same examples found there.

Indirect fulfillment of a type. Types are persons, events, procedures, oracles, or institutions (sometimes a combination of more than one of these) that anticipate a greater reality later in redemptive history. These types establish a pattern that is fulfilled with escalation, with such fulfillment sometimes including initial and final aspects. Some types are explicitly marked as forward looking (Isa 40:3–4//Isa 11:15–16+Exod 23:20–21), while others are only recognizable retrospectively in light of progressive revelation (2 Chr 2:13–14//Exod 31:2–6). See further the discussion in Chapter 6.

Blueprint/prototype. The donor text provides the outline or pattern for the receptor text. We have already noted two examples above (for Exod 15–18 as the pattern for Israel's later wilderness wandering, see Table 3-C above; for Rev 4–5 using numerous elements of Dan 7, see Table 3-D above). This use can take a number of different forms. The discussion above of the parallels between Adam (Gen 1–3) and Noah (Gen 9) is an example of extended echo effect, where a character, event, instruction, oracle, or the like naturally gets compared as a virtual simile to its counterpart, causing connotative transfer. These parallels can be (but are not necessarily) typological in nature. Synoptic parallels are places where the receptor text recounts the same event, law, teaching, and so on as the donor text using selectivity, arrangement, and verbal adaptation (much of 1–2 Chr is an example). Careful comparison of the donor and receptor texts often reveals theological shaping and key emphases in the receptor text (e.g. 2 Chr 27:1–9//2 Kgs 15:32–38). Paradigmatic shaping is the use of a donor text in a formulaic manner to shape the narrative structure of the receptor text in a broader sense, like the cycles of the judges or the kings who go from bad to good or vice versa in Chronicles, and so forth.[28] A frame narrative refers to the controlling narrative context of quoted or embedded elements therein. In Exod 32–34, the rebellion with the calf and its aftermath provides the frame narrative of the covenant renewal legal collection (Exod 34:11–26).[29] As such, the covenant renewal collection makes sense within its frame narrative. Another form of this blueprint/prototype category is narrative tracking, where one text echoes another by mimicking narrative structure rather than verbal parallels. However, the kinds of similarities allegedly evoked by these loose narrative similarities may largely fall short of exegetical interventions.

Affirming the sure fulfillment of a yet-unfulfilled prophecy. A receptor text cites or alludes to a donor text as a way of assuring that the yet-to-be-fulfilled

---

28. See Schnittjer, *Old Testament Narrative*, 75 (cycles of judges), 227 (paradigmatic reshaping in Chronicles).

29. See further Schnittjer, "Bequeathing Wrath," 106; *OTUOT*, 24–26.

promise or prophecy in the donor text will indeed be fulfilled (Zech 8:21–22// Mic 4:2–3; 2 Pet 3:11–14//Isa 65:17+66:22).

Analogical/Symbolic/Illustrative/Simile. The receptor text compares a present situation to a similar one in the donor text. The analogy invites the reader to observe both comparison and contrast. This use often emphasizes "a gnomic, broad, or universal principle"[30] (e.g. 1 Cor 9:9–10//Deut 25:4). For example, Isa 63:14 ("like cattle that go down to the plain, they were given rest by the Spirit of the LORD") adapts language from Exod 33:14 ("Yahweh replied, 'My Presence will go with you, and I will give you rest'" AT) that invites "the people of the failing restoration who need to look back to the new exodus and ask the same question"—"Where is he?" (Isa 63:11).[31]

Indicating an abiding authority. The receptor text uses the donor text to establish the ongoing authority of the truth expressed in the donor text. An obvious example is the re-statement of the Ten Commandments in Deut 5:1–21 (drawn from Exod 20:1–17), which points to their enduring authority for a new generation of God's people. The abiding authority of the donor text can also be a statement of God's character (Jonah 4:2//Exod 34:6–7) or a promise (Jer 31:33//Exod 6:7). Sometimes an author may use a series of donor texts as an abiding authority to prove a point (see Rom 3:10–18).

Legal exegesis. The receptor text explains and interprets the donor text in light of advances in revelation. In a broad sense, much of Deuteronomy is a form of legal exegesis, as it not merely restates earlier legislation from Exodus through Numbers but expands or clarifies that legislation (e.g., the dietary restrictions in Deut 14:1–21 expand and clarify those in Lev 11:1–45). Jesus uses a form of legal exegesis in the Sermon on the Mount (Matt 5:21–26//Exod 20:13; Matt 5:27–30//Exod 20:14; Matt 5:31–32//Deut 24:1; Matt 5:33–37// Lev 19:12+Eccl 5:2–7[1–6 H]; Matt 5:38–42//Exod 21:23–24+Lev 24:20+Deut 19:21; Matt 5:43–48//Lev 19:18).

Enhancement. This exegetical outcome takes various forms and works on a similar principle as legal exegesis but is used in nonlegal texts. The receptor text may further explain the donor text, such as in Ezek 34:4, which adds "harshly" (חָזְקָה) to explain the rare term "brutally" (פֶּרֶךְ) from the donor text (Lev 25:43). In Deut 7:9–10, Moses enhances the response of Yahweh as a jealous God in the image command (Exod 20:5//Deut 5:9) to emphasize his commitment to repay Yahweh-haters to their faces.

Extrapolation. Nahum extrapolates that Yahweh is an avenging God (1:2)

30. *HNTUOT*, 67.
31. *OTUOT*, 252.

based on his revelation of himself as a jealous God (Exod 20:5//Deut 5:9; cf. Exod 34:14).

Proverbial/Idiomatic. Over time a biblical word, phrase, or expression may become so widely known and used that it becomes idiomatic. In such cases, a word or phrase becomes disconnected from its original Old Testament context, "yet retains a common meaning that has its roots in that OT context."[32] This kind of lyrical diffusion is especially common in the Prophets, Psalms, and wisdom literature. As discussed above, some uses of language from the attribute formula in Exod 34:6–7 could reflect commonplace usage in the Psalms and Prophets. The phrase "Edom, Moab, the Ammonites" (originally used in 2 Sam 8:12) in Isa 11:14 and Dan 11:41 are likely examples of a stock-in-trade phrase referring more broadly to "all those who stand in antagonism to God's kingdom and people."[33]

Ironic/inverted. In this use of scripture, the receptor text uses the donor text with the opposite meaning of the donor text within its original context. Such irony can be used to ridicule as a means of highlighting judgment (Amos 4:4–5//Deut 14:28; 26:12+Lev 2:11; 7:13; Rev 13:4//Exod 15:11) or "to encourage the faithful, who, while suffering persecution and defeat, are ironically overcoming the world as they persevere faithfully."[34]

Summaries of Israel's stories. At various places in scripture, biblical authors will summarize the story of Israel up to that point.[35] The summaries highlight key events, individuals, institutions, divine promises, and divine acts in a chronological sequence that forms the basis of Israel's identity (e.g., Josh 24:1–13; Neh 9:1–38; Ps 106:6–46; Acts 7:2–53; 13:16–25).

Again it must be stressed that these are only a sample of the most common exegetical outcomes. They are provided as a starting point for considering the wide range of exegetical outcomes that interpreters have observed, but they should not be treated as an exhaustive list. Each passage and its potential exegetical outcome must be evaluated in its own right and described in light of the context of both the donor and receptor texts. Merely applying one of these labels is not enough, as the interpreter must explain the nature and significance of the exegetical outcome, regardless of whether one is writing a research paper or preparing a sermon. The goal is not merely to describe what the biblical author does but also to explain the passage's significance for understanding both the donor and receptor texts.

---

32. *HNTUOT*, 74.

33. Ibid., 75.

34. Ibid., 92. Irony and inversion are especially prevalent in Jeremiah (see *OTUOT*, 262–63).

35. For a helpful list of such places, see Hood and Emerson, "Summaries," 340–43 and Bruno, Compton, and McFadden, *Biblical Theology*. For a comparative chart, see *OTUOT*, 161.

THE TEXT FORM OF CITATIONS AND ALLUSIONS

One complication that arises when determining the presence of an allusion is determining what text form the biblical author uses. This aspect of evaluating potential allusions has not always received adequate attention. Careful study of how later authors of scripture use earlier scriptural texts quickly reveals that the wording of the quotation or allusion does not always match the source text exactly. Sometimes that is the result of an author adapting the donor text to fit the new context, such as changing the tense and mood of verbs (Mark 4:12//Isa 6:9–10), rearranging clauses (e.g., Rom 13:9//Exod 20:13–17, where Paul reorders the sixth, seventh, eighth, and tenth commandments), skipping portions of the donor text (e.g., Luke 4:18–19//Isa 61:1–2, which skips the line "to bind up the brokenhearted"), or using a synonym (John 12:15//Zech 9:9, changing "mounted" to "sitting").[36] Other times the variation in wording is the result of the biblical author offering an interpretive paraphrase of the donor text, which is sometimes even introduced with a citation formula (e.g., Neh 8:14–15//Lev 23:40, 42a; Mark 12:29–30//Deut 6:4–5; Rom 10:6–8// Deut 30:12–14).

A more challenging source of these differences is when a biblical author uses a text form different from what has come down to us as the Masoretic Text (MT). Do the variations represent interpretive interventions by the biblical author? Were the variations preexisting in version(s) of Israel's scriptures available to the biblical author? Responsible interpretation needs to begin by identifying, when possible, preexisting textual variations to explain the interpretive interventions. Caution must be used in drawing conclusions when evidence is lacking. Therefore, an important part of detecting allusions is being aware of the different text forms that may have been available to a biblical author.

Learning one's way around the evidence of versions of Israel's scriptures in circulation in the late Second Temple context may mean taking courses and studying current scholarship. A detailed study of varieties of scriptural traditions falls outside this present study. The goals here are limited to offering perspective and suggesting resources needed to interpret the Bible's use of the Bible.

Not all versions of Israel's scriptures available in the late Second Temple context were created equal. Students sometimes succumb to the temptation of thinking that "older is better." Sometimes it is. Much depends on the scribal culture in which the scriptures were being copied.

36. Lanier, *Old Made New*, 28.

Making copies of the scriptures caused a clash of ideals for ancient scribes. Ancient scribal culture in general served its constituencies by both copying and improving the texts being copied. But the emerging canonical authority of Israel's scriptures called for preservation. There is more to ancient scribal culture than this. But this will be adequate to keep in mind for the broad sketch presented here.

Proto-Masoretic Text. Ezra's return to Jerusalem may be seen as a beginning point for the preservationist copying of the authoritative scriptural scrolls in the temple and among their affiliated scribal guild.[37] Scribes in this setting were accountable for faithful copying of scrolls held in an emerging canonical esteem. The evidence of dramatically fewer accidental errors and fewer intentional "improvements" in proto-masoretic fragments found in the Judean desert at locations other than Qumran demonstrates a preservationist approach demanded of these copyist-scribes.[38]

Septuagint. The LXX or Septuagint is not a homogeneous version in the modern sense. Individual scrolls of Israel's scriptures were translated more freely or more rigidly, with Septuagintal Torah representing a midpoint.[39] The important point for the present discussion is that the production and copying of the Septuagint unfolded within a different scribal culture than the rigidness of the context which produced the proto-Masoretic Text.

The evidence shows greater freedom to make accidental errors and to make "improvements" in three phases of the Septuagint: copying the Hebrew parent text (*Vorlage*); translating the biblical scrolls; and copying the Greek translations of scripture.[40] Scribal improvements include grammatical, harmonistic, interpretive, and theological updating of the text.

The scribal freedom that allowed "improvements" in the Septuagint is one part of the basis of the text-critical general guideline that favors more difficult and nonharmonistic readings.[41]

Samaritan Pentateuch. In the main, the SP shares many tendencies with the Hebrew parent text (*Vorlage*) of the LXX. These include grammatical, harmonistic, and interpretive updating of the text. This suggests a scribal culture with freedom for accidental mistakes and intentional improvements by copyists. The evidence reveals that the distinctly sectarian alterations of the SP—making Gerizim the place for the temple in the tenth commandment and

37. See *TCHB*[4], 76. For a similar point, see Tov, "Textual Harmonization," 54–56.

38. See *TCHB*[4], 78; Tov, *Scribal Practices*, 25–26, 204, 252–53. See *OTUOT*, 863–65.

39. See Würthwein, *Text of the Old Testament*, 101.

40. Evidence that many variations of the Septuagint appear in its Hebrew parent text (*Vorlage*) includes Hebrew scriptural scrolls that align with the LXX—e.g., 4QSam[b]; 4QJer[b,d]. See *TCHB*[4], 231, 295.

41. See Strauss, *40 Questions*, 234–36.

kindred adjustments—appear in response to the destruction of the Samaritan temple by Hasmonean aggression (ca. 129 BCE).[42]

Sectarian Scriptural Scrolls. The present concern only relates to the scriptural scrolls discovered at Qumran, not the sectarian scrolls. Emanuel Tov has collated the evidence of all corrections of accidental and intentional variants in the biblical scrolls found at Qumran and contrasted these to the careful copying of the proto-Masoretic Texts found elsewhere in the Judean desert. The evidence demonstrates that the scribal culture at Qumran provided great freedom for both accidental errors as well as "improvements"—grammatical and interpretive.[43]

The scriptural scrolls found at Qumran bear resemblance to the proto-Masoretic Text, SP, and LXX. This suggests that the sectarians secured biblical scrolls wherever they could since they functioned outside the temple of Jerusalem and its sanctioned guild of biblical copyist-scribes.

Targums. The targums record the synagogal translation of scripture into Aramaic, plus interpretations. Two aspects concern us here. First, the translation of the Hebrew text itself offers an ancient witness to the version of Israel's scriptures mediated in local synagogues. Second, the sanctioned targumic plusses present early interpretive traditions of Israel's scriptures. Much caution is needed in evaluating the targumic plusses since they could be added at any time in the transmission process and may not reflect interpretive tendencies current in the late Second Temple context. These plusses and the challenges of dating them will be discussed in Resource Guide 5-E in Chapter 5.

Other important ancient versions of Israel's scriptures such as Syriac, Vulgate, and so on may be helpful at times but cannot be pursued here.

Before moving on it is important to remember that different scholars pursue different goals to evaluate the evidence of textual variations. These competing goals should be considered when evaluating "preferred readings." The present project uses the final text as the goal for textual criticism.[44]

In sum, the freedoms of ancient scribal cultures—outside the temple's preservationist setting for copyist-scribes of the proto-Masoretic Text—led to manifold interpretive traditions bound up with Israel's scriptures. Not all variations are of equal value. This means great care needs to be taken in evaluating

42. See Knoppers, "Parallel Torahs," 522, 524; idem, *Jews and Samaritans*, 182–90.

43. See Tov, *Scribal Practices*, 25–26, 204, 252–53. See summary and diagram in *OTUOT*, 863–65.

44. For an evaluative overview of five competing goals of OT textual criticism among scholars, see Waltke, "Aims of Textual Criticism," 93–108; cf. *TCHB*[4], 344–46, 396–98. See brief overview in Resource Guide 8-E in the Case Studies of the Bible's Use of the Bible near the end of this book. Waltke and Tov (both cited earlier in this footnote) advocate for the final text as the goal.

possible variations of the versions of Israel's scriptures known to and used by the biblical authors. Figure 3-F offers an overview of the preceding discussion.

Figure 3-F: Copying Israel's Scriptures in the Second Temple Period

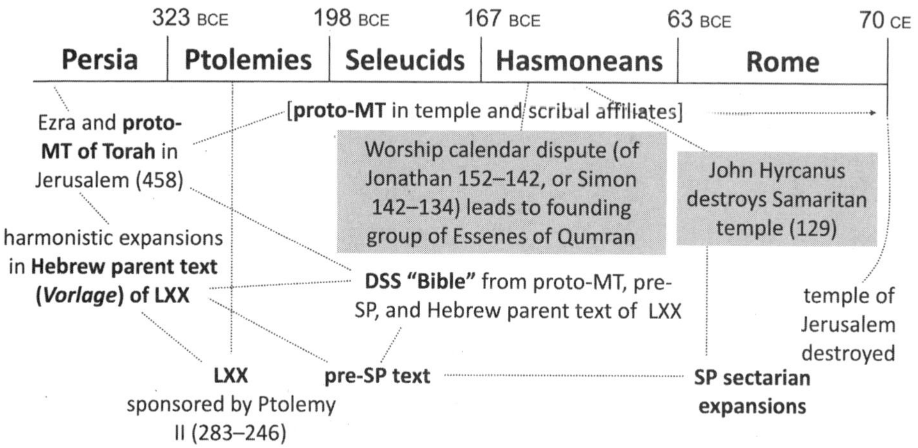

CASE STUDIES

Each of the case studies in this section highlights an aspect of detecting allusions. The first demonstrates the need to look for supporting evidence when evaluating a potential allusion. The second shows how John uses irregular syntax to signal the presence of an allusion in Rev 1:4–5. The third explores Paul's possible use of a targumic interpretive tradition in Eph 4:8. The final case study is for advanced students, showing the complexity of determining the text form of Amos 9:11–12 used in Acts 15:16–17. The last two were intentionally chosen because of their difficulties, so the conclusions reached will be far from definitive.

2 SAMUEL 23:5 IN JEREMIAH 23:5

Detecting allusions requires patience to seek corroborating evidence. One might suspect that the use of the verb "branch out" (צמח) in David's last words is a donor text for Jeremiah's famous expectation using the noun "branch" (צֶמַח).

> [David says:] "If my house were not thus with God, surely he would not have made with me an everlasting covenant, arranged and secured in every part;

surely he would not bring to fruition my salvation and **cause** my desire **to branch forth** [יַצְמִיחַ]." (2 Sam 23:5 AT)

"The days are coming," declares Yahweh, "when I will raise up for David a righteous **branch** [צֶמַח], a king who will reign wisely and do what is just and right in the land." (Jer 23:5 AT)

Though intriguing, this evidence of itself is not enough. A first step in investigating if it is more than a coincidence needs to be the immediate context. This reveals that David's last words include "When one rules over people in **righteousness** [צַדִּיק]" (2 Sam 23:3) which aligns with Jeremiah's expectation for a "**righteous** [צַדִּיק] branch" (Jer 23:5). This contextual evidence strengthens Jer 23:5 to the borderline between possible and probable allusion.

From here it helps to consider later uses of Jer 23:5 that may show an awareness of its allusion to David's last words. Jeremiah's own reworking of the righteous branch oracle in Jer 33 (an MT plus not in the LXX) provides helpful confirmation. Notice the way the Hifil stem of the verb "branch forth" is used with God as the subject just as in 2 Sam 23:5 which is paired with the noun form of "branch" as well as the modifier "righteous" just as in Jer 23:5.

In those days and at that time **I will cause a righteous Branch to branch forth from David's line** [אַצְמִיחַ לְדָוִד צֶמַח צְדָקָה]. (Jer 33:15a AT)

This evidence corroborates the initial observation that Jer 23:5 may have had David's last words in mind. This evidence not only strengthens the probability of an allusion but also provides a basis for evaluating a later allusion using both the verb "branch out" and the noun "branch" in Zech 6:12.

In sum, investigating potential subtle allusions requires attention to details, patience, and careful evaluation of corroborating evidence.[45]

EXODUS 3:14 IN REVELATION 1:4–5

Irregular syntax is a common feature in Revelation to indicate an allusion.[46] Three excellent examples are found in Rev 1:4–5. As part of the greeting, John writes:

45. For more detail on this case of potential allusion, see entries on Jer 23:5–6; 33:14–22; and Zech 6:11–14 in *OTUOTPL*. Also see 4Q252, 5.3–4 in *DSSSE* 1:504–5.

46. On this distinctive feature of Revelation, see Beale, *John's Use of the Old Testament*, 318–55.

> Grace and peace to you **from him who is** [ἀπὸ ὁ ὢν], and who was [ὁ ἦν], and who is to come [ὁ ἐρχόμενος], and from the seven spirits before his throne, and from Jesus Christ, who is the faithful witness [ὁ μάρτυς ὁ πιστός], the firstborn from the dead [ὁ πρωτότοκος τῶν νεκρῶν], and the ruler of the kings of the earth [ὁ ἄρχων τῶν βασιλέων τῆς γῆς]. (AT)

The object of the preposition "from" (ἀπό) should be in the genitive case (as it is in the phrase "from the seven spirits" [ἀπὸ τῶν ἑπτὰ πνευμάτων]). By using the grammatically incorrect nominative case instead, John forces the reader to slow down and notice the phrase as an allusion. The phrase "the one who is" (ὁ ὢν) alludes to Exod 3:14 LXX, where it occurs twice as part of the explanation of the divine name.[47]

> And God said to Moses, "I am **the one who is** [ὁ ὤν]" and he said, "Speak in this way to the sons of Israel, '**The one who is** [ὁ ὢν] has sent me to you.'" (Exod 3:14 LXX AT)

The same is true for "the faithful witness" (ὁ μάρτυς ὁ πιστός), which is in the nominative case to signal an allusion to Ps 88:38 LXX [89:37 E/38 H] instead of the expected genitive case to indicate it is in apposition to "Jesus Christ" (Ἰησοῦ Χριστοῦ) in the previous clause.

> And like the moon it will be established forever, as a faithful witness [ὁ μάρτυς . . . πιστός] in the sky. (Ps 88:38 LXX AT)

Similarly, "the firstborn" (ὁ πρωτότοκος) occurs in the nominative case instead of the grammatically correct genitive case, signaling an allusion to Ps 88:28 LXX [89:27 E/89:28 H], which has "firstborn" (πρωτότοκον).

> And I will appoint him as the firstborn [πρωτότοκον], higher than the kings of the earth. (Ps 88:28 LXX AT)

In each of the examples, John uses irregular syntax to mark an allusion. As Beale helpfully summarizes, "The author wants to keep the nominative to direct attention to the OT allusion, as well as, perhaps, because, as in v 4, the phrase is a designation for the Messiah (whether already in Judaism or as newly formulated by John). 'Firstborn' is changed from its OT accusative form either

47. Beale, *Book of Revelation*, 188.

because it has become a name or to conform to the nominative ὁ μάρτυς ὁ πιστός ("the faithful witness")."[48]

PSALM 68:18 IN EPHESIANS 4:8

One potential example of an Old Testament citation that may depend on a reading found in the targums is Paul's use of Ps 68:18 in Eph 4:8. Based on their shared belief in "one Lord, one faith, one baptism" (4:5), the apostle calls for unity within the body of Christ (4:1–7). This unity, however, is manifested in God giving different "grace gifts" to individual believers "according to the measure of Christ's gift" (ESV). This statement is grounded in a citation of Ps 68:18. But a quick comparison with the MT, the LXX, and targum reveals an important difference (bold emphases added):

> When he ascended on high, he took many captives and **gave gifts** to his people. (Eph 4:8)

> When you ascended on high,
> you took many captives;
> you **received gifts** from people,
> even from the rebellious—
> that you, LORD God, might dwell there. (Ps 68:18[19 H] MT via NIV)

> When you ascended on high, you took many captives, you **received gifts** from people. (Ps 68:18 LXX AT)

> You ascended to the firmament, O prophet Moses, you took captive, *you taught the words of the Law, you* ***gave*** *them as* **gifts** to *the sons of* man*;* even among the rebellious *who are converted and repent* does *the Shekinah of the glory* of the LORD God dwell. (Ps 68:18[19 H] ArBib, italics original, indicating interpretive differences from the MT; bold indicates similarity to Eph 4:8)[49]

Whereas both the MT and the LXX of Ps 68:18 portray Yahweh as *receiving* gifts from those whom he captured, Paul portrays Jesus as *giving* gifts to his people, which is how the targum presents it. If he is drawing upon a targumic reading, "Paul would then be working with a Moses typology, with Christ, the

48. Ibid., 192.
49. Italics adjusted because "gifts to. . .man" is in Hebrew but is italicized [*sic*] in ArBib.

greater Moses, giving gifts to the new Israel."[50] Conceptually this would further fit well with the typological correspondence between Moses as the giver of the law and Christ as the giver of the Holy Spirit that underlies the descent of the Spirit on the day of Pentecost. Since, however, we cannot be certain the targum reading existed in Paul's day or that he would have been familiar with it, all one can do is propose this as a possibility rather than a probability.

However, it should be noted that other plausible explanations have been offered. Paul may have borrowed "give" language from Ps 68:35[36 H], where God is described as the one who "gives power and strength to his people."[51] If so, this interpretive tradition could stem from an ancient tradition that both Paul and the targumist knew. Or Paul may have "applied Ps 68:18 to Christ in light of the psalm's typological expectation and its redemptive-historical fulfilment in Christ" based on retrospective and prospective elements within the psalm itself and possible allusions to Exod 15 and Judg 5.[52] The complexity of Paul's use of the Old Testament here likely means that interpretive consensus will remain elusive.

On the whole, then, the late date of the targums makes them of limited use when it comes to determining what Old Testament text an author is drawing upon. They are helpful, however, when it comes to identifying interpretive traditions that the New Testament authors may have been familiar with (see further in Chapter 5).

ADVANCED CASE STUDY: AMOS 9:11–12 IN ACTS 15:16–17

This case study is intended for advanced students—students new to textual difficulties may wish to skip this section and come back at a later time. It demonstrates the kind of complexities involved in studying the text form of some of the more difficult examples of the Bible's use of the Bible.

At the climactic moment of the Jerusalem Council, Luke presents James as affirming the arguments of Paul and Peter that God is at work among the Gentiles "to choose a people for his name from the Gentiles" (Acts 15:14). He supports this claim by stating that the words of the prophets agree with this conclusion, followed by a citation of Amos 9:11–12. This citation matches neither the LXX nor the MT exactly, though it is closer to the LXX than the MT, as the following comparison shows:[53]

---

50. Osborne, "Hermeneutics," 169. Although originally holding this position for many years, in this essay Osborne argues against this view.

51. This is the proposal of Lucas Whitson, provided in personal correspondence.

52. Greever, "Typological Expectation," 253–79.

53. A further challenge is determining the original reading of the LXX, which is difficult in light of the number of variants. See further Bauckham, "James," 154–84.

"In that day
I will restore **David's fallen** shelter—
I will repair its broken walls
and restore its ruins—
and will **rebuild** it as it used to be,
so that they may possess the remnant of Edom
and all the nations that bear my name,"
declares the LORD, who will do these things.
(Amos 9:11–12 MT via NIV, emphasis added)

"On that day I will raise up **David's fallen tent** and **rebuild** what has fallen of it and raise up its ruins, and rebuild it as the days of old so that the remnant of the people and all the nations upon whom my name has been called may seek me," says the Lord who does these things. (Amos 9:11–12 LXX AT)

"After this I will return and rebuild **David's fallen tent**. Its ruins I will **rebuild**, and I will restore it, that the rest of mankind may seek the Lord, even all the Gentiles who bear my name," says the Lord, who does these things. (Acts 15:16–17, emphasis added)

Although not immediately apparent from the English translations, in Amos 9:11 the LXX translator has taken some minor liberties in smoothing out grammatical incongruities in the Hebrew parent text that likely matched the proto-MT.[54] James seems to abridge and loosely paraphrase the LXX since he uses the same grammatical adjustments found in the LXX.[55] In short, the basic sense of Amos 9:11 is approximately the same in the proto-MT, the Hebrew parent text of the LXX, LXX translation, and even James's paraphrastic abridgement in Acts 15:16.

The situation is more complicated with Amos 9:12, however. Whereas in the MT David's fallen shelter possesses the remnant of Edom and the nations who bear Yahweh's name, in the LXX the remnant of the people and the nations who have been called by Yahweh's name seek him. Three observations may help explain the reason for the differences in the citation of Amos 9:12.

First, the initial verb of the Hebrew parent text of the LXX is apparently

54. Specifically, the proto-MT shifts the grammatical gender and number, "their [fp] breaches . . . its [ms] ruins . . . rebuild it [fs]" (AT), which the LXX translators smooth out to "its [fs] ruins . . . its [fs] destruction . . . rebuild it [fs]" (AT).

55. Acts 15:16 omits two entire clauses of the LXX and replaces the language of "raise up" with "rebuild." The result is a citation that does not match any known existing Hebrew or Greek text.

"and they will seek" (יִדְרְשׁוּ) versus "and they will possess" (יִירְשׁוּ) in the proto-MT (so LXX HPTAT). Another possibility is that the Hebrew parent text of the LXX was identical to the proto-MT and the LXX translator misread the *yod* (י) as a *dalet* (ד).[56] Either way, one can see how the Hebrew and LXX are not as far apart as the English translation might indicate.

Second, the Hebrew parent text of the LXX likely spelled "Edom" defectively as *'dm* (אדם) versus plene as *'dwm* (אדום), as in the MT. That is, the proto-MT and the Hebrew parent text of the LXX have an identical sense, with one spelled plene and the other defectively. Since the Hebrew text at the time would have been unpointed, it was up to the reader to determine the proper sense intended. In this case, the LXX translator may have vocalized the noun as "humankind" *'adam* (אָדָם) versus "Edom" *'edom* (אֱדֹם).[57] The likelihood of this variation created by the translator is more evident when comparing *'dm* (אדם) in the A line and "the nations" (הגוים) in the B line—this could easily suggest *'dm* (אדם) as "humankind" *'adam* (אָדָם). Thus James could be following what is already present in the LXX or could be making the interpretive move himself in light of the ambiguity of the Hebrew text. Regardless, what appears to be a significant difference between the English translations of the Hebrew and the LXX is shown to be textually less dramatic than it might initially seem.

Third, Acts 15:17 follows the LXX for the first two elements of Amos 9:12 noted above but makes an adjustment based on it. Specifically, the verb "they might seek" (ἐκζητήσωσιν) needs an object—seek what or whom? James supplies "the Lord" (τὸν κύριον) as the object whom they should seek. Not only does this make sense in light of "Lord" often being the object of this verb in the LXX,[58] but it makes sense in the context of Amos 9:12, which describes these converted nations/Gentiles as bearing Yahweh's name.

Finally, there are several additional potential echoes of Old Testament texts woven into James's wording here that may provide additional interpretive insight.[59] Although exploring these is outside the scope of this case study, those wishing to pursue this particular example of scripture using scripture must be sure to take these into account as well.[60]

The complexity of this example makes it difficult to draw firm conclusions regarding the specific text form being used. It may be that the LXX translation is based on a different version of the Hebrew text than the one reflected in the

56. Gelston, *BHQ*, 88*.
57. See Gelston, "Some Hebrew Misreadings," 498.
58. So Bauckham, "James," 162.
59. See the helpful summary in Marshall, "Acts," in *CNTUOT*, 591–92.
60. See *NTUOTPL*, ad loc.

MT.[61] Perhaps the differences are the result of James paraphrasing the LXX. Or perhaps Bauckham is correct when he concludes that the author, although familiar with the Hebrew text, saw the exegetical potential in the Greek text of Amos 9:11–12 "as a legitimate way of reading the Hebrew text of that verse."[62] This Greek version of the text allowed the author to establish even more clearly his point that Gentiles who call upon the name of the Lord Jesus Christ are part of the eschatological people of God without needing to become Jews.

Thankfully, the vast majority of citations and allusions in either testament do not involve this level of complexity when it comes to determining the text form used by the author. But this example from Acts 15 shows the value of paying careful attention to the potential text forms of the donor text for understanding what the receptor text is potentially doing with that donor text. Thus having a basic grasp of the issues involved in determining the text form of the donor text is an important aspect of faithfully interpreting scripture's use of scripture.

A CLOSING ENCOURAGEMENT

After this lengthy journey through the weeds of detecting allusions and sorting through different text forms, it could be easy to forget the big picture. Looking for the different kinds of evidence, evaluating that evidence carefully, and explaining the exegetical outcome is a helpful process for detecting allusions. Being aware of the different textual forms and the impact they can make on scripture's use of scripture is important. But even with such guidelines, one must not forget that detecting allusions is both art and science. One of the great benefits of consistently reading and studying scripture is that the interpreter begins to develop certain instincts and sensibilities for detecting connections between different parts of scripture.

Study Questions

1. What is the problem with approaches that emphasize the "scientific" aspects of detecting allusions to the neglect of the "artistic" aspects?
2. What is the problem with approaches that emphasize the "artistic" aspects of detecting allusions to the neglect of the "scientific" aspects?

61. Marshall, "Acts," in *CNTUOT*, 590.
62. Bauckham, "James," 161.

3. In what sense is detecting allusions an art and in what sense is it a science?
4. What are the different kinds of evidence one should look for when seeking to determine if an allusion is present?
5. What are the different tools for evaluating the evidence for a potential allusion?
6. Why is it valuable to check if others have detected a potential allusion?
7. Why is it helpful to distinguish between direct and indirect fulfillment?
8. Of the many different exegetical outcomes noted, which (if any) were you already familiar with? Explain at least one example in relation to a specific biblical passage.
9. Why is describing the exegetical outcome of a citation/allusion important?
10. Why is it important to examine the text form of the donor text used by the biblical author?
11. Based on the case study on Ps 68 in Eph 4, what is your own conclusion of the best way to explain what Paul is doing with the donor text?
12. Based on the case study on Amos 9 in Acts 15, what is your own conclusion of the best way to explain what Acts 15 is doing with Amos 9?

CHAPTER 4

HORIZONTAL CONTEXT
VERSUS
VERTICAL CONTEXT

This chapter presents a choice between the majority approach that investigates only the horizontal context of the donor text and the need to study both the horizontal and vertical contexts, whenever there is a vertical context.[1] This chapter promotes a both/and approach.

CHOICE

Horizontal context refers to the surrounding verses, paragraphs, and chapters. In one sense it may include entire books or even all of Israel's scriptures. **Vertical context** refers to the relationship between the earlier donor and later receptor texts created by an allusion in the receptor text.[2] Thus, it is a vertical relationship between contexts across time while a horizontal relationship denotes the surrounding passages within the same context.

Paying attention to vertical context is not something interpreters regularly do, even though vertical context is part of the context. Ignoring allusions (vertical context) is a commonplace way that interpreters take texts out of context.

All biblical texts have a horizontal context. Donor texts and receptor texts also have vertical context. Figure 4-A, though literarily too symmetrical to be realistic, illustrates the basic idea of vertical context. This figure displays the horizontal context of Texts A, B, and C, as well as the vertical context created

1. On the widespread problem of ignoring vertical context, see Schnittjer, "Long-Lost Grandparent Texts," 27–31; *OTUOT*, 851, n. 27.

2. The presentation of vertical context in this chapter is streamlined and student-friendly. For a more advanced explanation of how vertical contexts function, see Schnittjer, "Going Vertical," 114–42.

by the allusion of B to C and of A to B and, more subtly, A to C. The author of Text A interpreted donor Text B in relation to the deep context of Text B's donor Text C. The horizontal context of donor Texts B and C are both relevant to responsible interpretation of Text A.

Figure 4-A: Basic Concept of Vertical and Horizontal Contexts

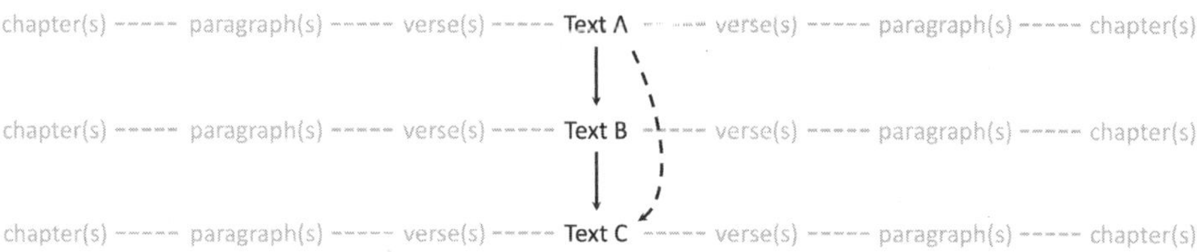

Vertical contexts are not all of one sort. In Figure 4-B, consider that Text X's interpretation of Text B may be influenced by Text A's earlier interpretation of Text B, even without evidence of direct dependence on Text A. Meanwhile Text A interprets Text B in the light of Text C—an interpretive blend. Text Y's interpretation of Text A may depend on the vertical context within Text A itself, alluding as it does to Texts B and C. And so on with Text Z. The highly allusive tendencies of the biblical writings means that all of these and other kinds of vertical context may be in play.

Figure 4-B: Multiple Vertical Contexts‡

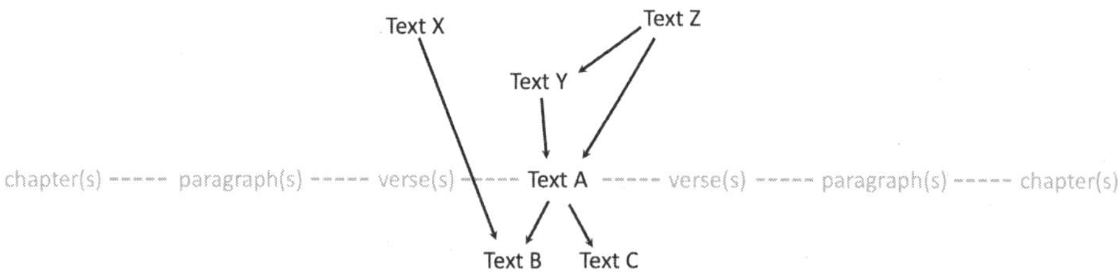

‡This figure has been simplified by only displaying the horizontal context of Text A. Texts B, C, X, Y, and Z all have horizontal contexts that are not being displayed.

The conceptual illustrations in Figures 4-A and 4-B need to be fleshed out with concrete examples. Figure 4-C lays out the horizontal and vertical contexts of 1 Kgs 11:1–4 that was discussed in the beginning of Chapter 2. The horizontal context of Solomon's wives in 1 Kgs 11:1–4 includes vv. 1–8 and then moves out to the precursors in the previous paragraph (1 Kgs 10:26–29) and to the consequences of Solomon's downfall in the following paragraphs (11:9–43).

The wider horizontal context includes the entire Solomon narrative (chs. 1–11) as well as the book of Kings, the Former Prophets, the Old Testament, and the entire Bible. The vertical context of 1 Kgs 11:1–4 includes its allusions to Deut 7:3–4; 17:17; 23:3, 7[4, 8 H], and the deep vertical context of the allusions within the donor texts to still earlier donor texts (Deut 7:1–5 to Exod 34:11–16 and Deut 23:1–8[2–9 H] to Num 22–24). The vertical context also goes upward from 1 Kgs 11:1–4 as a donor text to its receptor context in Neh 13:23–27.

Figure 4-C: Horizontal and Vertical Contexts of 1 Kings 11:1–4‡

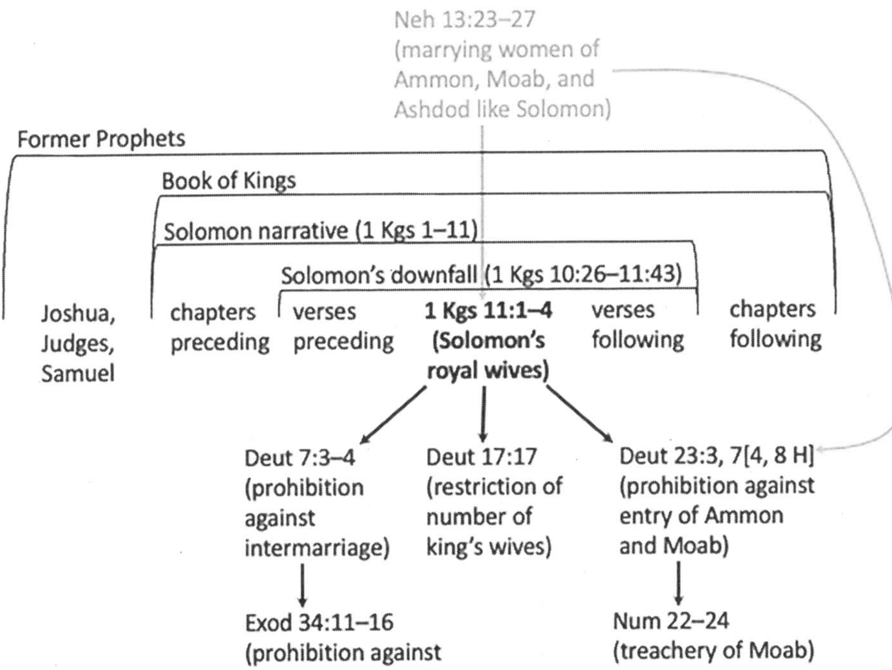

‡Though only the horizontal context of 1 Kgs 11:1–4 is displayed, all texts have horizontal contexts.

The most pressing horizontal context of 1 Kgs 11:1–4 is 10:26–11:8, though Solomon's downfall is one of the major turning points in Kings and the Former Prophets, connecting it to a wide horizontal context.[3] The critical issue of explaining the episode of Solomon's royal wives within its horizontal biblical context attracts the lion's share of interpretive effort in many studies. There is nothing wrong with this except when the author's intentional

3. See Schnittjer, *Old Testament Narrative*, 123–27.

contextualization of Solomon's downfall by an interpretive blend to Deut 7:3–4 (and likely Exod 34:16); 17:17; and 23:3, 7[4, 8 H] does not play a proportionate role in interpretation.[4] Responsible interpretation requires attending to all contexts, including vertical context.

Figure 4-D presents the vertical and horizontal contexts of some of the receptor texts that depend on Exod 23:20–21 as a donor text. Since this set of allusions has been discussed at the end of Chapter 1, the present point is restricted to a broad focus on vertical context. The allusion to Exod 23:20–21 in Isa 40:3 was likely suggested by the broad allusion in Isa 11:15–16 that detected an expectational analogy (typological pattern) between the exodus and the return from Mesopotamian exile. The allusion of Isa 40:3 to Exod 23:20 seems to be informed by Exod 33:14 since the way is not merely prepared for Israel but for Yahweh himself who promises to go with Israel. The ironic interpretive blend in Mal 3:1 enhances Isa 40:3 in the light of its vertical connection to Exod 23:20–21. The interpretive blend in Mark 1:2–3 depends on the horizontal context of each of its several donor texts: "gospel" (Mark 1:1; cf. Isa 40:9), Elijah figure (Mark 1:6; cf. Mal 4:5[3:23 H]; 2 Kgs 1:8), and identification of the Messiah as the Lord (Mark 1:3; cf. Exod 33:14; Isa 40:9).

Figure 4-D: Vertical and Horizontal Contexts Going Back to Exodus 23:20–21

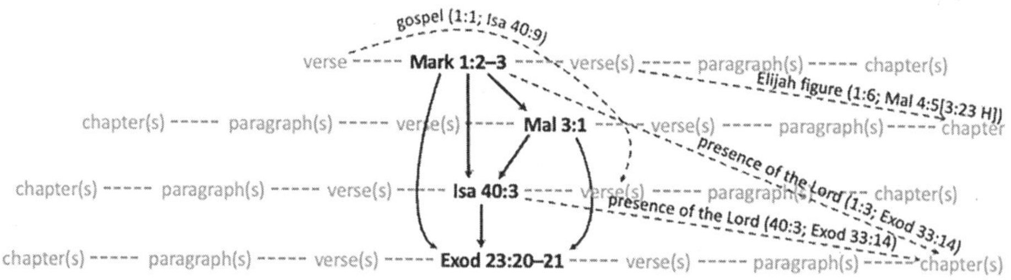

Allusions create vertical contexts that activate horizontal contexts in donor and receptor texts in relation to one another (see Figure 4-D). Before moving on, it is necessary to briefly consider how allusions function—in this chapter, allusion is used as inclusive of quotation, citation, and paraphrase. This will be followed by brief discussions of several kinds of vertical contexts: interpretive blends, synoptic contexts, networks, and deep context.

Allusion refers to purposefully evoking another context.[5] A biblical allu-

4. See detailed study in Schnittjer, "Overview of Composite Citations," forthcoming, and more briefly, see the beginning of Chapter 2 above.

5. See *OTUOT*, 889; Schultz, *Search for Quotation*, 222.

sion permanently connects the receptor and donor contexts because of emerging canonical consciousness. How do allusions work?

Allusions simultaneously activate the horizontal contexts of the donor and the receptor texts.[6] The texts tethered together by allusion in one place—at the point of allusion to the donor text—may indirectly evoke elements in the horizontal contexts of each other.[7] For example, the allusions to Exod 23:20–21, Isa 40:3, and Mal 3:1 in Mark 1:2–3 trigger a series of interrelations between the horizontal contexts (see black dotted lines with arrows in Figure 4-D).

The dynamic relationship between the texts is created by the dependence of the receptor text upon the donor text. Yet the connection between the receptor text and donor texts can cause or allow the donor text to enhance an aspect of the horizontal context of the receptor text and vice versa, if and when a pair of donor and receptor texts is interpreted together by a still later receptor text. For example, on the basis of the allusion to Deut 23:3, 7[4, 8 H] by 1 Kgs 11:1–2, Nehemiah's allusion in Neh 13:23–27 interprets the law of the assembly in Deut 23 as applying to apostasy marriages based on Solomon's apostasy marriages in 1 Kgs 11:1–2 (see Figure 4-C).

In sum, an allusion establishes a vertical context between receptor and donor contexts that activates the horizontal contexts of both texts in relation to one another. Still later authors can work up or down the vertical context of donor-receptor text pairs.

Interpretive blends refer to a receptor text that interprets one donor text in the light of one or more other donor texts. Two vertical contexts serve as tributaries to the receptor text, and they activate the horizontal contexts of all three texts in relation to the others. For example, the interpretive blend in Hab 2:14 reads together two distinct contexts from Isa 6:3 (judgment) and 11:9 (blessing) in a way that opens all three horizontal contexts to interpretive enhancements mediated by the vertical contexts. Notice the catchword ("holy") and catchphrase ("the earth is / will be full") in 6:3 and 11:9 that suggested reading these together (bold signifies near verbatim parallels and underlining, broken underlining, and wavy underlining signify verbal parallels).

And they were calling to one another:
"Holy, holy, holy is Yahweh Almighty;
the whole earth is full of his glory [מְלֹא כָל־הָאָרֶץ כְּבוֹדוֹ]."
(Isa 6:3 AT)

6. See Ben-Porat, "Poetics," 107, 127.
7. See ibid., 109–10.

> They will neither harm nor destroy
> on all my holy mountain,
> **for the earth will be filled with the knowledge of Yahweh** [כִּי־מָלְאָה הָאָרֶץ דֵּעָה אֶת־יהוה]
> **as the waters cover the sea.** (11:9 AT)

> **For the earth will be filled with the knowledge of** the glory of **Yahweh** [כִּי תִּמָּלֵא הָאָרֶץ לָדַעַת אֶת־כְּבוֹד יהוה]
> **as the waters cover the sea.** (Hab 2:14 AT)

Habakkuk converts the blessed knowledge of peace that fills the earth like waters cover the seas in Isa 11 to a knowledge of wrath against the Chaldeans based on the earth-filling wrath once brought against Judah in Isa 6.[8] This powerful imagery stands in the middle of the five woes of Hab 2:6–20 and helps explain the transition between the prophet's complaints in Hab 1 to his prayer acknowledging Yahweh's power in Hab 3.

Synoptic contexts within Israel's scriptures constitute another kind of vertical context.[9] Modern interpreters often compare the donor and receptor texts by asking: What's the same? What's deleted? What's added? What's different? And for all of these, why? There is nothing wrong with this modernist approach.

Aristotle's (ca. 335 BCE) observations concerning synoptic parallels offer an approach more suited to ancient synoptic narratives. Though Aristotle developed his analysis in relation to fiction, he regards historical narratives as functioning the same way. He says that "[T]he poet should be more a maker of plots than of verses . . . even should his poetry concern actual events, he is no less a poet for that."[10] Aristotle's important work can be summarized in three kinds of differences between the synoptic donor and receptor texts.[11]

- **Selectivity.** Authors decide what parts of the story to narrate (1456a, 6–9).

8. See *OTUOT*, 428.

9. Because the Old Testament was written over a period of one thousand years, the donor texts of synoptic narratives tended to have a measure of authority within the emerging canonical consciousness. The situation is different with the New Testament being written within two generations, though even within the New Testament there is evidence of an emerging canonical consciousness. While Old and New Testament synoptic narratives function identically, the latter was produced before the donor texts achieved the same level of canonical consciousness versus the synoptic donor texts of the Old Testament.

10. Aristotle, *Poetics*, 1451b, 27–30. Hereafter cited parenthetically.

11. This summary is condensed from Schnittjer, "Kadesh Infidelity," 104.

- **Arrangement.** Authors decide how to arrange narrative sequence—chronological versus dischronological, telescoping, and so on—as well as how to frame the story—biographical, thematic, and so on (1459a, 32–34).
- **Voicing.** Authors decide how to voice stories, including direct narration, background commentary, indirect speech, and embedded discourses (1460a, 7–8). Aristotle points out that altering even one word can shift the implications of the entire context (1458b, 18–21).

The Chronicler illustrates selectivity by beginning his narrative proper with Saul's death. He also illustrates voicing by revoicing the episode from embedded discourse in the donor text to narrative commentary. Chronicles uses the synonyms "seek" (בקשׁ) and "seek" (דרשׁ) to characterize those who seek Yahweh in worship. The Chronicler makes a wordplay on Saul's name (*sha'ul*, שָׁאוּל) and the prohibition against "asking [*sho'el*, שֹׁאֵל] ghosts." Notice the wordplay and revoicing (bold and underlining signify verbal parallels and broken underlining signifies marking):[12]

> There shall not be found . . . **one who asks** [שׁאל] ghosts or familiar spirits, or **seeks** [דרשׁ] the dead (Deut 18:10a, 11 AT).

> Saul **asked** [שׁאל] of Yahweh, but Yahweh did not answer him by dreams or Urim or prophets. Saul then said to his attendants, "Seek out [בקשׁ] for me a woman who consults ghosts, so I may go and **seek** [דרשׁ] of her." His attendants said, "Behold, a woman who consults ghosts is in Endor" (1 Sam 28:6–7 AT).

> Saul died because he was unfaithful to Yahweh; he did not keep the word of Yahweh and even **asked** [שׁאל] a ghost to **seek guidance** [דרשׁ], and did not **seek guidance** [דרשׁ] of Yahweh. So Yahweh put him to death and turned the kingdom over to David son of Jesse (1 Chr 10:13–14 AT).

The Chronicler not only chose this sin to typify Saul's infidelity because of the wordplay between "Saul" and "ask" but also to show readers the danger of insincerity of devotion. It is not enough for Saul to "ask" Yahweh if he does not "seek" him. David and Israel overtly refer to Saul's failure to seek Yahweh in worship according to Torah (1 Chr 13:3; 15:13; 16:11). In this way Saul embodies the problem of mere askers who do not seek Yahweh.

12. See *OTUOT*, 731–32.

Much confusion surrounds the work of scholars who try to make sense of New Testament synoptic narratives without attending to the many synoptic narratives within Israel's scriptures that the evangelists looked to as models. Michael Licona expresses his struggle with altered sequences of episodes between Matthew, Mark, and Luke, and so compares them to fictionalized Greco-Roman biographies. Licona's study distorts the issue and confounds students by neglecting the commonplace rearrangement of sequence, known as dischronological narration, in the synoptic narratives of Israel's scriptures, as well as other ancient Near Eastern narratives. The index to Licona's book includes zero scripture references to Old Testament synoptic narratives.[13] For an example of dischronological synoptic narration, see cases below.

Deep context makes up another part of vertical context. In many cases, later authors of Israel's scriptures cite donor texts that contain within them allusions to still earlier donor texts. For example, The Chronicler remixes and interpretively enhances three psalms from book four of the Psalter.

1 Chr 16:8–22	Ps 105:1–15
16:23–33	96:1b–10b, 11–13b
16:34–36	106:1, 47–48

All three of the psalms include a series of interpretive allusions to still earlier scriptural traditions. The international call to worship of Ps 96:7–8 features exegetical enhancements of the old call to worship before the storm in Ps 29:1–2. In this case, Ps 29:1–2 provides deep context that needs to be taken into account as part of understanding what the psalmist of Ps 96 had in mind. This deep vertical context sheds light on the Chronicler's psalm remix to celebrate the ark of the covenant coming into Jerusalem for the first time (1 Chr 16:1).[14]

Cases of deep vertical context—when the donor text is also a receptor text alluding to an earlier Old Testament text—apply to at least eighty allusions in the New Testament.[15]

The triumphal entry in Mark 11 makes allusion to both the prophecy of Zech 9:9 as well as the expectation for the ruler upon a donkey in the blessing

13. See Licona, *Why?* 190–96, and for the absence of references to OT synoptic contexts, see index, 303–8. The chapter on rearranged sequence of episodes in Licona's follow-up study *Jesus, Contradicted* includes zero references to dischronological narratives in the OT (129–48). For a list of biblical synoptic narratives, see Schnittjer, "Kadesh Infidelity," 96, n. 2, plus Table 1 (96); *OTUOT*, 80, n. 8, plus Table D1 (79). On dischronological narration in scripture, see Schnittjer, *Old Testament Narrative*, 10; *OTUOT*, 893; Glatt-Gilad, *Chronological Displacement*.

14. See Schnittjer, *Old Testament Narrative*, 235–36.

15. See Schnittjer, "Long-Lost Grandparent Texts," 31, n.6.

of Judah in Gen 49:11–12. Ignoring the vertical context leads to confusion by taking the passage out of context. Some scholars suppress the evidence of vertical context because Mark does not mark the allusion with a citation formula. This allows these New Testament scholars to discover that the zoological meaning of Mark 11:1–10 in its horizontal context does not relate to royal expectations but shows that Jesus is the Lord over creation because he rode on a young donkey.[16] Unlike these modern scholars, Matthew and John recognize the vertical context of the exegetical allusions that informs the horizontal context of Mark 11:1–10 when they insert a citation formula to Zech 9:9 (cf. Matt 21:4; John 12:14). The same problem of suppressing vertical context of the king riding a donkey appears among Old Testament scholarship as well.[17] Failure to account for vertical context and deep vertical context leads to exegetical distortions.

Zechariah's allusion to the blessing of Judah using rare donkey language helps his constituents situate the expectation for the saved and humble king that comes into Zion (Zech 9:9). The blessing spoken by Jacob depicts the Judah-king binding his mount to a vine. The incongruity illustrates that the overabundance of the vineyard of Judah requires hitching animals to vines (Gen 49:11). Zechariah's exegetical intervention extends the expectation by presenting a prequel of what comes before the ruler arriving and binding his mount—the coming of the king. Mark further extends the exegesis of Zechariah by connecting it to an ironic sequel within the horizontal context of his Gospel. The ironic allusions to Zech 9:9 (Mark 11:1–10) and to the deep vertical context of Gen 49:11 ("bind" and "unbind" 5x in Mark 11:2, 4, 5; cf. Gen 49:11 LXX) connect to the riddle of the vine growers who kill the vineyard owner's son by the use citations of Ps 118:25–26 and 118:22–23 in Mark 11:9–11 and 12:10–11. Table 4-E illustrates the intersection of deep vertical context and horizontal contexts by the prophet's prequel and the evangelist's sequel.

16. See Keener, "Unridden Donkey Colt," 40. In his zeal to make zoological observations, Keener suppresses the evidence of allusions to Gen 49:10–11 and Zech 9:9 (24). He claims Mark was not aware of the expectations in Israel's scriptures (25). Keener's argument from silence requires accepting that Mark five times coincidentally uses the term from Gen 49:11 LXX "bind" and "unbind" (cf. Mark 11:2, 4, 5). In addition, Keener does not investigate the research on the rare donkey language that definitively connects Gen 49:10–11 and Zech 9:9. See Way, "Donkey," 105–14. Also see related syntactical observations in Schnittjer, "Blessing of Judah," 28, n. 30.

17. For a detailed discussion of donkeys and mules in the Old Testament, but without recognizing the rare donkey language that Zech 9:9 adapts from Gen 49:10, see Boda, *Zechariah*, 568–71. Elsewhere Boda concludes Zech 9:9 alludes to the mule that Solomon rode (1 Kgs 1:38; cf. 2 Sam 16:2); see idem, *Haggai, Zachariah*, 417. On the rare donkey language that undermines Boda's proposals, see Way cited in previous footnote.

Table 4-E: Zechariah 9:9 as Prequel and Mark 11:1–10 as Set-Up to Ironic Sequel‡

[**Prequel** Humble king comes riding on a donkey (Zech 9:9)]	**Blessing of Judah** Judah-king enters his vineyard with his donkey (Gen 49:11)
Triumphal entry Messiah comes riding on a donkey (Mark 11:1–10)[a]	[**Sequel** Son of vineyard owner executed as king of the Jews (Mark 12:1–11; 15:26)]

‡Table adapted from Schnittjer, "Blessing of Judah," 29–30.
[a]Cf. allusions to Zech 9:9 in Matt 21:5; Luke 19:28–36; John 12:15.

Networks constitute a small but powerful kind of vertical contexts. An interpretive network refers to the cumulative exegetical interventions upon favorite biblical passages—favorites of the biblical authors. Repeated exegetical interventions on the same text do not exhaust but increase the generative capacities of donor texts for later receptor texts. The many interrelated texts of interpretive networks feature something like interpretive momentum for later biblical authors who make further exegetical interventions with the same texts, thus extending the network. Interpretive networks are dynamic engines of progressive revelation within scripture.[18]

An inductive study of exegetical interventions within Israel's scriptures uncovers at least twenty-one interpretive networks.[19] Representative interpretive networks include:

- Abrahamic covenant
- attribute formula
- Davidic covenant
- Judah-king
- new covenant
- new exodus
- the place Yahweh chooses for his name
- seventy years

18. For discussion of an interpretive network related to God's name, see Harmon, "Divine Identity," 3–19.

19. See *OTUOT*, 873–87, including description, diagrams, and a scripture index. For a detailed study of a major network with a summary of how networks function within scripture, see Schnittjer, "Blessing of Judah," 15–39. Networks are not developed by modern scholars and imposed on Israel's scriptures (contra Stovell, review of *OTUOT*, 17). Networks are based on repeated reuse of the same donor text by many later biblical authors (*OTUOT*, 874).

Most networks carry over into the New Testament, where authors put the network's interpretive momentum to good use.

The Davidic covenant network is well-developed, including numerous exegetical interventions with a favorite donor text at the end of Nathan's oracle in 2 Sam 7:11–15, as well as exegetical interventions with many of the oracle's receptor texts. Figure 4-F graphically depicts the primary relationships of this wide-ranging network. Several of the constituent texts of the Davidic covenant network are something like nexus texts because of their roles in other interpretive networks.[20]

Figure 4-F: Davidic Covenant Network‡

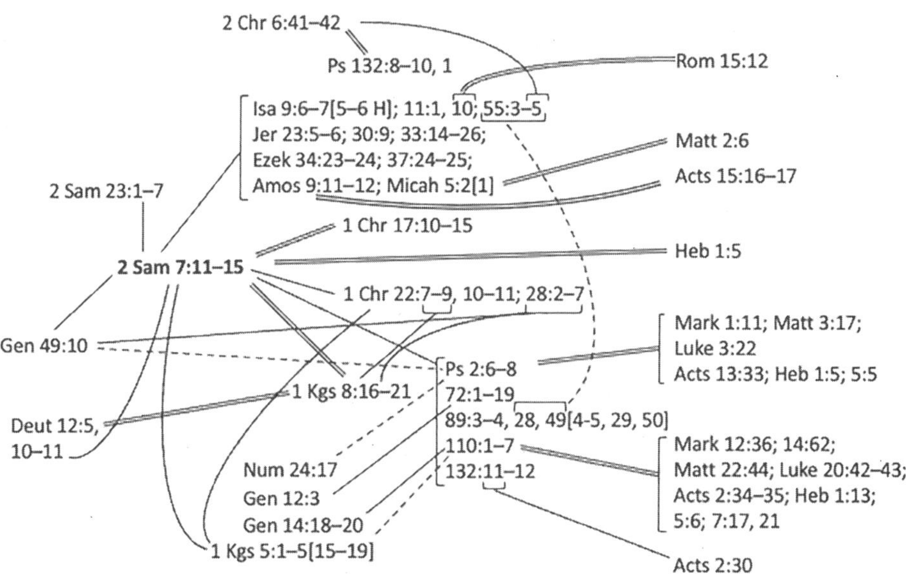

‡Double lines signify quotations, single lines signify probable allusions, and dotted lines signify possible allusions. Left and right as well as up and down do not indicate earlier or later texts or anything else. The placement merely is an attempt to graphically display network relations. Figure adapted with light modifications from *OTUOT*, 879.

An example of interpretive inertia that adheres to network relationships can be seen by tracing out the series of exegetical interventions with Nathan's oracle (2 Sam 7:1–17) by David and Solomon in Samuel, Kings, and Chronicles.[21] The

20. E.g., Gen 49:10 is part of the Judah-king network, Ps 72:17 is part of the Abrahamic covenant network, etc. See *OTUOT*, 879.

21. See esp., David, 2 Sam 7:18–29; 23:1–7; 1 Kgs 2:1–4; 1 Chr 22:6–19; 23:25–26; 28:2–7; Solomon, 1 Kgs 5:1–5[15–19 H]; 8:14–21; 2 Chr 6:1–11, 15–17.

long meditations and multiple exegetical interventions with Nathan's oracle eventually led David to conclude that he was not able to build the temple because he had shed too much blood (1 Chr 22:8; 28:3). David originally thought building a temple was his own idea because Yahweh claimed he had never asked for one (2 Sam 7:7//1 Chr 17:6). But after years of pondering and interpretation, David realized that building the temple had been part of Yahweh's sovereign will since the days of the Hebrew ancestors (1 Chr 28:4–6).[22]

In sum, vertical context conceptualizes a widely neglected context within biblical studies, namely, allusions. The vertical context created by allusions to earlier scriptures does not need to be added but is a native part of all scriptures with allusions. When allusions are ignored, the passage is taken out of its vertical context, leading to distortions of meaning.

Scriptural allusions create vertical context by linking receptor and donor texts. Scriptural allusions activate the horizontal contexts of the donor and receptor texts and cause other interrelations between them.

CASES

The choice in this chapter focuses on the danger of exclusive study of horizontal context while neglecting vertical context. The set of case studies included here illustrates how different sorts of vertical context work.

Allusions activate the horizontal context of the donor and receptor texts more widely than just the point of contact in the allusion itself. The refrain "everyone did what was right in their own eyes" (AT) in Judg 17:6 and 21:25 makes an allusion to the same phrase appearing in Deut 12:8–9.

Deuteronomy 12 is known as the place legislation because it requires that Israel only worship at the place Yahweh would choose. In Judg 17–18, Micah of Ephraim and the tribe of Dan disregard the place legislation and worship at places of their own choosing. The narrator borrows a phrase from Deut 12 to show the rebellion of the people in establishing their own places of worship (bold signifies verbal parallels).[23]

> You shall not act as we do today, **everyone doing what is right in their own eyes**, because you have not yet come to the resting place and to the inheritance that Yahweh your God is giving to you. (Deut 12:8–9 AT)

22. See Schnittjer, "Your House Is My House," 80.
23. See Schnittjer, *Old Testament Narrative*, 88.

> In those days there was no king in Israel. **Everyone did what was right in their own eyes**. (Judg 17:6 AT)

The reuse of the very same phrase in Judg 21:25 loads it with a new, much broader connotation, coming as it does after the sexual crime of Judg 19, the civil war of chapter 20, and the mass stealing of virgins from Shiloh in chapter 21. The Sodom-like rebellion in Gibeah of Benjamin in Judg 19 had nothing to do with worship and everything to do with the gruesome death of the concubine of a Levite from Ephraim. The deep irony comes with the solution of the eleven tribes who had gone to war against the Benjamites for their sins. The tribal leaders convince the men of Benjamin to abduct females from the town of Shiloh to repopulate their tribe after the civil war (21:20–21). Readers are slack-jawed at the flagrant hypocrisy of the tribes once outraged by gang rape now plotting mass stealing of virgin girls. The story closes on the well-known phrase borrowed from Deut 12.

The redeployment of "everyone did what was right in their own eyes" (AT) in Judg 21:25 extends the sense. The problem it addresses is not worshiping at the wrong place. It speaks of organized kidnapping and rape. This new kind of context for the same refrain invites a different contextualization. Over and over the narrator of Judges measures the rebellion of Israel against "the eyes of Yahweh" (AT). Notice how this juxtaposition affects the sense of "in their own eyes" (AT) (emphasis signifies verbal parallels).

> The Israelites **did** what was evil **in the eyes of** Yahweh (Judg 2:11//3:7//6:1 AT)

> Again the Israelites **did** what was evil **in the eyes** of Yahweh (3:12//4:1//10:6//13:1 AT)

> Everyone **did** what was right **in** their own **eyes**. (17:6//21:25 AT)

The two forms of the phrase that measured Israel doing evil in the eyes of Yahweh repeated seven times is not a good sign. But in Judges things never get better. What could be worse? Two things are worse than the rebellion that spans Judg 1–16. One, the standard of measurement, even for evil, is no longer the eyes of Yahweh but now each person's own eyes. Two, the rebellion in Judg 17–21 is no longer blamed on Israel collectively. Now, each individual does whatever they want. The powerful statement of high rebellion, "everyone did what was right in their own eyes," draws its force from its vertical context (Deut 12) connected to its horizontal context (Judg 1–16).

Interpretive blends draw upon dual vertical contexts simultaneously, and they can appear within networks. The interpretive blend in Balaam's third oracle at Num 24:9 represents an early exegetical nexus between the royal expectations of the Judah-king network and the Abrahamic covenant network. Notice how Balaam draws together two expectations from Genesis (bold and underlining signify verbal parallels and italics signify similar expressions).[24]

> [Yahweh to Abraham] I will bless those who bless you, and *whoever curses* [קלל] you I will curse [ארר]; and all peoples on earth will be blessed through you. (Gen 12:3)

> [Isaac to Jacob] May those who curse [ארר] you be cursed [ארר] and those who bless you be blessed. (27:29b)

> [Jacob to Judah] You are a lion's cub, Judah;
> you return from the prey, my son.
> **Like a lion he crouches** and *lies down* [רבץ],
> **like a lioness—who dares to rouse him**? (49:9)

> [Balaam] **Like a lion he crouches** and *lies down* [שׁכב], **like a lioness—who dares to rouse him**? May those who bless you be blessed and *those who curse* [ארר] you be cursed [ארר]! (Num 24:9 AT)

Genesis does not directly identify the expectations for the Judah-king with the covenant to Abraham. Yet the overlap in imagery between the (accidental) blessing on Jacob and the blessing of Judah suggests some kind of relationship between Gen 27:29 and 49:8, 10. The similarities move toward shared identity in Num 24:9. Balaam warns Balak of this dangerous lion-like people who stand under God's word of blessing. The connection established by Balaam gets reinforced by the psalmist who identifies the fulfillment of the Abrahamic and Davidic covenant together: "May his [God's king] name endure forever; may it continue as long as the sun. Then **all nations will be blessed through** him, and they will call him blessed" (Ps 72:17, emphasis signifies verbal parallel to Gen 12:3).[25]

Mark prepares readers for the interpretive blend that Jesus presents to the high priest by individual allusions in the contexts leading up to Mark 14:62.

24. See Schnittjer, "Blessing of Judah," 21–24; *OTUOTPL*, entry on Num 24:9.
25. See *OTUOT*, 489–92.

Jesus publicly pushes back against an incongruity of the religious scholars' view of Ps 110:1 in a way that accepts their identification of the son of David as messiah and that David is subordinate to messiah (Mark 12:35–37). Generally, the commonplace expression "son of a human being" means human, as in its plentiful use in Ezekiel, where the NRSVue appropriately renders it as "mortal."[26] Jesus privately teaches his followers to expect "the son of a human being coming on the clouds" (Mark 13:26 AT), thus identifying this expression with the figure in Dan 7:13 (see Chapter 1 on the singular/collective issue in Dan 7). Notice the interpretive intervention by the interplay of these two allusions in response to the high priest's question, "Are you the Messiah, the Son of the Blessed One?" (Mark 14:61).[27]

> Jesus said, "I am. You will see the son of a human being **seated at the right hand** [Ps 110:1 bold] of power and coming with the clouds of heaven [Dan 7:13 underlining]." (Mark 14:62 AT)

The phrase "coming with the clouds of heaven" activates Dan 7:13 as the donor text of the expression "son of a human being." And the combination of the verb "seated" with "at the right hand" activates Ps 110:1 as a donor text.[28] But this interpretive blend also alludes to Mark 12:36 and 13:26 with the interpretive outcomes Jesus had already worked out for both donor texts. All of these clues of allusion are needed to adequately apprehend both what Jesus is claiming and what the high priest thinks he is claiming.

Though interpretive blends are often based on catchwords, sometimes the linkage can be more complex. Carmen Imes demonstrates that 1 Pet 2:9 interprets together Exod 19:5 proto-MT and Isa 43:21 LXX by means of a connecting text or bridge text, Mal 3:17 proto-MT and LXX.[29] These donor texts have been identified with some confidence because of the relative rarity of "treasured possession" (סְגֻלָּה) in Israel's scriptures, including Exod 19:5 MT and Mal 3:17 MT (double underlined below) as well as the somewhat unconventional glossing of it as "to acquire/what is acquired" (περιποιέω/

26. See "בֵּן" sec. on בֶּן־אָדָם *DCHR* 2:185.

27. See Schnittjer, *Old Testament Narrative*, 181; Strauss, *Mark*, 656–57. On historical context, see Bock, *Blasphemy and Exaltation*, 220–33.

28. Only two places in Israel's scripture use "sit" (ישׁב, κάθημαι) + preposition *l-* (לְ, ἐκ) + "right hand" (יָמִין, δεξιός)—1 Kgs 2:19 and Ps 110:1. See collocation ישׁב לְ־ in "ישׁב" Even-Shoshan, 501 (nos. 622, 732). Cf. 1 Kgs 22:19//2 Chr 18:18; Ezek 16:46.

29. See Imes, "Treasured Possession," 15–36; idem, "Review Essay," 206–10. For other uses of the OT in 1 Pet 2:4–10, see Miller and Murawski, *1 Peter*, 119–25; cf. 41–41.

περιποίησις) in Isa 43:21 LXX and Mal 3:17 LXX (broken underlining below).[30] Notice how Peter makes this interpretive blend using the bridge text of Mal 3:17 (emphases signify verbal parallels and brackets enclose MT, LXX, and GNT).

> [Yahweh:] "Now if you obey me fully and keep my covenant, then out of all nations you will be my treasured possession [סְגֻלָּה, "for me a people special" μοι λαὸς περιούσιος]. Although the whole earth is mine [6]you will be for me a kingdom of priests and a holy nation [גּוֹי קָדוֹשׁ, ἔθνος ἅγιον]." These are the words you are to speak to the Israelites. (Exod 19:5–6)

> I provide water in the wilderness
> and streams in the wasteland,
> to give drink to my people, my chosen [עַמִּי בְחִירִי, "my *chosen race*" τὸ γένος μου τὸ ἐκλεκτόν],
> [21]the people I formed [עַם־זוּ יָצַרְתִּי, "my people whom I have acquired" λαόν μου ὃν περιεποιησάμην] for myself
> that they may proclaim my praise. (Isa 43:20b–21)

> "On the day when I act," says Yahweh Almighty, "they will be my treasured possession [סְגֻלָּה, "**acquisition**" εἰς περιποίησιν]. I will spare them, just as a father has compassion and spares his son who serves him." (Mal 3:17 NIV, divine name used instead of Lord)

> But you are a *chosen race* [γένος ἐκλεκτόν], a royal priesthood, a holy nation [ἔθνος ἅγιον], a people of God's **acquisition** [λαὸς εἰς περιποίησιν], that you may declare the praises of him who called you out of darkness into his wonderful light. (1 Pet 2:9 AT)

Peter's use of Mal 3:17 is a key, as observed by Imes, for two of his more important exegetical outcomes. First, Peter's use of "acquisition" (εἰς περιποίησιν) from Mal 3:17 invites the connotation of an eschatological remnant from Mal 3:17.[31] Second, the necessity of the Hebrew of Mal 3:17 to connect with Exod 19:5 by "treasured possession" (*segullah* סְגֻלָּה) invites the connotations of this rich term in Hebrew and in light of its Akkadian and Ugaritic counterparts, not

30. See six of eight uses in reference to Israel in this sense (Exod 19:5; Deut 7:6; 14:2; 26:18; Ps 135:4; Mal 3:17) in "סְגֻלָּה" Even-Shoshan 802 (nos. 1–5, 8); Imes, "Treasured Possession," 26–30; idem, "Review Essay," 208.

31. See Imes, "Treasured Possession," 42; idem, "Review Essay," 209–10.

merely as accumulated possessions but as cherished treasure with a vocational expectation.[32] Yahweh cherishes Israel, yes, but *segullah* is a technical term in treaty contexts that also refers to one who represents the suzerain.

In sum, the interpretive blend of Exod 19:5 and Isa 43:21 by the proto-MT and LXX connections of Mal 3:17 stand behind Peter's identification of God's people in Christ as his cherished eschatological remnant.

Synoptic contexts are a kind of vertical context that require special care. The natural impulse of many modern interpreters is to harmonize the differences with plausible scenarios to explain the variations. This impulse does not fit well with the evidence of biblical authors who interpreted synoptic narratives and prioritized the distinctives rather than trying to explain them away.

Numbers 13–14 emphasizes the collective responsibility of Israel for the rebellion at Kadesh that condemned an entire generation to die in the wilderness. Moses reframes these events in a synoptic version in Deut 1, emphasizing individual rebellion—not a quick public decision as in Numbers but a methodical and personal rebellion. The version of the events in Deut 1 warns God's people against lingering over discontent in the privacy of their own tents.[33] The psalmist does not seek to release the tensions moderns feel between the quick collective and the slow individual versions of the story. Notice how the psalmist emphasizes the dangers of both collective and individual rebellion (wavy underlining signifies what is shared by Num 14, Deut 1, and Ps 106; underlining signifies what is shared only by Num 14 and Ps 106; broken underlining signifies what seems like irony; and bold signifies what is only shared by Deut 1 and Ps 106):[34]

> Yahweh said to Moses, "How long will this people despise me? How long will they refuse to believe in me, even with all the signs I have done in their midst? (Num 14:11 AT)

> In this wilderness your corpses shall fall—all who were counted in the census from twenty years and upward, who grumbled [לון] against me. Not one of you will come into the land which I lifted up my hand for you to reside in it . . . the land which you rejected. But you, your corpses shall fall in this wilderness. (Num 14:29, 30a, 31b, 32 AT)

32. See *sikiltu* b3′, *CAD* 15:245; Greenberg, "Hebrew *segullā*," 174; *TLC* 2:79 (83, §5); *COS* 3.45i:95, nn. 53, 54 (lines 7, 12 "possession"); cf. *CTU*, 179 (2.39, lines 7, 12); and see Sarna, *Exodus*, 104; Imes, "Treasured Possession," 37–40, esp. nn. 113, 115.

33. See Schnittjer, "Kadesh Infidelity," 115; cf. 105–15.

34. See ibid., 116–17.

> **You grumbled to yourselves** [רגן] **in your tents** and said, "Yahweh hates us. He brought us out of Egypt to give us into the hand of the Amorites to destroy us" . . . But in spite of this word [of Moses's encouragement] you did not believe in Yahweh your God. (Deut 1:27, 32 AT)
>
> They rejected the pleasant land; they did not believe in his word. **They grumbled to themselves** [רגן] **in their tents**, and they did not obey the voice of Yahweh. So he lifted up his hand against them that he would make them fall in the wilderness. (Ps 106:24–26 AT)

Synoptic narratives often rearrange the sequence of episodes. This is not unusual. Many nonsynoptic narratives feature dischronological sequence for various narrative and theological reasons (see footnote 13 above for studies). The Chronicler follows the account in Samuel with regard to fronting David's capture of Jerusalem as his first act after being anointed king of all Israel (2 Sam 5:1–5, 6–10//1 Chr 11:1–3, 4–9). But the capture of Jerusalem is dischronological in Samuel. The battle with the Philistines occurred after David was anointed (2 Sam 5:17). The narrative sequence prioritizes David's most important accomplishment—capturing the city that Yahweh would choose for his temple.

The Chronicler not only fronts the capture of Jerusalem but rearranges the first part of bringing the ark of the covenant to Jerusalem. Notice the difference between 2 Sam 6:1–11 and 1 Chr 13:5–14 in Figure 4-G—in the Chronicler's version, David gets the ark before he defeats the Philistines. This fits with the Chronicler's emphasis on worship. But it also may be a trace of Ps 132:1–5, in which David makes a vow to provide a place for the ark (Ps 132:8 is the only explicit reference to the ark in the psalter).[35] That the Chronicler elsewhere uses Ps 132 in his narrative strengthens this possibility (2 Chr 6:40–41; Ps 132:8–10, 1).

Deep vertical context is important to investigate, including cases of interpretive blends. John splices together a marked allusion to Ps 34 with its deep vertical context and Zech 12 in his account of the crucifixion. This interpretive blend serves as a commentary on the soldier's choice to spear Jesus's torso because he was already dead rather than break his legs to end the crucifixion. The piercing provided an alternative that preserved his bones intact. Notice how John brings these together:

35. See Knoppers, *I Chronicles 10–29*, 590–91.

Figure 4-G: Synoptic Comparison from David's Anointing to the Davidic Promise‡

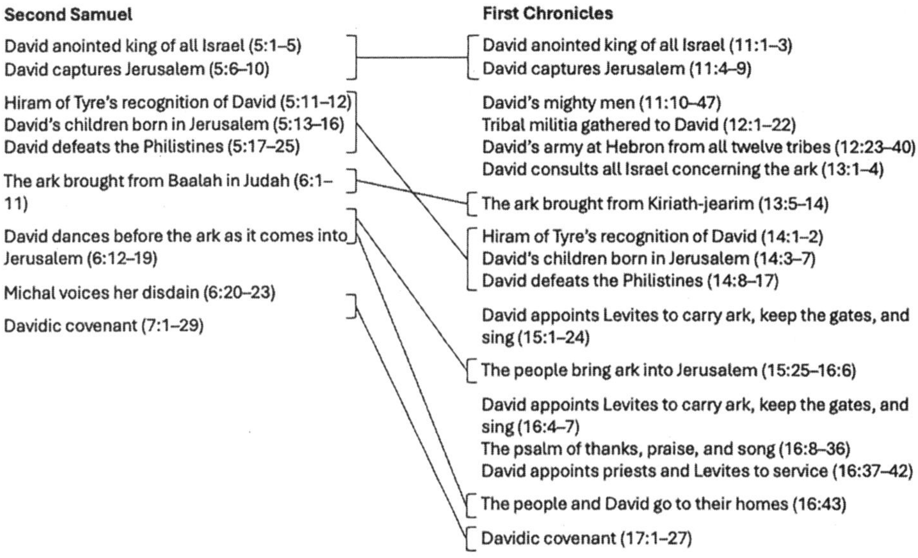

Second Samuel

David anointed king of all Israel (5:1–5)
David captures Jerusalem (5:6–10)

Hiram of Tyre's recognition of David (5:11–12)
David's children born in Jerusalem (5:13–16)
David defeats the Philistines (5:17–25)

The ark brought from Baalah in Judah (6:1–11)

David dances before the ark as it comes into Jerusalem (6:12–19)

Michal voices her disdain (6:20–23)

Davidic covenant (7:1–29)

First Chronicles

David anointed king of all Israel (11:1–3)
David captures Jerusalem (11:4–9)

David's mighty men (11:10–47)
Tribal militia gathered to David (12:1–22)
David's army at Hebron from all twelve tribes (12:23–40)
David consults all Israel concerning the ark (13:1–4)

The ark brought from Kiriath-jearim (13:5–14)

Hiram of Tyre's recognition of David (14:1–2)
David's children born in Jerusalem (14:3–7)
David defeats the Philistines (14:8–17)

David appoints Levites to carry ark, keep the gates, and sing (15:1–24)

The people bring ark into Jerusalem (15:25–16:6)

David appoints Levites to carry ark, keep the gates, and sing (16:4–7)
The psalm of thanks, praise, and song (16:8–36)
David appoints priests and Levites to service (16:37–42)

The people and David go to their homes (16:43)

Davidic covenant (17:1–27)

‡Figure adapted from *OTUOT*, 709.

> These things happened so that the scripture would be fulfilled: "Not one of his bones will be broken" **[Ps 34:20(21 H/33:21 G)]** and, as another scripture says, "They will look on the one they have pierced" **[Zech 12:10]**. (John 19:36–37)

The context of Ps 34 provides both help and puzzlement. The one whose bones are not broken is the righteous one (Ps 34:19[20 H]). The psalmist speaks of Yahweh rescuing the righteous one—it is in this sense that his bones will be unbroken (34:20[21 H]). A clue to John's allusion comes by considering a deeper context with overlapping imagery the psalmist may have used and that John has in view. The command to not break any bones of the Passover lamb (Exod 12:10, 46; Num 9:12) connects the logic of Ps 34:20[21 H] and John 19:36.[36]

The death of the Messiah in John with no bones broken brings a sense of closure to John the baptizer's statements: "Look, the Lamb of God, who takes away the sin of the world!" (John 1:29) and "Look, the Lamb of God!" (1:36).

36. The passive verb "will not be broken" matches in Ps 33:21 LXX [34:20 E/21 H] and John 19:36, apparently based on the active command in Exod 12:10, 46; Num 9:12. See "συντρίβω," LEH 596; BDAG 976. So also Köstenberger, "Exodus in John," 106; Hays, *Echoes of Scripture in the Gospels*, 317; Menken, *OT Quotations*, 148–52.

This also helps make sense of why John would build his crucifixion account around the alternate Judean time of the slaughter of the Passover lambs at the temple in John 19:14, 31 versus the Galilean timing used in Mark 14:12.[37] John takes good advantage of the dual systems of dating and sets the death of the Messiah at the very time Judean Passover lambs were being slaughtered. And that is why it is necessary to observe that he was pierced. None of his bones were broken. In this way deep vertical context can make sense of some very difficult uses of scripture.

In sum, it is easy to agree with the emphasis on studying horizontal context. This chapter has tried to demonstrate that responsible interpretation of scripture also must attend to vertical context.

Study Questions

1. In your own words, what is the choice at issue in this chapter?
2. What is horizontal context?
3. What is vertical context?
4. What are biblical allusions and how do they work?
5. What is an interpretive blend? What factors need to be considered to explain an interpretive blend?
6. Why are synoptic contexts within Israel's scriptures connected by vertical contexts?
7. What is an interpretive network and how does it work?
8. Select two kinds of vertical context discussed in this chapter and illustrate them with an example from scripture explained in your own words—the examples can be drawn from this chapter.

---

37. See m. Zebaḥim 1:3; cf. 1:1. The Galileans would bring Passover lambs to be slaughtered under a different designation (well-being or purification offering) since the Judeans did not celebrate the Passover until the next day. Because the fourteenth day of the Galilean calendar corresponds to the thirteenth day of the Judean calendar—used at the temple—Galileans would need to use a different sacrificial designation for their Passover sacrifices. "The Passover offering . . . without the appropriate designation, R. Joshua deems it valid, *as if it was slaughtered on the thirteenth*" (m. Zebaḥim 1:3, emphasis added). See Instone-Brewer, "Jesus's Last Passover," 122–23; Hoehner, "Chronological Aspects," 249–50; Casey, "Date of the Passover Sacrifices," 245; Thomas, "Examination of the Last Supper," 79–85; Schnabel, *Jesus in Jerusalem*, 146–47.

CHAPTER 5

BIBLICAL VERSUS EXTRABIBLICAL RELATIONSHIPS

The biblical authors did not live within a vacuum. As the authors of both testaments wrestled with the meaning of what God had already said in scripture, they were often part of interpretive communities. Beyond those interpretive communities were others who wrestled with the same texts or similar ideas. And beyond that, the biblical authors lived within a larger cultural context where even those who did not share their faith in the God of Israel still wrestled with larger ideals of what is right, what is good, and how to best pursue those ideals.

When it comes to studying both the Old and New Testaments, there is a staggering amount of background materials that helps to shed light on the everyday life and culture of the biblical world. Although knowledge of these background materials is not necessary for understanding the basic message of scripture, it is vital for gaining a fuller sense of what the biblical authors are trying to communicate—including their interpretation of earlier scriptures. Therefore, an important element of studying any citation or possible allusion is exploring how extrabiblical literature engages with that same donor text.

We have already discussed how some scholars appeal to the hermeneutical assumptions (Chapter 1) and exegetical methods (Chapter 2) of Second Temple Jewish literature to explain how the New Testament authors use the Old Testament. By contrast, we have argued that scripture's use of scripture establishes the foundation for both the hermeneutical assumptions and the exegetical methods that later biblical authors of both testaments use when engaging scripture. But this conclusion does not eliminate the value of extrabiblical literature for the study of the Bible's use of the Bible. Instead, it raises the specific issue of what role extrabiblical literature plays in understanding how later authors of scripture use earlier scripture when an extrabiblical text uses the same biblical text. While this issue is more pressing when it comes to how the New Testament authors use the Old Testament (as will be explained below), it also plays a role when studying the Old Testament use of the Old Testament.

THE CHOICE

The choice in this chapter is whether biblical or extrabiblical parallels should be prioritized when studying how a biblical author interprets Scripture. Because of the nature of this choice, it will help to begin with the debate surrounding the New Testament.

Scholars differ on the extent to which noncanonical texts are necessary or helpful for interpreting scripture. Some contend that such extrabiblical texts are essential for understanding how the New Testament authors use and interpret the Old Testament. Richard Longenecker is a well-known advocate of this position. He asserts that "it is *impossible* to give a fair hearing to the exegesis of the New Testament without also interacting with the various exegetical presuppositions and conventions found in the writings of Early Judaism—whether it be those found in the distinctive Dead Sea texts themselves, in the other pseudepigraphal and apocalyptic writings of Second Temple Judaism, or in the later rabbinic codifications of earlier Pharisaic teaching."[1] For Longenecker, the starting point for understanding how the New Testament authors use the Old Testament is careful study of not only extrabiblical Jewish texts but also the exegetical presuppositions and techniques found in those texts.

Following a similar approach, Herbert Bateman IV asserts in his study of Hebrews 1:5–13 that one cannot rightly understand what the author is doing with the Old Testament without understanding Jewish exegetical practices. After exploring Hebrews's use of the Old Testament through the lens of Second Temple Jewish hermeneutical practices (with particular emphasis on the so-called seven rules of Hillel), Bateman concludes: "The Holy Spirit moves and allows the author of Hebrews to use first century Jewish hermeneutical practices so that he might clarify, emphasize, and recontextualize the theological force of certain Old Testament citations as they are applicable to the one whom God called his Son."[2] Although Bateman does caution against overemphasizing the significance of such Jewish parallels, his approach strongly suggests the necessity of understanding Jewish hermeneutics for grasping Hebrews's use of the Old Testament.[3]

1. Longenecker, *Biblical Exegesis*, xxii (emphasis mine).
2. Bateman, *Early Jewish Hermeneutics*, 245. Also see idem, *Hebrews*, 59–60.
3. For a diagram of Bateman's approach, see fn. 12 in Chapter 2 above (p. 28).

By contrast, Michael Vlach argues that scholars who emphasize the necessity of Second Temple Jewish hermeneutical practices are often motivated by their conclusion that New Testament authors consistently use the Old Testament in noncontextual ways. But since closer examination of the New Testament use of the Old Testament reveals the authors did in fact use the Old Testament contextually, the need for appealing to first-century Jewish exegetical practices dissipates. Vlach affirms the conclusion of Paul Feinberg, who asserts that "If one is careful in the exegesis of the prediction and its fulfillment, paying particular attention to antecedent scripture and theology, *pesher* and *pesher midrash*, or any similar hermeneutical approach will not be needed."[4] Thus Vlach sees little if any need or benefit from drawing upon first-century Jewish exegetical practices to illuminate the New Testament use of the Old Testament.

We believe that there is a mediating position between these two extremes. As Doug Moo rightly notes, "the degree of influence of Jewish exegetical methods on New Testament procedure has often been considerably exaggerated. A vast gulf separates the often fantastic, purely verbal exegeses of the rabbis from the generally sober and clearly contextually oriented interpretations found in the New Testament."[5] Yet he goes on to note further that "study of Jewish exegetical procedures may help to explain what the New Testament authors sometimes do with scripture and why they do it; and it shows that Jesus and the writers of the New Testament often used methods that would have been familiar and acceptable to many of their contemporaries."[6]

It is certainly possible that a biblical author's engagement with a donor text has been influenced in some degree by extrabiblical literature. As Rosner notes, "Later portions of Scripture, and not just post-Biblical Jewish writings, may have mediated earlier portions of Scripture to Paul. In practice, whether the critical influence came directly from the Pentateuch, or the Prophets and Writings, or Jewish moral teaching may be difficult to determine. The stream of a given moral tradition may have flowed a fair way within the Scriptures before passing through Jewish moral teaching on its way to Paul."[7] That is to say, turning too quickly to extrabiblical literature may prevent the interpreter from seeing how the donor text has been further developed within scripture itself before it ever enters the streams of extrabiblical literature.

The ever-growing canonical consciousness seen within the biblical writings

4. Feinberg, "Hermeneutics," 116, cited in Vlach, *Old in the New*, 28.
5. Moo, "Problem of *Sensus Plenior*," 193.
6. Ibid., 194.
7. Rosner, *Paul*, 49, cited in Ciampa, *Presence and Function*, 23 n. 74.

shows that biblical parallels are more determinative than any other resources available to biblical authors. At the same time, an organic view of revelation means that investigating parallels from the biblical author's context can strengthen responsible interpretation of scripture.[8] The trick is how to make the best use of parallels from the historical context while prioritizing the biblical relationships themselves.

When it comes to the Old Testament, a one-size-fits-all approach to studying scriptural exegesis within Israel's scriptures in light of ancient Near Eastern literature offers less promise than handling things genre by genre, scroll by scroll, and case by case. Legal collections from competing ancient cultures offer a different kind of interpretive help than royal propaganda or mythological inscriptions or wisdom texts, for example. Of course, when it comes to proposed ancient Near Eastern parallels, it must be remembered that those parallels are not interacting with Old Testament scripture. Competing ancient Near Eastern texts rarely even acknowledge Israel, let alone its scriptures or faith traditions. This is entirely different from the Second Temple Jewish context of the New Testament that is dominated by interpreting Israel's scriptures. As a result, ancient Near Eastern parallels can only provide a point of comparison and contrast with how Old Testament authors engage similar themes or concepts.

When it comes to exploring the Old Testament use of the Old Testament, priority must be given to how other Old Testament texts interact with the donor text(s), as well as how later New Testament authors interpret the donor text. After working through the biblical context and connections, attention should then be directed to relevant ancient Near Eastern texts that address similar ideas/concepts.

One major problem stems from long prioritizing comparisons of New Testament and Second Temple Jewish exegetical methods while ignoring how both of these may rely upon exegesis within Israel's scriptures. The authors of the New Testament and authors of Second Temple Jewish literature both carefully studied Israel's scriptures. In a large number of cases, the use of scripture within Israel's scriptures provided models for exegesis of scripture in the New Testament and Second Temple Jewish literature. Similar exegetical tendencies may, at times, be a matter of coincidence when both sets of later authors are working out exegetical strategies that are commonplace within Israel's scriptures. This still leaves room to acknowledge the much rarer occurrence of exegetical tendencies shared by the New Testament and Second Temple Jewish literature but not evident in the Old Testament (see Figure 2-B in Chapter 2).

8. See Athas, *Bridging*, 5.

Thus when studying how the biblical author is interacting with scripture, the starting point must be how other *biblical* authors interact with the same or related donor text(s). Then and only then should one consult extrabiblical literature for insight into the larger exegetical and hermeneutical context in which the biblical author lived. Comparison of exegetical tendencies of New Testament authors and Second Temple Jewish literature needs to proceed in the light of exegesis within Israel's scriptures. In many cases where the New Testament and Second Temple Jewish interpretive traditions focus on the same Old Testament text, there will be contrasting rather than equivalent interpretive outcomes. Never prejudge outcomes. The primary value of researching Second Temple Jewish interpretive traditions is to reveal interpretive paths not taken by the authors of the New Testament. As such, they often provide a helpful reference point to compare and contrast how the biblical author engages with the donor text.

DIFFICULTIES

Perhaps the most noteworthy difficulty is establishing dates for extrabiblical literature. If one cannot conclude with some measure of confidence that the extrabiblical literature in view was contemporaneous with or written before the biblical author, that should be a red flag. This caution is especially necessary when it comes to the value of rabbinic literature for studying the New Testament use of the Old Testament. One must be extremely cautious in attempting to use potential parallels discovered in texts that date hundreds of years after the New Testament to illuminate how a biblical author is engaging scripture. Careful scholarship has demonstrated that at least some of the interpretive traditions present in the rabbinic literature were already present and known before and during the New Testament period. But in many cases it is impossible to demonstrate that a rabbinic interpretation of an Old Testament text was current or known during the period when the New Testament authors were writing (see further the discussion below under rabbinic texts).

A second difficulty is the availability of such extrabiblical literature to the biblical author(s). Simply demonstrating with reasonable confidence that the extrabiblical literature existed when the biblical author wrote is no guarantee that the biblical author was aware of its existence. We simply do not know the extent to which the surviving extrabiblical literature was known, so we must be cautious in concluding that a biblical author was familiar with a specific extrabiblical text. Even if one determines that a biblical author is familiar with ideas, themes, arguments, or interpretations found in a particular extrabiblical text, that does not automatically mean he was familiar with the specific document in question. He may simply be aware of that idea or interpretation "in the air" of his intellectual and cultural context.

A final difficulty is the danger of misunderstanding the proposed parallel if the modern interpreter does not understand the context of that potential parallel. Indeed, this was one of Samuel Sandmel's central concerns when he warned against "parallelomania," which he defined as "that extravagance among scholars which first overdoes the supposed similarity in passages and then proceeds to describe source and derivation as if implying literary connection flowing in an inevitable or predetermined direction."[9] Simply identifying a potential parallel itself is not enough. One must make the effort to understand how the proposed parallel fits within its own literary and historical context before assessing its relevance to how a biblical author is using the same biblical text or engaging with a similar biblical concept. Only then can one accurately compare and contrast how the donor text is used in that extrabiblical text with how a biblical author uses that same donor text.

Studying the ancient context of scripture is an important part of the interpretive process. But one must understand the limits of what extrabiblical texts can tell us about how the biblical authors use scripture. The dangers of "parallelomania" remain as real as when Sandmel first warned against it decades ago. The interpreter must be careful not to overstate potential dependence or connections between scripture and extrabiblical texts, while at the same time recognizing the value of these texts for comparison and contrast with how the donor text is interpreted within scripture itself.

EXTRABIBLICAL RELATIONSHIPS

Having a basic grasp of the different kinds of extrabiblical literature is helpful for any student of the Bible. Students will do well to take courses that introduce and work through major bodies of ancient literature of the biblical context. Students are encouraged to consult introductions for a general knowledge of these ancient sources. The purpose of this section is limited to explaining the significance of each body of literature for the study of the Bible's use of the Bible.

Interpreting any part of the Old Testament requires paying attention to its ancient Near Eastern context. This applies to passages that include interpretive interventions with earlier scriptures.

---

9. Sandmel, "Parallelomania," 1.

We also want to note that while many of the resources discussed below are available in various digital tools, some important resources remain accessible only in print form. Students should not make the mistake of neglecting these print resources simply because of their format.

The student will do well to make use of the standard reference collections of ancient Near Eastern literature. Theological libraries typically include: *Ancient Near Eastern Texts Relating to the Old Testament* (*ANET*), *The Ancient Near East in Pictures Relating to the Old Testament* (*ANEP*), *Context of Scripture* (*COS*), *Treaty, Law, and Covenant in the Ancient Near East (TLC)*, *Law Collections from Mesopotamia and Asia Minor* (Roth), and *The Persian Empire* (*PE*). Some of the shorter user-friendly collections of ancient literature are also helpful, such as *Stories from Ancient Canaan* (*SFAC*), *Myths from Mesopotamia* (*MFM*), *The Raging Torrent: Historical Inscriptions from Assyria and Babylonia relating to Ancient Israel* (*RT*), *Assyrian and Babylonian Chronicles* (*ABC*), and *Bound for Exile: Israelites and Judeans Under Imperial Yoke* (*BFE*). In the case of royal inscriptions of Mesopotamia, while the series The Royal Inscriptions of the Neo-Assyrian Period (RINAP) is extremely well done, older collections including *Ancient Records of Assyria and Babylonia* (*ARAB*) and *Assyrian Royal Inscriptions* (*ARI*) are accessible online.[10]

In many cases the better commentaries will cite standard collections of ancient Near Eastern writings listed in the previous paragraph, as well as others. When these citations relate to the donor text or receptor text, the student needs to take the time to look up the ancient writings and study them in their contexts. Though the present chapter only has space for brief illustrations in the cases below, a student who neglects the ancient context risks misinterpreting scriptural interpretation within Israel's scripture.

When it comes to an overview of the extrabiblical Jewish literature that is relevant for studying the New Testament, consult *Ancient Texts for New Testament Studies* (*ATNTS*), which not only summarizes each body of literature but also gives extensive bibliography through 2005. The *Handbook on the New Testament Use of the Old Testament* (*HNTUOT*) contains an extended chapter on relevant sources of Jewish literature relevant to scripture's use of scripture.[11] A good starting point for finding citations and allusions in extrabiblical literature is *Biblical Quotations and Allusions in Second Temple Jewish Literature* (*BQASTJL*). One can look up the Old Testament text under consideration and quickly find citations and allusions in Jewish literature, or look up a Jewish

10. *ARI* is available at archive.org and *ARAB* at https://isac.uchicago.edu/sites/default/files/uploads/shared/docs/ancient_records_assyria1.pdf.

11. See *HNTUOT*, 103–32.

text and see if there are any proposed citations/allusions to an Old Testament text. It even contains a section on "Uncertain Quotations and Allusions" that identifies less certain parallels. The *Commentary on the New Testament Use of the Old Testament* (*CNTUOT*) contains an index of every reference to each of the literature groups discussed below; by consulting this resource, the student can discover the New Testament text where an extrabiblical text is mentioned or discussed. Students should also consult the relevant articles in *Dictionary of the New Testament Use of the Old Testament* (*DNTUOT*) for each body of literature discussed below, as well as the scripture index of each body of literature, to discover where specific texts are mentioned or discussed. Good scholarly commentaries will also regularly mention extrabiblical Jewish texts that may be relevant for studying how a New Testament author is using scripture.

The earliest texts that may indicate interpretation of the Old Testament are translations of those texts. Differences between the Masoretic Text (MT) and the **Septuagint** (LXX) may simply indicate that the translator was working from a different Hebrew parent text (*Vorlage*), as discussed in Chapter 3. At times, however, the presence of differences may instead reflect an interpretive decision on the part of the translator. The definitive critical edition of the LXX is the multivolume project known as the Göttingen Septuagint, which provides not only a critical text but attempts to produce a comprehensive critical apparatus. Unfortunately, not every Old Testament book has been completed yet. The most commonly used contemporary edition of the LXX is Alfred Rahlfs, *Septuaginta*, originally produced in 1935 and most recently updated in 2006. It contains the complete text of the Greek Old Testament and a critical apparatus. Though the Cambridge LXX is a diplomatic versus an eclectic text, its thorough apparatus can be valuable and is available online.[12] With respect to English translations of the LXX, students should consult both Brenton (*The Septuagint Version of the Old Testament*) and *A New English Translation of the Septuagint* (NETS), which are both available online.[13]

Although not written down until after the New Testament period, the **targums** reflect interpretive traditions that often predate the first century CE. The standard critical edition is the four-volume *The Bible in Aramaic Based on Old Manuscripts and Printed Texts* (*TBA*). The standard English translation is *The Aramaic Bible: The Targums* (ArBib), which currently stands at twenty-two volumes. This resource helpfully italicizes interpretive additions to the Hebrew text. Since the targums are translations of the Old Testament, simply look

12. See archive.org.
13. See http://ccat.sas.upenn.edu/nets/edition/.

up the Old Testament text in the corresponding volume. Please consult the Resource Guide 5-E at the end of this chapter on targumic plusses.

The **Samaritan Pentateuch** can also provide a window into early interpretation of the Torah. An updated critical edition is partially available (see SP-G and SP-L). The standard critical edition is *Der hebräische Pentateuch der Samaritaner* (SP), which is available online.[14] A side-by-side comparison of the SP and MT in Hebrew is available in *The Torah: Jewish and Samaritan Versions Compared* (*TJSVC*). For a helpful side-by-side English translation that highlights differences between the SP and the MT, consult *The Israelite Samaritan Version of the Torah: First English Translation Compared with the Masoretic Version* (SP-Eng); portions of this book can be accessed through Google Books.

The **Dead Sea Scrolls** are valuable for both the biblical and sectarian texts. For biblical texts, consult *The Biblical Qumran Scrolls* (*BQS*) to compare the Hebrew text with the MT—available online.[15] A basic English-based equivalent is the Dead Sea Scrolls Bible Translations website,[16] which uses color coding to show differences. Also see the English translation in *The Dead Sea Scrolls Bible* (*DSSB*). For nonbiblical sectarian texts, *The Dead Sea Scrolls Study Edition* (*DSSSE*) contains the Hebrew text and an English translation on facing pages. Scripture indexes can be found in *A Catalog of Biblical Passages in the Dead Sea Scrolls* (*CBPDSS*) and at the back of Joseph A. Fitzmyer, *The Dead Sea Scrolls* (FDSS). Dan Gurtner's article on the "Dead Sea Scrolls, OT Use in" in the *DNTUOT* also provides a helpful list of Qumran manuscripts of Old Testament texts cited in the New Testament, as well as Old Testament texts cited in the both the New Testament and the sectarian texts of the Dead Sea Scrolls.[17]

For the **Apocrypha**, students should consult the Greek texts of the LXX (see above) for the text itself. An English translation is available online.[18] Students should consult *BQASTJL* for citations and allusions in these books. The collection known as the **Old Testament Pseudepigrapha** is most easily accessed in the two-volume *The Old Testament Pseudepigrapha* (*OTP*), along with the corresponding *A Scripture Index to Charlesworth's The Old Testament Pseudepigrapha* (*OTPSI*). At times it may also be worth consulting *Pseudepigrapha of the Old Testament* (*POT*), since volume 2 contains a topical index of both the Apocrypha and Pseudepigrapha.[19] Additional Old

14. See archive.org.
15. See https://archive.org/details/TheBiblicalQumranScrolls/mode/2up?view=theater.
16. The website is http://dssenglishbible.com/.
17. See *DNTUOT*, 173–76.
18. See the NRSVue at BibleGateway.com.
19. Available online for free at https://www.ccel.org/ccel/charles/otpseudepig.html.

Testament pseudepigraphal texts are available in *Old Testament Pseudepigrapha: More Noncanonical Scriptures* (*OTPMNS*), which helpfully contains a scripture index. Also worth consulting is the table of Old Testament texts cited in both the New Testament and the Pseudepigrapha found in Dan Gurtner's article "Pseudepigrapha: Comparison with the New Testament Use of the OT" in *DNTUOT*.[20]

As a contemporary of the New Testament writers, **Philo** provides a helpful window into a Hellenistic strand of first-century Jewish thought. Philo offers his own interpretation of virtually all of Torah. The ten-volume collection in the Loeb Classical Library (LCL), along with the two supplemental volumes, provides the Greek text and English translations on facing pages; note that volumes 1 and 10 contain scripture indexes. *The Works of Philo* translated by C. D. Yonge is handy for quick reference to the English text and includes a scripture index. A searchable online database is available through Biblindex.[21]

The first-century Jewish historian **Josephus** is a valuable source not only for the history of the Second Temple period, but also for how he himself interpreted scripture. The ten-volume Loeb Classical Library edition has the Greek text and English translation on facing pages. *Josephus: The Complete Works* is an accessible English translation that includes a scripture index.

As noted above, when dealing with **rabbinic literature** (by definition post-70 CE) students must exercise caution. Although these texts were written after the New Testament period, they do contain some exegetical and interpretive traditions that already existed during the New Testament period. Because this body of literature often has limited relevance to understanding how a New Testament author engages an Old Testament text, this is an area that can be skipped if one is pressed for time.

An excellent starting point for finding rabbinic references that are most relevant for the New Testament is *A Scripture Index to Rabbinic Literature* (*SIRL*). Two works by David Instone-Brewer are especially helpful for identifying material in rabbinic sources that may have its origins during or before the New Testament period: *Traditions of the Rabbis from the Era of the New Testament. Vol. 1, Prayer and Agriculture* (*TRENT1*) and *Traditions of the Rabbis from the Era of the New Testament. Vol. 2a, Feasts and Sabbaths* (*TRENT2a*). Both volumes contain scripture indexes. One of the most well-known sources for rabbinic references that may shed light on specific New Testament passages is *Kommentar zum Neuen Testament aus Talmud und Midrasch*, commonly

20. See *DNTUOT*, 664–65.

21. The website is https://www.biblindex.org/en. Simply select the "Patristic Tools" menu and click "Patristic authors" to find Philo of Alexandria.

referred to as Strack-Billerbeck (Str-B).[22] Recently it has been translated into English as *A Commentary on the New Testament from the Talmud and Midrash* (Str-BEng). Before using this tool, however, the student should read the "Introduction to the English Translation" that provides helpful background for this resource as well as important guidelines for using this resource properly.

Since the **Mishnah** (written around 200 CE) contains oral traditions that date back to the New Testament period, it is the most consistently valuable of the rabbinic sources for comparing scripture's use of scripture with Jewish interpretation. The standard Hebrew text is the six-volume Mishnah edited by Blackman.[23] An accessible English translation by Danby contains a scripture index that indicates where Old Testament texts are mentioned and is available online.[24]

While at times other rabbinic texts—such as the Tosefta, Babylonian Talmud, Jerusalem/Palestinian Talmud, and midrashic literature—may prove helpful for studying scripture's use of scripture, on the whole they are less valuable for this particular area of study. In the vast majority of cases, the resources already mentioned provide more than sufficient coverage of these rabbinic materials. Those who wish to go deeper into these rabbinic resources should consult the discussion in *HNTUOT*.[25]

These suggested resources should provide helpful insights into the ways that the authors of this extrabiblical literature interacted with the same Old Testament scriptures as the biblical authors. But primary consideration must be given to scripture's own use of scripture as a baseline even to evaluate extrabiblical literature and any potential insight such literature may provide.

CASE STUDIES

CASE STUDY 1—THE RELEVANCE OF ANCIENT NEAR EASTERN LITERATURE

Responsible interpretation of exegesis within Israel's scripture requires studying ancient Near Eastern context. Every case needs to be studied individually based on available evidence (Resource Guide 5-A). No formula or set of steps can be applied in a mechanical manner. Every case is different, subtle, and highly contested.

22. Available online at https://trove.nla.gov.au/work/797911.

23. Blackman, *Mishnayoth*.

24. Available online at https://archive.org/details/DanbyMishnah/page/806/mode/2up?view=theater. *The Oxford Annotated Mishnah* (see m. in Abbreviations) did not update Danby's scripture index.

25. *HNTUOT*, 118–21.

Resource Guide 5-A: Ancient Near Eastern Context

Where to Start:

- Look up ancient writings referred to in the better biblical commentaries

Suggestions to Identify Ancient Near Eastern Context to the Old Testament for English Bible and Hebrew Bible Students:

- Primeval Narrative: *MFM*
- Legal and covenantal contexts: Roth, *TLC*
- Conquest and Judges: *SFAC*
- Hebrew kingdoms and prophets: RINAP, *RT, ABC, ARAB, ARI, MFM*
- Exile and return: *BFE, PE, TAD*
- Comprehensive collections: *ANET, ANEP, COS*

The earliest version of the eighth military campaign of Sennacherib—made in the same year (691 BCE)—though somewhat unusual, offers a helpful point of comparison for the use of earlier scriptural traditions within the historical narratives of Israel's scriptures.

The Neo-Assyrian scribes enhanced Sennacherib's battle against the Elamites with imagery from several myths: the creation myth known by its first words *Enuma Elish*, "When on high" (second millennium BCE?); Erra and Ishum (eleventh to eight centuries BCE); and the prologue to the Law Collection of Hammurabi (ca. 1755 BCE). The allusions are probable based on rare language such as the use of "veins" as a kind of metonymy replacing "blood" in the standard stock phrases of the royal inscriptions.[26] Notice the Akkadian verbal parallels for all seven of these allusions in Table 5-B.[27]

While Sennacherib's boasting of horrific violence is commonplace, sustained

26. The conventional phraseology in Assyrian royal inscriptions of the enemy's "blood" (*dāmu*) flowing is replaced by the rare poetic term "veins" or "blood of veins" (*umunnû*) (RINAP 3.1:183 [22. vi.4]). See Weissert, "Creating," 196. This term appears in Erra and Ishum concerning Erra's savage acts in Babylon. See "*umunnû*," *CAD* 20:155.

27. The allusions in Table 5-B are based on Weissert, "Creating a Political Climate," 193–95. This discussion is indebted to Schnittjer, "Overview of Composite Citations." Translations and transliterations from: RINAP 3.1:181–83 (22.v.17–19, 28b–30, 67–75, vi.2–12), Akkadian from Luckenbill, *Annals*, 41 (v.18) (Sennacherib's royal inscriptions); Lambert, *Babylonian Creation Myths*, 70–71, 86–93 (Enuma Elish); *COS* 1.113:412, emphasis added, Akkadian from Cagni, *L'epopea di Erra*, 108 (Erra and Ishum); Roth, 76–77 (i.35–36) (Legal Collection of Hammurabi). Thank you to Nancy Erickson for feedback on the Akkadian parallels.

TABLE 5-B: Mythic Allusions in the Account of Sennacherib's Eight Campaign

Sennacherib's Royal Inscription	Enuma Elish
On my eighth campaign, after Šūzubu (Mušēzib-Marduk) had rebelled and the citizens of Babylon, evil gallû-demons [*gallê*], had locked the city gates, they plotted to wage war. . . . The Babylonians inappropriately placed him [*a-na la si-ma-ti-šu*] (back) on the throne (and) entrusted him with the lordship of the land of Sumer and Akkad. . . . I prayed to the deities . . . the gods who support me, for victory over (my) strong enemy and they immediately [*ur-ru-ḫi-iš*] heeded my prayers (and) came to my aid. I raged up like a lion, then put on armor (and) placed a helmet suitable for combat on my head [*a-pi-ra ra-šu-ú-a*]. . . . I took in my hand the mighty bow that the god Aššur had granted to me (and) I grasped in my hand an arrow that cuts off life [*pa-ri-iʾ nap-šá-ti*]. I roared loudly like a storm (and) thundered like the god Adad against all of the troops of the wicked enemies. . . . I slit their throats like sheep (and thus) cut off their precious lives like thread. Like a flood in full spate after a seasonal rainstorm, I made their blood [of the veins] flow [*ù-mun-ni-šú-nu*] over the broad earth. The swift thoroughbreds harnessed to my chariot plunged into floods of their blood (just) like the river ordeal. The wheels of my chariot, which lays criminals and villains low [*sa-pi-na-at rag-gi ù ṣe-ni*], were bathed in blood and gore. I filled the plain with the corpses of their warriors like grass. I cut off (their) lips and (thus) destroyed their pride. I cut off their hands like the stems of cucumbers in season.	The throng of devils [*gal-le-e*] who went as grooms at her [Tiāmat's] right hand . . . (IV.116) And you have improperly appointed him [*a-na la si-ma-ti-šu*] to the rank of Anuship [chief god] (IV.82) Soon [*ur-ru-ḫi-iš*] you will tread on the neck of Tiāmat (II.146, 148) And on his head [*a-pi-ir ra-šu-uš-šu*] he [Bel] wore an aura of terror (IV.58) They gave him an irresistible weapon that overwhelms the foe: (They said,) "Go, cut Tiāmat's throat [*nap-šá-tuš pu-ru-ʾ-ma*] (IV.30–31) **Erra and Ishum** You have made the blood flow like water in the drains of the public squares. You have opened their veins [*ù-mun-na-šú-nu*] and let the river carry off (their blood). (4.34–36) **Law Collection of Hammurabi** Hammurabi, the pious prince, who venerates the gods, to make justice prevail in the land, to abolish the wicked and the evil [*raggam u ṣēnam ana ḫulluqim*], to prevent the strong from oppressing the weak, to rise like the sun-god Shamash over all humankind, to illuminate the land. (i.35–36)

literary allusions to myths in Neo-Assyrian royal inscriptions are relatively rare.[28] The unusual enhancements suggest intentional propaganda to essentially cover over a military failure with grandiose imagery. The same battle recounted in Table 5-B is presented as follows in the standard Babylonian chronicles: "Mushezib-Marduk . . . effected an Assyrian retreat."[29]

Later copies of this inscription, after Sennacherib eventually defeated Mushezib-Marduk, do not always include the mythic imagery.[30] Weissert notes that part of the reason for the abridgement was likely due to space on the stone tablets versus the hexagonal prisms. But he also thinks the scribes may have removed the embarrassing mythic enhancements of a battle that Sennacherib lost.[31]

The unusual use of mythic traditions in Sennacherib's royal inscriptions can help us evaluate potential use of traditions in Exod 2. Interpreters routinely compare the birth narrative of Moses to several ancient Near East traditions, especially the legend of Sargon of Akkad (ca. 2300 BCE).

> My mother, a high priestess, conceived me, in secret she bore me. She placed me in a reed basket, with bitumen she caulked my hatch. She abandoned me to the river from which I could not escape. (5–7)[32]

And yet the account of Moses's birth and infancy contains several nonexegetical (literary) allusions to Genesis and Exodus, including a phrase from creation, "ark," which appears twenty-eight times in the account of Noah's flood and twice in Exod 3, and the term "reeds" (all emphases signify verbal parallels).[33]

> And God **saw** the light **that** it **was good** [וַיַּרְא אֱלֹהִים אֶת־הָאוֹר כִּי־טוֹב]. (Gen 1:4a AT; cf. vv. 10, 12, 18, 21, 25, 31)

> So make yourself an ark [תֵּבָה] of cypress wood. (6:14)

---

28. See Weissert, "Creating a Political Climate," 195–96.

29. *ABC* 1 iii 13, 18 (p. 80).

30. The hexagonal Jerusalem Prism of Sennacherib follows the Taylor Prism with its mythic allusions (RINAP 3.1:198–200 [23.v.9–11, 20b–22, 57–64, 77b–vi.9]). A more fragmentary hexagonal prism basically follows the Taylor prism (3.1:154–55 [18.v. 11–vi.1]). The abridged versions of Sennacherib's campaigns on the large stone tablet from Nineveh (3.1:224 [34.46–5a]) and on two stone tablet fragments presumably from Nineveh in the Berlin Museum (3.1:231–32 [35.44–52]) do not include the mythic allusions.

31. See Weissert, "Creating a Political Climate," 197–202.

32. Lewis, *The Sargon Legend*, 24–25. Much discussion surrounds the sense of the term here translated "high priestess." See "*ēntu* b" *CAD* 4:173.

33. On "ark," see "תֵּבָה" Even-Shoshan, 1218.

> The best of pharaoh's officers are drowned in the reeds sea [*yam suph* יַם סוּף]. (Exod 15:4b AT)

> And she [Moses's mother] **saw** him [Moses] **that** he **was good**" [וַתֵּרֶא אֹתוֹ כִּי־טוֹב הוּא]. . . . When she could no longer hide him she took an ark [תֵּבָה] of papyrus and sealed it with tar and pitch. She set the child in it and she set it in the reeds [*suph* סוּף] on the bank of the Nile. (2:2b–3 AT)

The evidence suggests that even if the story of Moses has been organized by motifs of the Sargon legend, the narrator's interest in using Genesis and Exodus imagery dominates the story.[34] This kind of use of imagery from other biblical traditions is commonplace in the Hebrew scriptures. This literary interconnectedness is one of many tendencies that sets biblical narrative apart from ancient Near Eastern counterparts.

Ancient Near Eastern legal standards from rival cultures sometimes can help make sense of legal exegesis within Torah. The case law of one who rapes a virgin requires careful consideration (bold signifies verbal parallels).

> **If a man** seduces a virgin **who is not pledged to be married** and sleeps with her, he must pay the bride-price, and she **shall be his wife**. If her father absolutely refuses to give her to him, he must still pay the bride-price for virgins. (Exod 22:16–17[15–16 H])

> **If a man** happens to meet a virgin **who is not pledged to be married** and rapes her and they are discovered, he shall pay her father fifty shekels of silver. **He must marry** the young woman, for he has violated her. He can never divorce her as long as he lives. (Deut 22:28–29)

Many modern interpreters take the law of the rapist in Deut 22 out of context by not reading it with the law of the seducer in Exod 22, which it supplements. Receptor legal standards do not replace but build on donor laws.[35] The father of the virgin who has been sexually assaulted receives the bridal price and he (and his daughter) retain the right to decide if the perpetrator must marry without the possibility of divorce (Deut 22:29) or shall not marry his daughter (Exod 22:17[16 H]). Beginning with ancient interpreters the right of the father (and daughter)

---

34. See Exod 2:3 NET text note.

35. In cases of amplification in the receptor text the details of the donor text do not need to be repeated but are understood. See *OTUOT*, 80–81, 137–38. For an analogous case of amplification in the Law Collection of Hammurabi, see Eichler, "Examples of Restatement," 387–88.

to refuse marriage to the rapist, even while receiving the bridal price, aligns with the prevailing protections for the vulnerable party in the legal standards of Torah. Philo (ca. 20 BCE–50 CE) regards the law of the rapist in Deut 22 as supplementing the law of the seducer in Exod 22 by granting the father the right to refuse or to accept this marriage for his daughter.[36] So too Josephus (ca. 37–100 CE) reads these two laws together granting the father the right to refuse marriage to the culprit even while accepting the bridal price of fifty shekels only mentioned in Deut 22:28–29.[37] The father (and daughter) retaining the right to refuse or accept marriage to the seducer or rapist remained the standard interpretation (cf. b. Ketub. 39b).[38] Other ancient legal standards provide perspective for shocked modern readers—marry her rapist?!—concerning the kinds of circumstances to which they applied as well as the kinds of severe punishments designed to protect the vulnerable party. If the rape were in the context of an elopement, on the analogy of various ancient legal parallels,[39] the father (and daughter) could consent to the marriage and receive the bride-price while the daughter's protections are strengthened by disallowing the husband the right to divorce. Rape is never acceptable in ancient Israel, even while the punishments protect the vulnerable rather than merely enact vengeance inclusive of collateral damage. The Middle Assyrian Laws (ca. 1076 BCE) deny the criminal any decisions, while he pays triple the bridal price and the father decides if they marry as well as the culprit handing over his wife to be raped (§A55 in Roth, 174–75).

The study of the use of earlier scriptures in Deuteronomy or Josh 24 should not neglect the shaping force of ancient Hittite treaties between a suzerain (ruler) and the suzerain's client or subjects (see Table 5-C). A recent reevaluation of the evidence has detected a means by which Hittite treaties overlap Israel's setting in Egypt. The treaty between the Hittite ruler Hattušili and Rameses II was not only written on the walls of the Amon temple in Karnak but was read aloud publicly in many places, including in 1259 BCE in the city of Rameses that Israel helped build (Exod 1:11). This shows how Israel could have been familiar with ancient Hittite treaty forms, whether directly or indirectly.[40]

36. See Philo, "Special Laws," III.69–70 (7:516–19).

37. See Josephus, *Antiquities*, 4.8.23 (4.252b).

38. See Greengus, *Laws in the Bible*, 64, 67; Tigay, *Deuteronomy*, 208. Contra the reading of the radical sectarians in 11QT/11Q19 66.10–11.

39. See Laws of Eshnunna §27 (ca. 1770 BCE) (Roth, 63); Law Collection of Hammurabi §128 (ca. 1750 BCE) (Roth, 105); Hittite Laws §28 (ca. 1500 BCE) (Roth, 221); as pointed out by Fleishman, "Shechem and Dinah," 15–17, 25. On legal consensual (seduction) and nonconsensual (rape) relations, see Darabi, "Provisions," 525–27. And on coercive sexual actions in biblical narrative, see Sharon, "Moral and Ethical," esp. 278–80.

40. See Johnston, "What Biblical Scholars Should Know," forthcoming; idem, "The Writing/Reading/Hearing of the Stone Tablet Covenant," 93–99.

Table 5-C: Comparing Ancient Hittite Suzerain Treaty and Biblical Covenant Forms[‡]

Hittite Treaties Late Second Millennium BCE	Hittite version of Treaty between Hattušil III and Ramesses II, ca. 1259 BCE	Egyptian version of Treaty between Ramesses II and Hattušil III, ca. 1259 BCE	Deuteronomy	Joshua 24
—	—	framing introduction	—	framing introduction (vv. 1–2a)
title/preamble	title/preamble	title/preamble	title (1:1–5)	title (v. 2b)
historical prologue	historical prologue	historical prologue	historical prologue (1:6–3:29)	historical prologue (vv. 2c–13)
stipulations	stipulations	stipulations	stipulations (4:1–26:19)	stipulations (vv. 14–15)
deposit of inscription and reading	—	—	reading (31:9–13) and deposit (31:24–26)	deposit (vv. 26)
witnesses	[lost]	witnesses	witnesses (30:11–20; 31:30–32:1)	witnesses (vv. 22, 27)
blessings and curses	curses and blessings	curses and blessings	blessings (28:1–14) and curses (28:15–68)	blessings (vv. 16–18) and curses (vv. 19–20)
oath and ceremony	—	—	ceremony (27:1–10) and oath (27:11–26)	oath (vv. 21, 24)
	—	additional stipulations	recapitulation (29:1–30:10), song (32), and blessing (33)	vv. 23, 25
	—	framing conclusion	framing conclusion (34)	framing conclusion (v. 28)

[‡] While ancient Hittite treaty forms have much consistency, there are variations. Table based on (with modifications): column 1, *TLC* 2:134; column 2, 1:573–82 (no. 71A); column 3, 1:583–94 (no. 71B); columns 4, 1:898 (no. 83); column 5, 1:906 (no. 84). Also see *TLC* 3:252–55. The idea for this comparison is indebted to Johnston, "What Biblical Scholars Should Know," forthcoming—see chart based on Johnston's research in chart in Schnittjer, *Torah Story*, 219.

The exegetical intervention with the blessing of Judah (Gen 49:8–12) in the Davidic promise sits at the intersection of the covenant's irrevocability and the obligations of the vassal (servant/son or client) (2 Sam 7:14–15).[41] Examples of ancient Hittite irrevocable covenants with obligations have helped interpreters make sense of biblical covenants while setting aside the older mistaken view of unconditional covenants with conditions.[42] The Hittite treaty of Tudhaliya IV with Ulmi-Teshup (Kurunta) in the thirteenth century BCE attests to harsh punishment within a permanent covenant.

> And even if some son or grandson of yours commits treason . . . they shall do to him whatever the king of the land of Ḫatti decides. . . . *But they may not take from him his "house"* (i.e., his dynasty). (*COS* 2.18:104, emphasis added)

This evidence corroborates the irrevocable promise with obligations to David: "When he does wrong I will punish him with *the rod* of mortals and with wounds inflicted by humans. But my covenantal loyalty *shall not depart* from him" (2 Sam 7:14b–15a AT, emphases signify allusions to Gen 49:10).

Responsible interpretation of scriptural exegesis within Israel's scriptures needs to attend to how ancient Near Eastern context bears on the biblical authors.

CASE STUDY 2—ZEAL IN GALATIANS 1:14

Responsible interpretation of New Testament use of scripture needs to consider the Second Temple Jewish context (see Resource Guide 5-D). We have already noted in Chapter 3 that Paul's reference to his preconversion zeal is likely an allusion to the zeal of Phinehas recounted in Num 25:11–13 (emphasis added).

> Phinehas son of Eleazar, the son of Aaron, the priest, has turned my anger away from the Israelites. Since he was as zealous for my honor among them as I am, I did not put an end to them in my zeal. Therefore tell him I am making my covenant of peace with him. [13]He and his descendants will have a covenant of a lasting priesthood, because he was zealous for the honor of his God and made atonement for the Israelites.

41. See Schnittjer, "Blessing of Judah," 24–26.

42. See ibid., 25–26, n. 22; idem, *Old Testament Narrative*, 106; idem, "Your House," 56–58; Block, *Covenant*, 2; Chisholm, *1 & 2 Samuel*, 218–19, 224–25; contra those who confuse the issue by speaking of "unconditional" covenants with conditions, e.g., Brettler, "Israel's Scriptures," 54.

> I was advancing in Judaism beyond many of my own age among my people and was extremely <u>zealous</u> for the traditions of my fathers. (Gal 1:14, emphasis added)

But rather than focus on how Num 25:11–13 is developed later in scripture, a number of scholars fixate on several references to Phinehas's zeal in Second Temple literature.[43]

Resource Guide 5-D: Second Temple Jewish Context

Where to Start:

- Broad indexes: *BQASTJL*, *OTPSI*, *CNTUOT*, *NTUOT*
- Kugel's *Traditions of the Bible*; Levine and Brettler, *The Bible with and without Jesus*
- Look up ancient writings referred to in the better biblical commentaries

Suggestions to Identify Second Temple Jewish Context to the New Testament:

[English Bible Readers]

- Biblical texts: NETS, SP-Eng, *DSSB*, ArBib (see Resources Guide 5-E)
- Nonbiblical texts: *DSSSE*, Apocrypha, *OTP*, m., Yonge's *Philo* and *Josephus*

[Greek New Testament Readers]

- Biblical texts: LXX Göttingen, LXX Cambridge, SP, SP-G, SP-L, *TJSVC*, *BQS*, *TBA*
- Nonbiblical texts: *DSSSE*, LCL Philo and Josephus, *OTP*

> And Mattathias saw this, and he became <u>zealous</u>, and his kidneys became stirred up. And his anger arose in judgment. And running, he slaughtered him on the altar and killed the agent of the king, who was forcing them to sacrifice at that time, and tore down the altar. And he became <u>zealous</u> in the law as Phinees had done against Zambri son of Salom. (1 Macc 2:24–26 NETS, emphasis added)

---

43. For a survey of scriptural contexts building on Phinehas's zeal in Num 25, see Schnittjer, *Torah Story*, 377–79.

> Remember the works of our fathers, which they did in their generations, and receive great glory and an everlasting name. Was not Abraam found faithful in temptation, and it was accounted to him as righteousness. . . . Phinees our father, by becoming zealous with zeal, received a covenant of everlasting priesthood. (1 Macc 2:51–52, 54 NETS, emphasis added)

> He told you about the zeal of Phinehas (4 Macc 18:12 AT)

> And Phinees son of Eleazar is third in glory, since he was zealous in the fear of the Lord and since he stood firm in the turning of the people, in the goodness of the eagerness of his soul; he also made atonement for Israel. (Sir 45:23 NETS, emphasis added)

Scholars like James Dunn interpret Paul's zeal against this Second Temple Jewish backdrop.[44] Indeed, Dunn devotes a total of three sentences to the Old Testament background of zeal in a three-page discussion of Paul's zeal. And even when mentioning such examples, he emphasizes references within Second Temple Jewish sources rather than the Old Testament texts themselves.

Yet what is often overlooked or not given proper attention is the reference to Phinehas's zeal in Ps 106:30–31. In a catalog of Israel's repeated covenant faithlessness, the psalmist notes how Israel provoked Yahweh's anger by yoking themselves to Baal-Peor (Ps 106:28–29, summarizing Num 25:1–6).

> But Phinehas stood up and intervened,
>   and the plague was checked.
> This was credited to him as righteousness
>   for endless generations to come. (Ps 106:30–31, emphasis added).

Although the word "zeal" is not used, the text explicitly refers to Phinehas and his actions to end the plague of judgment sent by Yahweh. But what is especially noteworthy is that the psalmist borrows language from Gen 15:6 to describe the outcome of his actions.

> Abram believed the Lord, and he credited it to him as righteousness. (Gen 15:6, emphasis added)

---

44. See Dunn, *Galatians*, 60–62.

Thus Ps 106:31 portrays Phinehas's zealous actions as an outworking of the same kind of faith that Abraham possessed and, as a result, pronounces the same outcome on Phinehas—it was credited to him as righteousness.[45] Indeed, a closer look at both 1 Macc 2:50–54 and Sir 45:23 (cited above) suggests they too are dependent on a blend of Ps 106:30–31 and Neh 9:8 rather than simply on Gen 15:6.[46]

The likelihood that Paul understood his preconversion zeal for the traditions of his fathers in light of Ps 106:28–31 is further strengthened by the prominent role that his citation of Gen 15:6 plays within the central argument of Gal 3:1–5:1. Given that Ps 106:31 is the only place in the Old Testament other than Gen 15:6 where the phrase "credited to him as righteousness" occurs, it makes sense that Paul was not only aware of this text but that it informed his preconversion self-understanding. As Ciampa helpfully notes, "Although Paul never cites [Ps 106:30–31], its justification language echoing Gen 15:6, tied to *the* figure renowned above all for his zeal for the law makes Phinehas a perfect life-model for the earlier Paul."[47] Recognizing this connection helps the reader see how Paul anticipates his discussion of justification by faith based on Gen 15:6 in Gal 3:1–5:1.

The point of this example is not to deny the value of the various Second Temple Jewish examples where Phinehas's zeal is mentioned. Rather, the point is that in the rush toward such sources, an important Old Testament use of Phinehas (Ps 106:30–31) can either be overlooked entirely or not given its proper weight. Furthermore, the possibility that at least two of the Jewish texts (1 Macc 2:50–54 and Sir 45:23) discussed also show signs of influence from Ps 106 (as well as Neh 9:8) demonstrates the necessity of considering the extent to which extrabiblical texts themselves are dependent on scripture's use of scripture. The Second Temple Jewish examples show the deep imprint that Phinehas's actions left within Israel's heritage, illuminating Paul's larger context. But one must begin with and prioritize scriptural examples (i.e., Ps 106:30–31) as the starting point for understanding Paul's use of zeal before moving on to extrabiblical literature.

CASE STUDY 3—GENESIS 15:6 IN JEWISH LITERATURE

As is well-known, Gen 15:6 is directly cited five times in the New Testament (Rom 4:3, 9, 22; Gal 3:6; Jas 2:23). In addition to the clear allusion to Gen 15:6 in Ps 106:31 noted above, there is also Neh 9:8.

45. See entries on Ps 106:28, 30, 31 in *OTUOTPL*.

46. On the significance of Neh 9:8 in these two passages, see McFadden, *Faith*, 62–63.

47. Ciampa, *Presence and Function*, 110 n. 18 (emphasis original).

> You found his heart faithful to you, and you made a covenant with him to give to his descendants the land of the Canaanites, Hittites, Amorites, Perizzites, Jebusites and Girgashites. You have kept your promise because you are righteous. (Neh 9:8, emphasis added)

Perhaps not surprisingly, Gen 15:6 left a significant mark with Second Temple Jewish literature.[48] A brief look at several examples within their original context illuminates the ways that Gen 15:6 and the related themes of righteousness and faith/faithfulness were understood within the Judaism of Paul's day. Careful study of these extrabiblical Jewish texts reveals some helpful context for the kinds of views that Paul may have been refuting in both Rom 3–4 and Gal 2–4.

A common theme in extrabiblical Jewish writings about Abraham is that he was declared righteous because he faithfully endured when tested.[49] In the previous case study, we noted an allusion to Num 25:11–13 in 1 Macc 2:51–54. In that same text, there is an allusion to Gen 15:6 as well.

> Was not Abraham **found faithful** when tested, and it was credited to him as righteousness? (1 Macc 2:52 AT)

Another Jewish text makes a similar connection:

> Abraam was a great father of a multitude of nations, and no blemish was found on his glory, who kept the law of the Most High, and he entered in a covenant with him; in his flesh he established a covenant, and in a trial **he was found faithful**. (Sir 44:19–21 NETS, emphasis added)

A similar line of thinking occurs in Jubilees 17:15–18, where the author highlights Abraham's faithful endurance of trials.

> Words came in heaven concerning Abraham that **he was faithful** in everything which was told him and he loved the LORD and **was faithful** in all affliction. . . . And the LORD was aware that **Abraham was faithful** in all of his afflictions because he tested him. . . . And in everything in which he tested him, **he was found faithful**. And his soul was not impatient. And he

48. What follows is adapted and expanded from Harmon, *Galatians*, 379–82.

49. The tradition of linking Abraham's faithful endurance of trials and being counted righteous is even more extensively developed in rabbinic texts that postdate the NT, several of which point to ten different trials (always culminating in the binding of Isaac [Gen 22]); see further the summary in Longenecker, *Galatians*, 110–12.

> was not slow to act because **he was faithful** and a lover of the LORD (*OTP* 2:90, emphasis added).

In contrast to Gen 15:6, which simply notes Abraham's trust in Yahweh and his promises, these texts connect Abraham being found "faithful" (πιστός) with endurance when tested (perhaps a reference to Gen 22). And as a result, that faithfulness to Yahweh when tested was credited to him as righteousness. This shift from Abraham as the subject of believing in Gen 15:6 to God as the implied subject finding Abraham faithful may stem from Neh 9:8, where a similar shift occurs. It appears that these Jewish interpreters may be explaining the allusion to Gen 15:6 in Neh 9:8 through the lens of Gen 22. As Watson helpfully notes regarding Jubilees 17:15–18, "The reference here to the occasions on which Abraham proved his faithfulness by obeying the divine command is closely related to the view that Abraham 'was justified by works.' Abraham's 'works' are his acts of faithfulness and obedience to the will of God."[50]

Perhaps the most illuminating Second Temple Jewish parallel is 4QMMT, which is "a sectarian polemic written to an influential leader in Jerusalem" framed in the form of a letter.[51] The central burden of this "letter" addresses mixing what is holy and what is profane, complete with twenty-four examples of how that was currently happening. Near the conclusion, the author explains that he has put forth "some works of the Torah which we think are good for you and for your people" (4Q399/4QMMT C 27 in *DSSSE* 2:803) that would be wise to follow. He concludes:

> And it shall be credited to you as righteousness when you do what is upright and good before him. (4Q399/4QMMT C 31 AT from *DSSSE* 2:802)

Since Abraham is not explicitly mentioned here, the citation could come from either Gen 15:6 or Ps 106:31. Regardless, the author has drawn from Gen 15:6// Ps 106:31 a generalized principle (someone being credited as righteous) but identified a very different means by which one achieves that status. As Gurtner summarizes, "So, where the biblical texts attribute 'righteousness' to the one who by faith believed the promises of God despite all external appearances (Abraham) or who acts in such a way on behalf of Israel to avert the righteous judgment of God (Phinehas), the Qumran text attributes it to the reader who

50. Watson, *Paul*, 223.

51. Daniel Gurtner, "Dead Sea Scrolls, OT Use in," *DNTUOT*, 178. The discussion that follows is indebted to ibid., 178–80.

(rightly) separates himself from the Jerusalem cult, where the sanctity of its worship is compromised by mixture with the profane."[52]

This background is especially helpful for Galatians. Paul not only cites Gen 15:6 as the starting point for his argument for justification by faith (Gal 3:6–9) but juxtaposes his view of being "justified by faith in Christ" with those who advocate being "justified by the works of the law" (Gal 2:16). Gurtner summarizes the "payoff" of examining this parallel from 4QMMT when he writes:

> Paul's appeal especially in Galatians may be in direct opposition to the kind of notion present in MMT. Paul's citation of Gen. 15:6 shows that it was the faith of Abraham that was regarded as righteousness (Gal. 3:6), and he insists that "works of the law" will by no means bring about justification (2:16). . . . Though there is no evidence of Paul directly opposing the Qumran sectarians, the common language of "works of the Law" does give evidence from antiquity that there were in fact some Jews, those responsible for 4QMMT, that regarded some aspect of obedience to Torah as taught by the Teacher as the means of acquiring righteousness.[53]

These examples from Jewish writings provide the interpreter with a sampling of the different ways Jews interpreted Gen 15:6 and the broader themes of righteousness and his faith/faithfulness. While we cannot know with certainty that Paul's opponents used the same hermeneutical practices and theological convictions evident in these texts, they provide a glimpse into Paul's larger intellectual context and a noteworthy contrast to the way that Paul himself interprets Gen 15:6.

CONCLUSION

The amount of extrabiblical literature can be overwhelming. But studying how biblical authors use scripture does not require mastery of these sources. A basic familiarity with these sources and how to access them is sufficient to provide the broader intellectual context of the biblical author as a starting point for comparing and contrasting how he is engaging earlier scripture.

In summary, we start with the Bible, evaluate relevant ancient Near Eastern or Second Temple Jewish literature, and return to the Bible. Sometimes it is difficult to demonstrate that a biblical author was actually aware of specific interpretive traditions or especially specific ancient Near Eastern or Second

52. Ibid.
53. Ibid.

Temple Jewish texts. Scripture's use of scripture provides a much more solid footing upon which to stand. Information gleaned from extrabiblical literature can provide valuable comparative material to situate what the biblical authors are doing within their interpretive environment.

Resource Guide 5-E: Oldest Interpretations in the Palestinian Targums of Torah

Targum interpretive traditions tend to be difficult to date. A significant difficulty is that interpretive traditions can be adjusted or added at any point in a targum's transmission history.

The evidence for the so-called Palestinian targums of the Torah have the right kind of evidence to detect the earliest of the interpretive traditions. These early targumic traditions should be used with caution since they do not necessarily date from the late Second Temple period.

The research is based on a synoptic comparison of the long plusses—at least a half a verse in length—in four complete witnesses to the Palestinian targums of Torah: Targum Neofiti (Tg. Neof.), Targum Pseudo-Jonathan (Tg. Ps.-J.), Fragmentary Targum-Paris (Frg. Tg.-P), and Fragmentary Targum-Vaticanus (Frg. Tg.-V).[54] When all four agree on the substance of an interpretive plus, it stands to reason that the plus predates the point when these targum traditions split off of their parent tradition. These can be called proto-Palestinian targum traditions. In addition, based on a series of deductions relative to agreements and disagreements of the four complete witnesses to the Palestinian targums, especially in Gen 49, Num 21–24, and Deut 32–34, the likelihood of interpretive traditions that may come from the Second Temple period can be extended to agreements between Targum Neofiti and Fragmentary Targum-Vaticanus.[55]

There are more than 150 proto-Palestinian targum traditions. The following list includes the proto-Palestinian targum interpretive traditions that appear in Targum Neofiti, Targum Pseudo-Jonathan,

54. See Flesher, "Translation and Exegetical Augmentation," 29–86; idem, "Mapping the Synoptic Palestinian Targums," 247–53. Also see Kugel, *Traditions of the Bible*, 943–44; Flesher and Chilton, *Targums*, 95–107, 154–60.

55. See Flesher, "Translation and Exegetical Augmentation," 65–67; cf. McNamara, "Early Exegesis," 67.

Fragmentary Targum-Paris, and Fragmentary Targum-Vaticanus, as well as those in italics that appear in Targum Neofiti and Fragmentary Targum-Vaticanus (whether or not they appear in Tg. Ps.-J. or Frg. Tg.-P).[56] These early interpretive traditions that appear in Targum Neofiti, Targum Pseudo-Jonathan, Fragmentary Targum-Paris, and Fragmentary Targum-Vaticanus can be accessed in user-friendly English translations.[57] Due caution is required even using these earliest targumic interpretive traditions.

Gen 1:2; 3:9, 15, 18, 19, 22, 24; 4:7, 8, *16*; 6:3; *10:2*, *4*; *11:1*, 4; 13:7; 15:1, 2, 12, 17; 16:5, 13; 18:1, *12*, 17, 21; 19:18; 20:16; 21:33; 22:10, 14; 24:62; 25:22, *34*; 26:35; 27:27, 40; 28:10, 12; 29:17, 22; *30:22*; *31:39*; 32:2[3 H], 26[27 H]; 34:31; *35:9*; 36:39; 38:25; 40:12, 18, 23; 41:43; 42:23, *36*; *44:18*, *19*; 45:28; *47:21*; *48:22*; 49:1, *2*, 3, *4*, *5*, *6*, 7, 8, 9, 10, 11, *12*, 15, 17, 18, 19, 20, 21, 22, 23, *24*, 25, 26, 27; 50:1, *19*.[58]

Exod 1:19, 21; 3:14; 4:25, 26; 10:28, 29; 12:33, 42; 14:13 (Frg. Tg.-P at 15:3), 15, 20, 25; 15:1, 9, 12, 17, *18*; *17:16*; 20:23[26 H]; 21:14; 23:2; *28:17–20*; 32:18, 25; 33:23; 34:26 (Frg. Tg.-V same as 23:19).

Lev 1:1; 10:19; 19:16; 22:27; 23:32; 24:12; *26:29*.[59]

Num *7:13–17*; *9:8*; 10:36; 11:26; *12:1*, 12, 16; *15:34*; *17:27*; *20:21*; *21:1*, *6*, *14*, *15*, 18–21, *28*, *29*, 34; 22:30; 23:9, *10*, *19*, 23, *24*; 24:3, 4, *7*, *8*, *10*, *14*, 15, *16*, 20, 23, 24; 25:4; 26:11; *27:5*; 28:2; 31:50; *33:9*; 34:6, *15*.[60]

Deut 1:1, 2; 3:29; *6:4*; 7:10; *15:11*; *22:4*; 25:13, *14*, 18; 27:8, 15; *29:15[14]*, 18[17]; *30:13*; 32:1, 2, 3, 4, 5, *10*, 14, *15*, 19, *24*, *27*, *30*, 31, *32*, *33*, *34*, *35*, *36*, *38*, *39*, *43*; 33:2, *3*, 4, 6, *7*, 9, *10*, *11*, *12*, 15, 16, 17, 18, *19*, *20*, 21, *22*, *24*, 25, *28*, 29.

56. List adapted from Flesher, "Translation and Exegetical Augmentation," 70–85; idem, "Exploring the Sources," 1:130–34. Adjustments (mostly minor typos) based on research and personal correspondence with Flesher.

57. For Tg. Neof. and Tg. Ps.-J., see ArBib. For Frg. Tg.-P and Frg. Tg.-V, see Klein, *Fragment Targums*.

58. Genesis 42:36; 48:22; and 50:19 are italicized because the interpretive tradition in Tg. Ps.-J. is not parallel to those in Tg. Neof., Frg. Tg.-P, and Frg. Tg.-V (Flesher, "Exploring the Sources," 131–33).

59. The plus in Tg. Neof. Lev 24:12 also appears with variations in Tg. Neof. Num 9:8; 15:34; 27:5. See ArBib 3:97, n. 6; 4:63, n. 6.

60. On the plusses in Tg. Neof. Num 9:8; 15:34 and 27:5, see previous footnote.

Study Questions

1. Why is it necessary and valuable to explore how a donor text is used in extrabiblical literature?
2. What is the danger of placing too much emphasis on Jewish exegetical practices when seeking to understand how the New Testament authors use the Old Testament?
3. What is the danger of ignoring extrabiblical literature when seeking to understand how scripture uses scripture?
4. What is the danger of turning too quickly to extrabiblical literature in an effort to understand how a receptor text uses a donor text?
5. How does the subject matter of Second Temple Jewish literature cause it to function differently for the context of the New Testament than the subject matter of ancient Near Eastern literature for the context of the Old Testament?
6. What is the primary value for comparing the use of a donor text in Second Temple Jewish literature and the New Testament use of that same donor text?
7. Why is the dating of extrabiblical literature an important element of determining its relevance for scripture's use of scripture?
8. Why must we be cautious about confidently asserting a biblical author is directly interacting with a particular extrabiblical source?
9. Why is it important to study the context of a Second Temple Jewish interpretive tradition that uses the same donor text as a biblical receptor text?
10. Why is the large body of rabbinic literature less relevant than other bodies of ancient literature for studying scripture's use of scripture?
11. For studying the use of scripture in Chronicles, what would be the five most relevant ancient nonbiblical resources to consult? Explain the reasons for your ranking.
12. For studying the use of scripture in the Gospels, what would be the five most relevant ancient nonbiblical resources to consult? Explain the reasons for your ranking.

CHAPTER 6

BACKWARD-LOOKING VERSUS FORWARD-LOOKING TYPOLOGICAL PATTERNS

Typology has a long and, in the view of at least some, checkered past within the history of the church. In their exuberance for typology, some interpreters have seen types lurking behind every corner in the biblical text. Often in response to such fanciful interpretations, other interpreters argue for a very limited number of types that are explicitly revealed in scripture. Because typology is a common feature of how scripture uses scripture, gaining a basic grasp of it is essential for understanding the unity and diversity of the Bible.

While definitions of typology will vary in their specific details,[1] our starting point will be the following:

> Typological patterns refer to intentional scriptural shaping to draw selective expectational analogies between persons, events, institutions, procedures, oracles, or a combination of these, within the historical framework of progressive revelation.

Understood this way, typology is one particular form of the larger promise-fulfillment structure that unites redemptive history across both the Old and New Testaments. It is an indirect form of fulfillment in that, rather than a

1. Cf. Davidson, "The Eschatological Hermeneutic," 8, who concludes that even among evangelicals there is disagreement on "the nature, function, and purpose of the typological approach." This is his summary of the conclusion reached by Glenny, "Typology," 627–38. If anything, the diversity has only increased since Glenny's article nearly twenty-five years ago.

direct verbal prophecy being fulfilled, it is the significance of a person, event, institution, or procedure that is being "filled up" later within redemptive history. Although the rest of the chapter will clarify the different aspects of this definition, a few observations will help orient our discussion.[2]

First, intentional scriptural shaping means that the author of the receptor text depicts the person, event, institution, and so on in a particular way to draw out the points of analogy between the donor and receptor text. The connections between the donor and receptor texts are rooted in authorial intent rather than the reader's response.

Second, there must be clear points of analogy that correspond between the type in the donor text(s) and the antitype in the receptor text(s). The nature and significance of those points of correspondence can vary, including, but not limited to, repeated words, phrases, and patterns of action. At times there are elements of the type in the donor text that are reversed or inverted in the antitype found in the receptor text. Not all forms of analogy or correspondence are typological in nature (see discussion below). We reserve the term "typological" for expectational patterns (i.e., patterns that point forward to a later reality).

Third, typology is rooted in history. That is, the points of correspondence are rooted in persons, events, institutions, and patterns that actually existed within history. Thus, typology is not the product of the interpreter producing connections on a merely literary level. Recognizing types within scripture rests upon God's sovereign rule over history. More specifically, types exist within redemptive history and are recorded in scripture because God organically designs people, events, and institutions in such a way that they anticipate greater realities later within redemptive history.[3]

Fourth, the nature of progressive revelation means that there is heightening or escalation between the type and the antitype. The fulfillment of the type in the antitype does not simply repeat the elements of the type but goes beyond it in significance and intensity.

Fifth, typological patterns selectively draw upon only certain details of the type as it is fulfilled in the antitype.[4]

A good example to begin with is Rom 5:12–21. In 5:14, Paul explicitly identifies Adam as a type (*tupos* τύπος, which the NIV renders "pattern") of Christ who was to come. He then draws a series of connections between Adam and Christ (see Table 6-A).

---

2. Compare the more expansive definition and discussion in *HNTUOT*, 14–22. Also see Naselli, "History of Interpretation: 1800 to Present," *DNTUOT*, 325.

3. So also Hays, *Echoes of Scripture in the Gospels*, 359.

4. See Moo, *Old Testament in the Gospel*, 380.

Table 6-A: Adam as a Pattern of Christ

Adam	**Christ**
Sin and death entered the world through Adam and spread to all people (5:12); many died through Adam's trespass (5:15)	God's grace and the gift that came by that grace overflows to the many through Christ (5:15)
The judgment that followed Adam's sin brought condemnation (5:16)	The gift of God's grace followed many trespasses and brought justification (5:16)
Because of Adam's trespass death reigned through him (5:17)	How much more do those who receive God's abundant grace and the gift of righteousness reign in life through Christ (5:17)
Adam's trespass resulted in condemnation for all people (5:18)	Christ's righteous act resulted in justification and life for all (5:18)
Through Adam's disobedience the many were made sinners (5:19)	Through Christ's obedience the many will be made righteous (5:19)
The law was brought in so sin might increase (5:20)	Where sin increased, grace increased all the more (5:20)
Sin reigned in death (5:21)	Grace reigns through righteousness leading to eternal life through Christ (5:21)

There is no question that Paul intentionally shapes his description of Christ in light of what he observes in Gen 1–3. Paul draws multiple points of connection between Adam and Christ, portraying them both as representative figures whose actions have eternal consequences for those identified with them.[5] But the respective actions of Adam and Christ, as well as the results of those actions for those represented by them, are presented as polar opposites. The nature of the connection between Adam and Christ assumes that Adam is a historical figure who not only existed but acted as the corporate head of all humanity, just as Christ is a historical figure who acts as corporate head for all who are identified with him by faith. In the movement from the type (Adam) to the antitype (Christ), Paul uses expressions like "how much more" (Rom

5. For a helpful summary of indicators in the text of Genesis, as well as later OT texts that indicate Adam is a type, see Davidson, "The Eschatological Hermeneutic," 23–28.

5:15, 17) and "all the more" (5:20) to demonstrate escalation in the movement from type to antitype.

As this example from Rom 5:12–21 shows, typology (and extended echo effect, for that matter) does not demand that every element of the donor text be reflected in the receptor text. Indeed, sometimes the differences between the type and the antitype are the central element of the comparison. The fact that Adam and Christ both represent a people and act in ways that have consequences for those whom they represent is the foundation for contrasting the different outcomes of that representation.

Another helpful example to consider is Jesus's temptation (Matt 4:1–11). Notice the combination of elements in Table 6-B that are identical along with elements that do not correspond (indicated by ≠).

Table 6-B: Contrasting Elements in Israel's and Jesus's Temptations

Israel	**Jesus**
God's son (Exod 4:22–23)	God's Son (Matt 3:17; 4:3, 6)
Led by God's presence into the wilderness (Exod 13:21–22)	Led by God's Spirit into the wilderness (4:1)
Tempted in the wilderness	Tempted in the wilderness by the devil (4:1)
In the wilderness 40 years	≠ In the wilderness 40 days and 40 nights (4:2)
Hungry in the wilderness (Exod 16:1–36)	Hungry in the wilderness (4:2)
When tempted by lack of food, Israel grumbles (Exod 16:2)	≠ When tempted to turn stones into bread because of hunger, Jesus resists by trusting God, citing Deut 8:3 (4:3–4)
When tempted by lack of water, Israel quarrels with Moses and tests Yahweh (Exod 17:1–3)	≠ When tempted to throw himself down from the pinnacle of the temple to test God's protection and provision, Jesus resists by trusting God, citing Deut 6:16 (4:5–7)
When tempted to go after other gods, Israel commits idolatry (Num 25:1–9)	≠ When tempted to receive the kingdoms of the earth if he will worship the devil, Jesus resists by trusting God, citing Deut 6:13 (4:8–10)

The very nature of the typological relationship between Israel and Jesus demands that there be enough points of similarity to establish the connection.[6] Both are sons of God led by God's Spirit into the wilderness to be tempted (Deut 8:2–5). The specific temptation each faces is different in the particulars though similar in the underlying issue of whether God's son will trust in Yahweh in the midst of significant hardship. But the whole point of drawing this connection is to highlight Jesus's obedience where Israel failed, identifying him as the obedient Son of God sent to fulfill Israel's mission. Thus, rather than undermining the typological connection, those differences are the means by which the antitype is revealed as greater than the type.

The approaches of biblical authors to typological patterns in earlier revelation should not be regarded as one-size-fits-all. Geerhardus Vos explains the interpretation of temporal and spatial patterns of typological revelation in the New Testament. For Vos both sorts of typological patterns can operate in forward-looking or backward-looking revelation—in his words: "a prediction or a prefiguration."[7]

Vos explains that temporal typological patterns emphasize "before and after."[8] In this case, the shadow or the type expects the reality or the antitype (Figure 6-C).

Figure 6-C: Temporal Type or Shadow before the Antitype or Reality

Type — Antitype

A temporal type may provide a forward-looking prediction, like the new covenant of Jer 31, or a backward-looking prefiguration, like David's suffering in Ps 22, which is discussed in case 2 below (Figure 6-D).[9]

Meanwhile, Vos explains that John, Paul, and especially the author of Hebrews interact with spatial typological patterns "between higher and lower," or celestial/heavenly and terrestrial/earthly.[10] Spatial patterns include the heavenly and earthly tabernacles that prefigure the temple and the saving work of the Messiah as well as Sabbath rest modeled on God's rest after creation that

6. With regard to the three specific temptations that Jesus faced, I have suggested a comparable temptation that Israel faced. Multiple examples could have been chosen for each one.

7. Vos, *The Teaching of the Epistle to the Hebrews*, 62; cf. 61. On Vos's views, see 55–65, or more detailed in idem, "Hebrews Part 2," 1–19.

8. Vos, "Hebrews Part 2," 9, 13.

9. See Vos, The *Teaching of the Epistle to the Hebrews*, 60, 62.

10. Vos, "Hebrews Part 2," 9; and see 10, 13–14.

Figure 6-D: Forward-Looking and Backward-Looking Temporal Types

together prefigure the rest awaiting believers.[11] The heavenly realities (A) cast their spatial shadows in Old Testament revelation (B) that prefigures the heavenly reality come to fulfillment in New Testament revelation (C) (Figure 6-E).

Figure 6-E: Spatial Shadow or Type of Heavenly and New Testament Realities‡

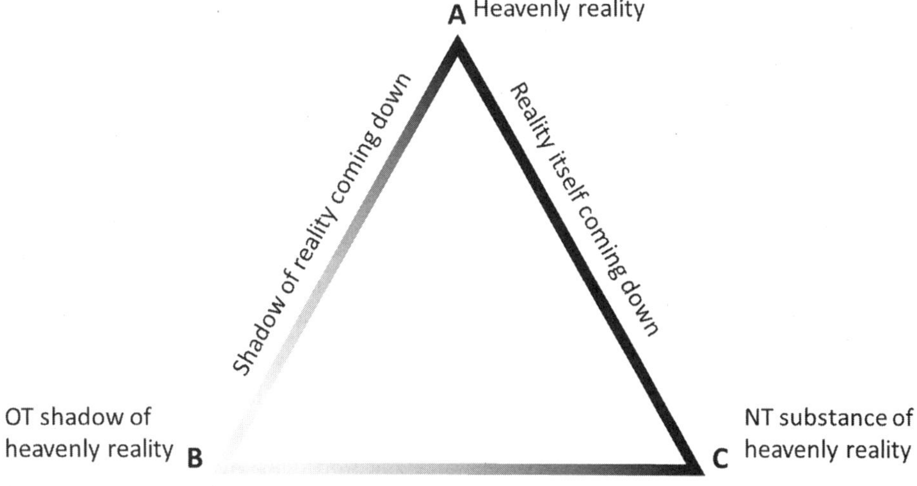

‡Figure based on Vos, *The Teaching of the Epistle to the Hebrews*, 57.

Care must be taken to avoid collapsing revelation of typological patterns into a monochromatic or static approach to revelation. The dynamics of progressive revelation include both temporal and spatial kinds of typological patterns. In certain cases, New Testament authors detect both kinds of typological patterns operating for the same historical person, event, or institution.

11. See ibid., 6, 11, 14

Vos observes that Melchizedek functions as a predictive (forward-looking) temporal typological pattern in Ps 110:4 and elsewhere as a spatial typological prefiguration (backward-looking) in Gen 14—both applied to Christ by the author of Hebrews (see case study 1 below).[12] Thus the interpreter should be attentive to both temporal and spatial forms of typology when considering the nature and function of a possible type.

Starting with these examples is helpful because they contain all the key elements of typology. Unfortunately, not all examples of typology are this straightforward.

CHOICE

Although there are a number of complex issues related to the study of typology within scripture, one of the most significant is whether types are forward-looking or backward-looking. Arguing for the latter, R. T. France contends that "A type is not a prediction; in itself it is simply a person, event, and so on recorded as historical fact, with no intrinsic reference to the future. Nor is an antitype the fulfilment of a prediction; it is rather the re-embodiment of a principle which has been previously exemplified in the type."[13] More recently, Richard Hays argues that "the discernment of a figural correspondence is necessarily retrospective rather than prospective. . . . Because the two poles of a figure are events within the 'flowing stream' of time, the correspondence can be discerned only after the second event has occurred and imparted a new significance to the first. But once the pattern of correspondence has been grasped, the semantic force of the figure flows both ways, as the second event receives deeper significance from the first."[14] Elsewhere Hays asserts typological patterns are "always" retrospective.[15]

By contrast, Richard M. Davidson argues for the prospective view when he defines Old Testament types as persons, events, or institutions "which God has specifically designed to correspond to, and predictively prefigure, their intensified antitypical fulfillment aspects (inaugurated, appropriated, consummated)

12. See ibid., 16; idem, *The Teaching of the Epistle to the Hebrews*, 59; idem, "The Priesthood of Christ, Part 2," 592–93.

13. R. T. France, *Jesus and the Old Testament*, 39–40. For a similar view, see Baker, *Two Testaments*, 183, who simply states "It is only in retrospect that an event, person or institution may be seen to be typical." Both quotes are taken from Caneday, "Biblical Types," 135.

14. Hays, *Echoes of Scripture in the Gospels*, 2–3.

15. See Hays, *Reading with the Grain of Scripture*, 73. Hays prefers the term "figural," by which he means "typological" (72, n. 6). Also see idem, "Figural Exegesis," 34–36.

in New Testament salvation history."[16] Along similar lines, James Hamilton argues that "when the biblical authors composed their writings, they intended to signal to their audiences the presence of promise-shaped patterns. Thus even if they did not fully understand the significance of the pattern and/or how the promise would be fulfilled (and see Eph 3:5 and 1 Pet 1:10–12), the Old Testament authors intended to draw attention to the recurring sequences of events, and they did so with a view to the future."[17]

So which is it? Is typology only forward-looking or only backward-looking? The answer is both. A proper understanding of typology requires recognizing that some types are expectational within their original context, while other types are nonexpectational in their original context but recognizable in light of later revelation. Biblical types are not rooted in the creativity of the interpreter; they are embedded by God himself within the text. While the degree to which the human author was aware that the person, event, institution, or pattern was pointing forward to someone or something greater can be debated, the larger redemptive-historical and canonical contexts indicate this in some fashion.

Examples of expectational types are present within both the Old and New Testaments. Oftentimes the forward-looking nature of the type is evident within the immediate context. The Song of the Sea (Exod 15:1–21) celebrates Israel's exodus, which culminated in their passing through the reeds sea waters while pharaoh's army drowned. Whereas the focus of 15:1–13 is on what Yahweh has already done, verses 14–18 look toward the future. Because of what Yahweh has done in the exodus, the peoples have heard and tremble in fear because the same powerful arm that brought them out of Egypt will now bring them into the promised land. The destruction of pharaoh's army and the rescue of Israel are portrayed as a pattern of what will happen in the conquest of the land. So it is not surprising when later texts in both the Old and New Testaments see the original exodus as a precursor for an even greater redemptive act (e.g., Isa 40:1–11; 43:16–21; Hos 2:14–23; Mark 1:2–3; Luke 3:4–6; 1 Pet 1:24–25). Isaiah makes the forward-looking expectational pattern of the historical exodus explicit with the preposition of analogy "like" or "as" (*ke-* כְּ) when he projects it forward onto the return from Mesopotamian exile (Isa 11:15–16).[18]

Sometimes the forward pointing element is found within the broader context, such as the promise in Deut 18:15–19 that God will raise up a prophet like

16. Davidson, "The Eschatological Hermeneutic," 12. This quote is also taken from Caneday, "Biblical Types," 136.

17. Hamilton, *Typology*, 5.

18. On "like, as" (כְּ), see GKC §118s; *IBHS* 11.2.9b.

Moses to whom the people must listen—using the preposition "like" (כְּ) as a literary signal of expectation. This promise invites the reader to look back at the life of Moses and anticipate a later figure who will do Moses-like things on an even greater level than Moses himself. This expectation is heightened as later biblical figures are portrayed as Moses-like figures, whether it is Joshua leading Israel into the promised land or the Isaianic servant leading the promised new exodus.[19] Thus when the New Testament both alludes to Jesus as the prophet greater than Moses (Matt 17:5) and then explicitly identifies him as such (Acts 3:22–23), the biblical authors are presenting Jesus as the one who fulfills both the promise of Deut 18:15 and the pattern of Moses-like actions displayed in several Old Testament figures.[20]

A good example of backward-looking typology occurs in John 19:28–29, where the apostle likely alludes to Psalm 69:21.[21]

> Later, knowing that everything had now been finished, and so that Scripture would be fulfilled, Jesus said, "I am thirsty." [29]A jar of wine vinegar was there, so they soaked a sponge in it, put the sponge on a stalk of the hyssop plant, and lifted it to Jesus's lips. (John 19:28–29, emphases added)

> They put gall in my food
> and gave me vinegar for my thirst. (Ps 69:21, emphases added)

Psalm 69 is a lament psalm in which David cries out for God to save him from the sorrows caused by his enemies. One way his enemies torment him is giving him vinegar when he thirsts, which, rather than satisfy the thirst, would likely intensify it. Nothing in the context of Ps 69 points forward to a future figure who will suffer these realities. They are simply the sufferings of David. Yet as he reflects on Jesus's statement of thirst and the response of the soldiers to give him wine vinegar, John sees the fulfillment of David's experience described in Ps 69:21. This claim rests on understanding David as a type of Jesus, his greater son. As a result, even those experiences of David which in their original context are not inherently expectational (as is the case with many, if not most of, the lament psalms) can in light of later revelation be seen as anticipating Jesus and, in particular, his suffering.[22] Elsewhere John makes explicit that the followers

19. See further Harmon, *Servant of the Lord*, 61–78, 109–42.

20. For more detail on the case of the prophet like Moses, see the first case study in Chapter 2.

21. On this allusion, see the discussion in Moo, *Old Testament in the Gospel*, 275–80.

22. On David's sufferings as a type of Christ's sufferings, see further Hoskins, *That Scripture Might Be Fulfilled*, 37–55.

did not connect other parts of Ps 69 to Christ until he was raised from the dead (cf. John 2:17). This theological insight is part of the postresurrection work of the Spirit (14:26),[23] as discussed in Chapter 2.

These brief examples of both expectational and nonexpectational types demonstrate that both are present in scripture. Recognizing and affirming both forms of typology shows the Spirit-inspired genius of the biblical authors and their understanding of God's work within redemptive history. As part of God's progressive revelation, Scripture uses both forward- and backward-looking typology to reveal the mystery of what had been hidden in plain sight (Eph 3:5; 1 Pet 1:10–12). Therefore the interpreter must be attentive to the presence of forward- and backward-looking forms of typology.[24]

DIFFICULTIES

The complex set of issues related to typology leads to a series of difficulties that the responsible interpreter of scripture must think through.

NATURE OF FULFILLMENT

Since types can be either forward- or backward-looking, one must further consider the nature of fulfillment when it comes to both expectational and nonexpectational forms of typology. As we noted above, a good starting point for understanding typology is to see it as one form of the larger promise-fulfillment structure that unites the Old and New Testaments.[25] As Doug Moo helpfully notes, fulfillment language "is used in the New Testament to indicate the broad redemptive-historical relationship of the new climactic revelation of God in Christ to the preparatory, incomplete revelation to and through Israel."[26] Thus, even when fulfillment language occurs in an introductory formula, "it does not mean that the author regards the Old Testament text he quotes as a direct prophecy."[27] Although fulfillment sometimes takes the form of a direct verbal prediction in the donor text that is fulfilled in the receptor text (Mic 5:2[1 H]//Matt 2:6; Zech 9:9//Matt 21:5), the way the biblical authors use the concept of fulfillment extends beyond such direct examples. Indeed, examples

23. On uses of Ps 69 in all four Gospels, see Moo, *Old Testament in the Gospel*, 354–55.

24. For a sample of the many typological patterns in the OT, see *OTUOT*, 715–16; Brettler, "Israel's Scriptures," 69–74; Fishbane, *Biblical Interpretation*, 350–79; Boda, "Legitimizing the Temple," 313–18. Also see Baker, *Two Testaments*, 171–72.

25. Similarly, Moo, "Problem of *Sensus Plenior*," 175–211.

26. Ibid., 191.

27. Ibid. On the sense of NT fulfilment formulas, see Schnittjer, "What's Old?" 73–78.

of uncontested direct prediction-fulfillment are somewhat rare in the New Testament.[28]

Thus when it comes to the concept of fulfillment, we can begin by affirming that fulfillment language, as used by the New Testament authors themselves, encompasses both direct predictions as well as broader typological relationships. In the latter case, the later biblical person, event, institution, and so on in some measure "fills up" the significance of its Old Testament precursor, often in ways unanticipated by the Old Testament author or original audience(s).[29] This understanding of fulfillment, it must be stressed, does not mean that the New Testament referent exhausts the significance of its Old Testament precursor; there may yet be further significance to be filled up before the Old Testament precursor reaches its complete and final fulfillment.[30]

DISTINGUISHING BETWEEN TYPOLOGICAL PATTERNS, EXTENDED ECHO EFFECT, AND ALLEGORY

The mere presence of analogy between a donor and receptor text does not automatically indicate typology. A later biblical author may use patterns from an earlier text for reasons other than drawing a typological connection between the donor and receptor texts. For example, "type-scenes" are cultural-literary templates with no expectational sense. The common biblical type-scene of the infertile wife (e.g., Sarah, Rebekah) or annoying little brother (e.g., Abel, Joseph) provide literary connections.[31]

Extended echo effect refers to "the connotative effects that derive from one context intentionally modeled after another, including multiple relations, often in the same sequence (a-b-c, a-b-c). A character, event, instruction, oracle, or the like naturally gets compared as a virtual simile to its counterpart, causing connotative transfer."[32] For example, the story of Abram lying about Sarai being his sister when he sojourns in Egypt and God protecting her despite this lie (Gen 12:10–20) is later echoed in the "she's my sister" stories of Abraham

28. See examples in Walton, *The Lost World of the Prophets*, 111–14.

29. On "fulfill" in scripture, see Schnittjer, "What's Old?" 74–76.

30. "The possibility of an OT precursor being referred to as fulfilled in the NT, and yet awaiting further significance/fulfillment should not be surprising given the already-not yet nature of much of NT theology. To cite just one example: when Paul claims that believers are a new creation (2 Cor 5:17), he is claiming that this fulfills God's promise of new creation in passages such as Isa 43:18–20; 65:17–18; 66:22–24. Yet the way in which he speaks of creation groaning because of its present bondage in Rom 8:20–25 makes it clear that Paul holds to a yet future fulfillment that will finally exhaust the OT promise of its significance" (Harmon, *She Must and Shall Go Free*, 38 n. 150).

31. See Alter, "Biblical Type-Scenes," 357–60.

32. *OTUOT*, 894.

(20:1–18) and Isaac (26:6–11). The intentional parallel descriptions between first-generation Israel in the wilderness (Exod 15–18) and the second generation in the wilderness (Num 10–17; 20–25) is another example of extended echo effect (see discussion in Chapter 3). In the New Testament, Luke intentionally echoes the miraculous works of Elijah (Luke 7:11–17//1 Kgs 17:17–24) and Elisha (Luke 7:11–17//2 Kgs 4:18–36; Luke 9:10–17//2 Kgs 4:42–44) when recounting some of Jesus's miracles, inviting the reader to see the actions of Jesus in light of his prophetic predecessors. Whether such correspondence is simply for literary effect or typological in nature is debated by scholars.

Indeed, sometimes it can be difficult to distinguish between typology and extended echo effect. A good example is the Joseph-like presentation of Daniel. The extensive parallels between Daniel (Dan 2:1–49) and Joseph (Gen 41:1–57) are evident even from a casual reading, and a close reading of the Hebrew/Aramaic text reveals even more parallels.[33] Schnittjer argues that these intentional points of correspondence are literary rather than exegetical, concluding that the "use of a scriptural tradition provides comparative connotation by which to measure the divine intervention on behalf of Daniel and the court sages. All of Nebuchadnezzar's pharaoh-like and Daniel's Joseph-like elements contribute to the literary development of the satirical story of the Neo-Babylonian court."[34] By contrast, Emadi sees a typological connection intended to "ignite hope among the exiled Jews for Israel's future. If the nation was birthed in exile in Egypt, then, despite all appearances to the contrary, it can experience new birth in exile in Babylon. If Joseph was a forerunner of the exodus, then Daniel, a new and better Joseph, portends a new exodus—one even greater than before."[35] Disagreements between scholars on the precise nature and significance of analogical correspondence between a donor and receptor text are common.

A further complication in distinguishing typology from extended echo effect is that, like extended echo effect, many typological patterns have additional installments of the person, event, institution, or pattern between the type and the antitype. These ectypes continue the pattern forward, sometimes with escalation, toward the ultimate fulfillment of the type in its antitype.[36] For

33. For a helpful summary chart see Emadi, *From Prisoner to Prince*, 110–11, who adapts the work of Philpot, "Was Joseph a Type of Daniel?" 681–96. For even more parallels, see Rindge, "Jewish Identity," 88–90.

34. *OTUOT*, 620.

35. Emadi, *From Prisoner to Prince*, 115.

36. Hamilton, *Typology*, 28. He defines an ectype as "an installment in a typological pattern between the archetype (or prototype), the initial instance, and the antitype, or final fulfillment to which the archetype and the ectype(s) pointed."

example, God's commission to Noah after he emerges from the ark (Gen 9:1, 7) both repeats and adapts the one given to Adam (1:28).

> Be fruitful and increase in number; *fill the earth* and subdue it. (1:28, emphasis added)

> Be fruitful and increase in number and *fill the earth.* (9:1, emphasis added)

> Be fruitful and increase in number; multiply on the earth and increase upon it. (9:7, emphasis added)

The obvious connection between these texts could be an example of extended echo effect, with the differences (e.g., eating meat, capital punishment) between the commissions and their larger contexts functioning on the literary level—within Genesis—to expand on the implications of creation and the residual image of God.[37] But these same connections—within a larger biblical context—could also be an installment (i.e., ectype) in a typological pattern that recurs throughout the Old Testament with a series of "Adam" figures that culminates in Christ as the last Adam.[38]

Typology should also be distinguished from allegory. Waters provides three helpful distinctions between typology and allegory.[39] First, whereas a typological correspondence is discernible from the letter of the text and rooted in the literary and historical context, allegory isolates words from their context in the interest of revealing a hidden meaning. Second, typology rests on historical correspondences that emerge from within the text itself, while allegory posits correspondences that are fundamentally ideological and imposed upon the text from the outside. Finally, whereas the escalation in typology is rooted in historical correspondence, in allegory "escalation is ahistorical and conceptual in nature. The lower realm points, in concealed and obscure fashion, to the comparatively pure truth or idea contained in the higher realm."[40] Thus, the "interpretive framework is not historical but philosophical."[41]

---

37. See *OTUOT,* 6–7.
38. See further Beale, *The Temple and the Church's Mission*, 93–121.
39. Guy Prentiss Waters, "Allegory," *DNTUOT,* 19.
40. Ibid.
41. Ibid.

Although not common, there are examples of allegory in the Old Testament.[42] Ezekiel 19 borrows language from the blessing of Judah (Gen 49:8–12) to construct an allegory of the lioness and her cubs, comparing them to a vine that became a scepter. Ezekiel 23 develops an elaborate allegorical portrait of Yahweh's two unfaithful sister wives Oholah/Samaria and Oholibah/Jerusalem using the broad biblical theme of rebellion rather than echoing specific scriptural texts. The allegorical scenario in Ezek 31 of Assyria as the greatest "tree" in the garden of Eden—used to speak judgment on pharaoh (31:18)—may echo the oracle of Yahweh chopping down Assyria in Isa 10:33–34. Whether allegory is present in the New Testament is debated. Although Paul uses the verb *allegoreo* (ἀλληγορέω) in Gal 4:24 to explain his reading of Gen 16–21, he appears to be signaling that he is reading Gen 16–21 through the lens of Isa 54:1 (cited in Gal 4:27). Thus Gal 4:21–5:1 is probably best understood as a combination of allegory (in the sense just described) and typology.[43]

Another key element that distinguishes typology from allegory is the selectivity of the details the receptor text uses from the donor text. As noted in Chapter 2, the lack of complete alignment between the details in the donor and receptor texts does not indicate a noncontextual use of the donor text. Because typological patterns are rooted in real historical people, events, and institutions, the receptor text only appropriates those details from the donor text that are related to the fulfillment of the type. Moo explains the selectivity of typological patterns in the passion accounts: "[T]he influence has proceeded from the history [of Messiah's death] to the text [cited from the Old Testament] rather than vice versa. The relatively small number of Old Testament passages utilized in the passion texts presumes *a strict selectivity*, conditioned by the circumstance of the passion events."[44] Such selectivity demonstrates the biblical authors' commitment to truthfully relating events while at the same time describing those events with their divinely intended significance. By contrast, the pesharim forms of scriptural engagement found at Qumran (e.g., 1QpHab; 4QpNah/4Q169) often allegorize the text because they attempt to find significance in every detail of the donor text.

In summary, typology, extended echo effect, and allegory all share the traits of analogous similarities. But each has a different function in scripture (Table 6-F).

42. These OT examples are adapted from *OTUOT*, 351–52.

43. See further Harmon, "Allegory, Typology, or Something Else?" 144–58.

44. Moo, *Old Testament in the Gospel*, 380, emphasis added. Cf. *OTUOT*, 862.

Table 6-F: Comparing Analogical Functions

Typological Patterns	Extended Echo Effect	Allegory
Selective analogical use of details of donor text	Selective analogical use of details of donor text	Nonselective analogical use of details of donor text
Respects the original context of the donor text	Respects the original context of the donor text	Little to no regard for the original context of the donor text
Depends on real historical events, people, and the like	Depends on real historical events, people, and the like	Depends on an extratextual philosophical or theological grid
Expectational	Literary (nonexpectational)	Ideological (expectational or nonexpectational)

While this chart is not exhaustive, it provides a starting point when attempting to distinguish between typology, extended echo effect, and allegory.

DISTINGUISHING BETWEEN TYPES AND ILLUSTRATIONS

Sometimes it can be difficult to determine whether a biblical author uses a donor text to identify a type or simply sees that person, event, and so on as an analogy used to illustrate a point. Indeed, Jude seamlessly moves between types and (nonexpectational) illustrations in his extended argument regarding the judgment coming on false teachers (Jude 5–16). He begins his argument with a look back to the exodus:

> Now I want you to remind you, even though you all once knew, that Jesus,[45] after saving a people from the land of Egypt, later destroyed those who did not believe. (Jude 5 AT)

Jude sees in the exodus a pattern of God saving a people out of bondage but later judging those who did not persevere in trusting Yahweh and his promises.

45. The Greek text of verse 5 contains one of the most well-known textual variants in Jude. Instead of saying that "Jesus" (Ἰησοῦς) saved the Israelites out of Egypt, other manuscripts say it was "God" (θεός) and still others say it was "the Lord" (κύριος). For helpful summaries of the textual evidence for each variant, see Wasserman, *The Epistle of Jude*, 160–62. Even if "Lord" is the original reading, the reference to "Jesus Christ, our only Sovereign and Lord" in the previous verse leads the reader to conclude that the "Lord" in view is Jesus Christ rather than a general reference to God.

By identifying the Lord Jesus as the one who rescued Israel from Egypt, Jude further tightens the typological connection between Israel's exodus and the redemption that believers experience through Jesus's death and resurrection. The connection moves from lesser to greater. Since the Lord destroyed those who did not persevere in faith when he rescued Israel from Egypt, how much greater will the judgment be on those who experience Jesus's even greater act of redemption through the new exodus of his death and resurrection and yet do not persevere in the faith? Like many other biblical authors before him, Jude sees the exodus as a type of the redemption accomplished by Jesus. But in line with 1 Cor 10:1–13 and Heb 3:7–13, Jude warns that just as the Lord judged the Israelites who did not persevere in faith, so too the Lord Jesus will destroy those who fall away from "the faith that was once for all entrusted to God's holy people" (Jude 3).

Yet later in the same letter Jude uses analogies to illustrate characteristics of his opponents. When he asserts that they "have taken the way of Cain; they have rushed for profit into Balaam's error; they have been destroyed in Korah's rebellion" (Jude 11), he is not asserting that Cain (Gen 4), Balaam (Num 22–24), and Korah (Num 16) are types. They are instead examples drawn from the Old Testament that illustrate an Old Testament precedent for similar behaviors and attitudes present within the false teachers. He is not presenting them as patterns that recur throughout scripture and intensify in their significance.

Matthew 12:38–41 provides a good example of a use of the Old Testament that scholars debate whether it is typology or illustration. In response to the request for a sign (12:38), Jesus answers,

> A wicked and adulterous generation asks for a sign! But none will be given it except the sign of the prophet Jonah. For as Jonah was three days and three nights in the belly of a huge fish, so the Son of Man will be three days and three nights in the heart of the earth. The men of Nineveh will stand up at the judgment with this generation and condemn it; for they repented at the preaching of Jonah, and now something greater than Jonah is here. (Matt 12:39–41)

Joel White sees this as a simple analogy.[46] He argues that neither Jesus nor Matthew refers to this as a type. Instead, it uses the explicit language of simile to make it clear "that this is simply an analogy drawn by Jesus."[47] Craig

46. Joel R. White, "Contextual and Noncontextual NT Use of the OT," *DNTUOT*, 122.
47. Ibid.

Blomberg agrees, concluding that "Jesus merely constructs a simple analogy based on the historical account of Jonah to illustrate what is going to happen to him."[48]

However, a good case can be made that this in fact typology.[49] Jesus identifies Jonah's three days and three nights in the belly of the fish as a type of his death and resurrection, an event designed by God and recorded in scripture as a sign of a person and event later in redemptive history. The points of correspondence are clear. Both Jonah and Jesus are prophets. Both spend three days and three nights in the depths of the earth. Both escape those depths. Both preach a message of coming judgment that leads to repentance. Jesus portrays these realities as real historical events that happened to a real historical person.

Yet even within those points of selective correspondence there are obvious elements of escalation between Jonah as the type and Jesus as the antitype. Although Jonah spent three days and three nights in the belly of the fish (Jon 1:17; Matt 12:40), he did not actually die. Furthermore, Jonah was in the belly of the fish because of his own disobedience to God's commission to proclaim the coming judgment on Nineveh and call for repentance. By contrast, Jesus actually dies and spends three days and nights in the depths of the grave. Rather than being there because of his own disobedience, Jesus was in the grave for the disobedience of his people. His commission was not merely to proclaim judgment and call for repentance in order to be saved but to actually accomplish the salvation of his people by experiencing the judgment they deserved. Jesus as the antitype far exceeds Jonah in the extent and cause of his suffering to fulfill a greater commission for a far larger number of people. Thus the escalation between Jonah and Jesus confirms the presence of typology.

In sum, expectational typological patterns differ from nonexpectational illustrations. The differences between types and illustrations can be subtle and contested. Interpreters should proceed with caution and humility.

CONTROLS

A common concern raised when discussing typology is the unrestrained zeal of some who seemingly find types everywhere they look. Such "hyper-typers"—as students sometimes call them—latch on to any potential point of correspondence and conclude that a type is present. A good example is the scarlet thread that Rahab hung outside of her window to prevent the Israelites from destroying

48. Craig L. Blomberg, "Matthew," in *CNTUOT*, 45.

49. See similarly France, *Matthew*, 489, and Gladd, *Handbook on the Gospels*, 45.

her home when taking Jericho (Josh 2:18), which Mitchell Chase (among others throughout church history) claims looks backwards to the blood placed on the doorposts at Passover and thus forward to the cross.[50]

A more measured approach to typology requires the use of controls to help evaluate the legitimacy of a proposed type. We suggest at least three controls.

First, consider the historical context of the donor text. Are there any indications in the broader context of the passage that suggest the potential type is pointing forward to realities later within redemptive history? Do later texts look back at the potential type and reveal indicators in the context of the proposed type that suggest greater realities later in redemptive history? The more central the proposed type is to the passage, the more likely it is to be a type.

Second, consider the larger redemptive patterns in scripture. Notice that the major expectational patterns revealed in scripture (e.g., Adam, the flood, exodus, tabernacle, Moses, David) are established on the macro-level of major elements rather than smaller incidental details. Those smaller details only take on typological significance in light of the major elements of correspondence. This control helps filter out what might otherwise be mistaken for fleeting typological allusions.

Third, typological patterns are secondary to the historical realities that establish the expectational patterns. As important as typological connections are, those connections must never eclipse the meaning of the text in its original context nor the larger redemptive message of scripture.

These controls cannot provide a foolproof method for legitimizing possible types. Still, they should caution us in cases that require too much imagination to sift through subtleties. We need to seek counsel from trusted resources and teachers. We also need to find gentle ways to set out guardrails to help well-meaning laity from getting carried away.

Geerhardus Vos provides an important reminder when he notes:

> The bond that holds type and antitype together must be a bond of vital continuity in the progress of redemption. Where this is ignored, and in the place of this bond are put accidental resemblances, void of inherent spiritual significance, all sorts of absurdities will result such as must bring the whole subject of typology into disrepute.[51]

---

50. Chase, *40 Questions*, 154. Vos rightly rejects this and other "accidental resemblances" (*Biblical Theology*, 146; and see below). For another example of typological excess, see the treatment of showbread in Street, *Believer-Priest*, 89. Also see Walton, *Wisdom for Faithful Reading*, 195–96.

51. Vos, *Biblical Theology*, 146.

CASE STUDIES

A brief look at three cases studies will help illustrate several key elements of our discussion.

CASE STUDY 1—AN EXAMPLE OF FORWARD-LOOKING TYPOLOGY

The Messiah's taunting of the interpretation of the scribes' reading of Ps 110:1 (cf. Matt 22:41–46; Mark 12:35–37; Luke 20:41–44) provides an excellent reason for the earliest Christians to study the entire psalm in relation to the Messiah. This naturally leads to reading the explicit forward-looking pattern of Melchizedek in v. 4 toward the Messiah.

Though many forward-looking typological patterns use the attached preposition of analogy "like" (*ke-* כְּ), Ps 110:4 uses the free-standing preposition "according to" (*'al* עַל) in its sense of alignment of otherwise unrelated elements.[52] The authors of Israel's scriptures used multiple kinds of literary signals to present expectational patterns of historical persons, offices, events, and the like.

Psalm 110 is one of eleven psalms with divine speech embedded in it—four of which enhance and extend elements of the Davidic promise (Pss 2; 89; 110; 132).[53] Whereas Ps 110:1 affirms the oracle of Nathan in 2 Sam 7 and may be an adaptation of it, v. 4 extends the sense of "forever" from the promise by connecting it with the priest Melchizedek, elsewhere known only in Gen 14.[54]

All of these factors help make sense of why the author of Hebrews gives extended attention to Melchizedek as an expectational pattern of Jesus the messianic priest.[55] Hebrews goes beyond the divine pronouncement of Ps 110:4 to extrapolate numerous elements of the typological pattern from the narrative of the historical priest Melchizedek that Abraham once met.[56] Most of the contested interpretive inferences of typology in Hebrews concern the handling of details from Gen 14:17–20 (cf. esp. Heb 7:1–10). Working out these exegetical extrapolations requires patience and caution. But this goes beyond the present purpose of highlighting the explicit forward-looking expectational pattern in Ps 110:4. One example will make the point at hand.

---

52. See GKC §119aa, n. 2; *IBHS* 11.2.13e; עַל BDB 754 (1.f.a); *HALOT* 1:826 (4).

53. See Gillingham, "New Wine," 380. For an extended exegetical discussion of Ps 110 that explores its typological significance, see Emadi, *The Royal Priest*, 89–128.

54. See *OTUOT*, 523. On Ps 110:1 as an interpretation of Davidic promise, see *OTUOT*, 521 and *OTUOTPL*, entry on 1 Kgs 5:1–5[15–19 H]. In a similar way, Zenger regards 110:4 as an interpretation of 2 Sam 7 (*Psalms*, 3:150).

55. See Heb 5:6, 10; 6:20; 7:17, 21; cf. 7:1–2.

56. On Melchizedek representing a better covenant based on Gen 14, see Vos, "The Priesthood of Christ, Part 1," 436–37.

The pattern of Melchizedek points to the everlasting priesthood of Jesus.[57] Notice how Hebrews builds both on the oracle and even the divine revelation citation formula of the psalmist (bold signifies a verbatim quotation of the LXX and broken underlining signifies a citation formula in the psalm carried over to Hebrews).

> **Yahweh swore and will not change his mind: "You are a priest forever,** in the order of Melchizedek." (Ps 110:4 AT of MT)

> And it was not without an oath! Others became priests without any oath, [21]but he became a priest with an oath when God said to him: **"The Lord has sworn and will not change his mind: 'You are a priest forever.'"** [22]Because of this oath, Jesus has become the guarantor of a better covenant. (Heb 7:20–22)[58]

Far from reading meaning back into Ps 110:4 that is not there, the author of Hebrews recognizes the explicit forward-looking elements of the psalm and identifies Jesus as the fulfillment. In doing so, he is simply following the lead of Jesus himself.

CASE STUDY 2—AN EXAMPLE OF BACKWARD-LOOKING TYPOLOGY

Psalm 22 is one of the most frequently alluded to texts in the Gospel passion narratives. Rather than reading the psalm allegorically, the evangelists do not follow the sequence of the psalm but draw on the psalm selectively as it speaks to specific elements of the crucifixion.[59] At a minimum there are at least three notable citations/allusions, the first of which comes from the opening lines of the psalm.

> My God, my God, why have you forsaken me?
> Why are you so far from saving me,
> so far from my cries of anguish? (Ps 22:1[2 H], emphasis added)

> About three in the afternoon Jesus cried out in a loud voice, "*Eli, Eli, lema sabachthani?*" (which means "My God, my God, why have you forsaken me?"). (Matt 27:46, emphasis added)

57. See ibid., 440; idem, "The Priesthood of Christ, Part 2," 594.
58. "God" is not in the Greek of Heb 7:21. The NIV supplies it from 5:10.
59. As observed by Moo, *Old Testament in the Gospel*, 363–64; Carey, *Jesus' Cry*, 164–65.

> And at three in the afternoon Jesus cried out in a loud voice, "*Eloi, Eloi, lema sabachthani?*" (which means "My God, my God, why have you forsaken me?"). (Mark 15:34, emphasis added)

The second use of Psalm 22 comes from much later in the psalm and is found in all four Gospels.

> They divide my clothes among them
> and cast lots for my garment. (Psalm 22:18[19 H], emphasis added)

> When they had crucified him, they divided up his clothes by casting lots. (Matt 27:35, emphasis added)

> And they crucified him. Dividing up his clothes, they cast lots to see what each would get. (Mark 15:24, emphasis added)

> And they divided up his clothes by casting lots. (Luke 23:34, emphasis added)

> "Let's not tear it," they said to one another. "Let's decide by lot who will get it." This happened that the scripture might be fulfilled that said, "They divided my clothes among them and cast lots for my garment." (John 19:24, emphasis added)

The final citation/allusion depicts the behavior of the bystanders.

> All who see me mock me;
> they hurl insults, shaking their heads.
> "He trusts in the LORD," they say,
> "let the LORD rescue him.
> Let him deliver him,
> since he delights in him." (Ps 22:7–8[8–9 H], emphasis added)

> Those who passed by hurled insults at him, shaking their heads. . . . In the same way the chief priests, the teachers of the law and the elders mocked him. . . . "He trusts in God. Let God rescue him now if he wants him, for he said, 'I am the Son of God'." (Matt 27:39, 41, 43, emphasis added)

> Those who passed by hurled insults at him, shaking their heads. (Mark 15:29, emphasis added)

> The people stood watching, and the rulers even sneered at him. (Luke 23:35, emphasis added)

That the Gospel writers portray Jesus's crucifixion in light of Ps 22 is beyond doubt. The question, however, is on what basis they do so. Psalm 22 is David's lament over his suffering at the hands of many enemies despite his innocence. The opening seems to pit the psalmist's misery against the assurance refrains of old, such as: "Yahweh your God goes with you; he will never leave you nor forsake you" (Deut 31:6 AT).[60] Although the psalm begins with an ironic cry of anguish questioning why God has forsaken him (22:1[2 H/G]), it concludes with an extended section calling others to join David in praising Yahweh for his deliverance (22:22–26[23–27 H/G]) and the confident assertion that the ends of the earth will worship Yahweh and proclaim his righteousness to generations yet to come (22:27–31[28–32 H/G]). The psalm itself makes no explicit statements that David's suffering points forward to the suffering of a future individual.[61]

How could a psalm about the psalmist's troubles serve as a pattern of the central moment in the messiah's suffering? The starting point is Jesus's own use of the opening of Ps 22 to express his anguish of abandonment. Moo observes: "Jesus is presented as making clear reference to every important OT background utilized in the passion sayings."[62] This starting point invited the earliest Christians to study the psalm in relation to the death of the Lord.

The New Testament authors see in David's sufferings a prefiguration of Jesus's sufferings.[63] This connection rests on Jesus being the promised son of David who would rule over an eternal kingdom (2 Sam 7:12–16; Matt 1:1). Because Jesus is David's greater son, the New Testament authors were able to look back at David's life and see how his experiences anticipate Jesus's experiences, particularly his suffering. As they reflected on the specific events of Jesus's crucifixion in light of Ps 22, they saw the now seemingly obvious ways that David's suffering foreshadowed the suffering of Jesus the son of David. These prefigurations were legitimately in the text, yet not capable of being recognized until later divine revelation made them evident.

At the same time, we should not underestimate the extent to which David himself understood his role within redemptive history. Yahweh promised him a descendant who would rule over an eternal kingdom in fulfillment of God's commission to Adam (2 Sam 7:12–16; cf. Gen 1:28; 12:1–3). Several

60. See *OTUOT*, 483–85; Carey, *Jesus' Cry*, 168–69.
61. So also Moo, *Old Testament in the Gospel*, 227–31.
62. Ibid., 357. Cf. 288–89; and see 271–75.
63. See ibid., 298–300.

key Davidic psalms connect this promise to Yahweh's anointed king ruling over creation, anticipating this future king from his line who would crush all his enemies and consummate God's purposes for creation (Pss 2; 8; 110; 132; cf. 72; 89). So when the New Testament authors identify David's suffering as a type of Christ's suffering, they are following the lead of the Old Testament itself, which Christ connected to himself.

CASE STUDY 3—TYPOLOGY AS INDIRECT FULFILLMENT

Matthew 2:15 remains one of the most contested cases of "fulfillment" in scripture. Matthew claims that Jesus's departure from Egypt "fulfilled what the Lord had said through the prophet: 'Out of Egypt I called my son,'" citing Hos 11:1, which in its original context describes the historical event of Israel (further identified as God's son; cf. Exod 4:22–23; Deut 1:31; 8:5) being brought out of Egypt in the original exodus. Although Hos 11:1 is not a prediction, Matthew asserts that Jesus coming out of Egypt indirectly fulfills this text based on the typological connection between Israel as God's son and Jesus as the true and ultimate Son of God.[64] Space does not allow summarizing or engaging the fierce debate concerning contextual versus noncontextual understandings of this case.[65] But both parts of this use of scripture require attention, namely, the use of a fulfillment formula and nonexpectational typological patterns. The purpose here is to present Old Testament precedents for both the use of fulfillment formulas and nonexpectational typological patterns as well as how the teachings of Messiah connect these interpretational tendencies to New Testament authors.

The Chronicler's fulfillment formula marks an interpretive blend of Jeremiah's seventy years and instruction in Lev 26 on the mandated Sabbath years for the land when Israel goes into captivity:

> *In order to fulfill* the word of Yahweh by the mouth of Jeremiah until **the land satisfied its sabbath rests it completed all the days of its *desolation*** *to fulfill seventy years*. (2 Chr 36:21 AT)

The bold words signify the Chronicler's verbal allusion to Lev 26:34–35, and the italicized words signify his verbal allusion to Jer 25:11–12 (cf. Jer 29:10).[66]

64. See Childs, "Prophecy and Fulfillment," 269–70.

65. See Beale, "Use of Hosea 11:1," 697–715; idem, "Finding Christ," 25–27, 30–35. Also see comparison of several ways Hos 11:1//Matt 2:15 is handled in the FAQs in Chapter 2.

66. See *OTUOTPL*, entry on 2 Chr 36:21; Schnittjer, "Individual versus Collective Retribution," 125–26.

The Chronicler's fulfillment formula, signified by underlining, borrows the language of fulfillment from the donor text in Jer 25:12. The Chronicler shifts the grammar from Jeremiah's use of "fulfill" in *qal* to "fulfill" in *piel* so it can function for fulfillment of the prophetic word, not just completion of time.[67] This interpretive move by the Chronicler establishes the kind of fulfillment formulas known in the New Testament, especially in Matthew and John, which rely upon Chronicles.[68]

Hosea interprets several nonexpectational Torah passages as prefigurations in relation to Israel. A good example is his shift from third-person singular in speaking about nonexpectational events in the life of Jacob recounted in Genesis to first-person plural in applying these historical events to his contemporary constituents.

> He [Jacob] struggled with the delegate and overcame him. He wept and he begged for his favor. He will find us at Bethel and will speak with us there—Yahweh God Almighty, Yahweh is his memorial. (Hos 12:4–5[5–6 H] AT, following MT)

The shift in person is signified by underlining. The main complications and interpretive issues have been explained elsewhere.[69] The only point that needs to be made here is that Hosea applies a prefiguration within a nonexpectational biblical narrative to his constituents who need to turn back to Yahweh.[70] Just as God met with their ancestor Jacob at Bethel and spoke with him, Hosea anticipates a day when God would meet his people Israel at Bethel—sometime after its golden calf is removed.

Based on the point at hand, we can look to a teaching attributed to Jesus in Mark's Gospel, of which Matthew makes extensive use, including the content quoted here. Jesus typologically applies nonexpectational prophetic discourse from Isaiah to his opponents:

> So the Pharisees and teachers of the law asked Jesus, "Why don't your disciples live according to the tradition of the elders instead of eating their food with

67. While Jer 25:12 uses "fulfill" (מלא) in *qal*—"To fulfill seventy years" (כִּמְלֹאות שִׁבְעִים שָׁנָה) (Jer 25:12 AT)—characteristic of fulfilling/completing a timespan, the Chronicler cites it as *piel*: "to fulfill seventy years" (לְמַלֹּאות שִׁבְעִים שָׁנָה) (2 Chr 36:21 AT). The *piel* of "fulfill" provides a bridge for the Chronicler's fulfillment formula, which needs to use "fulfill" in *piel* in the sense of accomplishing the prophetic word: "In order to fulfill (לְמַלֹּאות) the word of Yahweh" (AT). See Childs, "Prophecy and Fulfillment," 266; מלא *piel* no. 5 *HALOT* 2:584. For more detail, see *OTUOTPL*, entry on 2 Chr 36:21.

68. See Schnittjer, "What's Old?" 73–78.

69. See *OTUOT*, 362–66.

70. As observed in other contexts of Hosea by Garrett, "Hosea, Book of," *DNTUOT*, 338.

> defiled hands?" [6]He replied, "Isaiah was right when he prophesied about you hypocrites; as it is written: *'These people honor me with their lips, but their hearts are far from me. [7]They worship me in vain; their teachings are merely human rules.'* [8]You have let go of the commands of God and are holding on to human traditions." (Mark 7:5–8, carried over in Matt 15:7–9, emphasis added)

The typological interpretation by Jesus of nonexpectational prophetic discourse is not an innovation in Matt 15:7–9—he follows the framing in Mark 7:5–8. Amid a deeply ironic set of judgment oracles against Jerusalem, Isaiah pauses in Isa 29:13 to give voice to a nonexpectational scathing condemnation of his constituents. It is this nonexpectational condemnation of the people of Jerusalem in Isaiah's day that Jesus interprets as a typological pattern that he applies to the scholars who opposed his ministry.[71]

Matthew 2:15 puts together the precedents from Old Testament use of scripture and the precursors in the Messiah's exegetical use of scripture. Matthew follows Hosea's lead in using the exodus from Egypt as a prefiguration of return from Mesopotamian captivity (Hos 11:11; cf. 9:3; 11:5). In the tradition of the Chronicler (2 Chr 36:21), Matthew uses a fulfillment formula with the prophetic word as its object to lead into a typological interpretation of a nonexpectational historical comment in Hos 11:1 originally set amid a condemnation of Israel in Hosea's day (italics signify a fulfillment formula according to the precedent in 2 Chr 36:21 and bold signifies quotation of Hos 11:1 proto-MT as prefiguration according to the precedents of Hosea and Jesus).

> So he [Joseph] got up, took the child and his mother during the night and left for Egypt, [15]where he stayed until the death of Herod. *And so was fulfilled what the Lord had said through the prophet*: "**Out of Egypt I called my son**." (Matt 2:14–15, emphasis added)

It is easy to see how modern interpreters could take Matt 2:15 out of its historical and biblical context and impose modern standards on the passage. But we need to approach it according to the biblical precedents and precursors in the Old Testament and the teachings of Jesus, just like Matthew did. From this perspective, Matthew is reading Hosea typologically in exactly the way Hosea himself and Jesus interpreted earlier nonexpectational historical events recorded in scripture. Matthew advances revelation of the obedience of Jesus the Son of God with a Chronicles-like fulfillment formula introducing a

71. This observation comes from Craig Blomberg, "Jesus's Use of the OT," *DNTUOT*, 377.

Hosea-like reading of Hosea. In this light, Matt 2:15 can be regarded as plain sense exegesis. Matthew interprets Hosea and the life of Jesus in the very same way they interpret scripture.

CONCLUSION

When it comes to identifying types, the biblical text itself is the final authority. Because the biblical authors themselves identify types within scripture, we also should be attentive to the presence of typology within scripture. While the biblical authors themselves identify a large number of these types, we should not assume that every type within scripture is explicitly identified by the biblical authors. Since Jesus himself invites his followers to read the entirety of the Old Testament as a coherent narrative that points to his death and resurrection and the announcement of that good news to the ends of the earth (Luke 24:44–47), we should expect to find types that are legitimately in the text but not explicitly identified by the biblical authors themselves. But in doing so we must avoid two dangers.

The first is giving our proposed types the same authoritative status as the types explicitly identified in scripture. We may have a measure of confidence in our proposed types (depending, of course, on the strength of the evidence), but at the end of the day we should acknowledge that they cannot be asserted with the same level of authority as those types explicitly identified in scripture. Only biblical authors have been inspired by God and appointed to speak God's revealed will authoritatively across the generations. Thus, we must hold our proposed types with a measure of interpretive humility.

The second danger is hunting for "secret messages" in the Bible, as if God has embedded a complex code that only those who know what clues to look for can discover. Such an approach is a modern form of Gnosticism in which only the initiated possess the secret decoder ring that unlocks messages that God allegedly locked within scripture. Instead, our focus must remain on the plain sense meaning of the text within its literary, historical, social, redemptive, and canonical contexts.

With an awareness of these dangers and a firm grasp of the different aspects of typology, you will be well positioned to recognize how typology is one aspect that unites God's progressive revelation throughout both the Old and New Testaments.

Study Questions

1. How does typology relate to the promise-fulfillment structure of the scriptures?
2. What is the difference between direct and indirect fulfillment?
3. Identify and explain two examples of the kinds of correspondences that signal the possibility of a typological connection between a donor and receptor text.
4. What does escalation between a donor and receptor text mean?
5. What is the difference between temporal typological patterns and spatial typological patterns?
6. Identify and explain three ways that a donor text can indicate a forward-looking type?
7. When it comes to backward-looking typological patterns, on what basis do receptor texts identify typological patterns that are not immediately evident in the donor text?
8. What are the key differences between typological patterns, extended echo effect, and allegory?
9. Summarize in your own words the three controls suggested for avoiding identifying every potential analogy between a donor and receptor text as typology.
10. Select an example of a forward-looking type identified in this chapter and evaluate the biblical evidence for it.
11. Select an example of a backward-looking type identified in this chapter and evaluate the biblical evidence for it.
12. What two dangers must be avoided when proposing types that the biblical authors do not explicitly identify?

CHAPTER 7

HISTORICAL EXEGESIS VERSUS HISTORICAL AND PROSOPOLOGICAL EXEGESIS

CHOICE

The present chapter builds on the previous chapter by focusing on a tricky subset of typological patterns in scripture. The student who is unclear about typological patterns may want to review Chapter 6 before continuing in this chapter.

Prosopological exegesis is not something modern interpreters invented. The use of prosopological exegesis by biblical authors has been misrepresented by some, causing confusion. The reader new to this area of the Bible's use of the Bible will do well to be patient and cautious.

Here is a broad definition that will be fleshed out momentarily. Prosopological exegesis refers to the analogical use of earlier speeches in the Bible. Analogical speech is inclusive of typological speech. In this book we reserve the term "typological" for expectational patterns. Analogical speech includes both expectational/typological and nonexpectational speeches.

The choice is between the denial of prosopological exegesis in favor of exegesis confined to the historical context of donor texts and both historical and prosopological exegesis in scripture. This thorny hermeneutical decision requires great care. This chapter advocates for both historical and prosopological exegesis by the scriptural authors and emphasizes the common ground in the approaches of several leading scholars.[1]

1. Though each of the following interpreters takes a different angle and uses different terminology, they share substantial agreement regarding prosopological exegesis in scripture, namely, Franz Delitzsch, Geerhardus Vos, Madison Pierce, Brandon Crowe, James Hamilton, and the current authors (Harmon

The relatively recent renewed awareness of prosopological exegesis in scripture has run into difficulties. Some proponents of prosopological exegesis have intermixed it with nonessential elements. This has led to attacks that have denied prosopological exegesis altogether based on these nonessential insertions. This means a place to start for responsible interpretation is setting aside the nonessential elements that sometimes become intermixed into prosopological exegesis. To that end this section will be organized around a series of questions (the elements in these questions are defined below).

- What is prosopological exegesis in scripture?
- What nonessential elements have been intermixed with an approach to prosopological exegesis in scripture that leads some scholars to reject prosopological exegesis?
- What biblical evidence demonstrates that New Testament authors practice historical as well as prosopological exegesis of scripture?
- What precursors and precedents within Israel's scriptures and the life and teachings of the Messiah did New Testament authors follow in their prosopological exegesis?

What is prosopological exegesis in scripture? In this chapter, prosopological exegesis refers to a biblical author *reading an earlier biblical speech in the light of a new character.*[2] The new character can be the speaker and/or the referent and/or the auditor—the person(s) whom the speech is by, about, or to.

The term "prosopological" comes from the Greek word *prosopon* (πρόσωπον), meaning person or face. Prosopological exegesis is a subcategory of the interpretation of analogical patterns in scripture. Interpreters of prosopological exegesis in scripture emphasize the "face" or character that the author of the receptor text assigns as the allusion's speaker(s), referent(s), and/or auditor(s).[3] In that sense, prosopological exegesis is inclusive of extended echo effect and typological readings as these are reflected in *spoken* messages.[4] One scholar refers to prosopological exegesis as "typological speech."[5] But that is only half

and Schnittjer). We are grateful to Pierce, Crowe, and Hamilton for vigorous and extensive feedback and interaction with different drafts of this chapter. See footnotes below for each of their published works in this area. This chapter presents the views of the authors of this book and does not speak for anyone else.

2. This definition is indebted to Madison Pierce.

3. See Pierce, *Divine Discourse*, 4; idem, "Gospel Reading," 51.

4. For the distinction between extended echo effect and typological patterns, see Table 6-F in Chapter 6 and Glossary. Also see *OTUOT*, 894, 902; Schnittjer, *Torah Story*, 13, 18–19.

5. See Pate, "Who Is Speaking?" 732.

right because not all prosopological exegesis is expectational. It is more accurate to think of prosopological exegesis as *analogical speech*.

Prosopological exegesis appears in a few contexts of Israel's scriptures. As in the previous chapters of this study, the exegesis within Israel's scriptures that was studied by New Testament authors, and has been largely ignored by New Testament scholars, will serve as an important resource for interpretation. Several New Testament authors, especially the author of Hebrews, latched onto prosopological exegesis as an efficient way to unfold what the Messiah accomplished within God's redemptive will. Though prosopological exegesis in scripture is used for other things, many cases emphasize christological readings of donor texts.

As noted above, prosopological exegesis is not something modern interpreters do. It is an analogical and/or typological interpretation of speeches in biblical donor texts by authors of biblical receptor texts. An example may help. The psalmist of Ps 45 gives voice to what a royal bride says to and about her king (Ps 45:1[2 H]). In the spirit of royal hyperbole, she refers to her sovereign lord the king as "God" (*'elohim* אֱלֹהִים) who rules forever. She shows it to be hyperbole when she places God the human king under God, saying, "therefore God, your God . . ." (v. 7[8 H]). The psalmist gives voice to her praises:

> Your throne, O God, will last for ever and ever;
> a scepter of justice will be the scepter of your kingdom.
> You love righteousness and hate wickedness;
> **therefore God, your God**, has set you above your companions
> by anointing you with the oil of joy. (Ps 45:6–7[7–8 H], emphasis added)

In a famous contrast between celestial agents and Christ, the author of Hebrews analogically reassigns the speaker to God and the referent to the Son. The use of citation formulas is a key tool in many cases of prosopological exegesis. Notice how prosopological reframing serves the contrast the author of Hebrews is making.

> **But about the Son he [God] says,**
> "Your throne, O God, will last for ever and ever;
> a scepter of justice will be the scepter of your kingdom.
> You have loved righteousness and hated wickedness;
> therefore God, your God, has set you above your companions
> by anointing you with the oil of joy." (Heb 1:8–9, emphasis added)

By reassigning the speaker and the referent, the author of Hebrews provides an analogical interpretation of the speech of Ps 45:7[8 H] applied to the Son.[6]

The recognition of prosopological exegesis has been around a long time among modern interpreters even though it is not referred to as such.[7] Matthew Bates needs to be credited for reviving attention to the ancient designation of this biblical phenomenon as prosopological exegesis. But in so doing he added his own innovations.

What nonessential elements have been intermixed with an approach to prosopological exegesis in scripture that leads some scholars to reject prosopological exegesis? Bates builds several nonessential elements into his study of prosopological exegesis. These nonessential elements have instigated much confusion. One response to Bates's proposal rejects prosopological exegesis in scripture in favor of exegesis limited to the historical context of the donor text and denies the typological character of prosopological exegesis. All of these problems (added nonessentials, rejection of prosopological exegesis, denying the typological character of prosopological exegesis) need to be addressed briefly in order to explain the biblical authors' use of historical *and* prosopological exegesis.

The nonessential elements Bates includes in his presentation of prosopological exegesis are: (1) non-typological character of prosopological exegesis; (2) unmarked occasional Old Testament prophetic utterances that present a transhistorical theodrama (a term coined by Bates); (3) Jesus did not know who he was until he discovered his identity by prosopological exegesis; and (4) New Testament authors develop prosopological exegesis based on Greco-Roman background.[8] While all of these claims are problematic, only the first two will be taken up here due to space limitations and the focus of this chapter.[9]

Bates affirms that the scriptures use both typological patterns and prosopological exegesis. But, for Bates, they are two different kinds of

6. For examples of expectational typological speech, see Hamilton, *Typology*, 144–45 (Ps 22:21[22 H]+Isa 8:17–18 in Heb 2:12–13), 187–88 (Ps 16:8–11 in Acts 2:25–28).

7. See Delitzsch in K&D 5:117–18 (on Ps 102:24–29), 7:239 (on Isa 8:18); idem, *Hebrews*, 1:71–72, 82–84; 2:198–99; Vos, *The Teaching of the Epistle to the Hebrews*, 60–61.

8. See Bates, *The Hermeneutics of the Apostolic Proclamation*, 243, 252, 276, n. 133, 293, 300–4 and idem, *The Birth of the Trinity*, 9, 72, 117, 126 (non-typological character of prosopological exegesis); *Birth*, 34–35 and *Hermeneutics*, 350, and see 216, 243, 251–53, 268, 277 (prophetic utterances present a transhistorical theodrama); *Birth*, 65 (Jesus discovers his identity as the Son of God by prosopological exegesis); and *Hermeneutics*, 192–94 and *Birth*, 31 (Greco-Roman background). Bates admits that his own summaries of how Jesus puzzled out prosopological exegesis to understand who he is are "nothing more than a matter of speculation" (*Birth*, 65). Bates's studies are hereafter cited parenthetically in the next four paragraphs.

9. I am grateful to Matthew Bates for offering pointed feedback on multiple drafts of this part of the chapter including the version in the next four paragraphs.

things. He argues at length for typological patterns within Israel's scriptures (*Hermeneutics*, 135–48), though he prefers the expression "iconic mimesis (imitation)" because of problems with typology (135, 148). He affirms that Paul's use of typological patterns is ordinarily backward-looking—it is only "deliberately anticipatory" in retrospect (147–48). Bates rejects Richard Hays's backward-looking typological reading of Ps 69:9[10 H/68:10 G]—"zeal for your house devoured me [cf. John 2:17] and the insults of those who were insulting you fell on me [cf. Rom 15:3]" (Bates's translation of the LXX, 245)—because of a lack of analogy between David and Jesus (250) and because Hays's "convoluted" view relies upon David the individual representing Israel the collective (251).[10]

Typological patterns and prosopological exegesis are not mutually exclusive for Bates, since a context mainly of narrative correspondence could include a prosopological disjuncture. But, in Bates's view, an utterance can only be one or the other because typological patterns (iconic mimesis) require narrative correspondence and prosopological exegesis requires narrative disjuncture. He says, "[T]he sharing of a type demands that respective Old Testament and New Testament passages participate in a common image (iconic mimesis), and the prosopological reasoning is precisely that the actors do *not* appropriately share that image" (*Birth*, 182–83).

Bates's approach regards the prosopological utterance itself as emerging from the prophet's historical context, but the prophet speaks in the person of a theodramatic character from a different horizon in time (34). The theodrama occurs in a transhistorical setting other than that of the authors of Israel's scriptures. Bates says the prophets' words slip out of their historical context as they put on a *prosopon*/mask and voice part of the "*theodramatic production*" (*Hermeneutics*, 350, emphasis original).

The disjuncture between the surrounding context and the prosopological utterance can be so strong at times that Bates refers to it in terms of a dictation theory of revelation. He says, "the divine author was placing an in-character speech on the lips of the psalmist" (252) and "it is the Spirit who supplies the words to the prophet" (*Birth*, 34). There is no blanket view of prosopological inspiration. Bates approaches each occurrence on its own terms and most frequently characterizes prosopological utterances as the divine author speaking through the human author (e.g., *Hermeneutics*, 216, 217, 243, 251, 253, 268, 277, et passim). His strong emphasis on the divine author leads, at times, to less emphasis on the human authors. As Bates says of Rom 10:16, "[T]he

10. See Hays, *Conversion of the Imagination*, 115–17.

human prophet Isaiah is of very little hermeneutical significance to Paul as an individual, except inasmuch as he served as a faithful servant through whom the Holy Spirit could work" (349–50). Bates says this even though in this context Paul writes "for Isaiah says . . ." The focus on the divine author of the ahistorical prophetic utterances leads one reviewer to see Bates as making David "disappear" from his own psalms.[11]

Some of those who have critiqued Bates's bold proposal for understanding prosopological exegesis in scripture have rejected prosopological exegesis altogether. These rejections, unfortunately, are based on the nonessential elements added within Bates's view. Rejecting prosopological exegesis altogether results in a reading of scripture limited to the historical context of the donor text. The present purpose is to briefly describe the rejection of Bates's view and show that the confinement of the sense to the historical context of the donor text does not adequately handle the biblical evidence.

Peter Gentry says that in Bates's view New Testament authors move "beyond the original context in their interpretation of OT texts by employing prosopological exegesis."[12] Gentry admits that Hebrews cites scripture as the Father speaking to the Son and asks, "But is it prosopological exegesis?" (109) As part of his answer Gentry sketches out several areas at some length, including redemptive-historical framework, covenants, and his own view that Adam was a priest and a king (109–18). This leads Gentry to the conclusion that Peter's use of Ps 16 in Acts 2 and the use of scripture by the author of Hebrews are based on "the metanarrative" of scripture (redemptive-historical framework) and the covenants (118). These New Testament authors, claims Gentry, used typology within the canonical context of scripture (118). Gentry argues that the apostles cannot be using typology and prosopological exegesis at the same time (119–20). He concludes that the New Testament authors only interpret the Old Testament within the historical context of the Old Testament (120). Gentry answers his own question about prosopological exegesis (cited earlier in this paragraph): "They [New Testament authors] are arguing from the Scriptures. They are not making things up" (120).

William Dernell comes to virtually the same conclusions as Gentry.[13] But Dernell says: "there is little evidence, if any for PE [Prosopological Exegesis]

11. See Seitz, review of *The Birth of the Trinity* (by Bates), 765. He also says these emphases "evacuate the man David" (764).

12. Gentry, "A Preliminary Evaluation," 106; hereafter cited parenthetically in this paragraph. For another overview of this debate, see Streett, "New Approaches," 11–13.

13. See Dernell, "Typology," 137–61.

in the OT."[14] Dernell's confusion badly distorts the situation. See below for precursors and cases of prosopological exegesis within Israel's scriptures.[15]

It is easy to understand the need to argue against the nonessential elements that Bates included in his approach to prosopological exegesis in the New Testament. But in many cases receptor texts reread whom biblical speeches are by, about, and to in comparison to the donor text (see examples in Table 7-A below). In other words, prosopological exegesis is not something modern interpreters do to the Bible—it is in the Bible. The claim that New Testament authors could only use historical-typological exegesis but not prosopological exegesis on the same Old Testament texts does not fit with evidence (see next section below).[16]

Madison Pierce offers an approach to prosopological exegesis without the nonessential elements that Bates includes. Pierce wonders if, at times, Bates "was forcing a text or interpretation into a predetermined category."[17] Pierce explicitly sets aside Bates's nonessential elements in her own approach to prosopological exegesis.[18]

Two important elements have not been worked out in the debates about prosopological exegesis. The precursors of New Testament prosopological exegesis within Israel's scriptures and the evidence that prosopological exegesis does not replace the historical context both need attention. These will be picked up briefly in the next two subsections in reverse order.

What biblical evidence demonstrates that New Testament authors practice historical as well as prosopological exegesis of scripture? Though prosopological exegesis has been rejected by interpreters, such as Gentry and Dernell who confine the sense to the historical context of the donor text (see above), the New Testament affirms both historical and prosopological exegesis. The present approach likewise takes a both/and approach.[19]

The author of Hebrews provides evidence that supports interpreting Israel's scriptures in their historical context as well as approaching them by prosopological exegesis. The author of Hebrews tends to approach written scripture as spoken word. Notice the oral citation formula to a quotation of Ps 95:7–11 in Heb 3:7 (signified by underlining) with the citation of Ps 95:7b (signified by italics):

---

14. Ibid., 151.

15. Also see Crowe's contention for prosopological exegesis in the OT ("Prosopological Exegesis," *DNTUOT*, 645–46).

16. Other scholars argue both/and for prosopological exegesis and typological patterns. See, e.g., ibid., 646–47.

17. Pierce, review of *The Birth of the Trinity* (by Bates).

18. See Pierce, *Divine Discourse*, 20; idem, "Precedents for Prosopological Exegesis," 216, n. 26.

19. So also Crowe, "Prosopological Exegesis," *DNTUOT*, 646–47.

> So, as the Holy Spirit says:
> "*Today, if you hear his voice. . . .*" (Heb 3:7)

The author of Hebrews goes on to attribute the very same psalm to David (signified by underlining) to establish the temporal distance of "today" as encompassing Israel in the wilderness, the psalmist's constituents, and the readers of Hebrews:[20]

> . . . This he [Holy Spirit] did when a long time later he spoke through David, as in the passage already quoted:
> "*Today, if you hear his voice . . .*" (4:7b)[21]

The evidence in Heb 3:7 and 4:7 affirms the dual attribution of Ps 95:7 to David and the deity.[22] The author of Hebrews acknowledges the source of revelation as the Holy Spirit, but this does not replace the historical context of the rebellion in the days of Moses (3:16), the historical context of the psalm (4:7–8), or the human author (4:7). The point that the author of Hebrews is making about what the Holy Spirit said in Ps 95 depends on *not* collapsing any of these historical contexts.

The author of Hebrews does not merely read the Holy Spirit into the text. He follows the lead of Isa 63:11, 14 in seeing the Spirit among Israel in the wilderness.[23]

> Then his people recalled the days of old,
> the days of Moses and his people—
> where is he who brought them through the sea,
> with the shepherd of his flock?
> Where is he who set
> *his Holy Spirit among them?* (Isa 63:11, emphasis added)

---

20. This temporal observation is indebted to Madison Pierce. Also see Pierce, *Divine Discourse*, 144, n. 25; cf. 23, n. 57.

21. The NIV and NET wrongly add "God" to the beginning of Heb 4:7 (not quoted above). They do so for clarity by carrying down "God" from 4:3 which cites Ps 95:11. However, NIV/NET fail to notice that Heb 3:7 attributes Ps 95:7–11 to the Holy Spirit and within this citation the Holy Spirit shifts from third-person reporting in 3:7 to first-person embedded speech of God in 3:9–11 (God quoted by the Holy Spirit in Ps 95). Thus, the citation of Ps 95:7–8 in Heb 3:7–8, 15 is attributed to the Holy Spirit, and in 4:7 attributed to the Holy Spirit through David. Also see Pierce, *Divine Discourse*, 162; cf. 96, n. 11.

22. So also Vos, *The Teaching of the Epistle to the Hebrews*, 73; idem "Hebrews Part 1," 627. For a similar point on the dual referent of Ps 16 in Acts 2, see Hamilton, *Typology*, 187.

23. See Pierce, *Divine Discourse*, 163; cf. 146–48. Also see *OTUOT*, 251–52.

In sum, New Testament authors do not use prosopological exegesis to replace historical context, but they practice both prosopological and historical exegesis on the same passages.

What precursors and precedents within Israel's scriptures and the life and teachings of the Messiah did New Testament authors follow in their prosopological exegesis? The New Testament authors did not create prosopological exegesis ex nihilo. They expanded this form of analogical exegesis within Israel's scriptures and applied it to the Father, Son, and Spirit.[24] Israel's scriptures feature several precursors and precedents of prosopological exegesis. And, as with other kinds of scriptural interpretation, exegesis within Israel's scriptures connects with the New Testament by the life and teachings of the Messiah (see Chapter 1).

The headings on most psalms (about 100)—not the ones by modern Bible publishers but those in the Hebrew Bible—function as precursors to prosopological exegesis. These authoritative superscriptions have a literary function within the Psalter but do not constitute exegesis—more like apparatus or metadata.[25] The most well-known psalm headings are the approximately seventy-five "of David" superscriptions. The preposition "of" *le-* (לְ) features a similar semantic range in Hebrew and English: "(written) by," "about," "to," "for," and the like.[26] These psalms superscriptions cause all of these psalms to be considered in relation to David.[27] Did David write it? Is it about him? If it is for him or about him, who wrote it? Though the default reading for "of David" psalms by many interpreters is David-as-author,[28] some of these psalms contain elements from after David's historical context (e.g., Ps 5:7[8 H]; 51:18–19[20–21 H]; 65:1[2 H]; 68:29[30 H]; 122:1–2).[29] None of this needs to be sorted out here except for one thing. The headings of the psalms insert possible speakers, referents of the speeches, or auditors to these psalms. While this is more open-ended than prosopological exegesis, it is an important precursor.

The Chronicler takes excerpts from three psalms of book IV of the Psalter and sets them within the account of the ark coming into Jerusalem in the days

---

24. On trinitarian use in the NT, see Swain, "Covenant of Redemption," 120–21.

25. See *OTUOT*, 534–37.

26. See Joüon §130b, n. 5. For examples of *le-* (לְ) with the sense of "to," as in *given to*, from the eighth century BCE Samaria Ostraca, see, e.g., Aḥituv, *Echoes from the Past*, 269–71 (nos. 9, 10).

27. See Longman, *OT as Literature*, 169.

28. See GKC §129c; *IBHS* §11.2.10d (no. 17).

29. The view concerning "of David" psalms presented here is a standard view. See, e.g., Grisanti, "Psalms," 514.; VanGemeren, *Psalms*, 45–46; Goldingay, *Psalms 1–41*, 1:27–28. Although Longman affirms the range of meaning of "of" *le-* (לְ) he thinks that in the psalms headings it refers to authorship, but he cautions against dogmatism (*Psalms*, 25–26).

of David.[30] The Chronicler does not add a citation formula, allowing the psalm medley to function like a poetic interlude for readers. Notice the narrative framing:[31]

> Then on that day David first appointed Asaph and his associates to give praise to Yahweh. (1 Chr 16:7 AT)
>
> vv. 8–22//Ps 105:1–15
>
> vv. 23–33//Ps 96:1b–10b, 11–13b
>
> vv. 34–36//Ps 106:1, 47–48
>
> David left Asaph and his associates before the ark of the covenant of Yahweh to minister there regularly, according to each day's requirements. (16:37 AT)

The new narrative setting invites readers to consider the referents of the psalms excerpts and the worshiping community of Jerusalem of David's day and vice versa. This is especially the case with the use of the explicitly exilic perspective of 16:35 (Ps 106:47) that does not easily align with David's day. Though the psalms medley in 1 Chr 16 does not fully use prosopological exegesis, it offers another precursor within Israel's scriptures.

The reframing of Gen 12:3 in Ps 72:17 includes the implicit assigning of the auditor from Abraham to the Davidic heir. The psalmist says, "Then all nations *will be blessed through* him [the Davidic ruler], and *they will call him blessed*" (Ps 72:17b, emphasis added to signal allusive interpretation of Gen 12:3).

Approximately eleven psalms contain divine speech embedded in them, including four of the Davidic promise psalms.[32] The divine discourses in Pss 2; 89; 110; and 132 arguably have been reframed from the oracle of Nathan that appears in 2 Sam 7. Other cases of reframing Nathan's oracle as divine discourse to David without mentioning the prophetic intermediary include 1 Kgs 5:5[19 H]; 1 Chr 22:7–9; and 28:3, 6.[33]

Of the psalms with divine discourse, the allusion to 2 Sam 7:14–15 in Ps 2:6–7 includes a revoicing from speaking about the son of David in third person to the Davidic ruler recounting divine discourse directly to him.[34] Notice the poetic reframing of the Davidic promise (bold signifies verbal parallels and underlining signifies interpretive paraphrase):[35]

---

30. The evidence suggests that the postscript of book IV of the Psalter (Ps 106:48) was already in place when the Chronicler used these psalms. See *OTUOT*, 511.

31. See ibid., 736, 738–40.

32. See Gillingham, "New Wine," 380.

33. See *OTUOT*, 521; with further evidence in Schnittjer, "Your House Is My House," 63, 70.

34. So also more allusively, see Ps 89:26–27[27–28 H]; cf. 2 Sam 7:14.

35. See *OTUOT*, 480–81.

> [Yahweh says via Nathan] I will be a father for him and he will be a **son** to **me**. When he does wrong, I will punish him with a rod wielded by mortals, with floggings inflicted by human hands. (2 Sam 7:14 AT)

> [The Lord of heaven says] I have installed my king on Zion, my holy mountain. [The new king says] I shall recount the decree of Yahweh: He said to me, "You are **my son**. Today I have begotten you." (Ps 2:6–7, v. 7 AT)

The psalmist powerfully shifts perspectives to the time of the anointing of the Davidic ruler. The begotten language cannot be taken literally since infants do not hold conversations. Thus, the begotten imagery here more likely connotes divine adoption by anointing—a poetic exegetical advancement of Nathan's oracle. The point at hand is a shift from David's son as third-person object to direct address by a Davidic ruler himself. And this analogical shift appears within a poetic revoicing of the promise to the perspective of Davidic heir, the son of Yahweh. This case of prosopological exegesis sets the precedent for development in the New Testament.

Another important prosopological exegetical precedent within Israel's scriptures for the New Testament style of prosopological exegesis is 2 Chr 6:41–42. This will be explained in the cases below.

The connection between precedents for prosopological exegesis within Israel's scriptures and the New Testament is the life and teachings of the Messiah, as in other modes of scriptural exegesis (see Chapter 1). A voice, presumably from God the Father, employed prosopological exegesis in an interpretive blend at the baptism and transfiguration of the Lord.

> And a voice came from heaven: "You are my Son **[Ps 2:7]**, whom I love **[possibly Gen 22:2]**; with you I am well pleased **[Isa 42:1]**." (Mark 1:11; cf. Matt 3:17; Luke 3:22)

> Then a cloud appeared and covered them, and a voice came from the cloud: "This is my Son **[Ps 2:7]**, whom I love **[possibly Gen 22:2]**. Listen to him! **[Deut 18:15]**." (Mark 9:7; cf. Matt 17:5; Luke 9:35)

The Messiah used prosopological exegesis in an interpretive blend to declare of himself before the high priest: Jesus said, "I am [the Messiah, the Son of the Blessed One]. You will see the son of a human *sitting at the right hand* **[Ps 110:1, italics]** of the strong one and coming on the clouds of heaven **[Dan 7:13, underlining]**" (Mark 14:62 AT; cf. Matt 26:64; and see Chapter 4).

The evangelists accepted the Messiah's use of Ps 22:1[2 H]—"My God, my God, why have you forsaken me?" (Mark 15:34; cf. Matt 27:46)—as can be seen by the further typological use of Ps 22 in the narration (Mark 15:24; cf. Ps 22:18[19 H]; Mark 15:29, 31, 32b; cf. Ps 22:7[8 H]) (see Chapter 6). In these and other cases, the voice from heaven and the Messiah himself built on the precedents of analogical reading of whom scriptural speeches are by, about, and/or to within Israel's scriptures.

In sum, the life and teachings of the Messiah connected precedents for and early cases of prosopological exegesis in Israel's scriptures with the distinctive prosopological style of exegesis in the New Testament focused on the Father, Son, and Spirit.

CASE STUDIES

Two related cases of prosopological exegesis will be presented here, one from Israel's scriptures and one from the New Testament. This will be followed by a table listing many cases of prosopological exegesis in the Bible.

The Chronicler's use of scripture in 2 Chr 6:41–42 has all the characteristics of prosopological exegesis: (1) use of a preexisting opening and closing citation formula of the donor text (1 Kgs 8) and (2) the analogical shift of speaker and referents in the speech, as well as the auditors of Ps 132:8–10, 1+Isa 55:3 in 2 Chr 6:41–42. The extensive assortment of issues in the context of Chronicles needs to be set aside here to focus only on this case of prosopological exegesis.[36] The sense of the crucial last phrase of Isa 55:3 remains debated. Whether David should be seen as subject or object of covenantal loyalties does not alter the present argument concerning the analogical shift of referents of the speech.[37]

The placement of this interpretive blend into Solomon's prayer analogically shifts the speaker. Notice the interpretive blend within the recycled preexisting citation framework (emphases signify verbal parallels).

> Then *Solomon stood* before the altar of Yahweh in front of *the whole assembly of Israel, spread out his hands toward heaven, and said. . . . When Solomon finished praying. . . .* (1 Kgs 8:22–23a, 54a AT)

---

36. See *OTUOT*, 765–70.

37. For the subjective genitive view, see Lynch, *Monotheism*, 231, n. 73. For an objective genitive view, see *OTUOT*, 766. And see footnotes in both of these for leading proponents of this debate.

> A song of ascents. [paslmist:] Yahweh, remember David and all his self-denial. . . . [congregation:] "Arise, Yahweh, and come to your resting place, you and the ark of your might. May your priests be clothed with your righteousness; may your faithful people sing for joy." For the sake of your servant David, do not reject your anointed one. (Ps 132:1, 8–10 AT)

> Give ear and come to me; listen, that you may live. I will make an everlasting covenant with you [plural], **faithful love** promised **to David.** (Isa 55:3 AT)

> *Solomon stood* on the platform and then knelt down before *the whole assembly of Israel, spread out his hands toward heaven, and he said. . . .*
>
> Now arise, Yahweh God, and come to your resting place, you and the ark of your might. May your priests, Yahweh God, be clothed with salvation, may your faithful people rejoice in your goodness. Yahweh God, do not reject your anointed one. Remember **the faithful love to David** your servant.
>
> *When Solomon finished praying. . . .* (2 Chr 6:13b–14a, 41–7:1a AT)

The Chronicler's Solomon strategically cites the only explicit mention of the ark of the covenant in the Psalter (Ps 132:8), calling upon Yahweh to come just moments before fire falls from heaven upon the sacrifice and a second retelling of the glory coming into the temple (2 Chr 7:1–3; cf. 5:13–14; 1 Kgs 8:10–11). The Chronicler uses prosopological exegesis both to connect the Jerusalem temple with the forever commitment of Yahweh to his covenantal loyalty to David in Isa 55:3, as well as to provide loaded commentary on the promise to David as actualized by temple worship. The use of "you" plural in Isa 55:3 signals collective beneficiaries of Yahweh's covenantal loyalties to David. Embedding Isa 55:3 into Solomon's prayer underscores the role of temple worship as proximate fulfillment for the Chronicler's constituents at the Second Temple.

In his sermon at Pisidian Antioch, Paul analogically reads the son of Ps 2:7 as Jesus the Messiah, the auditors of the sermon as among the collective "you" plural of Isa 55:3, and the holy one of Ps 16:10 as the resurrected Jesus.[38] In other words, this compound set of prosopological exegesis explains what is fulfilled by the resurrection of Jesus. Notice how the three parts of Paul's introductory formula in italics correspond to the three citations—what was

38. See Bock, *Proclamation*, 244–45; followed by Marshall, "Acts," in *CNTUOT*, 585. For a series of catchword and catchphrase associations between the scriptures cited in this portion of Acts 13, see Johnson, *Septuagintal Midrash*, 45–46.

promised to the ancestors (Ps 2:7), for whom it is fulfilled (Isa 55:3), and the raising of Jesus (Ps 16:10).

> We tell you the good news: *What God promised our ancestors he has fulfilled for us, their children, by raising up Jesus.* As it is written in the second Psalm: "You are my son; today I have become your father" **[Ps 2:7]**. God raised him from the dead so that he will never be subject to decay. As God has said, "I will give you the holy and sure blessings promised to David" **[Isa 55:3]**. So it is also stated elsewhere: "You will not let your holy one see decay" **[Ps 16:10]**. (Acts 13:32–35, emphasis added)

The focus here is restricted to Paul's interpretation of Isa 55:3 LXX. Though the language of Isa 55:3 LXX makes several adjustments, especially from "my faithful love promised to David" (חַסְדֵי דָוִד הַנֶּאֱמָנִים) to "the holy things of David that are sure" (AT) (τὰ ὅσια Δαυιδ τὰ πιστά), it retains the essential sense of Isa 55:3 MT.[39] The most important correspondence, for the present point, is the use of "you" plural (ὑμῖν, dative) carried over from the MT (לָכֶם). Just as Isaiah promised "you" plural, the remnant, continuity with the enduring covenant of David even with no Davidic king in Jerusalem, so too Paul includes Jewish followers of Jesus as heirs of the covenant based on the resurrection of Jesus.[40]

The overlap and distinction between the use of Isa 55:3 in 2 Chr 6:42 and Acts 13:34 have not received adequate attention, especially in the light of their use of prosopological exegesis. The temple of Solomon in the narrative context of 2 Chr 6:42 and the Second Temple in the context of the reading constituents of Chronicles offer empirical evidence of Yahweh's faithfulness to his covenant with David. The glory of God with temple worshipers signifies the other blessings of the covenant as well, in a now and not yet sense of inaugurated fulfillment.[41] Paul includes the Davidic covenant as well as extends its implications to new covenant blessings of forgiveness of sins based upon the work of Jesus to "you" plural (Acts 13:38; cf. v. 34).

In sum, reuse of Isa 55:3 in 2 Chr 6 and Acts 13 demonstrates continuity and advancement of prosopological exegesis. Table 7-A summarizes representative cases of prosopological exegesis in scripture.

---

39. See Strauss, *The Davidic Messiah*, 166–68.

40. See ibid., 171. So also Crowe, *The Hope of Israel*, 55; Marshall, "Acts," in *CNTUOT*, 586; Bock, *Proclamation*, 255.

41. See the blessings of the Davidic covenant enumerated by Strauss, *The Davidic Messiah*, 171, namely, Davidic heir, Yahweh's favor, everlasting "house" (dynasty, temple), and rest from enemies.

CONCLUSION

The evidence shows that biblical authors retain a view of the historical context of earlier scripture in cases where they read it by prosopological exegesis. The evidence also shows how the life and teachings of Jesus built on the precedents and occasional prosopological exegesis in Israel's scriptures. Several New Testament authors further developed prosopological exegesis by applying it to the Father, Son, and Spirit.

Study Questions

1. In your own words, what is the choice at issue in this chapter?
2. How should prosopological exegesis in scripture be defined?
3. Why is it important to remember that analogical speech is a broader category than typological speech?
4. What are the dangers of a view that proposes that unmarked theodramatic speeches replace the historical context of selected Old Testament prophetic utterances?
5. What evidence shows that the author of Hebrews does not replace the historical context of biblical passages with prosopological exegesis but emphasizes both?
6. Explain one precursor of prosopological exegesis that appears within Israel's scriptures.
7. Explain one case of prosopological exegesis that appears in the life or utterances of Jesus.
8. Select any one example of prosopological exegesis in Table 7-A that was not explained in this chapter and briefly explain the prosopological exegesis in the receptor text.

Table 7-A: Examples of Prosopological Exegesis in Scripture[‡]

Donor text	Speaker	Auditor (a) or referent (r)	Receptor text
Num 13:1–2[a]	Yahweh	Moses (a)	Deut 1:22
2 Sam 7:14–15	Yahweh via Nathan	David (a), David's son (r)	Ps 2:6–7
Gen 12:3	Yahweh	Abraham (a)	Ps 72:17
Ps 132:8–10, 1 + Isa 55:3	psalmist; Yahweh via Isaiah	Yahweh (a); collective you (plur) via Davidic promise (r)	2 Chr 6:41–42
Isa 40:3–5	a voice	Yahweh (r)	Luke 3:4–6
Isa 61:1–2; 58:6	Spirit-anointed figure	constituents of the prophet (a)	Luke 4:18–19
Ps 69:9[10 H]	psalmist	Yahweh (a)	John 2:17
Isa 53:7–8	Isaiah	servant (r)	Acts 8:32–33
Isa 55:3	Yahweh via Isaiah	collective you (plur) via Davidic promise (r)	Acts 13:34a
Ps 69:9[10 H]	psalmist	Yahweh (a)	Rom 15:3
2 Sam 22:50//Ps 18:49[50 H]	psalmist	Yahweh (a)	Rom 15:9
Ps 116:10 LXX	psalmist	Yahweh (a)	2 Cor 4:13
Ps 2:7	Yahweh	Davidic heir (a)	Heb 1:5a
2 Sam 7:14	Yahweh via Nathan	David (a)	Heb 1:5b
Deut 32:43 LXX/DSS	Moses	celestial agents (a)	Heb 1:6

Citation formula	Speaker	Auditor (a) or referent (r)
Then all of you came to me and said	Israel	Moses (a)
He said to me	Yahweh as narrated by the Davidic king	Davidic king (a) as proclaimed by Yahweh who in turn is narrated by the Davidic king
—	psalmist	Davidic king (r)
He [Solomon] said . . . When Solomon finished praying	Solomon	Yahweh (a)
As it is written in the book of the words of Isaiah the prophet	voice is John	Lord is Jesus (r)
He [Jesus] began by saying to them, "Today this scripture is fulfilled in your hearing"	Jesus	congregation at Nazareth (a)
His disciples remembered that it is written	Jesus	God (a)
Then Philip began with this very passage of scripture and told him the good news of Jesus	Scripture	Jesus (r)
As God has said	God	Jesus (a)
For even Christ did not please himself but, as it is written	Christ	God (a)
As it is written	Christ	God (a)
It is written	Christ	God (a)
For to which of the angels did God ever say	God	Son (a)
Or again	God	Son (a)
And again, when God bring his firstborn into the world, he says	God	celestial agents (a)

Donor text	Speaker	Auditor (a) or referent (r)	Receptor text
Ps 104:4	psalmist	celestial agents (r)	Heb 1:7
Ps 45:6–7	royal bride via psalmist	(Davidic) king	Heb 1:8–9
Ps 102:25–27[26–28 H/101:26–28 G]	psalmist	Yahweh (a)	Heb 1:10–12
Ps 110:1	Yahweh	lord of psalmist (a)	Heb 1:13
Ps 22:22	psalmist	Yahweh (r)	Heb 2:12
Isa 8:17	Isaiah	Yahweh (r)	Heb 2:13a
Isa 8:18	Isaiah	Yahweh (r)	Heb 2:13b
Ps 95:7–11	psalmist (vv. 7–8), Yahweh (vv. 9–11)	congregation of psalmist (vv. 7–8), Israel (vv. 9–11) (r)	Heb 3:7–11
Ps 95:7	psalmist	congregation of psalmist (r)	Heb 4:7
Ps 2:7	Yahweh	Davidic heir (a)	Heb 5:5
Ps 110:4	Yahweh	lord of the psalmist (a)	Heb 5:6
Ps 110:4	Yahweh	lord of the psalmist (a)	Heb 7:17
Ps 110:4	Yahweh	lord of the psalmist (a)	Heb 7:21
Ps 40:6–8 LXX	psalmist	Yahweh (a)	Heb 10:5
Jer 31:33	Yahweh via Jeremiah	prophet's constituents	Heb 10:15
Jer 31:34	Yahweh via Jeremiah	prophet's constituents	Heb 10:17

[‡]The majority of examples in this chart come from research for this book. A few examples were added based on Hays, *Conversion*, 101–18; Pierce, "Gospel Reading," passim; idem, *Divine Discourse*, passim; Schnittjer, "Kadesh Infidelity," 111–13.

[a]Several other shifts in expressed agency occur in these contexts that may be referring to multiple speeches rather than the same speech, such as, encouragement to military action by Caleb (Num 13:30) and/or Moses (Deut 1:20–21), attempt to dissuade Israel from infidelity by Joshua and Caleb (Num 14:6–9) and/or Moses (Deut 1:29–33), and a few more. See Schnittjer, "Kadesh Infidelity," 111–13.

Citation formula	**Speaker**	**Auditor (a) or referent (r)**
In speaking of the angels he says	God	celestial agents (r)
But about the son he says	God	Son (r)
(continued)	God	Son (a)
To which of the angels did God ever say	God	Son (a)
He says	Jesus	God (r)
And again	Jesus	God (r)
And again he says	Jesus	"God (r)
So, as the Holy Spirit says	Holy Spirit	recipients of letter (vv. 7–8, 15), Israel (vv. 9–11; 4:3) (r)
he [Holy Spirit] spoke through David, as in the passage already quoted	God via David	congregation of psalmist (r)
But God said to him	God	Christ (a)
And he [God] says in another place	God	Christ (a)
For it is declared	—	our Lord (a)
God said to him	God	our Lord (a)
Therefore, when he came into the world, he said (AT)	Christ	God (a)
The Holy Spirit also testifies to us about this. First he says	Holy Spirit	recipients of the letter (a)
Then he adds	Holy Spirit	recipients of the letter (a)

CASE STUDIES OF THE BIBLE'S USE OF THE BIBLE

The following case studies offer step-by-step models of "how to" research for responsible interpretation of the Bible's use of the Bible. These models can be applied to research for papers, sermons, or studying the scriptures. Before presenting the cases, the way that the seven choices in the previous chapters fit together with hermeneutical basics needs to be explained.

HERMENEUTICS 101 AND SEVEN CHOICES TO STUDY THE BIBLE'S USE OF THE BIBLE

As noted in the Introduction, the seven choices build on what students learn in an introductory Hermeneutics 101 course. This section shows how.

Three methods of studying the New Testament use of the Old Testament presented in Table 8-A take the basics that anyone learns in introductory courses on biblical hermeneutics and apply these to two related texts—the donor and receptor texts. The core of all three methods is to study the donor and receptor texts in their biblical and historical contexts just like Hermeneutics 101.[1] The most important extra elements of these three methods that are not usually included in introductory hermeneutical courses are: determine the donor text as allusion/quotation (Evans, Beale) and analyze hermeneutical presuppositions (Snodgrass, Beale).

The methods summarized in Table 8-A need adjustment since the present concern goes beyond the New Testament to include the use of scripture in the entire Christian Bible. The present study, like the three methods summarized in Table 8-A, embraces the basic elements presented in any introductory

1. Also see Lanier, *Old Made New*, 19–40. Like the approaches in Table 8-A, Lanier does not treat the use of scripture within Israel's scriptures. His attempt to simplify three steps—identify the passage, double-click on the OT, and listen to the remix—skips many of the seven choices treated in this book. For example, Lanier does not deal with the deep vertical context of his main example to illustrate his approach: Isa 56:7+Jer 7:11 in Luke 19:45–46 (20–39). For the use of the law of the assembly (Deut 23) in Isa 56 and the Ten Commandments (Exod 20//Deut 5) in Jer 7, see *OTUOT*, 247–50, 270–71.

Table 8-A: Methods to Study the New Testament Use of the Old Testament‡

Evans	Snodgrass	Beale
Identify allusion		
Determine the OT text(s) being cited, including a conflation (interpretive blend).	--	Determine if the use is a quotation or an allusion.
Study donor text		
[textual]		
Determine the text-type being followed (Hebrew, Greek, Aramaic).	Compare the donor text in the MT, LXX, targums, and NT.	Compare the ancient versions of the donor text in the MT, LXX, and NT, including variants.
[contextual]		
Consider the larger OT context donor text.	Determine the original intention of the OT text in its own context.	Analyze the context of the donor text.
--	--	Analyze the hermeneutical presuppositions of the author of the receptor text.
[reception]		
Compare how the donor text was interpreted in second temple Judaic and other early Christian writings.	Compare how the donor text was used in ancient Judaic writings.	Compare how the donor text was used in ancient Judaic citations.
--	Determine the hermeneutical presuppositions that underly the interpretation of the donor text.	--
Study receptor text		
[textual]		
--	--	--
[contextual]		
Compare the function of the allusion to donor text with other biblical allusions in the receptor text.	--	Analyze the broad context of the receptor text.
Explain exegetical outcomes		
Determine the contribution of the allusion to the donor text within the receptor context.	Determine how the receptor text uses the donor text (divine proof, instruction, rhetorical effect, christological, eschatological).	Analyze the theological and rhetorical functions of the allusion to the donor text within the receptor text.

‡The methods are summarized, including some rearrangement and streamlining, from: Evans, "Function of the Old Testament," 170–71; Snodgrass, "Use of the Old Testament," 222–23; and Beale, "Method," *DNTUOT*, 520-26; *HNTUOT*, 42-43. This table is based on independent research for the present project. However, the idea for this table came from a similar table of these three methods in Keefer, "Meaning and Place," 75. After designing this table it was compared to Keefer's chart, though it serves a different purpose.

Hermeneutics 101 course. But this study works through seven choices that mostly start where introductory hermeneutics courses end. These seven choices target the special challenges of studying the Bible's use of the Bible. The three methods above do not adequately deal with choices 1, 2, 4, 6, 7 (see Table 8-B), when they deal with them at all (see Introduction for details). And these three methods do not focus on scriptural exegesis within Israel's scripture or adequately show how New Testament authors built their own scriptural exegesis upon the large body of earlier exegesis within their Bible. Despite these differences, the methods in Table 8-A do align with the steps of research of the present chapter.

Responsible interpretation of the Bible's use of the Bible includes four steps:

- Identify allusion
- Study donor text
- Study receptor text
- Explain exegetical outcomes

Table 8-B: Suggested Steps to Study the Bible's Use of the Bible‡

Step one, Identify allusion
- Determine the strength of allusion and if it is marked or unmarked (**3**).

Step two, Study donor text
[textual]
- Evaluate textual witnesses including MT, LXX, *BQS*, and (when applicable) SP (**3**).

[contextual]
- Evaluate vertical context including interpretive blends, synoptic parallels, deep context, and networks (**4**).
- Evaluate horizontal context (biblical, historical, and extrabiblical) (**5** and 101).

[reception]
- Evaluate Second Temple Jewish uses of donor text(s) (**5**).

Step three, Study receptor text
[textual and contextual]
- Evaluate textual witnesses (**3**).
- Evaluate context (biblical, historical, and extrabiblical) (101).
- Evaluate, as applicable, analogical patterns including backward-looking or forward-looking typological patterns (**6**) and prosopological exegesis (**7**).

Step four, Explain exegetical outcomes
- Explain how the receptor text uses the donor text in terms of exegetical and theological outcomes (**3** and cases in **1–7**).

Connected approach (**1**) based on advancement of revelation (**2**).

‡The numbers in parentheses refer to the chapters in this study where the choices are discussed—"101" means this is part of basic hermeneutics course(s) presupposed by the present study (see opening of the present chapter).

Table 8-B aligns these steps with the seven hermeneutical choices in the previous chapters. The case studies below follow this step-by-step approach to show how it all fits together. These cases illustrate some of the more difficult choices in the previous chapters.

LOVE THY NEIGHBOR—OLD TESTAMENT CASE STUDY

One of this case study's primary purposes is to evaluate the advancements of revelation that culminate in the command to "love thy neighbor" in Lev 19:18b. The other purpose is to work through the steps to study the Bible's use of the Bible summarized in Table 8-B. The closing section of this case study will briefly note one of the New Testament contexts that offers further exegetical advancements of Lev 19:18b.

Throughout this case study the phrase "Love thy neighbor" is shorthand for "Love thy neighbor as thyself. I am Yahweh" [וְאָהַבְתָּ לְרֵעֲךָ כָּמוֹךָ אֲנִי יהוה] (Lev 19:18b AT).

Step one, Identify allusion. "Love thy neighbor" does not drop out of the sky. It is the culmination of a series of exegetical allusions that lead up to it. Figure 8-C summarizes the basic set of allusions to be taken up here.[2]

Figure 8-C: Leviticus 19:18b as Culmination of a Series of Exegetical Allusions

The two "as yourself" (כָּמוֹךָ) clauses in Lev 19 vv. 18, 34 attract attention for good reason: they are the only appearances of the phrase in Leviticus.[3] More important is the rare syntax of the parallel phrases "love thy neighbor" and "love the residing foreigner." The verb "love" occurs more than two hundred times in the Hebrew Bible and normally uses the conventional accusative marker *'et* (אֵת) to denote the objects of the verb. Only three occurrences of finite forms of the verb use the preposition *le-* (לְ) to mark the object of "love": Lev 19:18, 34; and 2 Chr 19:2. This evidence makes it highly likely that vv. 18 and 34 are directly related by an allusion (Resource Guide 8-D). But which depends on which?

Nearly all scholars suggest that the command to love the residing foreigner (v. 34) depends on the command to love thy neighbor (v. 18). This is usually simply stated without any evaluation of the evidence. Milgrom is one of the few who evaluates the evidence. He argues that "as yourself" in the singular in v. 34 is incongruous with the plural context, suggesting that it is the receptor

2. For a detailed, advanced study of the scriptural exegesis in Lev 19:18b that goes beyond what can be presented here, to which the present discussion is indebted, see Schnittjer, "Going Vertical," 114–42.

3. For the other biblical occurrences, see "כָּמוֹ" Even-Shoshan, 548–49, nos. 74–102.

Resource Guide 8-D: Suggestions to Identify Allusions

- Tools to start: cross-references in an English Bible; *IBUB*; *OTUOTPL*; and *NTUOTPL*
- Resources for English Bible readers: *OTUOT*; *NTUOT*; and *CNTUOT*
- Additional resources for Hebrew Bible and Greek New Testament readers: the better commentaries; entries in dictionaries like *DCHR*, BDB, *HALOT*, LEH, BDAG; concordances like Even-Shoshan and R&H; and cross-references and the Appendix Loci Citati vel Allegati in NA[28]
- The best place to begin to detect allusions: Daily reading and study of the Bible

text.[4] This makes good sense because grammatical incongruity often appears in receptor texts that seek to keep the donor text intact. Notice the switch: "The residing foreigner [sg., הַגֵּר] residing with you [pl., לָכֶם] shall be treated like the citizen among you [pl., מִכֶּם]. *You shall love* [sg., וְאָהַבְתָּ] *them as yourself* [sg., כָּמוֹךָ] for you were [pl., הֱיִיתֶם] residing foreigners [pl., גֵרִים] . . ." (Lev 19:34 AT, emphasis added). However, a closer look at the evidence points in the opposite direction.

The term "citizen" (אֶזְרָח) is usually paired with "residing foreigner" (גֵּר)—fifteen of its seventeen uses—as it is here.[5] Both terms tend to be used as collective singulars, with the citizen and the residing foreigner signifying any and every one of these.[6] And, significantly, in thirteen of the fifteen instances of pairing these terms, the singular of residing foreigner appears in a plural context.[7] This evidence undercuts Milgrom's suggestion (see previous paragraph). If one of the two exceptions is examined, namely, Exod 12:48 (see footnote), the direction of dependence comes into focus.

The shift from the plural context of vv. 47 and 49 to the singular in v. 48 stems from the personal relationship between the citizen of Israel and the residing foreigner who lives in their household (Exod 12:48; cf. vv. 44, 46). And the evidence points toward Lev 19:33–34 alluding to Exod 12:48 and 22:21[20

---

4. See Milgrom, *Leviticus 1–16*, 1403, 1706–7.

5. See "אֶזְרָח" coll., *DCHR* 1:228; "אֶזְרָח" *HALOT* 1:28.

6. See *IBHS* §7.2.1d.

7. See Exod 12:19, 49; Lev 16:29; 17:15; 18:26; 19:34; 24:16, 22; Num 9:14; 15:14, 29; Josh 8:33; Ezek 47:22. The exceptions are Exod 12:48 and Num 15:30 (but cf. vv. 13, 29) ("אֶזְרָח" Even-Shoshan, 32).

H]—an interpretive blend. Of the three times in scripture that the verb "mistreat" is used with "residing foreigner" as its object, Exod 22:21[20 H] and Lev 19:34 also include the comparison to Israel as residing foreigners in Egypt.[8] This rationale clause combined with prohibitions against mistreating residing foreigners only appears in these two cases in scripture, making dependence almost certain. The catchword "residing foreigner" provides the basis to draw these texts together into an interpretive blend. Note the allusions (bold and underlining signify verbal parallels in Hebrew):

> **When residing foreigners reside with you** and want to celebrate Passover to Yahweh, all of their males shall be circumcised. Then they may come near and celebrate it **like any citizen** of the land. But no uncircumcised person shall eat of it. (Exod 12:48 AT)

> You shall not mistreat or oppress the residing foreigner, for you were residing foreigners in the land of Egypt. (Exod 22:21[20 H] AT)

> **When residing foreigners reside with you** in your land, you shall not mistreat them. Residing foreigners residing with you shall be treated **like** your own **citizens**. You shall love them as yourself, for you were residing foreigners in the land of Egypt. I am Yahweh your God. (Lev 19:33–34 AT)

Before moving on it is necessary to account for the relationship between Lev 19:34 and Deut 10:19 since some interpreters claim that the former depends on the latter. This suggestion fails to note the use of conventional syntax with the accusative marker *'et* (אֵת) in "love the residing foreigner" (AT) in Deut 10:19 versus the rare use of the preposition *le-* (לְ) in "love them [the residing foreigner]" (AT) in Lev 19:34, as noted above. Receptor texts tend to disambiguate, which provides convincing evidence that Deut 10:19 depends on Lev 19:34. Compare the evidence of two allusions to Lev 19:34 (bold and underlining signify verbal parallels and broken underlining signifies unconventional syntax):

> The residing foreigner residing with you shall be treated like your own citizens. **You shall love** them [וְאָהַבְתָּ לוֹ] **as yourself**, for you were residing foreigners in the land of Egypt. I am Yahweh your God. (Lev 19:34 AT)

8. See "ינה" BDB 413; Even-Shoshan, 473 (nos. 8, 11). It is worth noting that of the four uses of the rationale clause "for you were residing foreigners in the land of Egypt" (Exod 22:21[20 H]; 23:9; Lev 19:34; Deut 10:19 AT; see "גֵּר" Even-Shoshan, 243 [nos. 82–85]), Exod 23:9 is derivative of 22:21[20 H] and Deut 10:19 is derivative of Lev 19:34 (see below).

You shall love your neighbor [וְאָהַבְתָּ לְרֵעֲךָ] **as yourself.** I am Yahweh. (19:18b AT)

You shall love the residing foreigner [וַאֲהַבְתֶּם אֶת־הַגֵּר] for you were residing foreigners in the land of Egypt. (Deut 10:19 AT)

In sum, the evidence considered together confirms a set of allusions as well as direction of dependence. The command to love the residing foreigner in Lev 19:33–34 is an interpretive blend of the law of Passover participation in Exod 12:48 and the prohibition against mistreating residing foreigners in 22:21[20 H]. The command to love thy neighbor in Lev 19:18b builds on the command to love the residing foreigner in 19:34 (see Figure 8-C above).

Step two, Study the donor text.

Textual. The donor and receptor texts under consideration here have few variants (Resource Guide 8-E). Yet, considering these helps to reinforce the observations already made in the previous step on different grounds. The SP and (the Hebrew parent text of the) LXX (so LXX HPTAT) smooth out the grammar of Exod 12:48 by converting "with you personally" (sg., אִתְּךָ) in the MT to "with you collectively" (pl. אתכם, which would be pointed as אִתְּכֶם) (AT) (cf. *BHK*[3]/*BHS*). The more difficult reading in the MT is preferred. The same kind of smoothing out of grammatical number variation in the SP and LXX appears in 22:21[20 H] (cf. *BHK*[3]/*BHS* n. a). Again, the SP and LXX of Lev 19:33 use "with you collectively" (pl. אתכם, which would be pointed as אִתְּכֶם) to create grammatical agreement (cf. *BHK*[3]/*BHS*; *BHQ*). At Lev 19:33 Wevers affirms the LXX uses the plural "you" (ὑμῖν), agreeing with the SP-L rather than the MT.[9] All of this evidence supports the more difficult reading in the MT.[10] The shared and aligned grammatical incongruity in these texts confirms the allusion of Lev 19:33–34 to Exod 12:48 and 22:21[20 H]. And there are no substantial variants in Lev 19:18b.

In sum, the reading in the MT is preferred for Exod 12:48; 22:21[20 H]; Lev 19:18b; and 19:33–34. The evidence of the grammatical incongruities in the MT versus the smoothed-out grammar in the SP-L and LXX confirms the allusions summarized in the previous section.

Horizontal context. Study of the donor text's context may be the central

9. See *NGTL*, 309. Also see Himbaza, *BHQ*, 111*–12*; Lev 19:33 LXX HPTAT.

10. Though the ancient versions (LXX, *BQS*, targums, etc.) often "correct" singular/plural mixed grammar, as do some modern scholars, the evidence in Torah points another direction. Every legal collection in Torah freely intermixes second person singular and plural, often within the same verse. See Schnittjer, "Say You, Say Ye."

Resource Guide 8-E: Textual Criticism of the Hebrew Bible

[English Bible readers]

- NET tc notes (available at BibleGateway.com)
- Text notes in modern committee translations like the NIV and NRSVue
- NETS, SP-Eng, and *DSSB*

[Hebrew Bible readers]

- *Biblia Hebraica* apparatus (using both *BHQ* and *BHS* helps because they follow different text critical goals).[a] In addition, *BHK*^{3} with upper and lower apparatuses often sheds light on *BHS* decisions (upper apparatus is merely minor variants whereas the lower apparatus presents the editors' proposed textual emendations).[b]
- *NGTG*; *NGTE*; *NGTL*; *NGTN*; *NGTD*; LXX; *BQS*; SP; SP-G; SP-L; *TCHB*^{4}

[a]Waltke ("Aims of Textual Criticism," 93–108; cf. *TCHB*^{4}, 344–46, 396–98) presents five kinds of text critical goals: (1) original text (author) (older traditional approach); (2) final text (authorized editor) (e.g., *BHK*^{3}, *BHS*, NIV, NRSVue, NET; Waltke, "Aims of Textual Criticism," 107–8; *TCHB*^{4}, 398); (3) canonical text (proto-Masoretic ca. first century CE) (e.g., Childs); (4) earliest extant witness (e.g., *BHQ*, *HUB*); and (5) pluriformity (Qumran, LXX, SP) (e.g., scholars listed in *TCHB*^{4}, 345, n. 44; Waltke, "Aims of Textual Criticism," 102–7). The text critical goal accepted here is final form—with Waltke, Tov (*TCHB*^{4}), and the major translations (see no. 2 in this note).
[b]*BHK*^{3} (7th ed.) available at archive.org.

concern of the Bible's use of the Bible. Since the receptor text, the command to love thy neighbor (Lev 19:18b), and its primary donor text, the command to love the residing foreigner (vv. 33–34), both appear in the same chapter, the horizontal context of Lev 19 will be taken up below.

Vertical context. The present discussion targets specific elements within the series of donor texts of "love thy neighbor" that bear on the author's interpretive interventions. The arrows of Figure 8-F preview the elements of the vertical context of the command to love thy neighbor that will be taken up here.

The law of Passover participation begins categorically: "No foreigner may eat it" (Exod 12:43c).[11] In spite of the apparent sense, this prohibition does

11. See GKC §152b.

Figure 8-F: Vertical Context of Leviticus 19:18b and Its Horizontal Contexts

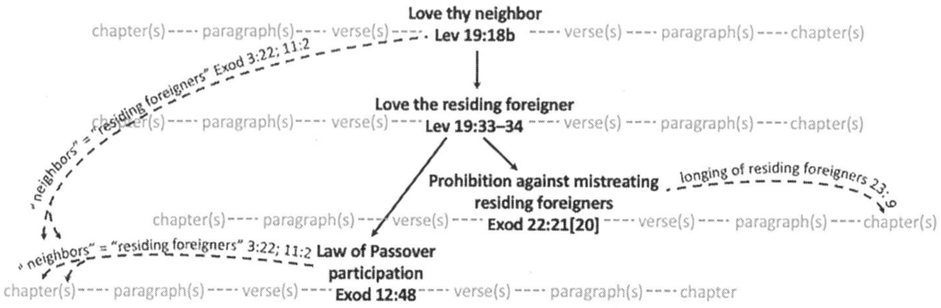

not refer to ethnic, racial, or genealogical otherness. The following verses go on to explain those ethnic others who may not and those who must participate in Passover. The uncircumcised are forbidden while the circumcised are required to participate in Passover like any citizen of Israel (12:44–45, 48). The expression for "foreigner" (בֶּן־נֵכָר) in v. 43 is different than the term "residing foreigner" (גֵּר) in v. 48. A residing foreigner connotes one who seeks asylum with Israel and, when circumcised, joins with the covenantal people as a non-citizen.[12] The importance of circumcision as the mechanism to sort who is in and out of the covenantal community is especially pressing in the context of a "mixed multitude" (12:38 NJPS).

The horizontal context of the law of Passover participation helps flesh out the sense of the circumcised residing foreigner who lives with you (12:48). Men and women alike are to ask their neighbors ("his neighbor" רֵעֵהוּ, "her neighbor" רְעוּתָהּ) for goods to take with them (11:2). This includes both Egyptians and foreigners residing within their own households (3:22).[13] The identification of residing foreigners as neighbors in the larger horizontal context of the donor text of the deep vertical context of Lev 19:18b (cf. Figure 8-F) helps explain the transposition between the command to love the residing foreigner in v. 34 and to love thy neighbor in v. 18.

The prohibition against mistreating the residing foreigner in Exod 22:21[20 H] gets collated with the prohibition protecting widows and orphans in vv. 22–24[21–23 H]. Elsewhere Levites also get collated with the protected classes (Deut 14:27, 29; 26:12). In a Venn diagram residing foreigners would be landless like orphans and Levites (while widows may inherit land) and manless like widows and orphans (in terms of an adult male citizen). The kind of otherness connoted by "residing foreigner" means they need the benevolence

12. See Block, "Sojourner; Alien; Stranger" *ISBE* 4:562.

13. See "גור I" obj. *DCHR* 2:377b; *HALOT* 1:184; cf. Schnittjer, "Say You, Say Ye," n. 10.

of landed-male-citizens within ancient patriarchal Israel like any widow or orphan. Israel knows what this is like.

A parallel prohibition (Exod 23:9; cf. 22:21[20 H]) within the covenant collection (Exod 21–23) explains the burden of the residing foreigner (cf. Figure 8-F above). The expansion in Exod 23:9b says emphatically, "*you yourselves know the longing* of the residing foreigner because you were residing foreigners in Egypt" (AT). This leads one interpreter to see the motive clause as a sort of negative golden rule; to paraphrase, "Do not do to the residing foreigners among you what the Egyptians did to you."[14] This commentary on the rationale clause in 23:9 helps fill out the exegetical upgrades of the interpretive blend in Lev 19:33–34.

The command to love residing foreigners in Lev 19:33–34 exegetically extrapolates and extends out of its donor texts (Exod 12:48; 22:21[20 H]). If the residing foreigner celebrates Passover like a citizen (Exod 12:48), it raises a question. How should Israel treat those who celebrate Passover like any citizen? The command to love the residing foreigner adopts the preposition of simile "like" or "as" *ke-* (כְּ) from the donor text. The treatment of residing foreigners like a citizen at Passover opens the opportunity for an exegetical intervention in Lev 19:34—love the residing foreigner as you would love yourself.[15]

The prohibition against Israel mistreating residing foreigners because of their own experiences as residing foreigners (Exod 22:21[20 H]) invites extension of the very same rationale to a positive counterpart. The exegetical intervention in Lev 19:33–34 explains that the command to love residing foreigners "as yourself" is grounded on Israel's own collective identity as residing foreigners in Egypt. Yahweh's redemption of Israel from their burden as residing foreigners places the command to love residing foreigners as a natural outgrowth of redemption.

The move from the command to love the residing foreigner to the command to love thy neighbor is part of the commonplace lesser to the greater in scripture (see Chapter 1). If the seducer must pay and do the bidding of the father and daughter, how much more the rapist (Exod 22:16–17[15–16 H]; Deut 22:28–29)? Human nature requires that the commands that should be understood need to be spelled out. If Israel is told you shall love the residing foreigner as yourself, how much more should Israel be expected to treat neighbors in the same way?

Like the law in Israel, the law collections of other ancient Near Eastern cultures sought to protect the disadvantaged. In ancient Ugaritic and

14. See Kelly, "The Ethics of Inclusion," 163.
15. See GKC §118s, v; *IBHS* §11.2.9b.

Mesopotamian writings, protected classes usually refer to widows, orphans, and the poor of one's own people. Hammurabi (1792–1750 BCE) says "that the strong might not oppose the weak, and that they should give justice to the orphan and the widow."[16] Protections extended to residing foreigners appear only rarely in ancient Near Eastern literature.[17] Thus, offering protections to residing foreigners alongside of widows and orphans sets apart Lev 19:33–34 and many kindred contexts in Torah.

Step three, Study the receptor text. Focus here will be restricted to two elements of the horizontal context of the receptor text—"Love thy neighbor" (Lev 19:18b)—that connect with its vertical context. The two aspects of horizontal context are the burden of holiness and the structure of Lev 19:17–18.[18]

Leviticus 19 explains the ethical obligations of the burden of holiness that Israel's laity shares with the priesthood. The highpoint of the ethical obligations appears midway through the chapter in the command to love thy neighbor.

The glory of Yahweh coming into the tabernacle triggered an entirely new situation for Israel. The people were transformed instantly into a congregation that needed to ever prepare to come into the courts of Yahweh. This situation explains why several legal instructions in Exodus invited exegetical upgrades in Leviticus.[19] The burden of holiness had been introduced at the mountain when Yahweh declared Israel a holy people (Exod 19:6).

Leviticus 19 opens with: "Yahweh said to Moses, 'Speak to the entire assembly of Israel and say to them: "*Be holy because I, Yahweh your God, am holy*"'" (Lev 19:1–2 AT). The holiness of Yahweh and his glory in the tabernacle translate into the demand for Israel to be holy. Whatever else Yahweh's holiness requires of Israel—such as sacrifices (chs. 1–7), ritual purity (11:44), and the holiness collection in Lev 17–26—it includes "Love thy neighbor."

The structure of Lev 19:17–18 helps define what it means to "love." This is the fifth of five units that end with "I am Yahweh" in vv. 11–18. A couple of scholars, such as Allbee and Milgrom, observe that vv. 17–18 is structured in two repeating panels (a-b-c, a-b-c). For Milgrom, this helps define love in v. 18 by comparing it with the parallel aspect of v. 17. This is a significant

16. Epilogue (xlvii.59–61) in Harper, *The Code of Hammurabi*, 99. And see Kitra 3.vi.45–49, in *SFAC*, 95. Also see Fensham, "Widow, Orphan, and the Poor," 176–92; Gordon, "The Background of Some Distinctive Values," 62.

17. See "The Instruction of Amen-em-opet," xxvi, 11, trans. John A. Wilson (*ANET*, 424b); Hittite instructions cited in Weinfeld, *Deuteronomy 1–11*, 439. On rareness of protections for strangers in the ancient Near East, see Tigay, *Deuteronomy*, 346, n. 68. On lack of protections for residing foreigners in the ancient Near East outside of Israel, see Milgrom, *Leviticus 17–22*, 1705.

18. For a fuller treatment of the horizontal context of Lev 19:18b, see Schnittjer, "Going Vertical," 116–20.

19. See *OTUOT*, 39–40.

observation as far as it goes. But the structure of vv. 17–18 loads much more onto the verb "love" than what results from scholars' use of the two-panel model. Figure 8-G modifies Milgrom's two-panel model to show how vv. 17–18 define love.[20]

Figure 8-G: Horizontal Context of Leviticus 19:18b‡

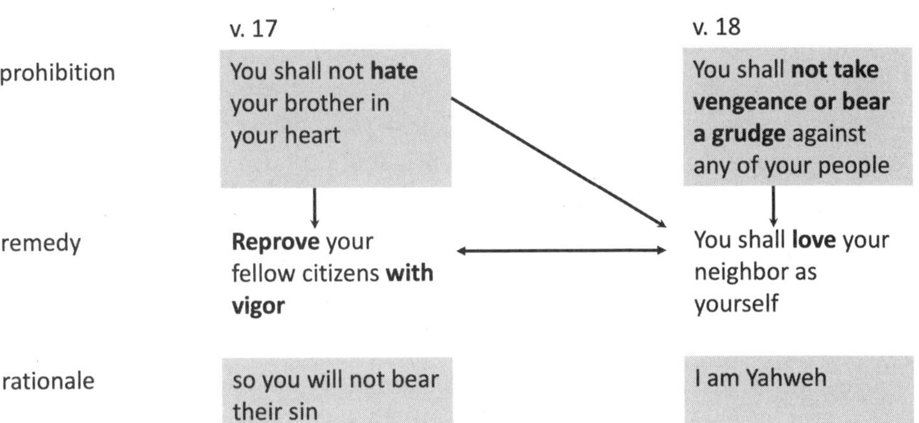

‡Mildly modified from Schnittjer, "Going Vertical," 119.

Love in Lev 19:18b naturally gets compared to and takes on new connotations from each of the four verbs that precede it in vv. 17–18. The contrast between "hate" in v. 17a and "love" in v. 18b loads the qualification of hate as "in your heart" onto love. The two-paneled structure invites aligning "reprove with vigor" in v. 17b and "love" in v. 18b. The ambiguous sense of "reprove with vigor" takes on a positive motivation based on its parallel with "love." It also suggests that love includes a verbal element. The two parts of v. 18 also invite a natural comparison. The two verbal ideas in v. 18a, "do not take vengeance" and "do not bear a grudge," suggest that the sense of the verb in v. 18b should be contrasted both to acts of vengeance and to an attitude or disposition against a person. In short, the structure of vv. 17–18 defines "love" as mental activity, verbal activity, action, and relational attitude.

If "love thy neighbor" is the answer, then vv. 17–18 ask four questions that point to it. If you shall not hate in your heart, what must you do? Love thy neighbor. If you shall vigorously reprove your fellow citizen, what will you

20. This figure is modified by using my own translation and adding arrows to make three comparisons versus Milgrom's single comparison. See Milgrom, *Leviticus 17–22*, 1402–3, 1646. Also see Allbee, "Asymmetrical Continuity of Love and Law," 162.

do? Love thy neighbor. If you shall not take vengeance, what must you do? Love thy neighbor. If you shall not bear a grudge, what must you do? Love thy neighbor. The structure of vv. 17–18 effectively spells out what it means to love. It is not just a feeling or an abstract ideal. To love one's neighbor requires mental activity, verbal activity, action, and relational disposition. Without all of this, it is less than the love that is demanded.

Step four, Explain exegetical outcomes. The horizontal context of "love thy neighbor" snaps together with its vertical context to produce its exegetical outcomes. The allusion that tethers together vv. 18b and 33–34 sends the connotations loaded onto love back down the vertical context. That is how allusions work. If the requirements to love thy neighbor include mental activity, verbal activity, action, and relational disposition, so too the requirements to love the residing foreigner.

Vertical contexts permanently connect scriptural teaching within the framework of emerging canonical consciousness. The vertical connection activates the horizontal contexts of the command to love thy neighbor and to love the residing foreigner in a way that causes mutual interplay between the horizontal context of the receptor text and the donor texts.[21]

In sum, the command to love thy neighbor did not appear ex nihilo. It is the culmination of a series of exegetical advances in Torah. The command to love thy neighbor *extends* the responsibility to love residing foreigners to neighbors—lesser to greater. The command to love thy neighbor also *enhances* the meaning of love, causing it to be inclusive of action, word, deed, and mental attitude.

But that is not the end. The culmination of exegetical advancements in the command to love thy neighbor turns out to be penultimate because the New Testament makes additional exegetical interventions upon it. This means we can build on the steps above and pick up with the last part of step two in order to focus on the New Testament use of this same teaching. The receptor text, Lev 19:18b, becomes a donor text of still later receptor texts that interpret it. The present discussion will be limited to an abbreviated explanation of one context that exegetically advances the command to love thy neighbor: Luke 10:36.

Study donor text—Reception. Studying extrabiblical uses of a donor text like the command to love thy neighbor often provides perspective to interpret a New Testament use of scripture. In many cases the differences between the uses of a donor text in Second Temple Jewish exegetical traditions and the New Testament strengthens the modern interpreter's sense of the exegetical outcomes by the New Testament author (Resource Guide 8-H).

---

21. See Ben-Porat, "Poetics," 107, 109–10, 127, as well as discussion of allusion in Chapter 4 above.

Resource Guide 8-H: Suggestions to Study the Reception of Donor Texts

- Tools to start: Kugel's *Traditions of the Bible*, 756–59; Levine and Brettler, *Bible with and without Jesus*, 424; *ATNTS*, 364; *BQASTJL*, 84; Daniel Gurtner, "Dead Sea Scrolls, OT Use in" *DNTUOT*, 173–76.
- Next steps: Scripture indexes of Philo, Josephus, and the Mishnah
- For more, see Chapter 5 and Resource Guide 5-D

The author of Jubilees, an imaginative rewriting of Genesis and the beginning of Exodus (second century BCE), regards the command to love thy neighbor as the epitome of the law.[22] Abraham spoke to his twelve sons:

> And he commanded them that they should guard the way of the LORD so that they might do righteousness and each one might *love his neighbor, and that it should be thus among all men so that each one might proceed to act justly and rightly* toward them upon the earth. (Jubilees 20:2, emphasis added)

In a similar way, Philo of Alexandria, a Hellenistic Jewish scholar (ca. 20 BCE–50 CE), singles out the commands to love God (Deut 6:5) and love others (Lev 19:18b) as the most important laws, which in a way summarize all the Mosaic laws.

> But among the vast number of particular truths and principles there studied, there stand out practically high above the others two main heads: *one of duty to God* as shewn by piety and holiness, *one of duty to men* as shewn by humanity and justice, each of them splitting up into multiform branches. (Philo, "Special Laws II," 63 [7:347], emphasis added)

The view of Jubilees and Philo is shared with other Jewish scholars of this era (Mark 12:32–33) as well as Jesus (Mark 12:29–31; cf. Matt 22:37–40). This exegetical tradition may build on the catchword "love," which only appears in

22. For many parallels treated here, see Kugel, *Traditions of the Bible*, 756–59. Also see Levine and Brettler, *Bible with and without Jesus*, 424; Akiyama, *Love*, passim; Livneh, "Love," 173–99.

commands five times in Torah with Yahweh, neighbors, and residing foreigners as objects (Lev 19:18, 34; Deut 6:5; 10:19; 11:1).[23]

Rather than defining love by the horizontal context of Lev 19:17–18 (see above), the author of Jubilees offers a common-sense intuitive explanation. Isaac says to Jacob and Esau:

> And among yourselves, my sons, *be loving* of your brothers as a man loves himself, with each man *seeking for his brother what is good for him*, and acting together on the earth, and loving each other as themselves (Jubilees 36:4, emphasis added).

The sense of "seeking . . . what is good" sounds much like the antithesis of "do not seek . . . their good" with reference to Israel's enemies in Deut 23:6[7 H] (AT).

Writings found among those of the Qumran sectarians interpret "neighbor" in Lev 19:18b ethnically by glossing it with "brother," even while downgrading the treatment of "residing foreigners" from love to help when impoverished.[24] This interpretive intervention seems to be based on the catchwords "love" (אהב), "residing foreigner" (גר), and "as" (כ) in Lev 19:18, 33–34, and 25:35. Note:

> ". . . for each one *to love* his brother [אחיהו] *as* himself and *to strengthen the hand* of the poor and needy and *the residing foreigner* [גר]" (4Q266/CD 6.20b–21 in *DSSSE* 1:558 AT, emphasis added to mark verbal parallels with Lev 19:18, 33–34 and 25:35).

Identifying "neighbor" as "brother" fits with the interchanging of "brother," "fellow citizen," "people," and "neighbor" in Lev 19:17–18.[25] But downgrading the treatment of residing foreigners from love to financial help requires suppressing the command to love the residing foreigner in Lev 19:33–34. In this way these Second Temple sectarians rejected the vertical context of "love thy neighbor."

In sum, the representative Second Temple Jewish writings surveyed here illustrate a variety of competing interpretive traditions. Many interpretive traditions extolled "love thy neighbor" as epitomizing the Mosaic law. Meanwhile, the sectarians read the commands selectively and against the sense of the text

23. See "אָהַב" Even-Shoshan, 19 (nos. 40–43, 78).

24. See Schnittjer, "Going Vertical," 118.

25. See Wenham, *Leviticus*, 267.

to maintain their ethnocentric ideology. In all of these cases, the hermeneutical mechanics follow those already well established in scriptural interpretations within Israel's scriptures (see Chapters 1 and 2).

Study New Testament receptor text—Textual context. The present case study only has space for one example of the command to love thy neighbor in a New Testament receptor text. The NIV and NET of Luke 10:25–37 do not contain any textual notes (Resource Guide 8-I). In addition, the *THGNT* does not include any black diamonds in the apparatus of vv. 25–37. Among the textual variants on this context in the NA[28] and UBS[5], only one variant in Luke 10:32 is noted in *TCGNT*—but the text critical outcome of it does not alter the use of Lev 19:18b.[26]

Resource Guide 8-I: Starting Points to Study Textual Criticism of the New Testament

[English Bible readers]
- NET tc notes (available at BibleGateway.com)
- Text notes in major modern committee translations like the NIV and NRSVue

[Greek New Testament readers]
- *TCGNT*
- Black diamonds in *THGNT* (see "Introduction," 515)
- Technical biblical commentaries
- For next steps see Resource Guide 8-K below.

Study receptor text and explain exegetical outcomes. To help guide the following abbreviated discussion, Figure 8-J provides a graphic summary of how Luke 10:36 works from horizontal contexts activated by the deep vertical context of love thy neighbor.

Only two persons cite scripture in Luke beside Jesus: the devil and the Torah scholar.[27] Jesus affirms the Torah scholar's connection between the commands to love God and to love neighbors in Luke 10:27. The Torah scholar's follow-up question on who his neighbor is prompts the Messiah's most famous

26. See *TCGNT*, 128–29.
27. See Powery, *Jesus Reads Scripture*, 217.

Figure 8-J: Vertical Context of Luke 10:36

Which was a neighbor?
chapter(s) ---- paragraph(s) ---- verse(s) ---- Luke 10:36 ---- verse(s) ---- paragraph(s) ---- chapter(s)
Love thy neighbor
chapter(s) ---- paragraph(s) ---- verse(s) ---- Lev 19:18b ---- verse(s) ---- paragraph(s) ---- chapter(s)
Love the residing foreigner
chapter(s) ---- paragraph(s) ---- verse(s) ---- Lev 19:33–34 ---- verse(s) ---- paragraph(s) ---- chapter(s)
Prohibition against mistreating residing foreigners
chapter(s) ---- paragraph(s) ---- verse(s) ---- Exod 22:21[20] ---- verse(s) ---- paragraph(s) ---- chapter(s)
Law of Passover participation
chapter(s) ---- paragraph(s) ---- verse(s) ---- Exod 12:48 ---- verse(s) ---- paragraph(s) ---- chapter
love the residing foreigner Lev 19:34
someone who hates you Exod 23:4–5
longing of residing foreigners 23:9
"neighbors" = "residing foreigners" Exod 3:22; 11:2
"neighbors" = "residing foreigners" 3:22; 11:2

riddle. The command to love the residing foreigner already goes beyond treatment of the Israelite neighbor. The riddle of Jesus further advances revelation.

The Messiah concludes his riddle of the good Samaritan with a question that collates the implications of the horizontal context of the deep vertical context of the command to love thy neighbor. Messiah asks: "Which of these three do you think *was a neighbor* to the man who fell into the hands of robbers?" (Luke 10:36, emphasis added) Without saying the word "Samaritan," the Torah scholar indicates it was the Samaritan in the riddle (v. 37). The Samaritan helped his enemy. The priest and the Levite did not help their neighbor, in order to avoid the risk of ritual impurity if the half-dead man happened to die (Luke 10:30–32; cf. Num 19:10b–13). The Messiah's question works from the lesser to the greater—if you shall help your enemy's animal when it is in trouble, how much more your enemy (cf. Exod 23:5)?—in the horizontal context of the prohibition against mistreating residing foreigners (22:21[20 H]; 23:9). The Messiah's exegetical advancement may use catchword logic based on "donkeys" in the narrative template of the good Samarians in 2 Chr 28:15—which he adapted for his riddle—and "donkey" in the command to help the animal in trouble, though Luke 10:34 uses a more generic term for a riding animal (emphases added).[28]

> If you see **the donkey** [חֲמוֹר MT, ὑποζύγιον LXX] of someone who hates you fallen down under its load, do not leave it there; be sure you help them with it. (Exod 23:5)

28. On the links between the good Samarians of 2 Chr 28 and the good Samaritan of Luke 10, see *OTUOT*, 807.

> The men [Samarians] designated by name took the prisoners [of Judah], and from the plunder they clothed all who were naked. They provided them with clothes and sandals, food and drink, and healing balm. All those who were weak they put on **donkeys** [חֲמֹרִים MT, ὑποζυγίοις LXX]. So they took them back to their fellow Israelites at Jericho, the City of Palms, and returned to Samaria. (2 Chr 28:15)

> He went to him and bandaged his wounds, pouring on oil and wine. Then he put the man on his own **animal** [κτῆνος], brought him to an inn and took care of him. (Luke 10:34 AT)

In this way the Messiah works from deep vertical context to *extend* the mandate to love beyond neighbor and residing foreigner to include even one's enemy (see Figure 8-J).

In sum, vertical context connects and activates horizontal contexts of donor and receptor texts. Still later biblical exegesis can rightly interpret together these horizontal contexts permanently connected by allusion within emerging canonical consciousness. The student will do well to do a close study of vertical context and its several interrelated horizontal contexts. The model above provides steps explaining "how to" interpret the Bible's use of the Bible.

CALLED FROM THE WOMB—NEW TESTAMENT CASE STUDY

In Gal 1:15–17 Paul recounts his encounter with the risen Jesus Christ that resulted in both his conversion and his commission as an apostle to the Gentiles.[29] Not surprisingly, Paul draws language from several Old Testament texts in doing so. This case study will focus on his use of Isa 49:1 in Gal 1:15, though along the way we will note how other Old Testament passages (including other portions of Isa 49) contribute to the larger picture (bold and underlining signify verbal parallels, broken underlining signifies portions of Isa 49 echoed elsewhere in Galatians).

Step one, Identify allusion. Responsible interpretation begins with identifying an allusion (see Resource Guides 3-E and 8-D). Describing his conversion, Paul writes this in Gal 1:15–17:

29. This example is adapted and expanded from Harmon, *She Must and Shall Go Free*, 78–86.

> But when God, who set me apart **from my mother's womb** [ἐκ κοιλίας μητρός μου] and **called** [καλέσας] me by his grace, was pleased [16]to reveal his Son in me [ἀποκαλύψαι τὸν υἱὸν αὐτοῦ ἐν ἐμοι] so that I might preach him among the Gentiles [ἐν τοῖς ἔθνεσιν], my immediate response was not to consult any human being. [17]I did not go up to Jerusalem to see those who were apostles before I was, but I went into Arabia. Later I returned to Damascus.

Now compare Paul's words to the description of the servant in Isa 49:1–6 (LXX, emphasis added):

> Hear me, O islands; pay attention, O Gentiles [ἔθνη]! After a long time it shall stand, says the Lord. **From my mother's womb** [ἐκ κοιλίας μητρός μου] he **called** [ἐκάλεσεν] my name [2]and made my mouth like a sharp dagger, and under the shelter of his hand he hid me; he made me like a chosen arrow, and in his quiver he sheltered me. [3]And he said to me, "You are my servant [δοῦλός], Israel, and in you I will be glorified [ἐν σοὶ δοξασθήσομαι]." [4]But I said, "I have labored vainly [κενῶς ἐκοπίασα], and I have given my strength in vain and for nothing; therefore my judgment is with the Lord, and my toil before my God." [5]And now thus says the Lord, who formed me **from the womb** [ἐκ κοιλίας] to be his own servant [δοῦλον], to gather Jakob and Israel to him; I will be gathered and glorified [δοξασθήσομαι] before the Lord, and my God shall become my strength. [6]And he said to me, "It is a great thing for you to be called my servant [κληθῆναί σε παῖδά μου] so that you may set up the tribes of Jakob and turn back the dispersion of Israel. See, I have made you a light for Gentiles [εἰς φῶς ἐθνῶν], that you may be for salvation to the end of the earth." (AT)

Paul uses this allusion and the residual echoes to pattern his own calling after the calling of the servant in Isa 49. The most direct verbal link between Gal 1:15 and Isa 49:1 is the phrase "from my mother's womb" (ἐκ κοιλίας μητρός μου). Paul claims that God separated him from his mother's womb, using the very same words found on the lips of the servant in the LXX of Isa 49:1. While the phrase "from the womb" (ἐκ κοιλίας) is somewhat common in the LXX (23x), only five occurrences (Judg 16:17; Ps 21:11 [22:11 H/E]; 70:6 [71:6 H/E]; Job 1:21; Isa 49:1) include the words "mother" (μητήρ) and "my" (μου). Of these five texts, there are additional residual echoes of Isa 49 that confirm that Paul alludes to this particular passage rather than simply using stock-in-trade language for a prophetic calling.

The first is the use of calling language that closely follows the phrase "from my mother's womb" (ἐκ κοιλίας μητρός μου) in both places, something that occurs nowhere else in the entire LXX. Whereas in Isa 49:1 "call" (καλέω) refers to Yahweh naming the servant, here in Gal 1:15 Paul uses the word in its theologically loaded sense of a divine summons to a specific task or position.[30] Paul claims that this calling was "through his grace" (διὰ τῆς χάριτος αὐτοῦ), an idea that although absent from Isa 49:1–6 is certainly consistent with it. Second, Paul's mission to preach the gospel "among the Gentiles" (ἐν τοῖς ἔθνεσιν; Gal 1:16) coheres with the servant's mission to be a "light of nations" (εἰς φῶς ἐθνῶν), as well as the call for the "Gentiles" (ἔθνη) to listen to the words of the servant (Isa 49:1). The exact phrase "among the Gentiles" (ἐν τοῖς ἔθνεσιν) Paul uses in Gal 1:16 is also found in the horizontal context of Isa 49. In Isa 52:5 (LXX), it refers to God's name being blasphemed among the Gentiles; this reality is reversed just a few verses later when Yahweh bares his arm (a reference to the servant; see 53:1–2) "before all the Gentiles" (ἐνώπιον πάντων τῶν ἐθνῶν; Isa 52:10 LXX[AT]).[31]

A third possible residual echo of Isa 49 may be found in Paul's claim that God delighted "to reveal his Son in me" (ἀποκαλύψαι τὸν υἱὸν αὐτοῦ ἐν ἐμοι). In Isa 49:3 Yahweh says to the servant, "in you I will be glorified" (ἐν σοὶ δοξασθήσομαι). If Paul saw himself as the Isaianic servant of Isa 49, the switch from "in you" (ἐν σοὶ) to "in me" (ἐν ἐμοι) makes sense in light of the change of context from Yahweh speaking to the servant (Paul) to Paul explaining what happened when Christ was revealed. This potential echo may explain the unusual use of the preposition "in" (ἐν) to indicate the sphere in which the revelation of God's Son takes place.[32] The possibility of a residual echo of Isa 49:3 is further strengthened by Paul's claim that the churches of Judea "were glorifying God in me" (ἐδόξαζον ἐν ἐμοὶ τὸν θεόν; Gal 1:24 AT), a more direct allusion to Isa 49:3. Carey Newman goes so far as to conclude that the expression "to reveal . . . in me" (ἀποκαλύψαι . . . ἐν ἐμοί; Gal 1:16) is in fact an echo of the phrase "in you I will be glorified" (ἐν σοὶ δοξασθήσομαι) found in

30. See, e.g., Coenen, "Call," *NIDNTT* 1:275–76; Eckert, "καλέω," *EDNT* 2:242–43. Of course, the notion of a divine summons to a specific task or position is at least implicitly present in Isa 49:1, and explicitly stated in Isa 49:6. On the importance of Isa 40–66 for the background of Paul's theologically loaded use of καλέω, see Dunn, *Galatians*, 40.

31. Paul actually quotes Isa 52:5 in Rom 2:24 as part of his condemnation of Jewish disobedience to the law.

32. In the eight other occurrences of the construction "reveal in" (ἀποκαλύπτω + ἐν) in the LXX/NT, not once does ἐν indicate the recipient of revelation. Instead it marks (1) the time when something is revealed (Num 24:4, 16; Dan 2:19; 1 Pet 1:5); (2) the sphere/location of a revelation (Judg 5:2; 1 Sam 2:27; Prov 11:13); or (3) the actions or being by which something is revealed (Ezek 16:36; 22:10); see further Harmon, *She Must and Shall Go Free*, 82. Murray Harris regards the use of "in" (ἐν) here as an "example of the basic locatival sense" of this preposition; see Harris, *Prepositions*, 118–19 and also Moo, *Galatians*, 104–5.

Isa 49:3.[33] At a minimum, then, it would seem that this expression is a strong thematic parallel if not an echo of Isa 49:3.

A fourth residual echo that might be easily overlooked is found in the final line before Gal 1:11–24. Paul asserts that he is not trying to be a people pleaser; instead, he is a "servant of Christ" (Χριστοῦ δοῦλος; Gal 1:10). In the LXX, both Isa 49:3 and 49:5 use this same Greek word (δοῦλος) to refer to the servant. These are the only two places in Isaiah where this Hebrew word for "servant" (עֶבֶד) is rendered with this Greek word (δοῦλος). It would seem, then, that Paul anticipates the use of servant language from Isa 49 to describe his conversion and calling by referring to himself as a servant of Christ in Gal 1:10.

Finally, and a bit further beyond the immediate context, there are two potential echoes of Isa 49:4 LXX, where the servant worries that "I have labored vainly" (κενῶς ἐκοπίασα, AT). In Gal 2:2 Paul explains that part of the motivation for his second postconversion trip to Jerusalem was to present before the church leaders in Jerusalem the gospel he preached, to be sure that "I was not running and had not been running my race in vain [κενὸν]." Galatians 4:11 also echoes the sentiment of Isa 49:4. Concerned over the dangerous spiritual condition of the Galatians, Paul fears "that somehow I have labored in vain over you [εἰκῇ κεκοπίακα]" (Gal 4:11).

The cumulative effect of these residual echoes is to confirm that when Paul describes his conversion and commission in Gal 1:15–17, he intentionally describes it using the language of Isa 49. The additional allusions and echoes in the surrounding context strongly suggest that the apostle has not only a specific phrase from Isa 49:1 in view, but the larger context of Isa 49 and the surrounding chapters as well. The primacy of Isa 49, however, does not preclude engagement with other texts from the surrounding context of Isaiah or other Old Testament texts as well.[34]

---

33. Newman, *Paul's Glory-Christology*, 205–7. Newman argues that "glorify" (δοξάζω) is often used to denote the manifestation of God's visible presence in the prophets, with elements of eschatological judgment frequently present. In such cases, "ἀποκαλύπτω ['reveal'] and δοξάζω ['glorify'], when speaking of God's eschatological self-manifestation, bear the same semantic cargo" (206). According to Newman, such language grows out of the early Jewish apocalyptic tradition of throne visions, which in turn stem from Ezek 1. As a result, Newman concludes that Paul "heuristically read his Christophany against the grid of mystical and apocalyptic Judaism, specifically the heavenly ascents of Jewish apocalypses, and therefore interpreted the Christophany as a throne vision in which the special agent of God was equated with the Glory of God." Although it is debatable whether Paul was as indebted to Jewish mysticism as Newman claims, the parallels between the passives of "glorify" (δοξάζω) and "reveal" (ἀποκαλύπτω) adduced by Newman are significant enough to suggest the presence of at least a thematic parallel between Isa 49:3 and Gal 1:16, and given the allusion to Isa 49:1 in Gal 1:15, an echo of Isa 49:3 here in Gal 1:16 cannot be ruled out.

34. See further Harmon, *She Must and Shall Go Free*, 78–86, for discussion of potential allusions/echoes of Isa 41:8–9; 42:1; and Jer 1:5 in Gal 1:15 and possible allusions/echoes to Isa 52:5, 7, 10; 53:1 in Gal 1:16.

Step two, Study donor text.

Textual. When it comes to the **textual** witnesses for Isa 49:1, there are no significant variants in the manuscript tradition (Resource Guide 8-E). The MT agrees with 1QIsa[a] and 1QIsa[b]/1Q8. Omissions in 4QIsa[d]/4Q58 make a true comparison difficult, but there does not appear to be any significant difference.[35] The LXX is a straightforward translation of the proto-MT, with only very minor variations that do not alter the meaning. As one might expect, there is a bit more variation in the targum (italics indicate variations from the MT), which reads "*Attend to my Memra, O islands*, and hearken, *you kingdoms* from afar. The Lord *appointed* me *before I was*, from the body of my mother [מִמְעֵי אִמִּי] he made mention of my name" (Isa 49:1 ArBib). Despite the variation in the opening lines of Isa 49:1, the targum reading retains the key expression that is the focus of our case study. Although Chilton renders the expression "from the body of my mother," the Aramaic word rendered "body" (מְעֵין) is a generic term that can more specifically refer to the womb.[36] The addition of the verb "appointed" (זַמֵּן) brings out explicitly what the MT implies: Yahweh's choice of the servant. This interpretive addition corresponds to Paul's language of God "setting him apart" and "calling" in Gal 1:15.

When it comes to understanding the call of the servant in Isa 49 within its **context**, one must begin by looking at servant language within the horizontal context of Isaiah.[37] In Isa 1–39, three specific individuals are identified as servants of Yahweh: Isaiah himself (20:3), Eliakim (22:20), and David (37:35). But in Isa 40–66 (and in particular chs. 40–55) the servant figure takes on far greater significance. After God announces comfort for his people (40:1–31), the idolatrous pagan nations are warned to fear the coming of Yahweh (41:1–7). By contrast, Israel should not fear because they have a special relationship with Yahweh, who calls Israel "my servant" (41:8–9). Isaiah 42:1–9 (the first of the four so-called Servant Songs) begins with a description of Yahweh's servant Israel (chosen, the object of his delight, and recipient of his Spirit) before laying out Israel's mission as the servant. Through Israel his servant, Yahweh will bring forth justice and establish him as a light for the nations in order to open the eyes of the blind and bring out prisoners from the darkest of dungeons. Unfortunately, Israel as a nation failed miserably in their commission as Yahweh's servant. In Isa 42:19, Yahweh asks, "Who is blind but my servant, and deaf like the messenger I send? Who is blind like the one in covenant with

---

35. See further the brief entry in *BQS*, 2:526.

36. See the entry in *DTTBYML*, 816.

37. What follows here is a brief summary of what is argued at much greater length in Harmon, *The Servant of the Lord*, 109–42.

me, blind like the servant of the LORD?" Instead of being a light to the nations, Israel has become blind; instead of being a herald of good news, they are deaf to God's words. Despite their failure, Yahweh remains committed to Israel his servant (43:10; 44:3, 21, 26; 45:4; 48:20), promising restoration.

Because of Israel's failure as his servant, Yahweh raises up a new servant. Isaiah 49:1–13 (the second servant song) introduces this new servant, with vv. 1–6 summarizing his commission and vv. 7–13 describing Yahweh's confirmation of his servant. Isaiah 49:1–6 can further be divided into two sections. Verses 1–4 recount the servant's call (49:1–3) and his concern at the prospect of failure in his mission (49:4). After summoning the nations to listen to him, this new servant says, "Before I was born Yahweh called me; from my mother's womb he has spoken my name" (49:1 AT). He further recounts what Yahweh directly said to him: "You are my servant, Israel, in whom I will be glorified" (49:3 ESV). After expressing concern that he may labor in vain (49:4), the servant reiterates that he was formed in the womb to be Yahweh's servant (49:5). He then recounts what Yahweh said to him: "It is too small a thing for you to be my servant to restore the tribes of Jacob and bring back those of Israel I have kept. I will also make you a light for the Gentiles, that my salvation may reach to the ends of the earth" (49:6). This commission has a dual focus: to restore Israel (thus making it clear that the servant is a new individual, for how can Israel as a failed servant restore Israel?) and to be a light for the nations so that Yahweh's salvation reaches to the ends of the earth. This shift from Israel as a collective servant to an individual as the servant is a good example of the interrelationship between individual identity and responsibility and collective identity and responsibility discussed in Chapter 1.

Although Isa 49:1 does not allude to any other Old Testament text, there is an element of vertical context to consider. Beginning with Adam, God uses a series of key individual servants (figures such as Moses, Joshua, and David) to advance his creational and redemptive purposes.[38] Through these individual servants—who to varying degrees exercise royal, priestly, and prophetic roles—God works to create a servant people. Understood against this backdrop, the individual servant of Yahweh identified here is another installment in this pattern, which culminates in Jesus Christ, the servant par excellence.

Reception. Once the context of the donor text has been examined, one must investigate the reception of the donor text, both within later scripture and texts outside the Bible (Resource Guides 5-D and 8-H). Identifying such texts where the donor text is cited or alluded to can shed helpful light on how the

38. See further Harmon, *The Servant of the Lord*, 7–221.

author of the receptor text understood the donor context and its surrounding context. Within the Old Testament, the servant's claim that Yahweh has called him from the womb (49:1, 5) finds a striking parallel in Jer 1:5.

> Listen to me, you islands; hear this, you distant peoples [לְאֻמִּים]: Yahweh **called me from the womb** [מִבֶּטֶן], from the belly of my mother [מִמְּעֵי אִמִּי] he named my name. (Isa 49:1 AT)

> And now Yahweh says, the one who **formed me from the womb** [יֹצְרִי מִבֶּטֶן] to be his servant to bring Jacob back to him and gather Israel to himself, for I am honored in the eyes of the LORD and my God has been my strength. (Isa 49:5 AT)

> Before I **formed you in the womb** [בְּטֶרֶם אֶצָּרְךָ בַבֶּטֶן] I knew you, before you came out of the womb [וּבְטֶרֶם תֵּצֵא מֵרֶחֶם] I set you apart; I appointed you as a prophet to the nations [לַגּוֹיִם]. (Jer 1:5 AT)

The similarities between these texts appear to be noninterpretive, making this an example of stock phrases used by prophets to communicate their divine commission as a prophet (cf. *OTUOT*, 255). Perhaps the most one could say about the reuse of Isa 49:1 in Jer 1:5 is that the language presents Jeremiah as the kind of prophet for his generation that Isaiah was for his.[39]

Within the sectarian texts of the Dead Sea Scrolls, there appear to be several echoes of language from Isa 49, though none likely rise to the level of an exegetically significant allusion. Perhaps the closest would be the possibility that in 1QH[a] 17:29–30, the Teacher of Righteousness may be drawing upon Isa 49:1 when he describes himself as known and chosen from the womb (ידעתני ומרחם [. . .] אמי). But this most likely is the use of stock language for a prophetic call rather than a specific allusion to Isa 49:1.

According to *BQASTJL*, there are no allusions to Isa 49:1 in the Apocrypha, Philo, or Josephus. In the *OTP*, Sib. Or. 3.710 overlaps with Isa 49:1 in referring to "islands" (*OTPSI*, 29), but this is hardly sufficient to establish even an echo. While there are a number of texts that refer to a servant figure (2 Bar. 70:10; 3 En. 10:3), Israel as Yahweh's servant (Pss.

39. Based on similar language between Jer 1:6–9 and Exod 4:10–12 plus Deut 18:18, Schnittjer concludes that "the call of Moses and Jeremiah may be related merely as type-scenes, especially the similar complaint about poor speaking (Exod 4:10; Jer 1:6)" (*OTUOT*, 267). But he further considers the possibility that "If the call of Jeremiah has been intentionally crafted after the call of Moses, the implication may relate to Jeremiah as a prophet like Moses in a general sense (Deut 18:15)" (ibid.).

Sol. 12:6; 17:21), Israel being a light to the nations (Sib. Or. 14.214; T. Levi 14:3), or an individual servant being a light to the nations (CšD II, 8) none can be confidently linked specifically to Isa 49 (*OTPSI*, *OTPMNS*). While *SIRL* (351) lists several rabbinic texts (Midr. Ps. 9.7; Midr. Ps. 58.2; Midr. Ps. 139.6), none of these are relevant here.

Isaiah 49 is both quoted and alluded to several times elsewhere in the New Testament. In Luke 1:15, the angel Gabriel announces to Zechariah that his soon-to-be-born son will be filled with the Spirit "from his mother's womb" (AT), which, in light of other Isaianic echoes within the broader context, may suggest a possible allusion to Isa 49:1. When Simeon takes the Christ child into his arms and blesses God, he borrows language from Isa 49:6 to identify Jesus as "a light for revelation to the Gentiles, and the glory of your people Israel" (Luke 2:32). After facing rejection by the Jews in the synagogue at Pisidian Antioch, Paul quotes Isa 49:6 as the Lord's commission to Barnabas and him: "For this is what the Lord has commanded us: 'I have made you a light for the Gentiles, that you may bring salvation to the ends of the earth'" (Acts 13:47). In 2 Cor 6:2 Paul cites Isa 49:8 to affirm that now is the "time of God's favor" and "day of salvation" promised by the prophet. Philippians 2:15–16 may contain two faint echoes of Isa 49. Paul describes believers as those who "shine . . . like stars in the sky" (2:15), language that may echo the description of the servant as a "light to the nations" (Isa 49:6, though an allusion to Dan 12:3 is more likely).[40] His desire to be proud that "I did not run or labor in vain" (Phil 2:16) likely echoes the concern of the servant that "I have labored in vain" (Isa 49:4; cf. Gal 2:2; 4:11). In Rom 14:11, Paul may be quoting Isa 49:18 in conjunction with Isa 45:23 to assert that Yahweh will be acknowledged by everyone as the sovereign ruler of creation.[41]

In summary, while there are some potential Old Testament and Second Temple Jewish texts that have similar language to Isa 49:1, none of them make exegetical use of such language. In the New Testament, however, there are a number of citations and allusions to Isa 49 that suggest its importance for both Luke and Paul.

Step three, Study the receptor text.

Textual. Regarding the **textual** witnesses for Gal 1:15–17, there are two modestly significant variants (see Resource Guide 8-K).

The first noteworthy variant is whether or not "God" (ὁ θεὸς) is original, and, as the brackets around the phrase in the NA[28] indicate, the textual

40. Though Dan 12:3 likely alludes to Isa 52:13+53:11; cf. *OTUOTPL*, entry on Dan 12:3.

41. For additional possible allusions and echoes of Isa 49 in the NT, see Loci Citati vel Allegati in NA[28].

Resource Guide 8-K: Next Steps to Study Textual Criticism of the New Testament

English Bible readers can consult the footnotes in most translations (NIV, ESV, NRSVue, NASB) to discover potential text-critical issues. The notes in the NET Bible are especially helpful for explaining different readings.

Those who are able should consult the textual apparatuses of the NA^{28} and the UBS^5, as well as the black diamonds in the *THGNT*. Helpful analysis on the most significant variants can usually be found in *TCGNT*. For advanced textual critical study, consult CNTTS apparatus (available in Accordance and Logos) and the *NTGECM* (where available).

witnesses are evenly split.[42] Metzger is probably correct that the most likely scenario is that a scribe added it to make the subject of "delighted" (εὐδόκησεν) explicit.[43] Regardless of whether it is original or not, this variant does not affect the meaning of the text and thus should not be considered major.

A second noteworthy variant is the omission of the phrase "and called [me] by his grace" (καὶ καλέσας διὰ τῆς χάριτος αὐτοῦ) at the conclusion of verse 15. Although present in most textual witnesses, the phrase is absent most notably from one of the earliest witnesses ($\mathfrak{P}^{46}$; it is also absent from 6. 1739. 1881). The overwhelming support of other strong witnesses, however, suggests an accidental scribal omission rather than other scribes adding the phrase. In the unlikely scenario that the phrase is not original, the notion of God's gracious call on Paul's life would no longer be explicit, though the concept would certainly be implied by the claim that God set apart Paul from the womb. The absence of the phrase would not undermine an allusion to Isa 49:1, though it would take away one of the subsidiary echoes of Isa 49 (the presence of the verb "called" [καλέω]).

Contextual. Within its broader horizontal context, Gal 1:15–17 is part of a larger section (1:11–2:21) in which Paul emphasizes the divine origin of the gospel he preaches and the legitimacy of his status as an apostle of Jesus Christ. Paul argues at length that he received that gospel directly through a revelation of the risen Christ rather than receiving it or being taught by others such as the apostles in Jerusalem (1:11–12). He supports this claim by describing four

42. While it is absent in $\mathfrak{P}^{46}$ B F G 629. 1505 lat sy^{p}; $Ir^{lat\ pt,\ arm}$ Epiph, the phrase is found in ℵ A D K L P Ψ 0278. 33. 81. 104. 365. 630. 1175. 1241. 1739. 1881. 2464 𝔪 sy^{h**} co; $Ir^{lat\ pt}$.

43. *TCGNT*, 521–22.

distinct events/period of time from his life: (1) his conversion and commissioning as an apostle to the Gentiles (1:13–17); (2) the early years of his ministry (1:18–24); (3) his second postconversion visit to Jerusalem (2:1–10); and (4) his confrontation with Peter in Antioch (2:11–14). Paul concludes the argument with a summary of the gospel message that he proclaims (2:15–21).

Paul's description of his conversion and commission falls naturally into two sections. In 1:13–14, the apostle describes his life in Judaism before encountering the risen Christ. Using a series of imperfect tense verbs, he highlights three activities: (1) persecuting the church, (2) trying to destroy the church, and (3) advancing Judaism beyond his peers through zeal for the traditions of his fathers. The one long Greek sentence that spans 1:15–17 describes the encounter with the risen Christ that resulted in his conversion and commission, as well as Paul's immediate actions in the aftermath. The main point is that God revealed his Son "in" Paul for the purpose of preaching the good news of Jesus among the Gentiles.[44] But before Paul had even been born, God had set him apart and called him by his grace for this very role. In response to his encounter with Christ, Paul did not consult with anyone (including the apostles in Jerusalem) but rather went off to Arabia before returning to Damascus.

Step four, Explain exegetical outcomes. Given our observation that somewhat similar language is found in Old Testament prophetic call narratives, one might conclude that Paul is simply using stock-in-trade language to present his conversion and apostolic calling in a similar light. Understood this way, Paul uses such language to legitimize his apostolic status much in the same way that the Old Testament prophets authenticated their prophetic commission from Yahweh. But if Paul is merely using such stock-in-trade language, it is difficult to explain why there are several additional echoes of Isa 49 within the broader context but none to other similar prophetic call narratives. Thus, whereas Jer 1:5–7 combines imagery and language that is broadly analogous to Isa 49, Exod 3, and 1 Sam 3 to portray Jeremiah's call as consistent with other prophets before him, Paul uses the particular language of Isa 49:1 along with residual echoes of that chapter to make the more specific claim that his calling is directly related to the calling of the servant in Isa 49.

But how then is he using Isa 49? In short, Paul's use of Isaiah can best be described as a form of indirect fulfillment. He sees his call to be an apostle to the Gentiles prefigured in the specific language of the Isaianic servant's call in Isa 49:1–6. As Paul reflected on his encounter with the risen Jesus in light of the Old Testament scriptures, he saw within Isa 49 his own ministry as the apostle

44. On the significance of God revealing his Son "in" Paul, see Harmon, *She Must and Shall Go Free*, 82.

to the Gentiles anticipated both in specific phrases as well as the broader scope of what the servant was commissioned to do: bring the good news of Yahweh's salvation to the Gentiles, even to the ends of the earth.

This conclusion does raise an additional question, however. Elsewhere, New Testament authors (including Paul himself in Gal 2:20; 3:13; 4:4–6) regularly describe Jesus in language borrowed from Isa 53. And as we have seen above, Luke 2:32 applies the language of Isa 49:6 directly to Jesus. Does that mean Paul identifies two distinct servants, with himself as the servant of Isa 49 and Jesus as the servant of Isa 53? Although a full answer is beyond the scope of our case study, Gal 2:20 provides the key to understanding Paul's conclusion. Paul states that "I have been crucified with Christ and I no longer live, but Christ lives in me. The life I now live in the body, I live by faith in the Son of God, who loved me and gave himself for me." Paul sees himself as the servant of Isa 49 because Jesus, the suffering servant of Isa 53, lives within him to fulfill the servant's mission.[45] In reading Isa 49 this way, Paul appears to have picked up on the interrelationship between individual identity and responsibility and collective identity and responsibility noted above. Jesus as the servant has produced servants, just as Isaiah had foretold.[46]

CONCLUSION

The two cases above provide step-by-step models for research and evaluation of the evidence. As mentioned in the Introduction, it would be a good idea to go to the library and look through any of the reference works to which the case studies refer. Thorough research and evaluation of the evidence are crucial.

Now that we have worked our way through the process modeled in these two case studies, it is time to get your hands dirty by studying the Bible's use of the Bible for yourself. Whether you are writing a research paper, preparing to preach or teach in the church, or simply seeking to grow in your understanding

45. For further unpacking of this conclusion, see Harmon, *She Must and Shall Go Free*, 106–22; and idem., *The Servant of the Lord*, 180–83.

46. Throughout Isa 40–53 the term "servant" (עֶבֶד) is consistently singular, regardless of whether it refers to Israel or the individual servant whom God raises up to fulfill Israel's mission. But once the individual servant has accomplished the redemption of his people through his suffering and vindication, Isaiah begins to speak of "servants" in the plural (e.g. 54:17; 56:6; 63:17; 65:8–9, 13–15; 66:14). Put succinctly, the work of the individual servant produces a servant people; see further Harmon, *The Servant of the Lord*, 137. For a similar dynamic between the individual servant of Isa 53 and the community described in Isa 57:14–19, see the helpful discussion in *OTUOT*, 244–46, where Schnittjer concludes that the individual servant's suffering is "a prototype for contrite citizens of restoration (57:15). His suffering models how redeemed ones should live. This use of the servant's suffering places it as something of a pivot to provide healing and to activate the new exodus and new creation" (ibid., 246).

of how scripture fits together, a firm grasp of these seven hermeneutical choices undergirds responsible exegesis in this specialized area of biblical studies.

As we put this knowledge and these skills to use, may it strengthen our love for God and obedience to his word. Our investment in studying the Bible's use of the Bible will prepare us to serve Christ and help those whom he has called us to serve.

Study Questions

1. What are the four steps to research a case of the Bible's use of the Bible? Where do the seven hermeneutical choices of this book fit into the four steps?
2. What reference tools can help an interpreter identify an exegetical allusion?
3. What reference tools can assist an English Bible reader with textual issues in the Old Testament? What reference tools can assist a Hebrew Bible reader with textual issues?
4. What reference tools help identify the reception of passages of Israel's scriptures within the Second Temple Jewish context?
5. What reference tools assist English Bible readers with textual issues in the New Testament? What reference tools assist Greek New Testament readers with textual issues?

GLOSSARY[1]

Advancement of revelation—see progressive revelation and Introduction.

Allusion refers to intentional evoking of a donor text by a receptor text. Allusion fits amid the sliding scale from quotation to paraphrase to allusion to echo to trace. Allusions include authorial intentionality, but echoes are too subtle to determine intentionality. In this book allusion serves as an umbrella term for quotations, paraphrases, and more subtle evoking of scriptures.

Atomization refers to exegesis of a scriptural unit interpreted in its own right without regard for its context.

Authorship, as it relates to the biblical authors' exegetical use of earlier scriptural traditions, is an umbrella term inclusive of authorial and editorial activities. **Author** refers to the agents responsible for composing texts. **Editing** refers to scribal interventions in representing source materials. Since scriptural exegesis of scripture requires donor and receptor texts, exegesis by authors naturally includes elements of editing within it.

The Bible's use of the Bible refers to scriptural authors of both testaments who present their teachings by means of allusion to earlier scriptural teachings. While it includes lesser allusions, this study focuses on exegetical use of earlier scriptures.

Canonical consciousness refers to the emerging esteem granted to authoritative scriptural texts. Canonical consciousness can be made explicit by overt marking, such as "as it is written."

Catchword, catchphrase refers to connecting two or more donor texts based on a shared root or word or phrase.

Citation—see marked.

Composite citation refers to a marked interpretive blend.

Connotation refers to that which is in, under, and with the denotation. The noun "rose" may denote a flower even while connoting innocence, fragility, love, or the like.

Covenant collection refers to Exod 21–23.

Deep context refers to an allusion within a donor text to a still earlier donor text. See vertical context and see Chapter 4.

Denotation refers to the referent of a signifier (e.g., word, expression). See connotation.

Diachronic refers to a focus on the author-text dialectic in the production of texts.

1. This Glossary is indebted in places to the glossary in *OTUOT*, 898–903.

Direction of dependence refers to determining the receptor text and its donor text(s).

Dischronological narrative refers to a narrative sequence that differs from the chronological sequences of the events. Examples include Moses entering the tent of meeting in Exod 33:7–11 that was not completed until 40:33 and John being arrested in Luke 3:20 before Jesus was baptized in v. 21.[2]

Donor text refers to the cited biblical text in a case of interpretive allusion.

Echo refers to potential evoking of a donor text by a receptor text. Echoes do not have adequate literary signals to decide between coincidence and intention. See allusion.

Ectype refers to "an installment in a typological pattern between the archetype (or prototype), the initial instance, and the antitype, or final fulfillment to which the archetype and the ectype(s) pointed."[3]

Editing—see authorship.

Excavative refers to the agenda of some diachronic studies to disassemble the biblical text seeking one or more elements of the production history of the text, such as theoretical editorial layer, theoretical source, and the like, and usually an attempt to date the theoretical elements.[4]

Exegesis in the narrow sense of the term refers to explaining and in the broad sense of the term refers to explaining, extending, expanding, extrapolating, enhancing, ironically qualifying, and the like. This study uses exegesis in its broad sense. Exegesis and interpretation are used identically.

Exegetical intervention is a broad expression referring to any kind of interpretive use of earlier scripture by the author of a receptor text.

Exegetical outcomes refer to the interpretations of donor texts within receptor texts. It is important to inductively describe all exegetical outcomes on their own terms. See Chapter 3 for a partial list of kinds of exegetical outcomes.

Expectational refers to messages with prophetic expectations.

Extended echo effect refers to the recurrence of similar elements from an earlier context in a later context usually in the same sequence (a-b-c, a-b-c). Extended echo effects are literary, not expectational. The purpose of extended echo effect is to project connotations from the earlier biblical context onto the later one. For example, the narrative of Cain's sin uses extended echo effect from the sin in the garden: e.g., desire/rule (Gen 3:16; 4:7); Where are you/is your brother? (3:9; 4:9); ground cursed (3:17; 4:11, 14); and banished to east (3:23–24; 4:16).[5] These parallels load Cain's sin with Adam-and-Eve-like connotations for literary and theological outcomes.

Figural means typological. See typological patterns.

Former Prophets refer to Joshua, Judges, Samuel, and Kings.

Frame narrative refers to the controlling narrative context of quoted or embedded elements therein. For example, the rebellion with the calf and its aftermath in Exod 32–34 provide the frame narrative that make sense of the covenant renewal legal collection (Exod 34:11–26).

---

2. See Schnittjer, *Old Testament Narrative*, 10; Glatt-Gilad, *Chronological Displacement*.
3. Hamilton, *Typology*, 28.
4. The term "excavative" comes from Alter, *Art of Biblical Narrative*, 14.
5. See Schnittjer, *Torah Story*, 67.

Haggadic—see halakic.

Halakic refers to legal interpretation versus haggadic which deals with interpretation of nonlegal scriptures, especially narrative.

Holiness collection refers to Lev 17–26.

Horizontal context—see vertical context.

Illocution—see locution.

Innerbiblical exegesis refers to receptor texts that make interpretive interventions with donor texts.

Interpretation—see exegesis.

Interpretive blend refers to a receptor text that interprets one donor text in relation to another.[6]

Intertextuality is a term coined by Julia Kristeva to refer to the general theory of interrelations between media (with all media referred to as "textual"). Kristeva acknowledges the broad use of the term "intertextuality" in various kinds of literary studies: "The term *inter-textuality* denotes this transposition of one (or several) sign system(s) into another; but since the term has often been understood in the banal sense of 'study of sources,' we prefer the term *transposition*."[7] In common practice of biblical studies, "intertextuality has come to be used as a synonym for 'echo' or 'allusion.'"[8] In scholarly use, "*intertextuality* is a vague and fluid term, which can cover *any* type of relations between texts, even those unconsciously evoked by authors, as well as those not recognized by their target audience."[9] The very broadness of intertextual relations, in part, accounts for the label being frequently redefined by individual scholars.

Inverted allusion—see Seidel's theory.

Jewish exegesis refers to interpretive standards in Second Temple sectarian texts (e.g., Dead Sea Scrolls, Pseudepigrapha, Samaritan Pentateuch, and so on). Many use this expression and/or kindred expressions like so-called rabbinic exegesis to refer to noncontextual interpretation. See atomization, midrash, and pesher, and see Chapter 2 ad loc.

Locution refers to an utterance. *Illocution* refers to the function of a locution to suggest, order, promise, commend, deceive, and so on, versus *perlocution* which refers to the accomplishment of the locution.

LXX—see Septuagint.

Lyrical diffusion refers to broad dissemination of stock phrases, refrains, stereotypical expressions, and the like that get detached from their biblical contexts of origin and become part of poetic idioms common in the prophets, psalms, and the like.[10]

Marked refers to the explicit acknowledgment of dependence, like "as it is written."

---

6. The expression interpretive blend is based on "legal blend," coined by Fishbane, *Biblical Interpretation*, 220. Legal blends make up a subset of interpretive blends which are commonplace in every genre of the Christian Bible. See Schnittjer, "Overview of Composite Citations," forthcoming.

7. Kristeva, *Revolution*, 59–60. And see van Wolde, "Texts in Dialogue with Texts," 1–4; Longman, *OT as Literature*, 157–59.

8. Theocharous, *Lexical*, 1.

9. Edenburg, "Intertextuality," 173, n. 16, emphasis original.

10. See detailed explanation in *OTUOT*, 216–17, 474.

Metanarrative refers to the storyline or framework within which a body of writings such as Israel's scriptures is interpreted.

Midrash means "interpretation" and refers to the genre of ancient Jewish writings that commonly include imaginative backstory and clever gap-filling of biblical traditions.[11] The common fictional gap-filling in this genre causes the term midrash to connote fictional traditions.

Narrative tracking refers to one text alluding to another by mimicking narrative structure rather than verbal parallels.[12]

Network refers to an interconnected set of interpretive allusions in several contexts.[13] Networks have an anchor passage to which all passages in the network are related directly or indirectly. For example, the passages in the attribute formula network all depend directly, or are related indirectly by some mediating allusion, to Exod 34:6–7.[14]

Noncontextual exegesis—see atomization and Jewish exegesis.

Oral Torah in rabbinic Judaism refers to the authoritative verbal interpretation of the written Torah that Moses received on Mount Sinai, in addition to the written Torah.[15] The oral Torah was passed on verbally generation by generation until it was written down in the Mishnah (ca. 200 CE), the Babylonian Talmud (ca. 600 CE), and the variety of midrashic and other Jewish writings in between.

Organic revelation—see revelation.

Paradigmatic shaping refers to broad formulaic narrative structure, like the cycle of the judges or presenting kings as going from bad to good in Chronicles or vice versa, and so on.[16]

Parent text refers to the text open before the author scribe or copyist scribe (*Vorlage*).

Perlocution—see locution.

Pesher comes from the Aramaic root *p-sh-r* (פשר) meaning "interpret" and refers to ancient sectarian writings that go verse by verse, allegorically explaining the fulfillment of mysterious meanings hidden in the biblical text (e.g., Habakkuk Commentary/1QpHab and 4QpNah/4Q169). See Chapter 2.

Plain sense exegesis refers to interpretation of biblical writings according to their contexts and their standards of interpretation of earlier scriptures. Plain sense exegesis excludes hermeneutical approaches that adjust meaning and/or adjust context. See Introduction and Chapter 2.

Prefiguration refers to the donor text in backward-looking typological patterns. See typological patterns.

Progressive revelation refers to authorized incremental disclosure of God's redemptive will. See revelation and Introduction.

---

11. See a list of ancient midrashim in Kugel, *Traditions of the Bible*, 926–28.

12. See Leonard, "Identifying Subtle Allusions," 96–97. Leonard uses Matt 2; Ps 78; and Ps 104 as examples (97–108).

13. See *OTUOT*, 873–887.

14. See ibid., 877.

15. See m. Avot 1:1; Jaffe, "Introduction: Avot," in m. 2:711; Avery-Peck, "Oral Tradition (Judaism)," *ABD* 5:34.

16. See Schnittjer, *Old Testament Narrative*, 75, 226–27; *OTUOT*, 715–16.

Prosopological exegesis is the analogical use of earlier speeches in the Bible, and it refers to a biblical author *reading an earlier biblical speech in the light of a new character.*[17] The new character can be the speaker and/or the referent and/or the auditor—the person(s) whom the speech is by, about, or to.

Quotation refers to intentional verbal repetition of a donor text within a receptor text. While in ordinary language the function of verbal repetition is left open, in this more specialized use, quotation signifies author-intended verbal repetition with "an exegetical purpose."[18]

Rabbinic exegesis—see Jewish exegesis.

Receptor text refers to the citing text in a case of interpretive allusion, paraphrase, or quotation.

Referent or reference refers to that which is signified by a term or passage.

Revelation refers to the disclosure of God's redemptive will in providence, divine acts, prophetic utterances, and scripture. Revelation advances toward its culmination in the teaching, death, and resurrection of the Messiah. The organic revelation of scripture by the Spirit stands in contrast to a mechanical dictation theory that treats biblical authors like mindless robots. A small yet vital subset of scriptural revelation is the Bible's use of the Bible.

Seidel's theory, or inverted allusion, named for the scholar who identified it, refers to the commonplace switching of the word order in the receptor text causing readers to pause and consider the allusion for an extra moment.[19] For example, when the prophet says, "gracious and compassionate God" (Jonah 4:2), he inverts the attribute formula's "compassionate and gracious God" (Exod 34:6).

Semantic function refers to what a linguistic sign does. A linguistic sign includes both signifier (word, phrase) and signified (referent/denotation and the associated connotations).

Sensus plenior refers to "the deeper sense of the words of scripture intended by God but not clearly intended by the human author—a sense uncovered only by further revelation or development of revelation."[20]

Septuagint refers to ancient Greek translations of the Hebrew scriptures. The term "Septuagint" means seventy and is often abbreviated by the Roman numeral LXX. The ancient Letter of Aristeas (ca. 250–100 BC) imaginatively tells of seventy-two scribes, six from each tribe of Israel, who independently translated the Torah in seventy-two days (vv. 39, 301–7). Philo (ca. 20 BCE–50 CE) added imaginative details claiming the translators independently made identical translations.[21]

Stock phrases refer to common figures of speech, refrains, formulas, and verbal repetitions, sometimes with variations, that are part of literary structure or style rather than signifying allusion or dependence.

Synchronic approach refers to study of the scriptures in their received form.

---

17. This definition is indebted to Madison Pierce.
18. See Schultz, *Search for Quotation*, 221.
19. See Beentjes, "Discovering a New Path," 49.
20. Brown, "Problems of *Sensus Plenior*," 460.
21. See Philo, *Moses II*, §37, 6:467.

Synoptic passages refer to two or more contexts that refer to the same event, law, poem, teaching, or the like.

Targums refer to Aramaic translations of the Hebrew Bible that began as oral traditions within the synagogues, allowing those who did not know Hebrew to understand what was being read. These translations often contain interpretive additions. Although written down after the New Testament period, sometimes they may provide insight into how the Hebrew Bible was interpreted in the late Second Temple period. See Resource Guide 5-E in Chapter 5.

Thematic similarities refer to parallels between a donor and receptor text that, rather than being based on shared vocabulary and syntax, are rooted in similar ideas/concepts.

Torah with a capital "T" is an English loanword from Hebrew that refers to the first five books of the Christian Bible, and torah with a lowercase "t" refers to instruction or teaching.

Trace refers to an unexpressed trigger (donor text) that suggests an interpretation. It falls at the far end of the continuum: quotation-paraphrase-allusion-echo-trace. An example is the likely trace of the new exodus of Isa 11:15–16 and 40:1–10 in Ezra 1:6 that builds on the return in Exod 12:35–36 as a typological pattern. That is, the connection between exodus and return in Ezra 1 may have been suggested by the new exodus contexts of Isaiah. Since traces are unexpressed, they have no evidence and can never be more than a guess.

Tradition, in the sense of a scriptural tradition, is a softer term used in recognition that the version of the donor text known by authors of the Hebrew scriptures may not be identical with the final canonical form. Yet, we only know of the scriptural traditions from the final form. Examples of inspired editorial updates include the reference to the establishment of the kingdom of Israel in Gen 36:31; looking back at some distance to the conquest of the land in Deut 2:12; and headings on the prophetic books and psalms.

Typological patterns refer to intentional scriptural shaping to draw selective expectational analogies between persons, events, institutions, procedures, oracles, or a combination of these within the historical framework of progressive revelation. Unlike allegory, only *selective* analogous elements get reused in typological patterns in scripture.[22] Some typological patterns are forward-looking and expectational, and other donor texts are nonexpectational in themselves with the backward-looking pattern recognized by the receptor text in light of its fulfillment. See Chapter 6.

Unmarked—see marked.

Use of scripture is a broad expression to refer to some kind of relationship while purposely avoiding issues of (in)direct dependence, authorial intention, and distinctions between echo, allusion, paraphrase, and quotation.

Verbal parallels, in the case of interpretive allusions, refer to the same phrases, words, and/or roots in donor and receptor texts. Content words (nouns, verbs,

22. See Moo, *Old Testament in the Gospel*, 380; *OTUOT*, 862.

and adjectives) count for verbal parallels not articles, prepositions, and other minor syntactical elements, though these may indicate syntactical dependence.

Vertical context refers to the temporal relationship (earlier and later) between two or more passages established by an allusion.[23] Whereas horizontal context refers to the surrounding verses, paragraphs, chapters, and book, vertical context is based on an allusion within a receptor text. Within emerging canonical consciousness, an allusion permanently tethers donor and receptor texts together so that later interpreters may work up or down vertical contexts of an earlier receptor text and its donor text(s). See Chapter 4.

23. See Schnittjer, "Going Vertical," 114–42.

BIBLIOGRAPHY

Adams, Sean A. and Seth M. Ehorn. "Composite Citations in Antiquity: A Conclusion." Pages 209–49 in *Composite Citations in Antiquity*, Vol. 2, *New Testament Uses*. Edited by Sean A. Adams and Seth M. Ehorn. New York: T&T Clark, 2018.

Aḥituv, Shmuel. *Echoes from the Past: Hebrew and Cognate Inscriptions from the Biblical Period*. Jerusalem: Carta, 2008.

Akiyama, Kengo. *The Love of Neighbor in Ancient Judaism: The Reception of Leviticus 19:18 in the Hebrew Bible, the Septuagint, the Book of Jubilees, the Dead Sea Scrolls, and the New Testament*. Ancient Judaism and Early Christianity 105. Leiden: Brill, 2018.

Allbee, Richard A. "Asymmetrical Continuity of Love and Law between the Old and New Testaments: Explicating the Implicit Side of a Hermeneutical Bridge, Leviticus 19.11–18." *JSOT* 31.2 (2006): 147–66.

Allen, David. "Introduction: The Study of the Use of the Old Testament in the New." *JSNT* 38.1 (2015): 3–16.

Allen, David, and Steve Smith. "Introduction." Pages 1–7 in *Methodology in the Use of the Old Testament in the New: Context and Criteria*. Edited by David Allen and Steve Smith. LNTS 579. New York: T&T Clark, 2020.

Allison, Dale C., Jr. "The Old Testament in the New Testament." Pages 479–502 in *The New Cambridge History of the Bible: From the Beginnings to 600*. Edited by James Carleton and Joachim Schafer. Cambridge: Cambridge University Press, 2013.

Alter, Robert. *The Art of Biblical Narrative*. Rev. ed. New York: Basic Books, 2011.

__________. "Biblical Type-Scenes and the Use of Convention." *Critical Inquiry* 5.2 (1978): 355–68.

Aristotle. *Poetics*. Edited and translated by Stephen Halliwell. LCL 199. Cambridge: Harvard University Press, 1995.

Athas, George. *Bridging the Testaments: The History and Theology of God's People in the Second Temple Period*. Grand Rapids: Zondervan Academic, 2023.

Baker, David L. *Two Testaments, One Bible: The Theological Relationship between the Old and New Testaments*. 3rd ed. Downers Grove, IL: IVP Academic, 2010.

Barr, James. *The Semantics of Biblical Language*. New York: Oxford University Press, 1961.

Barrett, C. K. "The Interpretation of the Old Testament in the New." Pages 377–411 in *The Cambridge History of the Bible*. Vol. 1, *From the Beginnings to Jerome*. Edited by P. R. Ackroyd and C. F. Evans. New York: Cambridge University Press, 1970.

Barrett, Matthew. *Canon, Covenant and Christology: Rethinking Jesus and the Scriptures of Israel*. NSBT 51. Downers Grove, IL: IVP Academic, 2020.

Bateman, Herbert W. IV. *Early Jewish Hermeneutics and Hebrews 1:5–13*. New York: Lang, 1997.

_________. *Hebrews*. KC. Grand Rapids: Kregel, 2021.

_________. *Jude*. Evangelical Exegetical Commentary. Bellingham, WA: Lexham, 2017.

Bates, Matthew W. *The Birth of the Trinity: Jesus, God, and Spirit in New Testament and Early Christian Interpretations of the Old Testament*. New York: Oxford University Press, 2015.

_________. *The Hermeneutics of the Apostolic Proclamation: The Center of Paul's Method of Scriptural Interpretation*. Waco, TX: Baylor University Press, 2012.

Bauckham, Richard. "James and the Gentiles (Acts 15.13–21)." Pages 154–84 in *History, Literature, and Society in the Book of Acts*. Edited by Ben Witherington, III. Cambridge: Cambridge University Press, 1996.

_________. *Jesus and the God of Israel: God Crucified and Other Studies on the New Testament's Christology of Divine Identity*. Grand Rapids: Eerdmans, 2008.

Bavinck, Herman. *Reformed Dogmatics*. Vol. 1, *Prolegomena*. Edited by John Bolt. Translated by John Vriend. Grand Rapids: Baker Academic, 2003.

Beale, G. K. *The Book of Revelation: A Commentary on the Greek Text*. New International Greek Testament Commentary. Grand Rapids: Eerdmans, 1999.

_________. "The Cognitive Peripheral Vision of Biblical Authors." *WTJ* 76 (2014): 263–93.

_________. "Did Jesus and His Followers Preach Right Doctrine from the Wrong Texts?" Pages 387–404 in *The Right Doctrine from the Wrong Texts?: Essays on the Use of the Old Testament in the New*. Edited by G. K. Beale. Grand Rapids: Baker Books, 1994.

_________. "Finding Christ in the Old Testament." *JETS* 63.1 (2020): 25–50.

_________. *John's Use of the Old Testament in Revelation*. JSNTSup 166. New York: Bloomsbury T&T Clark, 1998.

_________. "The Old Testament in Colossians: A Response to Paul Foster." *JSNT* 41.2 (2018): 261–74.

_________. *The Temple and the Church's Mission: A Biblical Theology of the Dwelling Place of God*. NSBT 17. Downers Grove, IL: InterVarsity Press, 2004.

_________. *The Use of Daniel in Jewish Apocalyptic Literature and in the Revelation of St. John*. Lanham, MD: University Press of America, 1984.

_________. "The Use of the Old in the Old as a Pattern for the Use of the Old in the New." Paper presented at the Evangelical Theological Society Annual Meeting. Denver, CO. 16 November 2022.

Beale, G. K., and Benjamin L. Gladd. *Hidden but Now Revealed: A Biblical Theology of Mystery*. Downers Grove, IL: IVP Academic, 2014.

Beentjes, Pancratius C. "Discovering a New Path of Intertextuality: Inverted Quotations and Their Dynamics." Pages 31–49 in *Literary Structure and Rhetorical Strategies in the Hebrew Bible*. Edited by L. J. de Regt, J. de Waard, and J. P. Fokkelman. Assen: Van Gorcum, 1996.

Beetham, Christopher A. *Echoes of Scripture in the Letter of Paul to the Colossians.* Biblical Interpretation Series 96. Leiden: Brill, 2008.

Ben-Porat, Ziva. "The Poetics of Literary Allusion." *PTL: A Journal for Descriptive Poetics and Theory of Literature* 1 (1976): 105–28.

Berding, Kenneth. "Conclusion." Pages 233–43 in *Three Views on the New Testament Use of the Old Testament.* Edited by Kenneth Berding, Jonathan Lunde, and Stanley N. Gundry. Grand Rapids: Zondervan Academic, 2007.

Blackman, Philip. *Mishnayoth: Pointed Hebrew Text, English Translation, Introductions, Notes, Supplement, Appendix, Indexes, Addenda, Corrigenda.* 2nd rev., corr., and enl. ed. 6 vols. Gateshead, UK: Judaica, 1977.

Block, Daniel I. *Covenant: The Framework of God's Grand Plan of Redemption.* Grand Rapids: Baker Academic, 2021.

Blomberg, Craig L. "Interpreting Old Testament Prophetic Literature in Matthew: Double Fulfillment." *TJ* 23 NS (2002): 17–33.

__________. *Matthew.* NAC. Nashville: Broadman & Holman, 1992.

__________. "The Historical-Critical/Grammatical View." Pages 27–47 in *Biblical Hermeneutics: Five Views.* Edited by Stanley E. Porter and Beth M. Stovell. Downers Grove, IL: IVP Academic, 2012.

__________. "Quotations, Allusions, and Echoes of Jesus in Paul." Pages 129–43 in *Studies in the Pauline Epistles: Essays in Honor of Douglas J. Moo.* Edited by Matthew S. Harmon and Jay E. Smith. Grand Rapids: Zondervan Academic, 2014.

Bock, Darrell L. *Acts.* BECNT. Grand Rapids: Baker Academic, 2007.

__________. *Blasphemy and Exaltation in Judaism: The Charge against Jesus in Mark 14:53–65.* Tübingen: Mohr Siebeck, 1998. Repr., Grand Rapids: Baker Books, 2000.

__________. "Evangelicals and the Use of the Old Testament in the New, Part 1." *BSac* 142 (1985): 209–23.

__________. "Evangelicals and the Use of the Old Testament in the New, Part 2." *BSac* 142 (1985): 306–19.

__________. "Opening Questions: Definition and Philosophy of Exegesis." Pages 23–32 in *Interpreting the New Testament Text: Introduction to the Art and Science of Exegesis.* Edited by Darrell L. Bock and Buist M. Fanning. Wheaton, IL: Crossway, 2006.

__________. *Proclamation from Prophecy and Pattern: Lucan Old Testament Christology.* JSNTSup 12. Sheffield: Sheffield Academic, 1987.

__________. "Scripture Citing Scripture: Use of the Old Testament in the New." Pages 255–76 in *Interpreting the New Testament Text: Introduction to the Art and Science of Exegesis.* Edited by Darrell L. Bock and Buist M. Fanning. Wheaton, IL: Crossway, 2006.

__________. "Single Meaning, Multiple Contexts and Referents." Pages 105–51 in *Three Views on the New Testament Use of the Old Testament.* Edited by Kenneth Berding, Jonathan Lunde, and Stanley N. Gundry. Grand Rapids: Zondervan Academic, 2007.

Boda, Mark J. *The Book of Zechariah.* NICOT. Grand Rapids: Eerdmans, 2016.

———. *Haggai, Zechariah*. NIVAC. Grand Rapids: Zondervan, 2004.

———. "Legitimizing the Temple: The Chronicler's Temple Building Account." Pages 303–18 in *From the Foundation to the Crenellations: Essays on Temple Building in the Ancient Near East and Hebrew Bible*. Edited by Mark J. Boda and Jamie Novotny. Münster: Ugarit-Verlag, 2010.

Brettler, Marc Zvi. "Israel's Scriptures in the Hebrew Bible." Pages 47–80 in *Israel's Scripture in Early Christian Writings: The Use of the Old Testament in the New*. Edited by Matthias Henze and David Lincicum. Grand Rapids: Eerdmans, 2023.

Brown, Jeannine K. *Scripture as Communication: Introducing Biblical Hermeneutics*. 2nd ed. Grand Rapids: Baker Academic, 2021.

Brown, Raymond E. "The History and Development of the Theory of a *Sensus Plenior*." *CBQ* 15.2 (1963): 141–62.

———. "The Problems of *Sensus Plenior*." *ETL* 43.3 (1967): 460–69.

———. "The *Sensus Plenior* in the Last Ten Years." *CBQ* 25.3 (1967): 262–85.

———. *The* Sensus Plenior *of Sacred Scripture*. Baltimore: St. Mary's University. Repr., Eugene, OR: Wipf & Stock, 1955.

Bruce, F. F. *This Is That: The New Testament Development of Some Old Testament Themes*. Exeter: Paternoster, 1968.

Bruno, Chris, Jared Compton, and Kevin McFadden. *Biblical Theology According to the Apostles: How the Earliest Christians Told the Story of Israel*. NSBT 52. Downers Grove, IL: IVP Academic, 2020.

Cagni, Luigi. *L'epopea di Erra*. Studi Semitici 34. Rome: Istituto di Studi del Vicino Oriente, 1969.

Caneday, Ardel. "Biblical Types: Revelation Concealed in Plain Sight to Be Disclosed—'These Things Occurred Typologically to Them and Were Written Down for Our Admonition.'" Pages 135–55 in *God's Glory Revealed in Christ: Essays on Biblical Theology in Honor of Thomas R. Schreiner*. Edited by James Hamilton, Denny Burk, and Brian J. Vickers. Nashville: B&H Academic, 2019.

Carey, Holly J. *Jesus' Cry from the Cross: Towards a First-Century Understanding of the Intertextual Relationship between Psalm 22 and the Narrative of Mark's Gospel*. LNTS 398. New York: T&T Clark, 2009.

Carson, D. A. "Mystery and Fulfillment: Toward a More Comprehensive Paradigm of Paul's Understanding of the Old and the New." Pages 393–436 in *Justification and Variegated Nomism: The Paradoxes of Paul*. Edited by D. A. Carson, Peter T. O'Brien, and Mark A. Siefrid. Grand Rapids: Baker Academic, 2001.

Carson, D. A. and H. G. M. Williamson, eds. *It Is Written: Scripture Citing Scripture: Essays in Honour of Barnabas Lindars*. New York: Cambridge University Press, 1988.

Casey, Maurice. "The Date of the Passover Sacrifices and Mark 14:12." *TynBul* 48.2 (1997): 245–47.

Chase, Mitchell L. *40 Questions about Typology and Allegory*. 40 Questions Series. Grand Rapids: Kregel Academic, 2020.

"The Chicago Statement of Biblical Hermeneutics." *JETS* 25.4 (1982): 397–401.

Childs, Brevard S. "Prophecy and Fulfillment." *Interpretation* 70 (1958): 259–71.

Chisholm, Robert B., Jr. *1 & 2 Samuel*. Teach the Text Commentary. Grand Rapids: Baker Books, 2013.

Chou, Abner. *The Hermeneutics of the Biblical Writers: Learning to Interpret Scripture from the Prophets and Apostles*. Grand Rapids: Kregel Academic, 2018.

Ciampa, Roy E. *The Presence and Function of Scripture in Galatians 1 and 2*. WUNT 2/102. Tübingen: Mohr Siebeck, 1998.

_________. "Scriptural Language and Ideas." Pages 41–57 in *As It Is Written: Studying Paul's Use of Scripture*. Edited by Stanley E. Porter and Christopher D. Stanley. SBL Symposium Series 50. Atlanta: Society of Biblical Literature, 2008.

Clark, David K. *To Know and To Love God*. Wheaton, IL: Crossway, 2003.

Cohick, Lynn. *The Letter to the Ephesians*. NICNT. Grand Rapids: Eerdmans, 2020.

Compton, Jared M. "Shared Intentions?: Reflections on Inspiration and Interpretation in Light of Scripture's Dual Authorship." *Themelios* 33.3 (2008): 23–33.

Crowe, Brandon D. *The Hope of Israel: The Resurrection of Christ in the Acts of the Apostles*. Grand Rapids: Baker Academic, 2020.

Darabi, Yuval. "The Provisions Regarding the Rape and Seduction of an Unbetrothed Girl." *VT* 73 (2023): 522–45.

Daube, David. "Rabbinic Methods of Interpretation and Hellenistic Rhetoric." *HUCA* 22 (1949): 239–65.

Davidson, Richard M. "The Eschatological Hermeneutic of Biblical Typology." *TheoRhēma* 6.2 (2012): 5–48.

Delitzsch, Franz. *Commentary on the Epistle to the Hebrews*. 2 vols. Translated by Thomas L. Kingsbury. Edinburgh: T&T Clark, 1874, 1872.

Dernell, William James. "Typology, Christology and Prosopological Exegesis: Implicit Narratives in Christological Exegesis." *SBJT* 24.1 (2020): 137–61.

Dharamraj, Havilah. "Reception-Centered Intertextual Approach." Pages 127–51 in *Five Views of Christ in the Old Testament: Genre, Authorial Intent, and the Nature of Scripture*. Edited by Brian J. Tabb and Andrew M. King. Grand Rapids: Zondervan Academic, 2022.

Dillard, Raymond B., and Tremper Longman III. *An Introduction to the Old Testament*. 2nd ed. Grand Rapids: Zondervan Academic, 2006.

Docherty, Susan. "Crossing Testamentary Borders: Methodological Insights for OT/NT Study from Contemporary Hebrew Bible Scholarship." Pages 11–22 in *Methodology in the Use of the Old Testament in the New: Context and Criteria*. Edited by David Allen and Steve Smith. LNTS 579. New York: T&T Clark, 2020.

_________. "Israel's Scriptures in the Dead Sea Scrolls." Pages 138–61 in *Israel's Scripture in Early Christian Writings: The Use of the Old Testament in the New*. Edited by Matthias Henze and David Lincicum. Grand Rapids: Eerdmans, 2023.

_________. "New Testament Scriptural Interpretation in its Early Jewish Context." *NovT* 57.1 (2015): 1–19.

Dodd, C. H. *According to the Scriptures: The Sub-structure of New Testament Theology*. New York: Scribner's Sons, 1953.

Driver, S. R. *A Critical and Exegetical Commentary on Deuteronomy*. 3rd ed. ICC. Edinburgh: T&T Clark, 1901.

Dunn, James D. G. *The Epistle to the Galatians.* BNTC. Peabody, MA: Hendrickson, 1993.

Duvall, J. Scott, and J. Daniel Hays. *Grasping God's Word.* 4th ed. Grand Rapids: Zondervan Academic, 2020.

Edenburg, Cynthia. "Intertextuality, Literary Competence and the Question of Readership: Some Preliminary Observations." *JSOT* 35.2 (2010): 131–48.

Eichler, Barry L. "Examples of Restatement in the Laws of Hammurabi." Pages 365–400 in *Mishneh Todah: Studies in Deuteronomy and Its Cultural Environment in Honor of Jeffrey H. Tigay.* Edited by Nili Sacher Fox, et al. Winona Lake, IN: Eisenbrauns, 2009.

Ellis, E. Earle. "How the New Testament Uses the Old." Pages 199–219 in *New Testament Interpretation: Essays on Principles and Methods.* Edited by I. Howard Marshall. Grand Rapids: Eerdmans, 1997.

_________. *The Old Testament in Early Christianity: Canon and Interpretation in the Light of Modern Research.* Tübingen: Mohr Siebeck, 1991. Repr., Grand Rapids: Baker Books, 1992.

_________. *Paul's Use of the Old Testament.* Grand Rapids: Baker Books, 1957.

Emadi, Matthew H. *The Royal Priest: Psalm 110 in Biblical Theology.* NSBT 60. Downers Grove, IL: IVP Academic, 2022.

Emadi, Samuel. *From Prisoner to Prince: The Joseph Story in Biblical Theology.* NSBT 59. Downers Grove, IL: IVP Academic, 2022.

Evans, Craig A. "The Function of the Old Testament in the New." Pages 163–93 in *Introducing New Testament Interpretation.* Edited by Scot McKnight. Grand Rapids: Baker Books, 1989.

Fee, Gordon D., and Douglas Stuart. *How to Read the Bible for All Its Worth.* 4th ed. Grand Rapids: Zondervan Academic, 2014.

Feinberg, Paul D. "Hermeneutics of Discontinuity." Pages 109–28 in *Continuity and Discontinuity: Perspectives on the Relationship between the Old and New Testaments.* Edited by S. Lewis Johnson and John S. Feinberg. Wheaton, IL: Crossway, 1988.

Fensham, F. Charles. "Widow, Orphan, and the Poor in Ancient Near Eastern Legal and Wisdom Literature." Pages 176–92 in *Essential Papers on Israel and the Ancient Near East.* Edited by Fredrick E. Greenspahn. New York: New York University Press, 1991.

Fishbane, Michael. *Biblical Interpretation in Ancient Israel.* New York: Oxford University Press, 1985.

_________. *Biblical Text and Exegetical Culture: Collected Essays.* Tübingen: Mohr Siebeck, 2022.

_________. *Haftarot.* JPSC. Philadelphia: Jewish Publication Society of America, 2002.

Fleishman, Joseph. "Shechem and Dinah—in the Light of Non-Biblical and Biblical Sources." *Zeitschrift für die alttestamentliche Wissenschaft* 116.1 (2004): 12–32.

Flesher, Paul V. M. "Exploring the Sources of the Synoptic Targums to the Pentateuch." Pages 101–34 in *Targum Studies.* Vol. 1, *Textual and Contextual Studies in the Pentateuchal Targums.* Edited by Paul V. M. Flesher. Atlanta: Scholars Press, 1992.

__________. "Mapping the Synoptic Palestinian Targums of the Pentateuch." Pages 247–53 in *The Aramaic Bible: Targums in their Historical Context*. Edited by D. R. G. Beattie and Michael J. McNamara. JSOTSup 166. Sheffield: Sheffield Academic, 1994.

__________. "Translation and Exegetical Augmentation in the Targums to the Pentateuch." Pages 29–86 in *New Perspectives on Ancient Judaism*. Vol. 3, *Judaic and Christian Interpretation of Texts: Contents and Contexts*. Edited by Jacob Neusner and Ernest S. Frerichs. Lanham, MD: University Press of America, 1987.

Flesher, Paul V. M., and Bruce Chilton. *The Targums: A Critical Introduction*. Leiden: Brill, 2011.

Foster, Paul. *Colossians*. BNTC. London: Bloomsbury T&T Clark, 2016.

__________. "Echoes without Resonance: Critiquing Certain Aspects of Recent Scholarly Trends in the Study of the Jewish Scriptures in the New Testament." *JSNT* 38.1 (2015): 96–111.

France, R. T. *Jesus and the Old Testament: His Application of Old Testament Passages to Himself and His Mission*. London: Tyndale Press, 1971.

__________. *Matthew*. NICNT. Grand Rapids: Eerdmans, 2007.

Gaffin, Richard B., Jr. "The Redemptive-Historical View." Pages 89–110 in *Biblical Hermeneutics: Five Views*. Edited by Stanley E. Porter and Beth M. Stovell. Downers Grove, IL: IVP Academic, 2012.

Gelston, Anthony. "Some Hebrew Misreadings in the Septuagint of Amos." *VT* 52.4 (2002): 493–500.

Gentry, Peter J. "A Preliminary Evaluation and Critique of Prosopological Exegesis." *SBJT* 23.2 (2019): 105–22.

Gillingham, Susan. "New Wine in Old Wineskins: Three Approaches to Prophecy and Psalmody." Pages 370–90 in *Prophecy and Prophets in Ancient Israel: Proceedings of the Oxford Old Testament Seminar*. Edited by John Day. LBHOTS 531. New York: T&T Clark, 2010.

Gladd, Benjamin L. *Handbook on the Gospels*. Handbooks on the New Testament. Grand Rapids: Baker Academic, 2021.

Glatt-Gilad, David A. *Chronological Displacement in Biblical and Related Literatures*. Atlanta: Scholars Press, 1993.

Glenny, W. Edward. "Typology: A Summary of the Present Evangelical Discussion." *JETS* 40.4 (1997): 627–38.

Goldingay, John. *Psalms 1–41. Baker Commentary on the Old Testament: Wisdom and Psalms*. Grand Rapids: Baker Academic, 2006.

Gordon, Cyrus H. "The Background of Some Distinctive Values in the Hebrew Bible." Pages 57–68 in *"Go to the Land I Will Show You": Studies in Honor of Dwight W. Young*. Edited by Joseph E. Coleson and Victor H. Matthews. Winona Lake, IN: Eisenbrauns, 1996.

Graves, Michael. *How Scripture Interprets Scripture: What Biblical Writers Can Teach Us about Reading the Bible*. Grand Rapids: Baker Academic, 2021.

Greenberg, Moshe. "Hebrew *segullā*: Akkadian *sikiltu*." *JAOS* 71.3 (1951): 172–74.

Greengus, Samuel. *Laws in the Bible and in Early Rabbinic Collections: The Legacy of the Ancient Near East*. Eugene, OR: Cascade Books, 2011.

Greever, Joshua M. "The Typological Expectation of Psalm 68 and Its Application in Ephesians 4:8." *TynBul* 71.2 (2020): 253–79.

Grisanti, Michael. "The Book of Psalms." Pages 512–26 in *The World and the Word: An Introduction to the Old Testament*. Eugene Merrill, Mark F. Rooker, and Michael A. Grisanti. Brentwood, TN: B&H Academic, 2011.

Hamilton, James M. *Typology: Understanding the Bible's Promise-Shaped Patterns*. Grand Rapids: Zondervan Academic, 2022.

_________. *What Is Biblical Theology? A Guide to the Bible's Story, Symbolism, and Patterns*. Wheaton, IL: Crossway, 2014.

Harmon, Matthew S. "Allegory, Typology, or Something Else? Revisiting Galatians 4:21–5:1." Pages 144–58 in *Studies in the Pauline Epistles: Essays in Honor of Douglas J. Moo*. Edited by Matthew S. Harmon and Jay E. Smith. Grand Rapids: Zondervan Academic, 2014.

_________. *Asking the Right Questions: A Practical Guide to Understanding and Applying the Bible*. Wheaton, IL: Crossway, 2017.

_________. "Divine Identity and the Resurrection in Galatians 1:1: An Exploration of the Intertextual Matrix Underlying Paul's Redefinition of God's Identity." Pages 3–19 in *Scripture, Texts, and Tracings in Galatians and 1 Thessalonians*. Edited by A. Andrew Das and B. J. Oropeza. Lanham, MD: Lexington Books, 2023.

_________. *Galatians*. Evangelical Biblical Theology Commentary. Bellingham, WA: Lexham, 2021.

_________. *She Must and Shall Go Free: Paul's Isaianic Gospel in Galatians*. BZNW 168. Berlin: de Gruyter, 2010.

_________. *The Servant of the Lord and His Servant People: Tracing a Biblical Theme through the Canon*. NSBT 54. Downers Grove, IL: IVP Academic, 2020.

Harper, Robert Francis, ed. and trans. *The Code of Hammurabi King of Babylon about 2250 B.C.* Chicago: University of Chicago Press, 1904.

Harris, Murray J. *Prepositions and Theology in the Greek New Testament: An Essential Reference Resource for Exegesis*. Grand Rapids: Zondervan Academic, 2011.

Hays, Richard B. "The Canonical Matrix of the Gospels." Pages 53–75 in *The Cambridge Companion to the Gospels*. Edited by Stephen C. Barton. Cambridge: Cambridge University Press, 2006.

_________. *Conversion of the Imagination: Paul as Interpreter of Israel's Scriptures*. Grand Rapids: Eerdmans, 2005.

_________. *Echoes of Scripture in the Gospels*. Waco, TX: Baylor University Press, 2016.

_________. *Echoes of Scripture in the Letters of Paul*. New Haven: Yale University Press, 1989.

_________. "Figural Exegesis and the Retrospective Re-cognition of Israel's Story." *BBR* 29.1 (2019): 32–48.

_________. "On the Rebound: A Response to Critiques of *Echoes of Scripture in the Letters of Paul*." Pages 70–96 in *Paul and the Scriptures of Israel*. Edited by Craig A. Evans and James A. Sanders. JSNTSup 83. Sheffield: Sheffield Academic, 1993.

_________. *Reading Backwards: Figural Christology and the Fourfold Gospel Witness*. Waco, TX: Baylor University Press, 2014.

_________. *Reading with the Grain of Scripture*. Grand Rapids: Eerdmans, 2020.

Henze, Matthias and David Lincicum, "Introduction." Pages 1–20 in *Israel's Scripture in Early Christian Writings: The Use of the Old Testament in the New*. Edited by Matthias Henze and David Lincicum. Grand Rapids: Eerdmans, 2023.

Hirsch, Eric Donald, Jr. *The Aims of Interpretation*. Chicago: University of Chicago Press, 1976.

_________. *Validity in Interpretation*. New Haven: Yale University Press, 1967.

Hoehner, Harold W. "Chronological Aspects of the Life of Christ. Part IV: The Day of Christ's Crucifixion." *BSac* 131 (1974): 241–64.

Hood, Jason B., and Matthew Y. Emerson. "Summaries of Israel's Story: Reviewing a Compositional Category." *CBR* 11.3 (2013): 328–48.

Hoskins, Paul M. *That Scripture Might Be Fulfilled: Typology and the Death of Christ*. Longwood, FL: Xulon, 2009.

Hubbard, Robert L. "Reading through the Rearview Mirror: Inner-Biblical Exegesis and the New Testament." Pages 125–39 in *Doing Theology for the Church: Essays in Honor of Klyne Snodgrass*. Edited by Rebekah A. Eklund and John E. Phelan, Jr. Eugene, OR: Wipf & Stock, 2014.

Imes, Carmen Joy. "Review Essay: *Exodus in the New Testament*." Pages 202–10 in *Exodus in the New Testament*. Edited by Seth M. Ehorn. LNTS 663. New York: T&T Clark, 2022.

_________. "Scripture Interprets Scripture: This Book Shows How." *Christianity Today*, 25 Feb 2022, https://www.christianitytoday.com/ct/2022/february-web-only/bible-reference-tool-old-testament-scripture-interpretation.html.

_________. "'Treasured Possession': Peter's Use of the Old Testament in 1 Peter 2:9–10." Unpublished MABS thesis, Gordon-Conwell Theological Seminary, Charlotte, NC, May 2011.

Instone-Brewer, David. "Jesus's Last Passover: The Synoptics and John." *Expository Times* 112.4 (2001): 122–23.

Johnson, Elliot. "Author's Intention and Biblical Interpretation." Pages 409–29 in *Hermeneutics, Inerrancy, and the Bible*. Edited by Earl D. Radmacher and Robert D. Preus. Grand Rapids: Academie Books, 1984.

Johnson, Luke Timothy. *Septuagintal Midrash in the Speeches of Acts*. Milwaukee: Marquette University Press, 2002.

Johnson, S. Lewis, Jr. *The Old Testament in the New: An Argument for Biblical Inspiration*. Grand Rapids: Zondervan, 1980.

Johnston, Gordon. "What Biblical Scholars Should Know about Hittite Treaties." In *TORAH: Treaty, Law, and Ritual in the Hebrew Bible in Its Ancient Near Eastern Environment*. Edited by David C. Deuel, Richard S. Hess, Richard E. Averbeck, et al., forthcoming.

_________. "The Writing/Reading/Hearing of the Stone Tablet Covenant in the Light of the Writing/Reading/Hearing of the Silver Tablet Treaty." Pages 71–99 in *Write That They May Read: Studies in Literacy and Textualization in the Ancient Near East and in the Hebrew Scripture, Essays in Honour of Professor Alan R. Millard*. Edited by Daniel I. Block. Eugene, OR: Pickwick, 2020.

Kaiser, Walter C., Jr. "The Current Crisis in Exegesis and the Apostolic Use of Deuteronomy 25:4 in 1 Corinthians 9:8–10." *JETS* 21.1 (1978): 3–18.

_________. "Response to Enns." Pages 218–25 in *Three Views on the New Testament Use of the Old Testament*. Edited by Kenneth Berding, Jonathan Lunde, and Stanley N. Gundry. Grand Rapids: Zondervan Academic, 2007.

_________. "Single Meaning, Unified Referents." Pages 45–89 in *Three Views on the New Testament Use of the Old Testament*. Edited by Kenneth Berding, Jonathan Lunde, and Stanley N. Gundry. Grand Rapids: Zondervan Academic, 2007.

_________. *The Uses of the Old Testament in the New*. Chicago: Moody, 1985.

_________. *Toward Old Testament Ethics*. Grand Rapids: Academie Books, 1983.

Keefer, Arthur. "The Meaning and Place of Old Testament Context in OT/NT Methodology." Pages 73–85 in *Methodology in the Use of the Old Testament in the New: Context and Criteria*. Edited by David Allen and Steve Smith. LNTS 579. New York: T&T Clark, 2020.

Keener, Craig S. "The Unridden Donkey Colt: Mark 11:2 in Light of Equine Development and Pedagogy." *BBR* 32.1 (2022): 17–40.

Kelly, Joseph Ryan. "The Ethics of Inclusion: The גר and the אזרח in the Passover to Yhwh." *BBR* 23.2 (2013): 155–66.

Knoppers, Gary N. *I Chronicles 10–29*. AB. New York: Doubleday, 2004.

_________. *Jews and Samaritans: The Origins and History of Their Early Relations*. New York: Oxford University Press, 2011.

_________. "Parallel Torahs and Inner-Scriptural Interpretation: The Jewish and Samaritan Pentateuchs in Historical Perspective." Pages 507–31 in *The Pentateuch: International Perspectives on Current Research*. Edited by T. B. Dozeman, K. Schmid, and B. J. Schwartz. FAT 78. Tübingen: Mohr Siebeck, 2011.

Köstenberger, Andreas J. "Exodus in John." Pages 88–108 in *Exodus in the New Testament*. Edited by Seth M. Ehorn. LNTS 663. New York: T&T Clark, 2022.

Kristeva, Julia. *Revolution in Poetic Language*. Translated by Margaret Waller. New York: Columbia University Press, 1984.

Kugel, James L. "The Beginnings of Biblical Interpretation." Pages 3–26 in *A Companion to Biblical Interpretation in Early Judaism*. Edited by Matthias Henze. Grand Rapids: Eerdmans, 2012.

_________. Review of *Biblical Interpretation in Ancient Israel,* by Michael Fishbane. *Prooftexts* 7 (1987): 269–83.

_________. *Traditions of the Bible: A Guide to the Bible As It Was at the Start of the Common Era*. Cambridge: Harvard University Press, 1998.

Lambert, W. G. *Babylonian Creation Myths*. Winona Lake, IN: Eisenbrauns, 2013.

Lanier, Greg. *Old Made New: A Guide to the New Testament Use of the Old Testament*. Wheaton, IL: Crossway, 2022.

LaSor, William Sanford. "The *Sensus Plenior* and Biblical Interpretation." Pages 260–77 in *Scripture, Tradition, and Interpretation: Essays Presented to Everett F. Harrison by his Students and Colleagues in Honor of his Seventy-fifth Birthday*. Edited by W. Ward Gasque and William Sanford LaSor. Grand Rapids: Eerdmans, 1978.

Leonard, Jeffery M. "Identifying Subtle Allusions: The Promise of Narrative Tracking." Pages 91–113 in *Subtle Citation, Allusion, and Translation in the Hebrew Bible.* Edited by Ziony Zevit. Sheffield: Equinox, 2017.

Levine, Amy-Jill, and Marc Zvi Brettler. *The Bible With and Without Jesus: How Jews and Christians Read the Same Stories Differently.* New York: HarperOne, 2020.

Lewis, Brian. *The Sargon Legend: A Study of the Akkadian Text and the Tale of the Hero who was Exposed at Birth.* Cambridge: American Schools of Oriental Research, 1980.

Licona, Michael R. *Jesus, Contradicted: Why the Gospels Tell the Same Story Differently.* Grand Rapids: Zondervan Academic, 2024.

__________. *Why Are There Differences in the Gospels?: What We Can Learn from Ancient Biography.* New York: Oxford University Press, 2017.

Lindars, Barnabas. "The Place of the Old Testament in the Formation of New Testament Theology." *NTS* 23.1 (1976): 59–66.

Livneh, Atar. "'Love Your Fellow as Yourself': The Interpretation of Leviticus 19:17–18 in the Book of Jubilees." *Dead Sea Discoveries* 18.2 (2011): 173–99.

Longenecker, Richard N. *Biblical Exegesis in the Apostolic Period.* 2nd ed. Grand Rapids: Eerdmans, 1999.

__________. "Can We Reproduce the Exegesis of the New Testament? *TynBul* 21 (1970): 3–38.

__________. *Galatians.* WBC 41. Dallas: Word, 1990.

Longman, Tremper, III. "Christotelic Approach." Pages 73–100 in *Five Views of Christ in the Old Testament: Genre, Authorial Intent, and the Nature of Scripture.* Edited by Brian J. Tabb and Andrew M. King. Grand Rapids: Zondervan Academic, 2022.

__________. *The Old Testament as Literature: The Foundations of Christian Interpretation.* Grand Rapids: Baker Academic, 2024.

__________. *Psalms.* TOTC. Downers Grove, IL: IVP Academic, 2014.

Luckenbill, Daniel David. *The Annals of Sennacherib.* Chicago: University of Chicago Press, 1924.

Lunde, Jonathan, and Kenneth Berding. *Three Views on the New Testament Use of the Old Testament.* Grand Rapids: Zondervan Academic, 2007.

Lynch, Matthew. *Monotheism and Institutions in the Book of Chronicles: Temple, Priesthood, and Kingship in Post-Exilic Perspective.* FAT II/64. Tübingen: Mohr Siebeck, 2014.

Macaskill, Grant. "Israel's Scriptures in Early Jewish Literature." Pages 109–37 in *Israel's Scripture in Early Christian Writings: The Use of the Old Testament in the New.* Edited by Matthias Henze and David Lincicum. Grand Rapids: Eerdmans, 2023.

Marshall, I. Howard. "An Assessment of Recent Developments." Pages 1–21 in *It Is Written: Scripture Citing Scripture: Essays in Honour of Barnabas Lindars.* New York: Cambridge University Press, 1988.

McFadden, Kevin W. *Faith in the Son of God: The Place of Christ-Oriented Faith within Pauline Theology.* Wheaton, IL: Crossway, 2021.

McKnight, Scot. *Five Things Biblical Scholars Wish Theologians Knew*. Downers Grove, IL: IVP Academic, 2021.

McNamara, Martin, "Early Exegesis in the Palestinian Targum (Neofiti 1) Numbers 24." *Proceedings of the Irish Biblical Association* 16 (1993): 57–79.

Menken, Maarten J. J. *Old Testament Quotations in the Fourth Gospel: Studies in Textual Form*. Kampen: Kok Pharos, 1996.

Milgrom, Jacob. *Leviticus 17–22*. AB. New York: Doubleday, 2000.

Miller, Timothy E., and Bryan Murawski. *1 Peter*. KC. Grand Rapids: Kregel, 2022.

Moo, Douglas J. *The Old Testament in the Gospel Passion Narratives*. Sheffield: Almond Press, 1983.

__________. "The Problem of *Sensus Plenior*." Pages 175–211 in *Hermeneutics, Authority, and Canon*. Edited by D. A. Carson and John D. Woodbridge. Grand Rapids: Academie Books, 1986.

__________. *A Theology of Paul and His Letters*. Grand Rapids: Zondervan Academic, 2021.

Moo, Douglas J., and Andrew David Naselli. "The Problem of the New Testament's Use of the Old Testament." Pages 702–46 in *The Enduring Authority of the Christian Scriptures*. Edited by D. A. Carson. Grand Rapids: Eerdmans, 2016.

Morales, Michael. *Numbers 1–19*. ApOTC. Downers Grove, IL: IVP Academic, forthcoming.

__________. *Numbers 20–36*. ApOTC. Downers Grove, IL: IVP Academic, forthcoming.

Motyer, Stephen. "Old Testament in the New Testament, The." Pages 582–85 in *Evangelical Dictionary of Biblical Theology*. Edited by Walter A. Elwell. Grand Rapids: Baker Books, 1996.

Moyise, Steve. *The Old Testament in the New: An Introduction*. 2nd ed. New York: Bloomsbury, 2015.

__________. "Latency and Respect for Context: A Response to Mitchell Kim." Pages 131–39 in *Paul and Scripture: Extending the Conversation*. Edited by Christopher D. Stanley. Early Christianity and Its Literature 9. Atlanta: Society of Biblical Literature, 2012.

Newman, Carey C. *Paul's Glory-Christology: Tradition and Rhetoric*. NovTSup 69. Leiden: Brill, 1992.

Noonan, Benjamin J. "Unraveling Hebrew שַׁעַטְנֵז." *JBL* 135.1 (2016): 95–101.

Ortlund, Dane C. *Zeal without Knowledge: The Concept of Zeal in Romans 10, Galatians 1, and Philippians 3*. London: T&T Clark, 2012.

Osborne, Grant R. "Hermeneutics and Paul: Psalm 68:18 in Ephesians 4:7–10 as a Test Case." Pages 159–77 in *Studies in the Pauline Epistles: Essays in Honor of Douglas J. Moo*. Edited by Matthew S. Harmon and Jay E. Smith. Grand Rapids: Zondervan Academic, 2014.

Osborne, William R. "Conclusion." Pages 311–20 in *The Prophets and the Apostolic Witness: Reading Isaiah, Jeremiah, and Ezekiel as Christian Scripture*. Edited by Andrew T. Abernethy, William R. Osborne, and Paul D. Wenger. Downers Grove, IL: IVP Academic, 2023.

_________. "Emulating the Apostles: Reading Ezekiel as Christian Scripture in the Footsteps of the Apostles." Pages 249–69 in *The Prophets and the Apostolic Witness: Reading Isaiah, Jeremiah, and Ezekiel as Christian Scripture*. Edited by Andrew T. Abernethy, William R. Osborne, and Paul D. Wenger. Downers Grove, IL: IVP Academic, 2023.

Packer, J. I. "Infallible Scripture and the Role of Hermeneutics." Pages 321–56, 412–19 in *Scripture and Truth*. Edited by D. A. Carson and John D. Woodbridge. Grand Rapids: Zondervan, 1983.

Pate, Brian. "Who Is Speaking?: The Use of Isaiah 8:17–18 in Hebrews 2:13 as a Case Study for Applying the Speech of Key Old Testament Figures to Christ." *JETS* 59.4 (2016): 731–45.

Philo. *Life of Moses II*. Edited and translated by F. H. Colson. LCL 289. Cambridge: Harvard University Press, 1934.

_________. "Special Laws." Books II and III. Pages 304–471, 472–607 in *Philo*. Vol. 7. Edited and translated by F. H. Colson. LCL 320. Cambridge: Harvard University Press, 1937.

Philpot, Joshua M. "Was Joseph a Type of Daniel? Typological Correspondence Genesis 37–50 and Daniel 1–6." *JETS* 61.4 (2018): 681–96.

Pierce, Madison N. *Divine Discourse in the Epistle to the Hebrews: The Recontextualization of Spoken Quotations of Scripture*. New York: Cambridge University Press, 2020.

_________. "Gospel Reading and Prosopological Exegesis in Luke-Acts." Pages 48–67 in *Gospel Reading and Reception in Early Christian Literature*. Edited by Madison N. Pierce, Andrew J. Byers, and Simon Gathercole. New York: Cambridge University Press, 2022.

_________. "Precedents for Prosopological Exegesis and Features of Its Use in the Epistle to the Hebrews." Pages 124–32 in *Practicing Intertextuality: Ancient Jewish and Greco-Roman Exegetical Techniques in the New Testament*. Edited by Max J. Lee and B. J. Oropeza. Eugene, OR: Cascade Books, 2021.

_________. Review of *The Birth of the Trinity*, by Matthew W. Bates. *Reviews of Biblical and Early Christian Studies*, 2015, https://rbecs.org/2015/10/17/bt/

Powery, Emerson B. *Jesus Reads Scripture: The Function of Jesus' Use of Scripture in the Synoptic Gospels*. Biblical Interpretation 63. Leiden: Brill, 2003.

Rad, Gerhard von. *Old Testament Theology*. 2 vols. Translated by D. M. G. Stalker. New York: Harper & Row, 1965.

Rindge, Matthew S. "Jewish Identity under Foreign Rule: Daniel 2 as a Reconfiguration of Genesis 41." *JBL* 129.1 (2010): 85–104.

Rosner, Brian S. *Paul, Scripture and Ethics: A Study of 1 Corinthians 5–7*. AGJU 22. Leiden: Brill, 1994.

Sandmel, Samuel. "Parrallelomania." *JBL* 81.1 (1962): 1–13.

Sarna, Nahum M. *Exodus*. JPSTC. Philadelphia: Jewish Publication Society, 1991.

Schnabel, Eckhard J. *Jesus in Jerusalem: The Last Days*. Grand Rapids: Eerdmans, 2018.

Schnittjer, Gary Edward. "The Bad Ending of Ezra-Nehemiah." *BSac* 173 (2016): 32–56.

_________. "Bequeathing Wrath: Exegetical Use of Scripture in Exodus 34." *Journal for the Study of Bible and Violence* 2 (2023): 104–20.

_________. "The Blessing of Judah as Generative Expectation." *BSac* 177 (2020): 15–39.

_________. *Ezra-Nehemiah*. Baker Commentary on the Old Testament: Historical Books. Grand Rapids: Baker Academic, forthcoming.

_________. "Going Vertical with Love Thy Neighbor: Exegetical Use of Scripture in Leviticus 19.18b." *JSOT* 47.1 (2022): 114–42.

_________. "Individual versus Collective Retribution in the Chronicler's Ideology of Exile." *JBTS* 4.1 (2019): 113–32.

_________. "Kadesh Infidelity of Deuteronomy 1 and Its Synoptic Implications." *JETS* 63.1 (2020): 95–120.

_________. "Long-Lost Grandparent Texts of the New Testament." *Didaktikos* 5.4 (2022): 27–31.

_________. *Old Testament Narrative Books: The Israel Story*. Brentwood, TN: B&H Academic, 2023.

_________. "An Overview of Composite Citations in the Hebrew Bible with a Case Study from 1 Kings 11:1–4." In *Composite Allusions in Antiquity*. Edited by Sean A. Adams and Seth M. Ehorn. LNTS. London: Bloomsbury, forthcoming.

_________. "Say You, Say Ye: Individual and Collective Identity and Responsibility in Torah." *Center for Hebraic Thought*, 9 March 2022, https://hebraicthought.org/individual-collective-identity-responsibility-torah/.

_________. *Studying Scripture by Its Connections: An Introduction to Interpretation*. Brentwood, TN: B&H Academic, forthcoming.

_________. *Torah Story*. 2nd ed. Grand Rapids: Zondervan Academic, 2023.

_________. "What's Old about New Testament Exegesis of Scripture?: Fulfillment Citations in Chronicles and the Gospels." *CTR*, NS 21.2 (2024): 61–80.

_________. "Your House Is My House: Exegetical Intersection within the Davidic Promise." *BSac*, 180 (2023): 54–80.

Schultz, Richard L. *The Search for Quotation: Verbal Parallels in the Prophets*. JSOTSup 180. Sheffield: Sheffield Academic, 1999.

Seitz, Christopher. Review of *The Birth of the Trinity*, by Matthew W. Bates. *CBQ* 78.4 (2016): 763–66.

Sharon, Diane M. "Moral and Ethical Values in Structural Patterns of Coercive Acts in Hebrew Bible Narrative." *JSOT* 48.3 (2024): 265–84.

Shepherd, Michael B. *The Text in the Middle*. New York: Lang, 2014.

Shively, Elizabeth Evans. "Israel's Scriptures in Mark." Pages 236–62 in *Israel's Scriptures in Early Christian Writings: The Use of the Old Testament in the New*. Edited by Matthias Henze and David Lincicum. Grand Rapids: Eerdmans, 2023.

Snodgrass, Klyne. "The Use of the Old Testament in the New." Pages 209–29 in *Interpreting the New Testament: Essays on Methods and Issues*. Edited by David Alan Black and David S. Dockery. Nashville: Broadman & Holman, 2001.

Stead, Michael R. *The Intertextuality of Zechariah 1–8*. LHBOTS 506. New York: T&T Clark, 2009.

Stemberger, Günter. "From Inner-biblical Interpretation to Rabbinic Exegesis." Pages 190–217 in *The New Cambridge History of the Bible: From the Beginnings to*

600. Edited by James Carleton and Joachim Schafer. Cambridge: Cambridge University Press, 2013.

Stovell, Beth M. Review of *Old Testament Use of Old Testament,* by Gary Edward Schnittjer. *Didaktikos 2021 Fall Books Preview* (2021): 14–17.

Strauss, Mark L. *The Davidic Messiah in Luke-Acts*. JSNTSup 110. Sheffield: Sheffield Academic, 1995.

__________. *40 Questions about Bible Translation*. Grand Rapids: Kregel Academic, 2023.

__________. *Mark*. ZECNT. Grand Rapids: Zondervan Academic, 2014.

Street, Harold B. *The Believer-Priest in the Tabernacle Furniture*. Chicago: Moody Press, 1946.

Streett, Andrew D. "New Approaches to the Use of the Old Testament in the New Testament." *SwJT* 64.1 (2021): 9–24.

Swain, Scott R. "Covenant of Redemption." Pages 107–25 in *Christian Dogmatics: Reformed Theology for the Catholic Church*. Edited by Michael Allen and Scott R. Swain. Grand Rapids: Baker Academic, 2016.

Tabb, Brian J., and Andrew M. King. *Five Views of Christ in the Old Testament*. Grand Rapids: Zondervan Academic, 2022.

Theocharous, Myrto. *Lexical Dependence and Intertextual Allusion in the Septuagint of the Twelve Prophets: Studies in Hosea, Amos, and Micah*. LHBOTS 570. New York: Bloomsbury, 2012.

Thomas, Joel. "An Examination of the Last Supper in the Light of Jewish Cultural Backgrounds." Ph.D. dissertation, Dallas Theological Seminary, 2007.

Thomas, Robert. "The New Testament Use of the Old Testament." *The Master's Seminary Journal* 13.1 (2002): 79–98.

Tigay, Jeffrey. *Deuteronomy*. JPSTC. Philadelphia: Jewish Publication Society, 1996.

Tooman, William A. "Scriptural Reuse in Ancient Jewish Literature: Comments and Reflections on the State of the Art." Pages 23–39 in *Methodology in the Use of the Old Testament in the New: Context and Criteria*. Edited by David Allen and Steve Smith. LNTS 579. New York: T&T Clark, 2020.

Tov, Emanuel. "Hebrew Scripture Editions: Philosophy and Praxis." Pages in 247–70 in *Hebrew Bible, Greek Bible, and Qumran: Collected Essays*. Texts and Studies in Ancient Judaism 121. Tübingen: Mohr Siebeck, 2008.

__________. *Scribal Practices and Approaches Reflected in the Texts Found in the Judean Desert*. Atlanta: Society of Biblical Literature, 2009.

__________. "Textual Harmonization in the Five Books of Torah: A Summary." Pages 32–56 in *The Bible, Qumran, and the Samaritans*. Edited by Magnar Kartveit and Gary N. Knoppers. Berlin: De Gruyter, 2020.

Tucker, W. Dennis, Jr. *Malachi*. ZECOT. Grand Rapids: Zondervan Academic, 2024.

Ulrich, Dean R. *Now and Not Yet: Theology and Mission in Ezra-Nehemiah*. NSBT 57. Downers Grove, IL: IVP Academic, 2021.

VanGemeren, Willem A. *Psalms*. EBC. Grand Rapids: Zondervan Academic, 2017.

Vanhoozer, Kevin J. *Biblical Authority After Babel: Retrieving the* Solas *in the Spirit of Mere Protestant Christianity*. Grand Rapids: Brazos, 2016.

_________. *Is There a Meaning in This Text?: The Bible, the Reader, and the Morality of Literary Knowledge*. Grand Rapids: Zondervan Academic, 2009.

_________. "Lost in Interpretation?: Truth, Scripture, and Hermeneutics." *JETS* 48.1 (2005): 89–114.

_________. *Mere Christian Hermeneutics: Transfiguring What It Means to Read the Bible Theologically*. Grand Rapids: Zondervan Academic, 2024.

_________. "The Semantics of Biblical Literature: Truth and Scripture's Diverse Literary Forms." Pages 49–104 in *Hermeneutics, Authority, and Canon*. Edited by D. A. Carson and John D. Woodbridge. Grand Rapids: Academie Books, 1986.

Vermes, Géza. "Bible and Midrash: Early Old Testament Exegesis." Pages 199–231 in *The Cambridge History of the Bible*. Vol. 1, *From the Beginnings to Jerome*. Edited by P. R. Ackroyd and C. F. Evans. New York: Cambridge University Press, 1970.

Vlach, Michael. *The Old in the New: Understanding How the New Testament Authors Quoted the Old Testament*. Sun Valley, CA: Master's Seminary Press, 2021.

Vos, Geerhardus. *Biblical Theology: Old and New Testaments*. Grand Rapids: Eerdmans, 1948.

_________. "Hebrews, The Epistle of the *Diatheke*: Part 1." *PTR* 13.4 (1915): 587–632.

_________. "Hebrews, The Epistle of the *Diatheke*: Part 2." *PTR* 14.1 (1916): 1–61.

_________. "Inaugural Address." Pages 3–40 in *Inauguration of the Rev. Geerhardus Vos, Ph.D., D.D, as Professor of Biblical Theology*. New York: Randolph, 1894.

_________. *The Mosaic Origin of the Pentateuchal Codes*. New York: Armstrong, 1886.

_________. "The Priesthood of Christ in the Epistle to the Hebrews, Part 1." *PTR* 5.3 (1907): 423–47.

_________. "The Priesthood of Christ in the Epistle to the Hebrews, Part 2." *PTR* 5.4 (1907): 579–604.

_________. *The Teaching of the Epistle to the Hebrews*. Grand Rapids: Eerdmans, 1956.

Waltke, Bruce. "Aims of Textual Criticism." *WTJ* 51.1 (1989): 93–108.

Walton, John H. *The Lost World of the Prophets: Old Testament Prophecy and Apocalyptic Literature in Ancient Context*. Downers Grove, IL: IVP Academic, 2024.

_________. *Wisdom for Faithful Reading: Principles and Practices for Old Testament Interpretation*. Downers Grove, IL: IVP Academic, 2023.

Wasserman, Tommy. *The Epistle of Jude: Its Text and Transmission*. ConBNT 43. Stockholm: Almqvist & Wiksell, 2006.

Watson, Francis. *Paul and the Hermeneutics of Faith*. 2nd ed. New York: Bloomsbury T&T Clark, 2016.

_________. "Scripture in Pauline Theology: How Far Down Does It Go?" *JTI* 2.2 (2008): 181–92.

Way, Kenneth C. "Donkey Domains: Zechariah 9:9 and Lexical Semantics." *JBL* 129.1 (2010): 105–14.

Weinfeld, Moshe. *Deuteronomy 1–11*. AB. New York: Doubleday, 1991.

Weissert, Elnathan. "Creating a Political Climate: Literary Allusions to *Enūma Eliš* in Sennacherib's Account of the Battle of Halule." Pages 191–202 in *Assyrien im Wandel der Zeiten*. Edited by Hartmut Waetzoldt and Harald Hauptmann. Rencontre Assyriologique International 39. Heidelberg: Heidelberger Orientverlag, 1997.

Wenham, Gordon J. *The Book of Leviticus*. NICOT. Grand Rapids: Eerdmans, 1979.

__________. *Numbers: An Introduction and Commentary*. TOTC 4. Downers Grove, IL: IVP Academic, 2008.

White, Joel R. "N. T. Wright's Narrative Approach." Pages 181–204 in *God and the Faithfulness of Paul: A Critical Examination of the Pauline Theology of N. T. Wright*. Edited by Christoph Heilig, J. Thomas Hewitt, and Michael F. Bird. Minneapolis: Fortress, 2017.

Wilcox, Max. "On Investigating the Use of the Old Testament in the New Testament." Pages 231–43 in *Text and Interpretation: Studies in the New Testament Presented to Matthew Black*. Edited by Ernest Best and R. McL. Wilson. New York: Cambridge University Press, 1979.

Witherington, Ben III. *Isaiah Old and New: Exegesis, Intertextuality, and Hermeneutics*. Minneapolis: Fortress, 2017.

__________. *Psalms Old and New: Exegesis, Intertextuality, and Hermeneutics*. Minneapolis: Fortress, 2017.

__________. *Torah Old and New: Exegesis, Intertextuality, and Hermeneutics*. Minneapolis: Fortress, 2018.

Wold, Benjamin. "Old Testament Context: Insights from the Dead Sea Scrolls." Pages 115–25 in in *Methodology in the Use of the Old Testament in the New: Context and Criteria*. Edited by David Allen and Steve Smith. LNTS 579. New York: T&T Clark, 2020.

Wolde, Ellen van. "Texts in Dialogue with Texts: Intertextuality in the Ruth and Tamar Narratives." *Biblical Interpretation* 5.1 (1997): 1–28.

Wray Beal, Lissa M. "Emulating the Apostles: Reading Jeremiah as Christian Scripture in the Footsteps of the Apostles." Pages 143–62 in *The Prophets and the Apostolic Witness: Reading Isaiah, Jeremiah, and Ezekiel as Christian Scripture*. Edited by Andrew T. Abernethy, William R. Osborne, and Paul D. Wenger. Downers Grove, IL: IVP Academic, 2023.

__________. *1 & 2 Kings*. ApOTC. Downers Grove, IL: IVP Academic, 2014.

Wright, N. T. *The New Testament and the People of God*. Minneapolis: Fortress, 1992.

__________. *Paul and the Faithfulness of God*. Book II, Parts III & IV. Minneapolis: Fortress, 2013.

Würthwein, Ernst. *The Text of the Old Testament: An Introduction to the Biblia Hebraica*, 3d ed. Edited by Alexander Achilles Fischer. Translated by Erroll F. Rhodes. Grand Rapids: Eerdmans, 2014.

Yonge, C. D., trans. *The Works of Josephus*. Peabody, MA: Hendrickson, 1987.

__________. *The Works of Philo*. Peabody, MA: Hendrickson, 1993.

Zahn, Molly M. "The Samaritan Pentateuch and the Scribal Culture of Second Temple Judaism," *Journal for the Study of Judaism* 46 (2015): 285–313.

Zakovitch, Yair. "Inner-biblical Interpretation." Pages 27–63 in *A Companion to Biblical Interpretation in Early Judaism*. Edited by Matthias Henze. Grand Rapids: Eerdmans, 2012.

Zenger, Erich, and Frank-Lothar Hossfeld. *Psalms 3*. Hermeneia. Minneapolis: Fortress, 2011.

ACKNOWLEDGMENTS

We are grateful to the Lord for the opportunity and strength for this project.

Each of us wrote the first draft of half of the chapters, and we each contributed elements to the other chapters—along with a lot of editing and discussion. Any reader familiar with our writing may be able to pick out the chapters and places where each of us is the primary initial contributor. Many of the contested issues required give and take as well as pushing back and inviting pushback. We both felt free to disagree and suggest something different, including do-overs in the case of two chapters. The highlights of working together are the face-to-face meetings at the conferences every year and especially the taxing yet enjoyable shoot for the videos that accompany the book. We are grateful for what we have learned by collaborating with a professor of the other testament. Both of us recognize that we still have a long way to go.

Thank you to several scholars who took time for critical feedback on drafts of chapters at various stages including Keith Plummer (introduction and chapters 1 and 2); Kevin McFadden (chapters 6 and 7); Brandon Crowe (chapter 7); James M. Hamilton, Jr. (chapter 7); Matthew Bates (chapter 7); Madison Pierce (early draft of chapter 7 and a later draft of the entire manuscript); Jonathan Master (entire manuscript); Ben Gladd (entire manuscript); and the blind peer reviewers and blind academic readers (entire manuscript). Thank you to Matt Lynch for pointing out a glitch in chapter 2, to Carmen Imes for suggesting a tweak in chapter 4, and to Alan Hultberg for suggesting an entry for the glossary.

Thank you to Herbert Bateman IV for permission to represent his chart in a footnote in chapter 2.

We are grateful to several scholars for graciously providing pre-publication copies of their forthcoming works including Ben Gladd as an editor of *Dictionary of the New Testament Use of the Old Testament*; Michael Morales's two-volume commentary on Numbers; Tremper Longman III's *The Old Testament as Literature*, with its chapter emphasizing intertextuality in the wisdom writings; Kevin Vanhoozer's *Mere Christian Hermeneutics*; and Gordon Johnston's essay on Hittite covenants.

We are grateful to Gary's research assistant Kimberly Ellis for proofreading the entire manuscript and making suggestions for the glossary. Kimberly also devoted much time to producing instructor's materials for the textbook and videos.

We thank Barbara Arnold for looking up every verse reference in the book to check for errors as well as offering many helpful suggestions.

We express our gratitude to Jenny Moo for producing outstanding indexes and for detecting many errors for correction.

It is a pleasure to work with the team at Zondervan Academic. They brought the right mix of professionalism and friendship into this project. We are grateful for the work of Nancy Erickson. She oversaw this project through the entire process from the initial idea through several editorial stages until going to press. Nancy's expert editing and insightful questions and advice have improved this book including its usefulness to students. Thank you to Sara Colley for interior design. We are grateful to Liz England and the film crew for careful production of the videos, with much good humor. We thank Kent Hendricks for a lively breakfast conversation about typological patterns in scripture, and especially for telling us about Vanhoozer's new book. Thank you to Emily Bruff for helping us with the title, cover, marketing, and the initial promotion of the book and videos.

—Gary Edward Schnittjer and Matt Harmon

I express my gratitude to Cairn University for several kinds of support for this project. I am grateful for the distinguished professorship that allocates half of my time for research and writing. Cairn continues to provide for conference and travel expenses, annual book budget, teaching and research assistants, as well as costs for indexing this project. All of these elements were necessary to complete this project. Thank you to the university's board, president, provost, and dean of the School of Divinity for supporting scholarship that serves students.

Thank you to Caroline Master, Lauren Raab, and Michelle Matthias for many scans and trips to the library, as well as support from Laurie Handzlik and Nancy Rivera. I express my appreciation to the staff of Cairn's library for securing numerous resources quickly and with good cheer.

I am grateful for spirited discussions over the decades with students about the Bible's use of the Bible. The give and take with students who wrestle through research and interpretation of difficult passages has helped me consider the scriptures from many different angles.

I benefitted much from critique and interaction by Richard Schultz and

Greg Beale, along with a few good laughs, during a panel review of *OTUOT* at the Hermeneutics section of the Evangelical Theological Society. The spirited feedback and pushback by scholars regarding numerous conferences papers on the Bible's use of the Bible that I delivered in the runup to this book have been a great help—a few of these have been published and are listed in the bibliography. I also benefitted by questions and feedback and warm reception in PhD seminars I visited to discuss Old Testament use of Old Testament at Midwestern Baptist Theological Seminary and Lancaster Bible College and Graduate School.

I offer my gratitude to Cheri. Her support goes back to my student days when she put me through seminary so I could devote myself fully to study, which continues to pay dividends including this project. She also made possible for me to do postgraduate studies twice—at University of Pennsylvania and at Westminster Theological Seminary—both of which were essential for this project. During the years of working on this project, Cheri has managed many aspects of our lives and actively protected time for research and writing. Beyond the mechanics, is the encouragement during our walks along shaded paths and talks about biblical interpretation and the views of students and scholars. For all of this and more, I thank you.

—*Gary Edward Schnittjer*

God has blessed me with wonderful support for my research and writing at Grace College and Theological Seminary. I am especially grateful for the encouragement from the president, the provost, my dean, and my colleagues. The reduced teaching and administrative load enable me to devote time and energy to projects like this. For this project, the administration went above and beyond by helping to fund the cost of indexing this project. Thank you for your ongoing partnership with me to help people know Christ and make him known.

The primary audience for this book is students. The interactions I regularly have with them in the classroom, during office hours, and in personal conversations have spurred me on to write this book. Their thoughtful questions and insights have helped me refine my own thinking on how the biblical authors use scripture. For that and much more I am grateful to them.

My approach to the Bible's use of the Bible has been most significantly shaped by two scholars. The first is Doug Moo, who served as my PhD supervisor at Wheaton College. The second is Greg Beale, who also taught at Wheaton during my doctoral studies. Together these two scholars have pushed me to do the hard work in the text to demonstrate the presence of an allusion or echo, while at the same time pushing me to explore the range of possible allusions and their exegetical and hermeneutical significance. I consider it an honor to call both of these men not only mentors but friends.

In the process of writing this book I was invited to present a paper on typology for the Scriptural Use of Scripture section at the annual meeting of the Evangelical Theological Society. I am grateful for the gracious and thoughtful interaction from Darrell Bock, Cynthia Westfall, and David Firth, which helped me sharpen my thinking on this challenging topic.

My wife Kate is my biggest encourager. Her love and support throughout the years have been a constant source of strength and joy. She models Christlike love and service to me, my sons, her church family, her students at Lakeland Christian Academy, and many others. Kate, you will always be my favorite.

—Matthew S. Harmon

INDEX OF TABLES, FIGURES, AND RESOURCE GUIDES

INDEX OF SCRIPTURE AND OTHER ANCIENT LITERATURE

OLD TESTAMENT

Exodus

Leviticus

Numbers

Deuteronomy

Proverbs

Ecclesiastes

Isaiah

Jeremiah

Ezekiel

NEW TESTAMENT

Matthew

Mark

Luke

ANCIENT NEAR EASTERN TEXTS

DEUTEROCANONICAL BOOKS

PSEUDEPIGRAPHA

DEAD SEA SCROLLS

ANCIENT JEWISH WRITERS

RABBINIC WORKS

GRECO-ROMAN LITERATURE

SUBJECT INDEX

AUTHOR INDEX

How to Study the Bible's Use of the Bible Video Lectures

Gary Edward Schnittjer,
Matthew S. Harmon

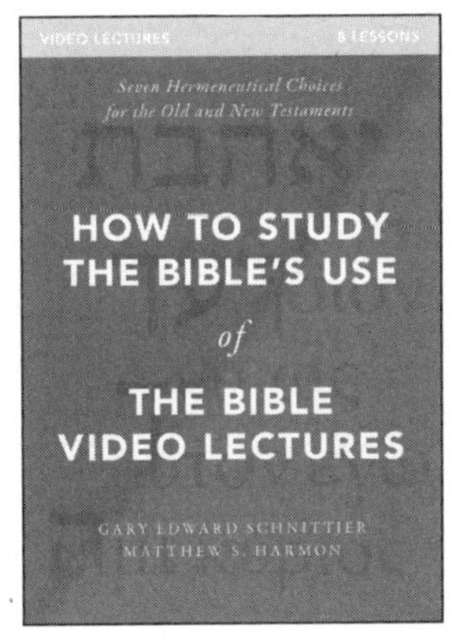

How to Study the Bible's Use of the Bible Video Lectures by Gary Edward Schnittjer and Matthew S. Harmon is an essential resource aimed at teaching a hermeneutic for understanding the Bible's use of the Bible. Intended for students of both testaments, the series' innovative approach demonstrates how the Old Testament use of Scripture provides resources for the New Testament authors' use of Scripture. Lessons provide students with a clear approach to handling the Bible's use of itself through seven key hermeneutical choices organized into individual videos. Each lesson introduces a hermeneutical choice and then provides several examples of the Old Testament use of Old Testament and the New Testament use of Old Testament. The plentiful examples model for students the need to ground hermeneutics in biblical evidence and provide insight into understanding why the Bible's use of the Bible is important.

https://zondervanacademic.com/seven-choices

Torah Story, Second Edition

An Apprenticeship on the Pentateuch

Gary Edward Schnittjer

The gospel story begins in Torah. What culminates at Golgotha starts with the rebellion in the garden. The Torah's story can be framed as a question: How will the word of God overcome the human revolution?

Torah Story offers a student-friendly introduction to the redemptive narrative housed in the first five books of the Bible. Every main chapter introduces a section of Torah with attention to its basic structure. This is followed by another look at how this portion of Torah connects to the rest of the Christian Bible.

The dynamic design includes opportunities in every chapter to make the most of Torah study including:

- Helps for getting started (focus questions, key terms, outline)
- An interactive workshop with challenge questions and advanced questions
- Suggestions for research projects
- Next steps for further study

A refreshingly new approach to the Torah—neither an introduction nor a commentary—*Torah Story* provides an apprenticeship on the Old Testament's first five books. But it also provides a model of how to read Scripture intertextually with an eye to the New Testament Gospels. It leaves no doubt as to the overarching unity of the message and composition of the Pentateuch. The second edition is streamlined and simplified throughout, with updated examples and new sidebars and imagery.

The Torah Story Video Lectures

An Apprenticeship on the Pentateuch

Gary Edward Schnittjer

A working knowledge of the Torah is essential for every serious student of the Scriptures. Presented in an engaging and accessible manner, even while digging into difficult and complicated matters at a sophisticated level, *The Torah Story Video Lectures* by Gary Schnittjer feature 29 lessons on 4 DVDs. The lectures emphasize the content of the text itself, moving beyond debating dates and theories of authorship into understanding how these five key books of the Bible help us understand the story of salvation.

A companion to the *Torah Story* textbook, *The Torah Story Video Lectures* provides a model for how to read Scripture intertextually. It leaves no doubt as to the overarching unity of the message and composition of the Pentateuch.

Accessibly formatted and focused on the most significant topics and discussions in the textbook, *The Torah Story Video Lectures* is designed with the learner in mind, and each lecture is approximately 15 to 20 minutes. These lectures are an indispensable resource for students and independent learners alike.

Session Titles and Runtimes:

1. An Apprenticeship on the Torah (29 min)
2. Introducing the Torah (28 min)
3. Macroview of Genesis (24 min)
4. The Beginning (28 min)
5. The Garden and Exile (24 min)
6. The Flood and the Nations (30 min)
7. The Abraham Narratives (37 min)
8. The Jacob Narratives (29 min)
9. The Sons of Jacob Narratives (33 min)
10. The Last Days (23 min)
11. Macroview of Exodus (30 min)
12. The River and the Bush (24 min)
13. The Plagues and the Sea (32 min)
14. The Wilderness and the Mountain (29 min)
15. The Rebellion and the Dwelling (26 min)
16. Macroview of Leviticus (25 min)
17. Sacrifice (29 min)
18. Purity and Worship (34 min)
19. Holy Living (35 min)
20. Macroview of Numbers (26 min)
21. The First Generation on the Plains of Moab (30 min)
22. Two Generations in the Wilderness (29 min)
23. The Second Generation on the Plains of Moab (21 min)
24. Macroview of Deuteronomy (25 min)
25. The Words (26 min)
26. The Ten Words and the Command (23 min)
27. The Rules and Regulations (30 min)
28. A View of the Other Side (28 min)
29. Reintroducing the Torah (21 min)

https://zondervanacademic.com/masterlectures/torah-story

Old Testament Use of Old Testament

A Book-by-Book Guide

Gary Edward Schnittjer

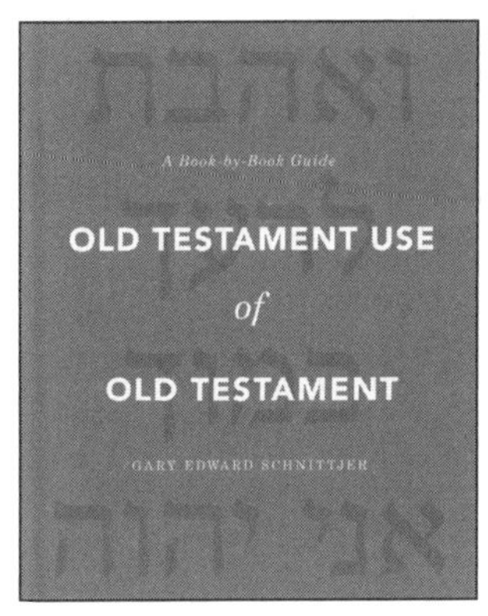

SOUTHWESTERN JOURNAL OF THEOLOGY 2021 BOOK OF THE YEAR IN BIBLICAL STUDIES

CENTER FOR BIBLICAL STUDIES AT MIDWESTERN SEMINARY 2021 BOOK OF THE YEAR IN OLD TESTAMENT

Old Testament Use of Old Testament, by Gary Edward Schnittjer, surveys the hundreds of Old Testament allusions within the Old Testament and provides hermeneutical guidance for interpreting these interrelated Scriptures.

The handbook takes an easy to navigate book-by-book approach. Schnittjer provides a list of Scripture allusions for each book and follows with an interpretive profile of how that book uses passages from elsewhere in the Old Testament. Specific criteria are applied to each allusion, providing readers with evaluation of the significance of each interpretive allusion. Minor allusions caused by style, figures of speech, and other minor elements are not included.

Responsible exegesis requires careful attention to interrelated Scriptures, yet there is a host of interpretive difficulties related to Scripture's use of Scripture. Designed for ease-of-use for any serious student of the Bible, *Old Testament Use of Old Testament* offers a thorough, systematic tool to aid in evaluating scriptural interpretation of Scripture.

This dynamic tool equips students of the Bible to:

- Understand how the Old Testament uses the Old Testament
- Easily find the most important Old Testament allusions
- Grasp the complexity of Scripture's use of Scripture
- Evaluate the significance of interpretive allusions
- Gain exegetical insight into the study of interrelated Scriptures